The Customs of Mankind

In 2 Volumes

Lillian Eichler

Vol II

GIAN PUBLISHING HOUSE
Delhi-110 007

First Published in 1988 Reprint 2017 in India by
Gyan Publishing House,
5, Ansari Road, Darya Ganj,
New Delhi-110002
Phones : 011-47034999, 9811692060
E-mail: books@gyanbooks.com
Website: www.gyanboks.com

Lasser Type Setting by: Quick Media, Delhi
Printed at : G. Print Process, Delhi

CONTENTS

CHAPTER PAGE

Vol II

CHAPTER XIII

The Tale of Table Manners

Ages before man felt the need of indigestion remedies, he ate his food solitary and furtive in some corner, hoping he would not be espied by any stronger and hungrier fellow. It was a long, long time before the habit of eating in common was acquired; and it is obvious that the practise could not have been taken up with safety until the individuals of the race knew enough about one another and about the food resources to be sure that there was food sufficient for all. When eating in common became the vogue, table manners made their appearance and they have been waging an uphill struggle ever since. —Richard Duffy.

FOOD AND CIVILIZATION

MAN was created hungry. And being hungry he ate.

To satisfy hunger needs no reason; it is as natural an instinct as sleep. But to store up food for future use, to cultivate it, to cook it and make it palatable—all this requires a degree of reasoning which came only after long ages of development. And to make of eating a ceremony, a social pleasure to be enjoyed with one's fellows, requires a degree of cultural advancement which followed but slowly in the path of reason.

Eating, then, knows no other origin than hunger and the natural instinct to satisfy that hunger. But eating habits, or manners, have been moulded by a million external influences through the ages of human existence. The development of eating habits has kept pace with man's own development.

Take any people in the world, study their eating habits from the earliest times to the present day, and you have a pretty fair picture of their social progress. The French and the English, who have reached what we consider a high degree of civilization in the social sense, have excellent table manners. The Australians and the Africans, who are still groping at the bottom rung of civilization's great ladder, eat with their hands or with crude implements.

As surely as a compass points the direction a floundering ship must take, the eating habits of a people point to the direction those people have trod in the path of civilization.

Luncheon with Primitive Man.—Early man subsisted upon berries, roots, raw fruit, insects. He had meat when he could pick up a dead animal or kill one himself.

We can see him prowling through primitive forests, this brute-man ancestor of ours, searching for something to satisfy the hunger that gnaws at his stomach like hundreds of insects trying to tear it apart. In the beginning, it did not matter so very much what he ate. And to the manner in which he ate, he gave not the slightest thought.

Perhaps he finds a berry tree or some roots that are good. Perhaps he comes, suddenly, upon the remains of an animal upon which some beasts have gorged. Or perhaps he is fortunate and is able to kill some small forest creature that crosses his path. Gazing quickly and furtively around, he sits down to his "luncheon."

We handle our food delicately. But early man's instinct was to "wolf" his food—eat it quickly and stealthily before some other hungrier fellow happened along. Therefore, if we are to be unseen guests at his luncheon, we must hide behind a primeval tree and be silent, lest we frighten him away.

He has felled a bird with a stone. See how he tears at it savagely, just as a starving cat might tear at a sparrow. He crouches low under the berry tree and crunches the slender bones between his powerful teeth. A low growl escapes him as he hears a twig crack. We shrink back into the shadows. It would never do to let him see us. To protect his bit of food he would jump at us like a tiger. And who are we, of an artificial age, to compete with the great savage man-beast of primitive times?

But we make up in reason what we lack in strength, so we wait until the fellow has gorged himself with bird and roots and berries, and we watch him while he sprawls out on the ground with a grunt of contentment and falls almost instantly into slumber. And we come a little closer to examine him.

Here he lies, stuffed to exhaustion like any animal, the man upon whose shoulders all later civilization is built. See how clean he has picked the bones of his bird. Not a speck of flesh remains. His strong, sharp teeth have done a good job. No need for forks and knives here! We take a bit of the bone for a souvenir and steal softly away, knowing the fellow will sleep until he is hungry again. And we walk on to meet the next stage of development.

Man Begins to Eat Leisurely.—We are going to dine with a group of cave people on the hill. These people live in a favourable climate, as you notice, and there is plenty of food for all. Therefore the social instinct has made itself felt; and as we climb the forbidding path to the cave home above, we see that there are half-a-dozen figures grouped about the fire. It would appear that a large beast of some kind has been killed.

Taking our place silently at the head of the group, we watch the men around us for a cue as to how we shall eat. There are no eating implements. The men squat in a semi-circle around the fire. We see them tear huge pieces of flesh from the beast, devouring immense mouthfuls. Marrow bones they crack open and suck out the juices. They glance about them furtively, now and then, as though expecting to be attacked; but they have none of the stealth and half-starved fear that we saw in the earlier man.

The meal completed, the men sit out under the stars for a while, silent, or playful like well-fed animals, according to their nature. Then they enter the cave, rolling a huge rock against its mouth to keep out the dangerous beasts. In a few moments they are sleeping soundly.

And we leave them sleeping so, knowing that they will

waken hungry again, go hunting, return with the kill, eat and sleep once more. From such rude beginning has grown our complex and highly polished routine of living.

Not all peoples were quick to welcome company while they ate. The food resources of the locality in which a people found itself had very much to do with it. Where food was plentiful, men formed early the habit of eating together. But where food was scarce, men for a long time retained the habit of eating stealthily and in solitude.

Just as the modern small boy eats his piece of cake or candy in some corner, hiding it selfishly from his playmates, primitive man ate alone because he was afraid of having someone steal his food from him. Habit, as we have seen in an earlier chapter, becomes custom. In later life we find it custom even for kings and priests to eat by themselves.

The King of Abyssinia still dines alone. In Loango any person who sees the king eat is put to death. In Tonga everyone turns his back upon the king while he eats or drinks. The king of the Congo always eats and drinks in secret. It is said that the Emperor of Germany never ate in public but sat out every banquet before an empty plate.

We venture that customs such as these, existing as they do in many places throughout the world, had their origin in man's first fear of having his food stolen. But we find, as we turn a few pages in the book of life, that another element enters into this seemingly widespread preference for eating alone.

This element, which characterized almost everything else which primitive man did, is fear. It appears to have been a common belief among savages, and still is to a great extent to-day, that evil could enter the body with food. Bad food or too much raw meat causing the tortures of indigestion would give rise to just such a belief. Unable to understand the pains and aches that followed his careless eating, primitive man would have blamed it on evil spirits. And those evil spirits, according to his primitive reasoning, must have entered his body with the food.

Thus great caution attended the eating and drinking of these early men. They avoided their fellows. They found their own food and ate it alone. The kings and chiefs particularly took great caution in eating, fearful of the enemies who envied them their power. Many authorities believe that it was this fear which led early rulers to eat in solitude rather than the fear of having their food stolen. To us it would seem that eating alone as a habit, handed down from very primitive times, came first; and that in later primitive times the habit became custom, law, when man conceived the idea of evil entering the body with the food.

For instance, it was at one time the habit of all the natives of Loango to eat alone. This was when food was scarce and fear of having the food stolen was paramount. Later, when food became more plentiful the natives began to eat together, but it had become by that time the custom for the king to eat by himself. To-day it is a law that the king of Loango may not be seen eating or drinking under pain of death.

Man did not begin to eat leisurely and in comfort until he came to realize that there was food enough for all. This realization, of course, did not come until comparatively late, and it came only to those who actually had an abundance of foodstuffs. To them it gave freedom from the fear of starvation, and they began to think of ways to improve the taste of their food, means of eating in greater comfort.

Eating habits came into being, and they have been struggling step by step with civilization ever since.

DEVELOPMENT OF THE CULINARY ART

The first men did not cook or prepare their food, any more than an animal does to-day. They had hazelnuts and beechnuts, wild cherries and gooseberries, crabapples, birds, eggs, snails, frogs, fish, caterpillars (still relished by the Chinese), and small animals such as the rabbit, the hare, the rat. They ate to satisfy their hunger and with no sense of delicacy. We are told that they ate even the putrid, ill-smelling flesh of dead animals, developing a taste for it which has survived to the present day. The epicure will tell you that certain kinds of game and many kinds of cheese must be semi-putrid before they taste right!

For a long time there was no change in the eating habits of man. He was hungry and he ate whatever he could procure in whatever form it was procurable. Then came fire and its tremendous influence upon the daily life of man. He was able to cook his food and store it away for periods of famine. We see him, during this next great stage, at his "squatting place" as Wells calls it, around his fire, preparing the food before devouring it. He has stone implements. He roasts the ox and the bear. He eats still in his savage, animal-like fashion but more leisurely than before; *and he has a knife made of flint* to help him crack the bones and cut apart the beast.

Mr. Wells says:

> The most probable way in which fires were started was by hacking a bit of iron pyrites with a flint amidst dry dead leaves; concretions of iron pyrites and flints are found together in England where the gault and chalk approach each other.

Sir John Lubbock and Ludwig Hopf advance the same theory. We have already seen how natural phenomena, such as a conflagration caused by lightning, or spontaneous combustion caused by fermenting vegetable materials, made known to man the power of fire (see p. 14). The use of fire for cooking food, first for purposes of preservation and later to improve the taste, seems to be of great antiquity.

There are many curious traditions concerning the origin of fire. The Maoris tell this tale: The great Maui was given fire as a gift by his old blind grandmother, Mahuika, who drew it by magic from the nails of her fingers. Maui wanted a stronger fire, so he pretended they had all gone out and prevailed upon his grandmother to draw him a new one from her great toe. It was a fierce fire she gave him, and everything melted before it. Even Maui began to burn, but a deluge was sent from heaven to save him—and the world. (A curious interpretation of the deluge myth.) But Maui managed to preserve a few sparks of the fire, before it was all extinguished, and imprison them in some trees. From these trees, so the Maoris believe to-day, men draw their supply of fire.

Finnish mythology tells us how "fire, the child of the sun, came down from heaven, where it was rocked in a tub of yellow copper, in a large pail of gold."

The legends of the North American Indians describe how the great buffalo, hurrying across the plains, made sparks fly into the night. These sparks set the prairie ablaze wherever the buffalo's hoofs hit the rocks, and the Indians were given the secret of fire. The same idea prevails in Hindu mythology.

The Dakotas claim that their ancestors obtained fire from the sparks which a friendly panther struck with its claws upon a stony hill.

Origin and Development of Bread-Making.—Strangely enough, bread, which is to-day a staple and practically universal item of diet, is one of the most ancient forms of food. The calcined remains of bread or cakes made from coarsely ground grain have been found in regions around the Swiss lake dwellings. Authorities estimate these cakes as dating back to the Stone Age.

These cakes appear to have been made of a sort of bruised grain. Round-shaped stones have been found in the lake dwellings which were doubtless used for pounding or crushing the grain into a kind of coarse flour. It was probably the custom of the lake dwellers to place the dough on a flat or convex-shaped stone which was heated, covering the cake with hot ashes so that it would bake through.

Perhaps the earliest form of bread was prepared from acorns and beechnuts pounded to a powder. There are to this day remnants of Indian tribes on the Pacific slopes who eat a sort of cake prepared from crushed acorns. Most of the Indians, however, used maize for their cakes.

The early Egyptians used a charcoal fire to cook their meats. They made bread and caraway-seed cakes. Like the Israelites they were highly advanced in the art of preparing food, and they appear to have been among the first to know of meat-curing. Four thousand years ago the Egyptian noonday meal "usually consisted of a soup made of onions, garlic, and beef, although the flesh of the ibex or gazelle were used as favourite dishes."

The Israelites made bread, we know, for Abraham said to Sarah, "Make ready quickly three measures of fine meal, knead it, and make cakes." (Genesis, XVIII, 7.)

With the cultivation of wheat, oats, and rye, and the use of yeast, bread-making became an art. The baker became a highly respected member of the community. Bread, in many varieties, of course, became the foundation food of mankind. One might say that civilization itself has been nourished and has grown big on bread. It is one of the oldest, most widely used and most nourishing foods of man.

Concerning the Stove.—The first stoves were simply hot stones. In using his flint knife, man evidently discovered that stone held heat, and soon we find him utilizing this discovery. Huge, round stones have been found which appear to have been used for purposes of cooking food. Some are flat, some concave. A large pot, of a later period, has been found containing several smooth round stones. It is believed that early man heated water by dropping hot stones into it.

In early times, the fire was built in the centre of the cave; and for a long time the cook fire occupied the centre of the home. But later the fire was moved to the side of the home, and in the 12th century chimneys to supply draughts and to lead smoke and fumes out of the house were introduced.

Closed stoves of brick or porcelain tile have been in use in Holland, Russia, Germany, and other northern countries of Europe since the end of the Middle Ages. Prior to that period there was no way of leading the smoke out of the house, and the doors of cottages were made in two sections. The lower section was kept closed to prevent the chickens and pigs from entering; the upper section was swung open to let the smoke escape.

Cast-iron stoves were known in Alsace as early as 1490, but they did not come into general use until considerably later. For many generations the brick and tile stoves were in use.

The early colonists, we are told, did their cooking in open fireplaces. They had large swinging cranes on which to suspend their pots. For baking they used brick ovens. In 1744 Benjamin Franklin invented the portable fireplace of iron.

To-day we have gas ranges, electric toasters, grills, a wide and astonishing array of highly perfected stoves. But when the palate tires of the *camouflaged* foods of civilization, it can still taste the wholesome tang of foods cooked plainly and simply in the primitive way—over a roaring bonfire or buried in hot ashes. Campers will tell you they prefer such food to the highly seasoned and richly sauced foods of the modern table.

Cooking as an Art.—The ancients, though great eaters, had none of the subtle refinements of taste which we associate with food and with eating. They ate because they were hungry, and simple hunger does not produce the art of cookery. Food was not disguised to tempt the palate until man was sufficiently advanced to have acquired taste.

As we study the development of the culinary art throughout the centuries, we cannot fail to see how closely cookery is bound up with the physical possibilities of the various countries, and of course with its products. Where caterpillars were plentiful a taste was acquired for them. In China, for instance, even to-day dried caterpillars are sold at the market and they are prepared for eating in various ways. The Chinese have also a taste for eggs that have been so long buried that they are black, hard, and tasteless.

We who find it difficult to understand such grotesque tastes as the Chinese have must remember that they have been accustomed to eat such food from the very earliest times, and they would consider our taste for rich pastries and creamy sauces quite as grotesque.

In the United States, pig and chicken are eaten daily by great multitudes of people. But among the Samoans a pig or chicken is never killed unless there are important guests to be feasted. The difference is that in the United States pig and chicken are plentiful, while among the Samoans both are scarce.

With increasing culture man developed a pampered appetite. By the time of the Greek and Roman civilizations, man was eating not only to satisfy his hunger but to please his palate. We know the sumptuous character of the Greek banquets. Athenæus took pains to get whatever information he could concerning the manner in which delicacies for the table were prepared by various peoples. There appear to have been many food connoisseurs, prominent among them being Hegemon, Philogenes, Numenius, and in the third century before the Christian Era, the great Epicurus.

The Romans borrowed from the Greeks their ideas of food and food preparation. We have already seen how the Romans sent messengers far and wide to secure for their feasts choice fruits and rare viands (see p. 325). They added a note of luxury and extravagance to the table; but they did not add any notable subtleties to the art of cookery. They did, however, invent a baking pan with six spaces for baking batches of small cakes.

It is interesting to note how old cheese is. The early Greeks appear to have been familiar with cheese as a foodstuff long before they knew how to make butter. The Romans evidently copied from the Greeks the method of cheese-making, for they too are known to have had cheese in their dietary. It was known also to the early Egyptians and is mentioned in the Bible.

The Beginning of Modern Cookery.—Cookery, as we know it to-day, cannot be said to have started before the Renaissance in Italy; and Italy was indeed its birthplace. Possibly because of the traditions surrounding Rome, possibly because of the geographical location and the natural products, possibly because of a natural skill in cookery, the Italians became highly advanced in the art. It is apparently to the Italians that the development of cooking in Europe was due.

According to Montaigne, Catherine de' Medici brought Italian cooks to Paris and introduced there a new kind of cookery. Abraham Hayward, in his "Art of Dining," tells us that the Italians were the first to introduce ices into France. As France was by this time the inspiration of social Europe it did not take long for Italian ideas to spread into foreign kitchens.

According to the records that have come down to us, the Italians not only developed the art of cookery but the art of dining. They were among the first to use forks. Coryate, writing his "Crudities" in the time of James I, says that his friends mocked him and called him "furcifer" because he used "those Italian neatnesses called forks."

One of the greatest advances in cookery took place in France during the reign of Louis XIV. Béchamel was the king's *maître d'hôtel,* and he is said to have created many new and tempting dishes. He is particularly famous for his sauce.

Madame de Sévigné relates a rather pathetic tale of Vatel, one of the most famous chefs of this period. So conscientious was he in the preparation of foods that, when a fish that he ordered for part of a dinner he was arranging failed to come in time, he committed suicide. He wel-

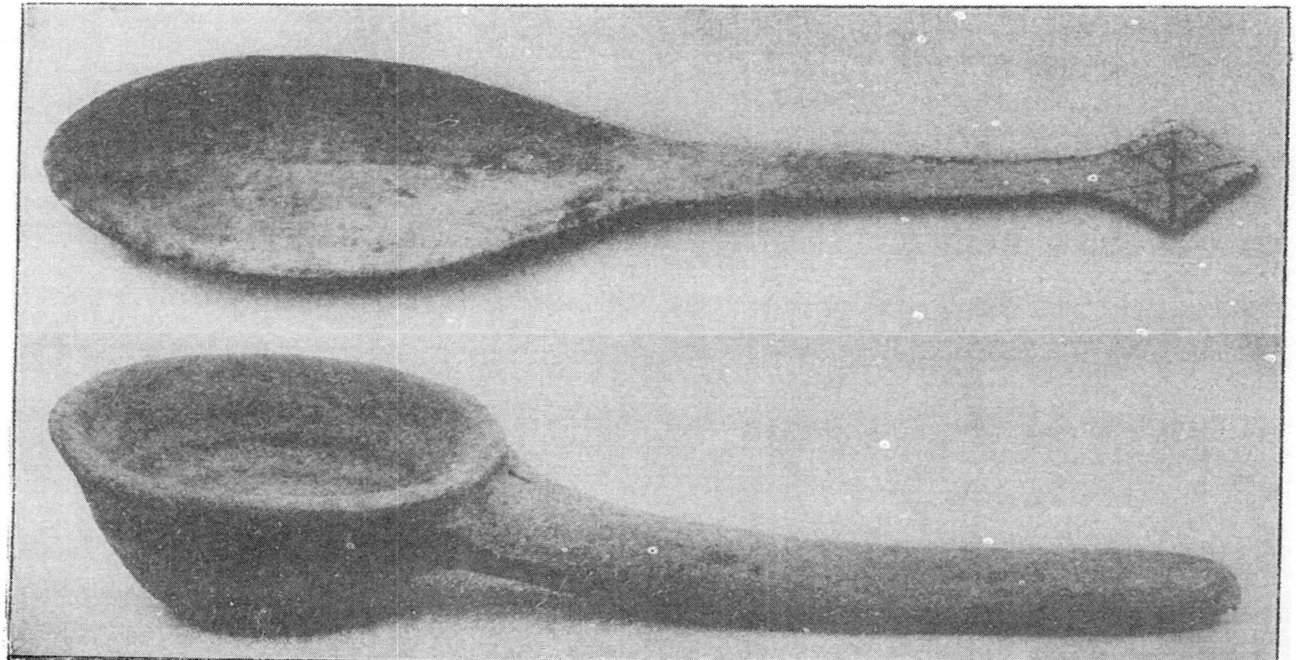

(Courtesy of Metropolitan Museum of Art)

Egyptian spoon and ladle of the Coptic period; coarse red ware. From the monastery "Priest Elias."

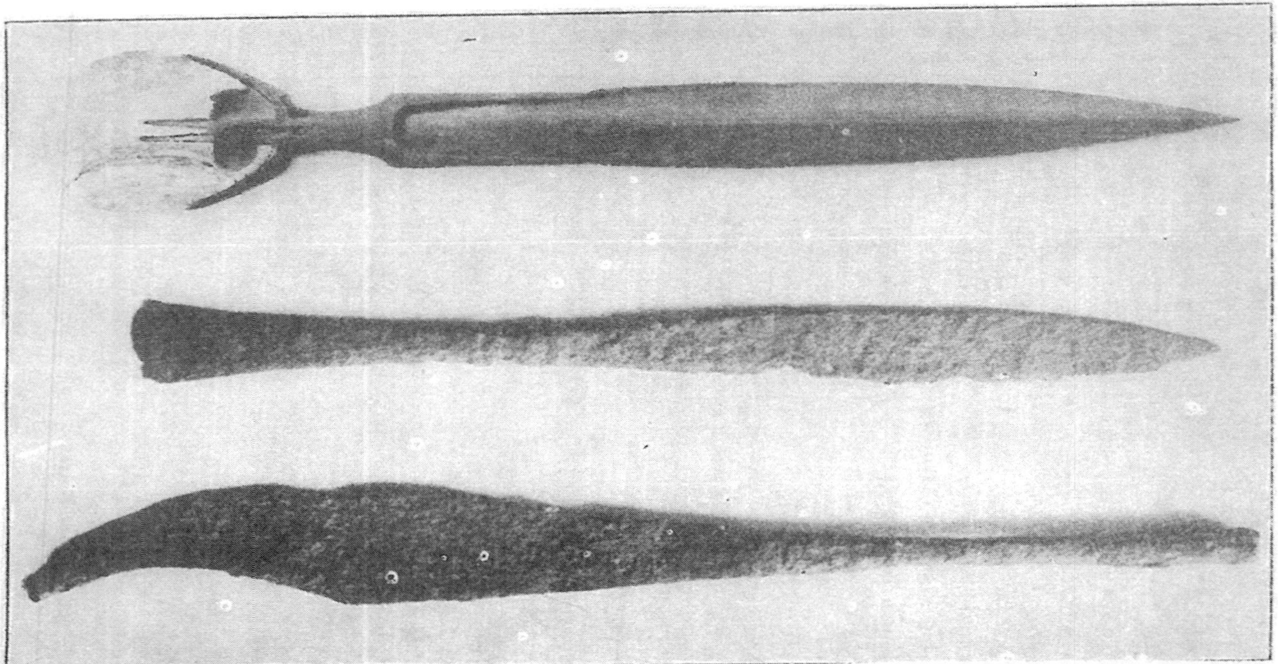

(Courtesy of Metropolitan Museum of Art)

(Upper) ***Bronze dagger, Egyptian, 17th Dynasty.***
(Lower) ***Ancient Egyptian knives of iron. Probably used for cutting or carving purposes at table.***

comed death rather than the disarrangement of his menu.

Another great advance took place under Louis XV, who was a glutton if there ever was one. He ate for the sheer pleasure of eating rather than to satisfy any hunger. His reign saw many new developments.

Mayonnaise, for instance, is credited to Richelieu. Originally it was known as *mahonnaise*. Various rich sauces of the time were named for la Pompadour. It appears to have been the custom to name new dishes for celebrities of the day, and we meet with such names as "*potage à la Condé,*" "*poulets à la Villeroi,*" "*chartreuses à la Mauconseil,*" etc.

So did French cookery develop, until the Revolution. From the beginning of the Revolution until the early 19th century the art suffered a decadence. But it was revived about 1825 by the celebrated Carême who has been at different times chef to Tsar Alexander I, George IV, and Baron Rothschild. Carême appears to have been an artist in dinner-giving. An account of one of his dinners can be found in Lady Morgan's "France," vol II, p. 414. Carême was the author of the famous volume known as "Maître d'hôtel français."

An important development of the Revolution was the appearance of many public restaurants in Paris. The first is said to have appeared in the rue des Poulies in 1770 under the name of "Champ d'oiseau." Twenty years later, in 1790, there were more than a hundred restaurants. In 1804, when the Revolution was over and Bonaparte sat at the head of France, there were about six hundred. By 1815 the restaurants had attracted the best culinary artists of Paris.

England appears to have had more authors of cookbooks than famous chefs. "The Accomplisht Cook," by Robert May, appeared in 1665. May was the son of a cook and is said to have studied abroad under his father. In the preface of his book he criticizes the elaborate dishes of the French which, he indicates, were created as much to amuse and astonish as to satisfy the appetite.

Dr. Pegge's "Forme of Cury" (1780) is a rare and delightful old English work. It has between its covers many interesting reflections concerning the historical background of food and eating. He says, in one instance,

> We have some good families in England of the name Cook or Coke. Depend upon it, they all originally sprang from real professional cooks, and they need not be ashamed of their extraction any more than Porters, Butlers, &c.

Though the English became skilled in certain phases of cookery, they never quite equalled the French. We quote from the "Encyclopædia Britannica":

> At the present time, whatever the local varieties of cooking, and the difference of national custom, French cooking is admittedly the ideal of the culinary art, directly we leave the plain roast and boiled. And the spread of cosmopolitan hotels and restaurants over England, America and the European continent, has largely accustomed the whole civilized world to the Parisian type. The improvements in the appliances and the appurtenances of the kitchen have made the whole world kin in the arts of dining, but the French chef remains the typical master of his craft.

Luncheon with primitive man—and a noonday meal at a modern restaurant. What a tremendous cultural stretch separates the two!

WHEN MAN BEGAN TO DINE

By no stretch of the imagination can we possibly call the eating of primitive man dining. True dining had its inception when man began to eat leisurely, when he began to use tables instead of the ground, when he had table implements, no matter how crude. When he thought not only of what he ate, but of how he ate it, man commenced to dine in the finer sense of the word.

Richard Duffy relates an interesting anecdote of the World War which we cannot resist quoting here. He says:

In the midst of the war, some French soldiers and some non-French of the Allied forces were receiving their rations in a village back of the lines. The non-French fighters belonged to an army that supplied rations plentifully. They grabbed their allotments and stood about while hastily eating, uninterrupted by conversation or other concern. The French soldiers took their very meagre portions of food, improvised a kind of table on the top of a flat rock, and having laid out the rations, including the small quantity of wine that formed part of the repast, sat down in comfort and began their meal amid a chatter of talk. One of the non-French soldiers, all of whom had finished their large supply of food before the French had begun eating, asked sardonically: "Why do you fellows make such a lot of fuss over the little bit of grub they give you to eat?" The Frenchman replied: "Well, we are making war for civilization, are we not? Very well, we are. Therefore, we eat in a civilized way."

The "civilized way" seems to be on tables, out of dishes, and with knives and forks instead of fingers. Let us see how these appointments were given to civilization.

Chairs and Tables.—Who knows what comfort-loving savage first sat upon one stone and used another for a "table"? The first chairs and tables will never be known. Primitive man, of course, had at first no furniture. The earth was his table, and the sky his ceiling. For eating implements he had his ten fingers and his great, strong teeth. But at about the time primitive man took to cave homes, the first crude forms of chairs and tables of which we have record made their appearance. The table was just a huge flat rock in the centre of the cave; the chairs, smaller fragments of rock (see p. 19).

Development of the chair and table, and of appointments for the table, followed very naturally in the wake of culinary development. Where food was eaten raw, in solitude, and without preparation of any sort, the fingers remained the only implements and the earth remained the table. But where cookery lent itself to subtler development, becoming an art, dining too took on all the lights and shadows of advancing taste.

For instance, in Rome, where every meal was a luxurious banquet for those who could afford it, we find rich and beautiful tables, dining couches, and drinking vessels of magnificent artistry.

It was the ancient custom, among both the Romans and the Greeks, to recline on couches while eating. This custom undoubtedly originated with the Greeks who were wont to go first to the public baths, then to pass immediately from bath to couch. While resting on the couches they were usually served some light repast. From this, very possibly, grew the general custom of eating in careless, recumbent position, on dining couches.

The ancient tables were very beautiful, particularly those of the Romans. Most of them were square with four legs or oval with three connected legs. They resemble modern tables, except that they are lower. Necessarily so, for high tables would not have been convenient to reclining persons. It is to be noted that the ancients used tables chiefly, if not solely, for purposes of eating, and not for reading or writing. Writing tables came later, when writing itself was general.

The materials used for table-making were wood, at first —particularly maple wood—and later, bronze, precious metals, and ivory were introduced. From characteristic examples in the museums it would seem that the ancients were fond of imitating the legs of animals in making the legs of their tables. Most table legs were given claws at the end. Evidently we have not outgrown this peculiarity, for modern furniture is frequently made with clawed legs, usually around a ball.

Among the Romans there was usually a place of honour at the head of table. The highest in rank sat at the head, next in rank at the upper end, next at the lower end. Everyone washed his hands at the table before eating, and this ceremony began with the highest in rank and ended with the lowest. Foods were brought in and placed, as to-day, before the man at the head. Fruits were brought in baskets which were placed on the floor beside the table. According to records, the Romans sometimes used several tables, one of them being the "honour table" reserved for the host, hostess, and special guests.

Ray S. Lineham, in "The Street of Human Habitation," tells us that the Egyptians, who feasted in long halls, sat on chairs and were served by the household slaves. The Egyptian host supplied one whole chair for each single guest, but married people got only one between them!

The development of the chair and the table was rapid, and by the opening of the Christian Era it was an established custom among European peoples to eat from the table. It had various forms, of course, and sometimes was simply a board running around the side of the house. The mantelpiece is said to have originated with this old dining board. Apparently the North American Indians used just such a board, for we read that the wife of the chief, Granganimeo, took the English explorers, Philip Amidas and Arthur Barlow, into the house, washed them, gave them every comfort, and served venison and roasted fish on a board that stood along the side of the house (see p. 335). But for the most part the earth served our Indian brothers as table.

Although the chair reached a high degree of development among most European peoples, becoming rich and elaborate in one generation, simple and crude in another, it failed entirely to gain a foothold among various other peoples. For instance, the Chinese and Japanese to this day have very little use for the chair. We speak now of the native Chinese or Japanese, in his original environment; not of the Americanized man who has adopted, to a great extent, the manners and customs of this country.

Tablecloths were used by the Romans during the period of the last Emperors. They were of linen, striped with purple and gold. They had napkins, too, which were used for a very different purpose than we use napkins to-day. The guest at a dinner would wrap delicacies from the table and fruit baskets in his napkin and so carry them home. It was a general custom to carry away food in this manner; the guest who neglected to do so took the risk of hurting his host's feelings.

Origin of the Spoon.—The true origin of the spoon must be for ever lost in antiquity. We know, however, that it is of very remote origin, and that in its earliest forms it was crude, very much like a rough ladle.

There are in the museums spoons of wood, stone, and ivory which were found in ancient Egyptian tombs. Possibly the spoon goes back even farther; spoon-like implements belonging to the Palæolithic Age have been found. The photographs reproduced are of actual "finds" to be seen at the museums.

The Greeks and Romans used spoons of bronze and silver. Some examples are beautiful, exquisitely wrought by the hands of masters now long forgotten.

The spoons of the early Christian Era were of wood. During the Middle Ages the materials used for spoon-making were bone, wood, and tin, while the wealthy had elaborate spoons of beaten silver. The Chinese, in addition to their chopsticks, had little porcelain spoons which were usually painted.

"Chopstick" is so-called pidgin-English for the small, tapering stick used by the Chinese and Japanese in eating. The sticks are used in pairs. "Chop." is pidgin-English for "quick," the Chinese word for the sticks being *kwai-tsze* (the quick ones)

Held between the thumb and fingers of the right hand, the chopsticks are used as tongs to take up portions of food. Among the Chinese and Japanese, food is brought to table cut up into small and convenient pieces. The chopsticks are commonly made of wood, bone, or ivory.

There are complex rules of etiquette concerning the chopsticks, just as there are rules of etiquette concerning the use of the spoon or the fork. They are used also as a secret code of signalling. For instance, to place the chopsticks across the top of the bowl and leave them so is a sign that the guest wishes to leave the table. With us it was one time the custom to indicate the same thing by turning the plate upside down.

The Chinese use chopsticks because they consider the knife and fork barbaric. "We sit at table to eat, not to cut up carcasses," they say.

The Knife and Fork.—The use of the knife and fork marks a great advance in the progress of dining. This advance, however, did not come until late; only 300 years ago knives and forks were curiosities. In England they were rare; in France everyone ate with his fingers until the 17th century. At the courts of Francis I and Henri II, and even at the magnificent court of Louis XIV, forks for eating purposes were unknown.

Nevertheless, both knives and forks have been in existence since very early times. It seems surprising that they did not come into general use until so late a time.

Most authorities are of the opinion that the primitive savage used a natural fork in the shape of a small pronged twig. Others believe that the fork originated with the arrow—that it was, at first, a sort of stick, or toothpick, which was used to remove food from between the teeth. This skewer would be easy to make by people who were already making arrows.

The first actual forks appear to have been long, two-pronged affairs which were used only in cooking and for holding the joint of meat while it was being carved. They were very much like our carving forks, but much cruder, of course. They were made of iron, bone, and hard wood.

We cannot be certain when the fork was first introduced to the table for eating purposes, but we can be reasonably sure that it was not until after the Christian Era. Leandro Alberti, in "Urbis Venetæ Descriptio" (Venice, 1626), mentions that the wife of the doge Domenico Silvio (sister of the Emperor Nicephorus Botaniates, 11th century) was too dainty to touch her food with her fingers. Therefore she used a small golden fork for eating. She is described as being "luxurious beyond belief" and we are told that "instead of eating like other people, she had her food cut up into little pieces, and ate the pieces by means of a two-pronged fork."

A Milanese friar, known as Fra Bonvicino da Riva, wrote about 1290 and left us a curious, versified manual of fifty common courtesies for the table. Mention of the fork appears nowhere in the poem; but the use of a spoon as a fork is indicated: "Suck not with the mouth when thou eatest with a spoon." It appears that one spoon is given the guest at the beginning of the meal, and it must suffice throughout. It is also clearly indicated, in this rare old manual, that each guest is expected to bring his own knife.

The fork was not entirely unknown in mediæval France, but it was very rarely used at the table. It was used sometimes for serving; but it was not until the time of Henri III that the fork was used in the modern fashion. In England, however, the fork was used through the Middle Ages as an article of luxury for eating fruits and preserves.

Thomas Coryate is the first to mention forks in England (1611). He tells us that when he used a fork for eating in England he was ridiculed for his daintiness.

A 16th-century writer says:

> At Venice each person is served, besides his knife and spoon, with a fork to hold the meat while he cuts it, for they deem it ill manners that one should touch it with his hand.

From the 17th century, after Coryate's fork caused so much excitement, the development of table accoutrements is rapid. We see silver forks being used in Italy. We see table appointments keeping step with the developing culinary art. And by the end of the 18th century, we find that table manners as a whole have reached a fairly high degree of cultivation.

As for the knife, we know that the original cutting implements used by the human race consisted of fragments of flint or other stone, rudely chipped to a cutting edge. There are many such cutting instruments in existence. It

Bringing in the boar's head at a Saxon feast. A dainty rarely lacking on the Saxon table of the 9th and 10th centuries.

seems that the knife, or rather the cutting tool, was one of the first implements to be devised by man.

Of course, the knife took many forms and was made of many materials during the course of its development. During the Stone Age knives were made of flint, very much similar to the arrowheads that the Indians were using when the white man "discovered" them. There were also knives of bone, and in the Bronze Age, knives of bronze.

At first the knife was made for general cutting purposes. There was no such thing as a table knife in early times. Even as late as 300 years ago the table knife was a rarity. It is quite a recent development. For a long time each person carried about with him, usually in his belt or shoe, a knife of his own for general purposes, much as modern man carries around a pocket knife. Whenever large portions of food were served him, he cut them up with his knife and returned it to his belt.

The greatest advance in the table knife took place after the 17th century. Silver knives for table use were introduced in England and became popular. Sheffield, England, became one of the greatest cutlery manufacturing centres in the world and has retained that proud title without challenge.

The Use of Dishes: Pottery.—If our earliest primitive ancestors used dishes of any kind, they were natural, not man-made. It is very likely that a broad leaf was used by the savage as we use a plate; that a gourd was used as we use a bowl; that a halved cocoanut shell was used as we use a cup. These "dishes" were created, no doubt, as needed. In tropical climates, even to-day, uncivilized people use such natural objects as the cocoanut, the gourd, and the calabash for drinking vessels.

The tribal chief probably had his drinking vessel decorated and ornamented to distinguish it from those everyone could have, from the simple cocoanut shells that his subjects were permitted to use. From this custom of ornamenting the vessel for the chief it would seem that the idea for making separate vessels and jars evolved.

The making of pottery is one of the oldest arts of man. Even in early prehistory man knew of the uses of clay and made for himself jars, jugs, and drinking vessels.

Primitive man found clay on the surface of the ground and near the river beds. He spread it out upon a stone slab to remove the foreign substances. He beat it with stones and trod upon it with his feet to make it of a fairly uniform consistency, and then he fashioned it rudely with his hands, moulding it according to his whim. The rays of the sun made it hard.

Then came the great discovery of what fire would do. Man baked his pottery, made it hard and substantial. He began to make really beautiful jugs and vessels. A great deal of this early clay work has been preserved and gives us much of our knowledge concerning these ancient peoples.

The early Babylonians were skilled and clever in pottery-making. Clay was familiar to them, though for a long time they used it only in brick-making. When they perceived it to be suitable for other purposes, they began to mould it into lamps, pots, drinking vessels of all sizes and shapes. They used a rather coarse clay, mixing it with chopped straw to give it cohesion.

Some primitive genius invented the first crude potter's wheel, and the idea was copied by the Babylonians. They sought out and found a finer clay, and with the help of the potter's wheel they modelled vases, lamps, jugs.

Among the Greeks, Romans, Assyrians, and Egyptians, pottery developed as a fine art, and some of the examples that have come down to us are magnificent. The Grecian pottery is of surpassing beauty, and one marvels that it could have been created with such crude and simple materials as were available. The Mexicans and the Peruvians also made beautiful pottery.

Some writers accredit the Egyptians with the discovery of glass-blowing, for the Egyptians had glass drinking vessels and vases 4000 years ago. But glass-blowing was not invented until shortly before the Christian Era, and the beautiful glass objects made by the early Egyptians and miraculously preserved were modelled by hand over a core.

AT THE RIGHT, A MAN SHAPES A POT WITH HIS RIGHT HAND WHILE WITH HIS LEFT HAND HE KEEPS IT TURNING ON THE POTTER'S WHEEL. AT THE LEFT IS AN OVEN ON WHICH POTS ARE BAKED. ABOVE ARE SHOWN THE POTS ALREADY COMPLETED.

FROM WALL-PAINTING IN TOMB OF KHNUMHOTEP AT BENI HASAN. DYN. XII (ABOUT 2000 B.C.)

MANUFACTURE OF POTTERY

Courtesy of the Metropolitan Museum of Art.

With the invasion of the barbarians, the fine arts died in Rome and Greece. During the Middle Ages whatever pottery was made was crude and inartistic, except that of the Moors in Spain. Then came the great revival, led by Italy. The Italians made an exquisite decorated enamelled pottery known as majolica. A variety of this type of pottery, made in Faenze, Italy, is known as faience.

During the first half of the 9th century, the Chinese

began to make fine porcelain, for which they have since become famous. The poet Tu, living in that era, writes:

> The porcelain of Ta-yi kilns is light and yet strong. It rings with a low jade note and is famed throughout the city.

Tu might have been an advertising writer had he lived in the 20th century!

Trading with China, the Dutch gained a knowledge of pottery. This they combined with the knowledge of glazing which they borrowed from Italy. Then they learned how to make a blue colour by using oxide of cobalt, and they began to manufacture a clean blue and white pottery known as Delft, from the Dutch city. This blue and white pottery they were able to produce at a much lower price than they could secure Chinese wares. Thus chinaware came to be distinguished from ordinary earthenware —a distinction it has held ever since.

Before leaving the subject of pottery we cannot refrain from mentioning the two men who have, in comparatively recent times, contributed greatly to the beauty and utility of pottery. The first of these is Bernard Palissy who lived in 16th-century France. The second is Josiah Wedgwood who lived two centuries later in England.

Palissy was a potter at Saintes, France. He devoted a lifetime to a vain attempt to create a certain kind of white enamel, but in his experiments he made other discoveries which made his name forever famous in the history of pottery. He discovered the process of making beautifully coloured enamels by colouring the glazes before putting them over the baked clay. The former process had been to use a white enamel and then paint it. He made some very remarkable vases and dishes decorated with this coloured enamel. Other minor discoveries of his contributed largely to the beauty and artistry of pottery.

Josiah Wedgwood (1730–95) was one of the greatest potters the world has ever known. Authorities believe his classic vases, ornamented by the sculptor Flaxman, to be some of the finest specimens ever produced. Wedgwood was the originator of the famous dinnerware known as Queensware. He was the first to introduce cheap china in England, so making it possible for everyone to have clean, pretty tableware.

Although pottery was a highly developed art even in early times, and our ancestors had many pots, jugs, plates, and even cups and saucers, as modern excavations show, the use of separate dishes for each person is comparatively new. For a long time it was the general custom, among the high-bred as the low, for food to be brought in on large platters, divided by the steward, and placed on the bare table. The steward used the fork and knife to carve the meat; the diners used their fingers. Fruit and pastries were placed in baskets on the floor by the tables, and the guests helped themselves as they liked.

Concerning Table Manners.—Manners of any kind, but particularly table manners, belong to an advanced age. When food was simply food, and man ate to satisfy his hunger, there was no etiquette of the table. But when the culinary art developed and gave us jellies, custards, salads, ices, puddings, and when eating became something of a ceremony, table etiquette bowed itself into the social scheme. Foods have so disguised themselves that a recent writer on etiquette is moved to include an article headed "Attacking a Complicated Dish," in which she says:

> When a dinner has been prepared by a chef who prides himself on being a decorative artist, the guest of honour and whoever else may be the first to be served have quite a problem to know which part of an intricate structure is to be eaten, and which part is scenic effect!
>
> The main portion is generally clear enough; the uncertainty is in whether the flowers are eatable vegetables and whether the things that look like ducks are potatoes or trimming. If there are six or more, the chances are that they are edible, and that one or two of a kind are embellishments only. Rings around food are nearly always to be eaten; platforms under food seldom, if ever are. Aspics and desserts are, it may be said, occasionally Chinese puzzles, but if you do help yourself to part of the decoration, no great harm is done.

It was inevitable that, as foods changed, becoming more and more elaborate, more and more disguised, the eating manners of man should have changed also. When foods were quite plain and simple, man's eating manners were in accord. But when foods became elaborate, man's mode of eating those foods lost their simplicity and took on a wholly new social significance.

When forks and knives first made their appearance on the dinner table we can be certain that it was on the tables of the wealthy and the powerful. The humbler classes did not have knives and forks until considerably later.

We can understand how these first users of the knife and fork felt themselves quite fashionable and superior. They made of eating a certain ceremony. In their conscious importance they told one another what was correct and what was incorrect.

And later, when the use of knives and forks became general, the people patterned themselves after those who were accustomed to using the implements. They were clumsy at first. They did not know in which hand to hold the fork, in which the knife. They found it easier to eat in the primitive manner of their ancestors. Yet, as always, they wanted to be "with the crowd"—they wanted to do what everyone else, and particularly what the wealthy classes, were doing.

So the use of the knife and the fork, and the new custom of ceremony in dining, left the courts and found their way even into the humblest of homes. The new order of things seeped through the cities and into the smaller towns. Civilized man accepted table manners, but having them, he wondered how to use them. So originated the books on etiquette, manuals for the masses.

The Correct Use of Table Silver.—Table manners are still quite young, and man is by no means entirely at ease with them. In his own home and among his own kind of people he eats as he is accustomed, in the manner that seems most comfortable and natural to him. But let him find himself among people of a different social caste, and he is conscious of a vague unease. He wonders if he is holding his fork correctly, if a spoon or a fork should be used for the melon, if olives may be taken with the fingers. Furtively he watches the others, and is unutterably pathetic in his embarrassment.

Books on etiquette lay particular stress upon correct table manners. The writers realize that nothing can reveal as quickly as one's table manners the environment and the habits of life to which one has been accustomed.

> Spoons [says "The Book of Etiquette"] are used when eating grapefruit and fruits served with cream. Jellies, puddings, custards, porridges, preserves, and boiled eggs are always eaten with spoons. The spoon is used also with soup, bouillon, coffee and tea. In the case of the three latter beverages, however, the spoon is used only to stir them once or twice and to taste them to see that they are of the desired temperature. It is never allowed to stand in the cup. Nor is it permissible to draw up a spoon full of soup or coffee and blow upon it; one must wait until it is sufficiently cooled of itself.

Of course, rules such as these cannot possibly give exquisite table manners to one who has for a lifetime been accustomed to doing what is uncultivated and incorrect. Grace, poise, and ease come through practice and through association with cultured people. Etiquette is simply the master key that must be fitted to the lock and turned.

The greatest value of a book on etiquette is that it helps avoid conspicuous and embarrassing blunders. One cannot help being embarrassed if melon is served and one is not certain whether melon should be eaten with the fork or the spoon. It is not the most comfortable thing in the world to watch others for a clue. Books on etiquette tell what is correct according to the accepted standard.

Concerning knives and forks, "The Book of Etiquette" says:

> The first rule to be remembered is that the knife is never used for any purpose other than cutting food. It is unforgivable to use a knife to convey food to the mouth.
>
> The knife is held in the right hand and the fork in the left. When

the desired morsel of food is cut, the knife is laid aside temporarily and the fork is shifted to the right hand.

Custom has made this a rule in the United States; in most European countries the fork remains in the left hand and food is so conveyed to the mouth.

The foods eaten with the fork are meats, vegetables, fish, salads, oysters and clams, lobster, ices, frozen puddings, and melons. Hearts of lettuce and lettuce leaves are folded up with the fork and conveyed to the mouth. If the leaves are too large to be folded conveniently, they may be cut with the blunt edge of the fork—never with a knife.

Civilization has not entirely eliminated the use of the fingers in eating. We still have what are known as "finger foods." French artichokes, corn on the cob, lobster claws, celery, radishes and olives, raw fruits, bread, crackers, and some kinds of cake are taken in the fingers.

Origin and Use of the Finger Bowl.—Strangely enough, finger bowls, or their forerunners, have been in use from the time when infant civilizations were learning to enjoy the luxury of dinner-giving. Among the early Greeks it was considered ill-bred to sit down to table (or rather lie down to table!) at once; first there was a period of entertainment, then small ewers of water were brought in and the guests washed their hands. Not until they had done so were they ready to dine. The same custom seems to have prevailed among the Romans and Egyptians.

Among the Romans all guests washed their hands before and after dinner. Small basins were used for this purpose, and usually a flower or two was dropped into the water to make it fragrant. This is a custom which we seem to have borrowed from them, for modern writers on etiquette say, "A fragrant leaf may be added to the water" (in the finger bowl).

The Egyptian guest at a dinner party was welcomed by a special servant who anointed his head and washed his hands. Sometimes the process was repeated during the course of the dinner, which lasted several hours. Before leaving the table the hands were always washed, whether

(Courtesy of Metropolitan Museum of Art)

An ornamented drinking vessel, bronze age. Cypriote.

A silver cup for drinking. Cypriote, 500 B. C.

(Courtesy of Metropolitan Museum of Art)

Blown glass, from Rome.

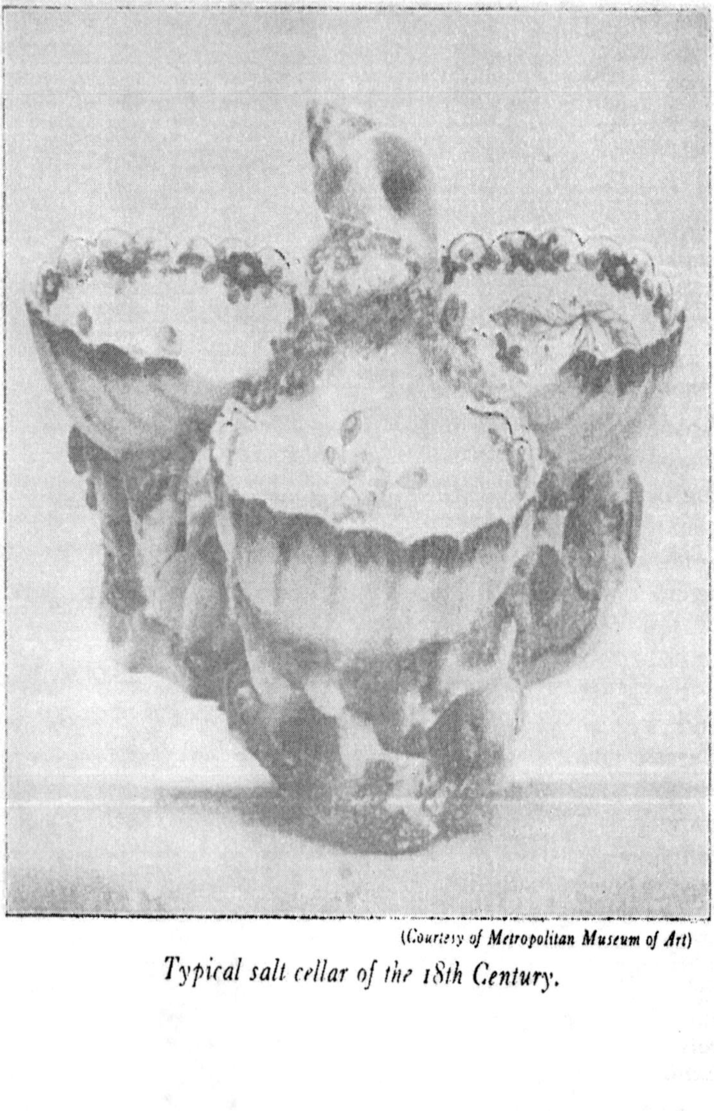

(Courtesy of Metropolitan Museum of Art)

Typical salt cellar of the 18th Century.

for purposes of cleanliness or because of established custom we do not know.

The Hebrews made of hand-washing a sort of ceremony. Before eating the hands were washed; upon returning from a funeral the hands were washed before reëntering the home; before making burnt offering or sacrifice at the tabernacle the hands were washed. The Bible contains many laws concerning the ablutions required of the people of Israel.

And he set the laver between the tabernacle of the congregation and the altar, and put water there for washing. And Moses and Aaron and his sons washed therefrom their hands and their feet. (Exodus XL, 30, 31.)

The finger bowl, as we know it, probably made its first appearance in the 15th century. In 1455 at the Court of Anjou (third son of Louis II, King of Sicily) it was the custom to wash the hands just before leaving the dining room. It appears that during that year the custom became general and popular. For these ablutions, scented water —usually rose water—was brought into the dining room in ewers of precious and delicately wrought metals. Pages or squires handed the ewers to the ladies in silver basins to hold the water as it was poured over the hands.

From the Court the custom spread through the cities and was adopted by the wealthier and the fad-seeking classes. Finger bowls thenceforth appeared upon all fashionable tables. But instead of disappearing in the customary manner of the fad, the use of the finger bowl has remained and is to-day an accepted custom.

Whenever fruits are served the finger bowl should follow. It is always used at the completion of the dinner. The bowl is always filled with tepid water and set upon a plate. The fingers are dipped lightly in the bowl, one hand at a time, and then dried on the napkin. It is a mark of ill-breeding to splash the water about, to put both hands into the bowl at once, or to wet the entire palm of the hand. Only the finger tips should touch the water.

Setting the Table.—The ancient Greeks took great pride

in their table appointments. They used elaborate bowls and beautiful drinking vessels. From the Odyssey (IV, 614–18) we learn that the choicest gift that Menelaus could offer to Telemachus when he took his departure from his court was a richly wrought bowl such as the wealthier classes were then using on important occasions—as we use our choicest chinaware and finest silver on occasions of importance. We quote Homer's description:

> Of all the chattels that my house contains,
> The noblest and most beautiful, a bowl
> Wrought deftly, all of silver, but with lips
> Gold-sprinkled, by Hephæstus shaped and framed
> Which Phædimus once gave me, Sidon's king.

The Greeks ate three meals daily, according to William Swinton. Their tables were uncovered, and they ate reclining on couches, using their fingers in primitive fashion. They had no knives or forks for table use, but spoons were fairly common.

Among the Egyptians the guests sat around a table and dipped bread into a common dish placed in the centre. This mode of eating from a common dish, widely prevalent among early peoples, still exists in Cairo and throughout the East.

A study of existing savage races reveals many peculiar contradictions, as, for instance, the case of the Niam-Niam. Here is a people hopelessly savage; the Niam-Niam are, or were until recently, cruel cannibals; they are known to desert their sick and their aged. Yet they have a strict etiquette regulating the reception of guests. And when several of them drink together "they are observed each to wipe the rim of the drinking vessel before passing it on."

One is impressed by the extremes of barbarity which are sometimes found among peoples who have some habits of culture and refinement. The Ahts are known occasionally to sacrifice one of their number to the gods; they desert the aged; they are cruel and savage. Yet after meals they invariably offer to the guest water and cedar bark for washing the hands and mouth! And they keep small mats of bark strips on which strangers can wipe their feet.

But as a rule early peoples, savage or semi-civilized, gave little thought to table appointments. They were more interested in the food than in the manner in which it was served. The Greeks and Romans were possibly an exception to this rule; but even they, gourmands that they were, looked to the contents of the dish before they concerned themselves with the dish itself.

As the centuries rolled by and the culinary art reached a high degree of development, table appointments began to show a new influence. Curious dishes, for holding spices and condiments, sauces and relishes, made their appearance. Even great artists, whose fame still rings in our ears, thought it not the least beneath their dignity to lend their genius to the painting of dishes and salt cellars. Tables became crowded not only with new kinds of foods —or rather, old foods served in different dress—but with new and elaborate appointments.

Only a quarter of a century ago it was still customary to load the table with all sorts of appointments—glasses, tiny dishes for olives and salted nuts, ornate silver bowls, napkin rings, hand-painted chinaware and enough forks, knives, and spoons at each place for at least a dozen courses! Scarcely a square inch of the white tablecloth showed through.

But to-day, good taste demands precisely the opposite. Nothing is placed on the table that is not actually needed. Services are of silver, and china is simple in design but of the finest quality. A centrepiece of glass, china, or silver is generally used, on top of which is placed the floral decoration. When adjusted, this floral centrepiece may be used as a mathematical base for all the rest of the table appointments.

The early colonists used tall, slender candlesticks on their dinner tables, because they had no other means of illumination. But we like to continue the old custom despite electricity and its clever conveniences, because of the traditions that surround the mellow candle gleam, because of the romances and the memories that lurk in its ring of light.

And so we place four candlesticks equidistant around the centrepiece—stately guardians of the dinner table. And we light the candles just before the guests arrive. Between the candlesticks are located the salt and pepper dishes; and with this mathematical centre correctly arranged, we proceed to set the places for the guests.

The knives and spoons are placed at the right, in the order in which they are to be used. The proper number of forks is placed to the left. Not more than three forks should ever appear on the table at one place. This custom originated a century ago when the introduction of many new dishes threatened to swamp the table with forks. Etiquette writers then helped to establish the rule that no more than three forks appear on the table at one place, and that other forks be brought in as needed.

Saying Grace before Eating.—The custom of saying grace before eating did not originate as an expression of thankfulness. Early peoples offered prayer before eating, to avert any deleterious influence that the food might possess.

Primitive peoples sometimes made sacrifice to their gods before a feast to make sure that the foods upon which they intended feasting would not poison them or cause them injury. Probably out of this custom grew the later one of making prayer before every meal—a custom found among many savage races. The Mois of Cochin China always "ask for a blessing upon their food" before eating and drinking. The Tahitians and other South Sea Islanders offer a prayer before eating.

The Israelites appear to have been among the first to offer prayer before eating, *out of gratitude for having food to eat.* The Egyptians, a scrupulously religious people, apparently copied the notion from them. We find that they rarely sat down to meals without saying grace; and, like the Israelites, they offered food to their gods before eating themselves.

Like the custom of saying grace, fasting has a primitive background. In primitive life, when a crisis of some sort was at hand, when it was necessary to coax food from an obdurate god or insure success in war, fasting was a means of magic persuasion. The savage did not fast because he liked to; we can be certain of that. He fasted to avoid danger to himself.

Out of this first custom of fasting to avoid danger and evil influences evidently grew the idea of fasting being good for body and nerves. Thus the early Christians referred to fasting as "a means to prevent evil spirits entering the body."

The religious element of fasting by no means began with the Christians. In India it was anciently the custom for fakirs to starve themselves and inflict upon themselves all sorts of bodily torture. This was a form of worship among them. The Eskimo are forbidden by their religion to make use of certain seals at certain times; and even though a community may be on the point of starvation, no one will kill one of the seals. One is amazed at the amount of self-control shown by these people whom we are inclined to think of as savages.

The Toast.—There are several different stories, all interesting, concerning the origin of the toast. Most authorities, however, are of the opinion that the custom of "drinking to the health" of a person originated with the practice of drinking first to show that the drink is not harmful. This little ceremony of drinking first would predispose the other to friendliness and good-will.

Among both the Romans and the Greeks healths were drunk to guests. Some writers say that the custom originated with the Greeks and was copied by the Romans, but of this we cannot be certain. We know that both drank healths, and that both had the custom of proving the wine unpoisoned by having the host drink first. Neither a Greek nor a Roman would pass the cup to his friend without having first tasted of it to prove its safety. Thus drinking together came to be a sort of pledge to friendship and amity.

Roman gallants had a pretty drinking custom. Among them it was the custom to drink as many glasses of wine as there were letters in their sweethearts' names. For instance, Martial's bit of verse:

> Six cups to Naevia's health go quickly round
> And he with seven the fair Justina crowned.

A great many early peoples offered a goblet of wine to a guest the moment he entered the house, possibly as a sign of good-will. We have already seen how drinking together constituted a form of friendship among early races (see pp. 323-324). At the tables of the rich in early Egypt wines were offered to the guests before eating to excite the palate. The Chinese are said to have offered wine to guests before eating from the earliest times. Among the Romans, when a late comer was announced by the servants (yes, the early Romans and the early Egyptians both announced guests, even as we do!) he was immediately given a goblet of wine as a sign of welcome.

Before Volstead discovered America it was quite a general custom to offer a cocktail to a dinner guest before entering the dining room. The Greeks, the Romans, and the Egyptians set this happy precedent; Volstead destroyed it; but let us hope it won't affect our hospitality!

It was an ancient custom, not only to drink to healths, but to make oaths with food or drink. In Madagascar, for instance, parties taking oath drink together, each praying that the liquid turn to poison for him who breaks the vow. In Ceram it is customary to take oath by eating food in which a sword has been placed. The Timorese taking oath drink water which has been mixed with gunpowder and earth, saying, "May I die of sickness, by powder or the sword if I swear falsely." The Malays swear alliance, truth, fidelity, etc., by drinking water in which daggers or spears have been dipped. Other savage peoples cut open a vein, mix the blood with water, and take oath with this horrid drink.

Doubt surrounds the true origin of the word "toast." One writer says that in the reign of Charles II a piece of toasted bread was dropped in the wine, and a wit, seeing that the wine had been quaffed, remarked, "If I cannot drink the wine, at least I can have the toast."

Others tell us that at Bath, during this reign, a celebrated beauty of the court of Charles was in the Cross Bath. One of the crowd took a glass of the water in which she stood and drank her health to the company. A gay fellow is said to have jumped up saying, "I like not the liquor, but I shall have the toast." Since then, we are told, it has been the custom to call this type of drinking a toast.

Still another theory concerning the origin of the word has been advanced. It was a general custom to drink by the fireside, bread being toasted while the men drank. Some writers believe that the word, in connection with drinking healths, originated in this way.

An entirely unrelated tale concerning the origin of drinking healths has been found, in which Edward the Martyr, who came to the throne of England in 975, figures. It appears that on the 18th of March, 978, the King was hunting in Dorset Forest, near the old Corfe Castle, where Elfrida lived. He decided to pay her a visit. Riding up to the castle unattended, he was greeted affectionately by the Queen and engaged in a conversation with her. She asked him to dismount, but he refused. Whereupon she handed him a cup of wine with her own hands, and while he was drinking caused him to be stabbed in the back. He died of his wounds.

This, we are led to believe, gave rise to a form of health drinking. It became customary throughout England when drinking at parties or dinners to pass around one large cup. Each person to receive the cup rose and drank from it. The man beside him rose also, as his "pledge" to protect him from "being stabbed in the back as was the Martyr Edward." This was known as drinking health. The cup which went the round of the table came to be known as the "loving cup." Such cups came to be looked upon as the proper tribute of an inferior person to one of superior rank. The "loving cup" to-day is given to the winning team, to the individual or the club which proves itself superior.

Drinking toasts from a slipper dates back to the 18th century. In certain parts of Hungary it was the custom for a groom to drink a toast to the bride out of her slipper on the wedding night. The slipper was publicly removed, filled with wine and given to the groom. He made a toast to his bride, drank the wine and threw the slipper to the guests. The custom spread to other localities, and in the 19th century every gallant felt it his duty to drink a toast to some lady out of her shoe. To-day the custom is almost obsolete, having faded into the background with Elizabethan ruffs and Victorian "receptions."

Customs of Politeness.—"The hostess must see that all her guests are comfortable and well taken care of."

The early Romans and Greeks evidently followed this precept, voiced by a writer who came many generations later, when these twin civilizations were already dead, and forgotten by all save the student. The Romans rarely invited guests to their dinners, which were simple repasts; but they almost invariably had visitors at the most important meal of the day—the supper.

These early Roman suppers held from three to seven courses. The host gave each guest an exact list of the courses and all the dishes of which the feast was composed —a forerunner of the menu card. Each guest was presented with a wreath of flowers and was given a goblet of wine to drink.

The Roman host made every effort to please his guests and supply them with every comfort. At first chairs or stools were used: but after their association with the Greeks and Asiatics, the Romans adopted the dining couch. Three of these beds, or couches, were placed at one table, the fourth side usually being left open to receive the service. Four people could dine comfortably from one couch. They were low, without backs and covered with rich fabrics. Some were in the shape of half-moons. The host sat at the head table with the guest of honour and his wife; the other guests took places at the other two tables according to rank.

The Greeks also provided carefully for the comfort of their guests. Servants brought in ewers of water as soon as the guests arrived so that they might freshen themselves. Like the Roman guests, they were given goblets of wine before the feast.

The Greeks ate reclining on couches, but usually one person to a couch and not several as among the Romans. They had no knives and forks, but water was provided several times during the course of the meal for washing the hands.

The Egyptians were fond of entertaining, and the Egyptian host delighted in pleasing and amusing his guests. Dinner was served at midday and supper at night. The food, the best that the host was able to afford, was placed in the centre of the table and the guests helped themselves. They were provided with comfortable couches on which they stretched for hours, eating, drinking, and enjoying the music and entertainments which the host provided.

When invited to a dinner, the ancient Egyptian brought his servants. One carried his stool, another his writing tablet, another his sandals. It was considered polite for the guest to bring with him whatever he would need during his stay.

Upon their arrival, guests gathered in the sitting room. The host and hostess sat side by side and each guest, as he arrived, approached them to receive their welcome and good wishes. Then he joined the others, was given a goblet of wine, and enjoyed the music and dancing provided for his entertainment. Both the Egyptians and the Greeks considered it ill-bred to sit down to table immediately upon arrival. They felt that it was a form of politeness to assemble first for a period of chatting and entertainment. We still feel that it is somehow impolite to eat the moment we reach the house of a friend or acquaintance.

It is interesting to note that the host and hostess never entered the dining room until all their guests had preceded them. They considered it impolite to do so. With us,

> The host leads with the lady who is to sit at his right; the hostess ends the "procession" with that lady's husband. If there is one more woman than men in the party, the customary thing is for the hostess to enter the dining-room alone after all her guests have entered.

The custom of "coupling" guests, that is, placing them at the table in couples, was introduced during the age of Chivalry. At about 1455 it became the custom to place a gentleman and a lady together, each couple having one cup and one plate, from whence comes our phrase "to eat from the same plate."

But the Egyptians, who invited ladies to their dinners, had a sort of double chair which followed the use of the dining couch. The single guest was permitted to occupy one of these chairs; but a married couple was obliged to share it. We see here a very early form of "coupling" guests.

Among the Egyptians it was a form of politeness to offer one another a flower from one's bouquet. The Greeks and Egyptians always had flowers at their parties, but it was the Egyptians who made the flowers tokens of friendship. Hostesses to-day like to have a small decorative bouquet at the place of each woman guest at their formal dinner parties.

In the United States and elsewhere, the guest is expected to taste of every dish served. Several writers suggest that this custom had its origin among the early Iroquois Indians.

Whether hungry or not, the Iroquois guest was obliged

to taste of every dish presented to him. He was also expected to say *"Hz-në-a-weh,"* which means "I thank you." To refuse a dish was to indicate enmity.

Similarly, among certain tribes of Siam—notably the Steins, a Shan tribe—a visitor was expected to eat whatever was set before him. He was expected to drink out of the common cup through his bamboo tube. If he neglected to do so he was usually killed, for the others suspected him of being an enemy. Even to-day the stranger who refuses to eat what is placed before him takes the risk of being knifed before he has gone very much farther.

Among civilized peoples it is considered ordinary politeness to taste of each dish served. "The Book of Etiquette" says,

> It is better to accept a little of each course on one's plate and eat a bit of it although one does not particularly care for it, than to refuse it entirely.

Which brings to mind the old pressing hospitality of the French bourgeois which seemed to spread everywhere. The hostess heaped food upon the guest's plate, assuming that the guest was too timid to ask for it himself. This was a form of vanity, of course, induced by the selfish desire to see one's good things appreciated. Some hostesses carried this custom to such extremes that the guest was obliged to turn his plate upside down. It is still a custom to-day, when a course is completed, to place one's knife and fork on the plate to indicate that one has had sufficient.

But the old pressing hospitality is gone and is rarely, if ever, to be found among the fashionable and well-bred classes. Nevertheless, books on etiquette still find it necessary to admonish:

> Ten-course dinners are quite out of fashion, and the "groaning board" belongs to the past. The correct hostess of to-day does not take the attitude that the guest has come to her home half-starved.

And again:

> To insist, on the part of the host or hostess, after the guest has refused a second helping, is overdoing the bounds of hospitality, and perilously borders on the verge of incivility.

Whom to serve first is a problem of great concern to the modern hostess. In some homes the hostess is served first; in others the guests are served before the hostess. Both forms are correct, but it is interesting to note their origins.

It has always been the custom among savage peoples for the host to take the first bite or drink, to "take the fetish" from the food. In other words, he proves by taking the first bite that the food is safe and unpoisoned.

In the Banks Islands it has always been the custom for the host to take the first bite of any food, to take any risk of poisoning upon himself. In New Guinea it is a mark of courtesy and friendship to offer water to a stranger; but before presenting it the natives drink themselves to prove that the water is not dangerous in any way. Among the Basutos, when food or drink is offered to a guest and he is in no doubt as to whether or not it is safe, he may ask the host to eat first. The host, out of politeness, is obliged to do so. Similar customs are to be found in Central Africa, among the Damaras, among the Iddahs, among the Zulus. In Soudan the housewife always takes the first drink of any beverage to "take the fetish" off it. Throughout the Middle Ages, when it was a simple matter to dispose of one's unwelcome guests by poisoning, polite hostesses served themselves first to prove that *their* food at least was safe to eat!

But as civilization advanced, courtesy came to mean more than tradition, and gradually the custom of serving guests first came to be recognized as a form of politeness. Yet even to-day we find in many homes that the hostess is invariably served first. Custom lives on long after its original meaning or purpose has been forgotten. In fashionable homes, however, preference is usually given to the more polite form of guests first.

From a 17th-Century "Civilite."—We have previously mentioned two rare old *Civilités* which are now in the hands of an English art collector (see p. 111) There are in one of these volumes, dated 1695, many rules of etiquette concerning manners at the table, and we are able to glean from them an interesting picture of table manners in the 17th century. We know you will find some of these rules amusing.

Here, for instance, is one bit of advice. "One ought sometimes to look off the meat, yet without looking on the meat which is before others." Dinners must have been most lively affairs in the 17th century!

The guest is further admonished that "he must not lick his fingers or wipe them on the bread." A later *Civilité* (1782) reminds the fashionable hostess that "viands are served with the fork and not with the hand."

We are led to wonder what sort of soup was served in the 17th century when we read, "Do not try to eat soup with a fork." Evidently table forks were so new that people did not know just how to use them.

According to the *Civilité*, when a lady drank at the table an attendant stood beside her and held a napkin under her chin. It was only at the tables of the wealthy that every guest had an individual glass. These glasses were not placed on the table but were ranged on a sideboard. Guests were obliged to call for the drink as they desired it. It was only about the middle of the 18th century that the glass found its way to the table and took its place at the right of the guest.

Our *Civilité* takes great pains in warning the guest not to criticize the host's viands. To do so, we are informed, would be both ill-bred and impolite. Modern books on etiquette voice the same thought.

Guests washed their hands before dining, and the *Civilité* naïvely suggests that "a dry corner be left [on the towel] for the person who is to use it afterwards."

Among other things, the guest is exhorted not to scratch

himself in company, not to snuff the candle with his fingers, not to blow in his soup, not to return the meat to the dish after smelling it. He must not pocket the fruit at dessert, and he must not put a second morsel into his mouth before the first has been swallowed.

Persons of good breeding never swallow before masticating [we are told]. If the plate before you is not quite clean do not scrape it with your fingers; ask for another. Make as little noise as possible in swallowing. Do not pile up your plate till it will hold no more. Do not on any account clutch your plate as though you feared that someone would snatch it from you.

We wonder how our etiquette books will seem to those who read in 2200!

Conversation at the Table.—Louis Étienne St. Denis, in his personal recollections, gives us some very interesting sidelights upon the personality and upon the social life of the great Bonaparte. In his book, "Napoleon, from the Tuileries to St. Helena," (translated from the French by Frank Hunter Potter) he tells us how important the Emperor's dinner hours were to him and how he liked to fill them with light, gay conversation. He always liked dinner served early, and he always invited as guests those whose conversation he enjoyed. Subjects of importance were rarely discussed at his dinner table; he was fond of gay witticism and jolly "drawing-room conversation." He found such conversation a great relaxation.

Most frequently when the Emperor came out of his room he would be accompanied by some important person—a Minister or someone —with whom he would continue his conversation till the Empress arrived, for when she was present all serious discussion was banished and playful chat took its place.

The Egyptians were among the first to realize the pleasures to be derived from dinner-hour conversation. The Egyptian host felt it his duty to keep the conversation interesting and animated, and the guests felt it their duty to respond.

But on the contrary, most early peoples ate in silence,

and there are even to-day certain peoples who never talk while at their meals. The Japanese, Chinese, and other Orientals eat in silence. The Ahts, Maoris, Siamese, and Hindus rarely talk when eating. The Arabs of Syria mutter a *Bismillah* before eating, then take their meals in absolute silence. The Buddhist priests say that "to eat and talk at the same time is sin."

Everything is relative, however, and social life is something like a moving picture. The scenes change as the story develops, but the plot remains the same. Thus, a quarter of a century ago any Southern gentleman would have told you that the carving of a chicken or a duck was an art, and an art which every gentleman must possess. Yet to-day in almost ninety-nine families out of one hundred the carving is done in the kitchen, simply because it has been found more convenient and expeditious. Fifty years ago a young woman was considered well bred when she knew how to enter a drawing room correctly. To-day, instead of carrying books on her head in practice to gain poise and haughty bearing, she opens the books to find out what is inside. And instead of sitting demurely near her chaperon until someone invites her to dance, she uses the information obtained from the books to ensnare the handsome young college professor and engage him in an animated conversation concerning Palæolithic fossils, or perhaps the theory of relativity!

And so, too, has it been with dinner conversation. Among some peoples it was, and is, customary to eat in silence. Among us it was at one time customary to bar all intellectual conversation at the dinner table and "engage in simple, pleasant, light talk that everyone can enjoy."

To-day the clever hostess chooses her guests carefully, with a regard for their tastes in talk as in other things, and she permits them to introduce whatever subjects they themselves enjoy talking about, whether it be the latest Parisian fad or the newest best-seller. She makes no attempt to "lead" the conversation unless she finds it lagging. And if the talk veers to things intellectual and her guests discuss the possibility of life on Mars, or of Japan joining other lost lands for ever at the bottom of the Pacific, so much the better! It is a reflection upon her good sense in inviting guests; for only a well-selected group of people can begin, and carry on for any length of time, an interesting intellectual discussion.

The first rule, then, is to choose your guests well. The rest will follow.

(Courtesy of Metropolitan Museum of Art)

Scene from a Greek oinochoe, 450 B. C. Return of Hephaistos to Olympus. Notice the loving cup, and notice also the musician with his double reed pipes who precedes to frighten away evil spirits.

(Courtesy of Metropolitan Museum of Art)

Bronze bell of about the 4th Century, B. C., Greece.

CHAPTER XIV

HOLIDAYS AND THEIR CUSTOMS; HOW THEY ORIGINATED

Our harvest being gotten in, our governor sent four men on fowling so that we might after a special manner rejoice together after we had gathered the fruits of our labours. They four killed as much fowl as with a little help beside served the company about a week. At which times among other recreations we exercised our arms, many of the Indians coming amongst us, and among the rest their greatest king, Massasoyt, with some ninety men, whom for three days we entertained and feasted, and they went out and killed five deer which they brought and bestowed on our governor, and upon the captain and others.

—EDWARD WINSLOW (to a friend in England).
December 11, 1621

THE PLAYDAYS OF HUMANITY

MAN was once free as the birds. He jumped and danced and shouted as his instincts prompted. He slept when the sun made him drowsy and ate when he found his food. He laughed at the dancing moonbeams. He beat his breast in proud defiance of the rain. He jumped in glee from stone to stone, rocked wildly from the limb of a tree, gave animal vent to the instincts and impulses that crowded through him. So, short and happy, went the span of his life.

Then came civilization. Life was cut into slices and handed to some on a silver platter, to some on a wooden spoon. The powerful cut little squares from the heart of the universe and called them laws. Factories and offices grew where forests used to be. Days were divided into hours, each hour with its special duty. Man stifled his natural instincts, and walked silent with the masses.

But beneath the smoothness that is civilization there smoulders a great unrest. Man longs for the freedom that once was his. Sometimes, while civilization still was young, that longing became intense and mass madness resulted. The many trampled upon the few. And the few, being wise, created holidays.

We are taught that these great playdays of humanity are really holy days, special days set aside in which to honour some person or some memory, which is, of course, partly true. But we cannot help seeing that these holidays —playdays—are brief periods during which the mass spirit frees itself from the shackles of life, and dances as it did when the world was young.

Festival days have been set aside and observed in all ages, and among practically all peoples. Writers tell us that such-and-such a holiday was established because of some event connected with the religious life of the people, or some great natural event such as the return of spring. But these are the excuses, not the causes. The one great cause is that man needs regular playdays, fun days. He has not yet learned to stifle his natural instincts without brief periods of freedom.

The ancient Druids celebrating May Day by building huge fires and dancing wildly around them; the joy-crazed Paris mobs celebrating the Festival of the Fools in the shadow of Notre Dame; the English peasantry kindling fires, roasting nuts, and making merry though ghosts walk abroad on Hallowe'en—are they not all but glorified forms of "mob relief"? Can't you almost hear the revelling masses take a deep breath as they throw off the grim realities of their daily life, and play?

We of a later and more artificial civilization have learned to control a little better than our forefathers the instincts and impulses that crowd through us. Therefore, our festival days have less madness, more dignity. But they are, nevertheless, playdays, no matter what religious or reverential significance we may choose to attach to them.

The earliest festivals appear to have been connected with the dead. Among primitive peoples, when a death occurred, fires were kindled and drums were beaten to frighten away the evil spirits. Gifts were made to the dead man to carry with him to the next world, and offerings were made to the gods. Thus death was the occasion for a sort of festival. Often feasting and dancing accompanied other ceremonies.

Later festivals came to be connected with the sun and the moon. The moon particularly, because of its changing aspects, inspired many forms of worship and festivity in man. In some parts of New Britain it is even now the custom to bow to the new moon. In the Hervey Islands superstitious people plant their cocoanuts at the full of the moon, sometimes with festivity and celebration.

Then came the celebrations connected with seed-time and harvest-time, festivities for the changing seasons. The Romans celebrated Lupercalia in spring and Saturnalia in midwinter. These two holidays were marked by games, amusements, the exchange of gifts. The Greeks had feasts to celebrate the two most important seasons of the year—harvest-time and spring-time. These two seasons symbolized to them the time of plenty and the time of promise. In their festivals they honoured the god of the vineyard, Dionysus (Bacchus). To show their worship they danced, sang, and made sacrifice. At the winter festival, bands of revellers marched in high glee through the village, chanting rude choruses.

These early festivals were, in a sense, religious. Feasting was a part of the celebration and the good things were shared with the gods. But it was not a religious instinct that inspired the celebration in the first place; it was a natural instinct. We can understand how the sudden beautiful flowering of nature in the spring, how the rich bounties of harvest-time, would have created a certain joyousness in the multitudes. And this joyousness inspired the ancient festivals which survive in our May Day and Thanksgiving.

Holiday meant originally holy day, since the gods played a conspicuous part in the festivals. The holiness of the holiday has survived to a great extent, particularly in such holidays as Easter and Christmas. But fundamentally the holiday is a day of merrymaking and celebration.

Political holidays, holidays celebrating a momentous victory, the beginning of a new period, or the birth of some great leader, are all of a later growth and belong to a more advanced stage of progress. With their advent we sense a new element entering into the holiday spirit—sentiment. Sometimes it is the sentiment of one person, or perhaps of one party or class; more frequently it is the sentiment of the nation, of the people.

Holidays Celebrated in the United States.—The manner in which a people observes its holidays is an excellent reflection upon the character of that people. The Japanese with their *O Hina Sama* (Dolls' Festival) show an inherent love of children. The French with their *Poisson d'avril* (April Fool) show an appreciation of the practical joke. The Chinese with their Festival of the Dragon Boats (at New Year) show a love of the grotesque, the unusual, the magical.

In the United States holidays have a certain dignity. There are no legal national holidays, although Congress does name special holidays, and it is the privilege of the various states to make them legal.

Practically all states make New Year's Day legal. Other holidays made legal by state action are:

Washington's Birthday	(Feb. 22)
Memorial Day	(May 30 in North, April 26, June 10 in Southern states)
Independence Day	(July 4)
Labour Day	(First Monday in Sept.)
Thanksgiving	(Last Thursday in Nov.)
Christmas	(Dec. 25)

State action sometimes makes these popular holidays legal:

Arbour Day	(Fixed by governor)
Lincoln's Birthday	(Feb. 12)
Flag Day	(June 14)
Columbus Day	(Oct. 12)
Armistice Day	(Nov. 11)

There is still another class of holidays, entirely different from those mentioned above. They have no legal recognition. But, with their customs, they are firmly rooted in the folklore and the traditions of the people, and they continue to be observed from one generation to another. These holidays are:

Valentine's Day	(Feb. 14)
St. Patrick's Day	(March 17)
April Fool's Day	(April 1)
Easter Day	(Usually in April)
May Day	(May 1)
Mother's Day	(Second Sunday in May)
Hallowe'en	(Oct. 31)

Let us see precisely how these holidays originated and what the customs connected with them—customs we still religiously observe—mean. We will start with New Year's Day and trace each holiday to its source. And we will concern ourselves not only with the origins of these holidays and their interesting customs, but with modern methods of entertainment and celebration.

NEW YEAR'S DAY

The custom of celebrating the New Year is very old. Some accredit it to the Chinese, some to the ancient Germans, some to the Romans.

The Chinese have always made of the New Year an extravagant and elaborate celebration. They have, at the New Year, their Feast of the Lanterns, their gay Festival of the Dragon Boats, their Fisherman's Festival. Their New Year begins several days later than ours, and the attendant celebrations last over a period of days.

The New Year of the ancient Germans was established as a result of the changing seasons. At first the German year was divided simply into summer and winter, one winter and one summer being counted a year.

It is important to remember that the German winter actually began about the middle of November, which was the period when the ground began to freeze. About this time, which was the time of flock-gathering and harvesting, the people were inclined to celebrate with feasting and festivity. We can understand their joyousness at gathering together, after the separation and work of the summer months, building fires, enjoying the fruits of their harvest, enjoying above everything else their brief span of freedom from toil.

Thus the ancient Germans came to look upon this period as the beginning of the New Year—the putting aside of old troubles and old worries, the welcoming of new duties and the promise of new bounties. The change, very naturally, was one to be celebrated with feasting and merrymaking. This original New Year's festivity would have taken place about the end of November when winter was beginning to set in and the harvest was garnered.

Then came the invasion of the Romans. And though the old German division of the year with its quaint festivities is still observed in rustic localities, the New Year came to be celebrated on the first of January.

The early Romans made much of the New Year. To them it symbolized the putting aside of an old life, the taking up of a new. They presented one another with branches of trees as tokens of good luck for the coming year. Some authorities are of the opinion that the custom of decorating houses and churches with evergreens at this period of the year originated with the old Roman practice of presenting tree branches.

Savage peoples greet the beginning of a new year with great rejoicing. Among the Zulus the opening of the year is celebrated with the Feast of the First Fruits. The men are gorged with the flesh of the bull or ox, they are feasted and fêted, that they may be strong and prosperous during the coming year.

The Cherokees have an elaborate New Year's festival. On the day that the new year is supposed to begin they build huge fires and burn all the old clothes and utensils.

The cabins are made scrupulously clean. Old fires are extinguished, the dirt removed, and new fires built in their place.

The following day the festivities begin. Everyone wears new apparel; new corn is cooked; new beads and headdresses are displayed. Everything old is cast aside, to symbolize the passing of the old year.

For three or four days there are music, feasting, and ceremonious dancing. Visits are made to neighbouring villages. Prisoners are pardoned. Everyone rejoices that a new year is to begin, and that he has been favoured by the gods and permitted to live on in this next year.

It is a most colourful and picturesque celebration and it gives us an excellent idea of the common notion concerning the New Year. The multitudes recognize the period as an auspicious one for beginning all over, starting a new lease on life, casting off the old and welcoming the new. That they celebrate with feasting and merrymaking is natural enough, knowing what we do of human instincts.

The New Year's Resolution.—The New Year's resolution undoubtedly had its origin in the notion that the coming year represented an entirely new period of life to the individual, with which he might do as he pleased. What was already passed he put out of his mind, for it was something over which he had no control. But on the coming year he concentrated in earnestness. It spread out like a golden vista before him. It was a period of promise. And he probably found himself making solemn avowals concerning what he would do with his next year of life.

In ancient England it was the custom to clean out the chimneys on New Year's Day so that luck could descend and, of course, remain all year. With us it is customary to speak of "cleaning the slate" (of life) and making good resolutions so that the "slate" will remain clean throughout the year.

The making of New Year's resolutions became quickly a common practice. We can understand why a custom such as this would appeal to the popular fancy and remain throughout the generations. To a mass mind, no period of the year could be more timely for a change in one's mode of living than that period which represents the beginning of the year. A new year—a new life.

The New Year's Gift.—The exchange of gifts at New Year's probably had its origin in the desire to invite prosperity during the coming year. First the gifts would be to the gods, with a little prayer that one may be happy and prosperous during the year. Then the idea would expand, and gifts would be exchanged promiscuously.

The ancient Romans were accustomed, at New Year's time, to present small gifts to the senators under whose protection they were placed. Here again we see the desire to invite safety and protection during the coming year by making gifts. The Romans also gave one another branches of trees as tokens of good luck for the year, as we have already seen (see p. 394).

The Persians have a custom of presenting one another with eggs on New Year's Day. The egg, of course, typifies creation, the beginning of life, and hence, the beginning of a new period of life. The same thought is conveyed by our Easter egg, as we shall presently see.

In France and Spain, New Year's Day has always been the proper time for exchanging gifts. The people make calls upon one another, extend their good wishes for the coming year, and make small gifts. From the earliest times, and always throughout the ages, the exchange of gifts seems to have prevailed to a greater extent at New Year's than at any other time.

The kinds of gifts have varied at different times and among different peoples. For a long time the glove was considered the appropriate New Year's gift. In more recent times the box of candy has become popular. Calendars are peculiarly appropriate because a new calendar is needed at the beginning of a new year. The book, too, has become a popular New Year's gift; and lately there appears to be a tendency to sign up a friend's name for a year's subscription to a magazine, as a New Year's remembrance.

The Round of Calls.—Since the days of the early Romans when it was customary to visit the senator under whose protection one was placed and carry him a New Year's gift, it has been customary to make a round of calls on this day—or at least, at this period of the year.

Among the Chinese, the New Year's call is carefully regulated by caste. The men receive calls from those who are acknowledged below them in the social scale, and they in turn make calls upon those above them. It is not necessary with them, as it is with us, to return calls.

The early English never failed to make calls on New Year's Day, for the purpose of expressing their good wishes for the next twelvemonth. It must have been curious, indeed, to see the villagers trooping from house to house, in one and out another, to pay their calls. We wonder how anyone found anyone else at home!

The custom of making a round of calls on New Year's Day was brought to us by the New Amsterdam Dutch. These people, whose hospitality, particularly on New Year's Day, was limitless, taught the New Yorkers the custom of calling upon one another to offer good wishes for the coming year. And for several centuries New York observed this social custom, discontinuing it only recently. To-day the New Year's call is not an absolute necessity, though some people like to observe it. The round of calls is quite out of fashion, however; it went out with the victoria and the bustle.

In an account of a New Year's Day in Colonial times, Marquis de Chastellux tells how a hundred or so young people assembled under his windows, fired several shots from their muskets, and knocked on the door. The landlord was obliged to give them some of the Marquis' wine and some money before they would leave. The account reads, in part:

I learnt from my landlord that it was the custom of the country for the young folks, the servants, and even the negroes to go from tavern to tavern, and to other houses, to wish a good New Year, and ask for a drink, so that there was no particular compliment to me in this affair. In the morning, when I went to take leave of General Clinton, I met nobody but drunken people in the streets.

The accepted method of "wishing a good New Year" is to clasp hands and say cordially, "A happy New Year!" Other peoples have different modes of expressing the same thought. The Chinese, for instance, say *"Sui-hi,"* which means, "May joy be yours."

Waiting for the Chimes.—We all like to sit up on New Year's Eve and listen for the chimes that "ring out the old, ring in the new."

This custom of ringing bells on New Year's Eve originated in England long ago. It was customary to ring muffled bells just before twelve o'clock, and at twelve to remove the wrappings and permit the bells to ring out loudly. This symbolized the thought that the old year was weak and feeble, that the new was strong and powerful.

"Of all sounds of all bells," says Charles Lamb, "most solemn and touching is the peal which rings out the old year." We like to hear the bells peal out the news that the New Year has started. It seems a death knell to the old year—a welcome to the new. And while the echo of the chimes still lingers in our ears we are making our resolutions!

The ringing of a bell has been, from the very earliest times, a method of announcing death. Even early savages beat upon drums or rang bells to announce the fact that one of their number had died. The ancient Egyptians believed that bells tolled at the time of death kept spirits from wielding an evil influence—upon the dead and upon the living. The superstition found its way to Italy, to Scotland, to Ireland, to England. In Paris hundreds of years ago it was the custom to ring the bells of Notre Dame whenever a prisoner was led to execution. The ringing of the bells on New Year's Eve was apparently intended to announce the death of the old year.

We sit up and wait for the chimes because of an inherent curiosity that has been bred in us for many generations. We don't want to miss anything. And we have a secret little superstitious feeling that something, anything, might happen on New Year's Eve. Our early Anglo-Saxon ancestors climbed to the roof on New Year's Eve, "to see what would happen when the New Year came in."

The New Year's Din.—In Petrograd it was at one time the custom to usher in the New Year with a cannonade of a hundred shots fired at midnight. Various Scandinavian cities still celebrate the advent of the New Year with the noise of firearms.

The early savages always had noise and din during their periods of celebration. In various sections of Australia the bullroarer is used (pp. 181-182). This is a peculiar instrument made usually of a bit of wood, and it makes a low, sharp, whirring noise that grows louder and louder as the instrument is twirled around rapidly on a string. The bullroarer was, and is, used as a sacred instrument in religious ceremonies, and its use has spread to New Mexico, New Zealand, and Africa. It was known to the ancient Greeks: it became the plaything of the peasant boy of early England.

The horn is the bullroarer in modern celebrations, particularly in the United States. On New Year's Eve the street revellers have horns of every size and description with which they make a great din—much to the satisfaction of their savage instincts.

How the World Celebrates the New Year.—Every country celebrates the New Year in its own way. In several countries, the New Year's celebration is the most important of the year, for instance, in France and in Scotland.

To the French the New Year is a more important holiday than Christmas. It is true that the peasant child places its *sabot* on the hearth for a gift at Christmas time; but it is not until the New Year that the adults exchange gifts among one another. The first three days of the New Year represent one of the most important social seasons. There are parties and gay entertainments. People stop one another on the street to extend good wishes for the year. And there is a great deal of informal visiting.

Scotland still retains the custom of "open house" at New Year's. There is a quaint old superstition among the people that he who is the first to visit a family in the New Year will be lucky and prosperous throughout the year. Therefore, everyone visits everyone else on New Year's Eve, revellers usually making a scramble to be "first foot," as it is called, when the clocks strike twelve. The more dignified make their calls on New Year's Day.

The midnight revellers in Scotland always carry with them, as they go from house to house, boxes of cakes and spiced ale. At each house the host is regaled with a bit of the cake and a sip of the ale. No guest enters a friend's house empty-handed, for to do so would be to frighten away prosperity for the year.

The Chinese celebrate all their holidays for the year at once. At the beginning of their New Year, they shut down all industry and close their shops for a period of several days. During this period they parade the streets in brand-new clothes, exchanging good wishes with everyone they meet. Sometimes in rural sections they carry tiny ornamented boxes of tea, which is considered an ideal New Year's gift. The box of tea is supposed to invite prosperity not only to him who receives it but to the donor.

During their celebration the Chinese have fireworks and gay revelry. There are feasting and funmaking from dawn until long after dark.

The Japanese have very gay New Year's celebrations. Every gatepost is ornamented with pines and green bamboos, and red lobsters hang over the doorways. Scarlet tangerine-like fruits are also used tor decoration. The pines, bamboos, and lobsters are symbolical of long life, strength, and happiness; the fruits are symbolical of prosperity.

No matter how poor he may be, every Japanese on New Year's Day dons a new suit and visits his friends. They in turn visit him, and there are many parties and entertainments. Even strangers accost one another on the streets during the New Year's festivities to exchange good wishes for the year. The Japanese celebration generally lasts for three days.

In the United States, New Year's Day is celebrated in various ways. There are many who still observe the old custom of "open house" and make a round of calls on this day, although as a general custom this is now practically obsolete. Each rural district, each city, has its own peculiar customs, its own methods of celebration. On New Year's Eve there is usually a great deal of street revelry, dancing and theatre parties, private dinners and public banquets. Each church has its own New Year's "watch-night" services —a custom borrowed from the Hebrews whose great watch night, Passover, ushers in their New Year.

But in the United States, as everywhere, the New Year is a period of social activity. There are parties and entertainments of every nature. To entertain at a dinner or a dance seems the proper way to usher in the New Year.

Some Suggestions for Entertainment.—Many hostesses, particularly in Chicago, New York, and other big cities, plan jolly midnight supper parties for New Year's Eve. Sometimes the parties are held at hotels or restaurants, for the convenience of the hostess and the entertainment of out-of-town guests. Frequently they are held at home, the drawing room and dining room being decorated with bells and winter greens for the occasion.

If it is to be a midnight supper, the guests do not assemble until about nine o'clock. The hostess who is wise arranges some sort of entertainment so that interest will not begin to lag at ten o'clock or so. There are many appropriate New Year games from which she can select.

An amusing New Year's game is called "I Resolve." Each guest is provided with a sheet of paper and a pencil. On the paper he is required to write a list of ten New Year's resolutions—whatever silly, foolish things occur to him, such as:

"I resolve not to wear a high silk hat when I go to church."
"I resolve not to marry until I am twenty-one."
"I resolve, during the coming year, to live up to my ideal—Charlie Chaplin."

These lists are folded and placed in a hat or jar. Each person draws one out in turn, and in turn reads his list to the assemblage. There is much laughter, of course, as the resolutions always seem funnier when applied to the person who is reading them.

After all the resolutions have been read, a vote is taken and the cleverest list of resolutions passed upon. The person who wrote the list is then requested to step forward and receive his prize—a handsome calendar. To the one who read the list is awarded the booby prize—a tiny bisque "kewpie" doll with an inscription of the year across it.

An enjoyable game to play at about eleven o'clock is called "Ghost." One of the guests is blindfolded and he or she must sit in the centre of the room. One by one the guests pass before the blindfolded "King Ghost" and recite a bit of verse or sing a little tune. They may disguise the voice in any way they like. The "King Ghost" must call out the name of the person who is reciting or singing, and until he does, the reciting continues. All the guests are "ghosts" and continue to be "ghosts" until their names are guessed correctly.

The guests enter the dining room a little before midnight. Each guest finds at his place when he enters a horn, whistle, bell, or other "noise-maker" for use in ushering in the New Year. It is interesting to have place cards in the form of pasteboard bells, of the kind that can be purchased from most stationers. On the back one might inscribe this pertinent sentence:

Use *this* now; save the others until midnight!

A menu that is always appropriate for the New Year's supper is: Hot bouillon in cups, chicken or turkey salad, nut-bread sandwiches, fruits, cakes and candies. Of course there must be plenty of nuts—for nuts are an age-old symbol of bounty in connection with the New Year. During the Christmas and New Year's season magazines usually carry interesting entertainment and menu suggestions. They are recommended to the hostess who is in doubt.

A popular form of entertainment on New Year's Eve is the masquerade ball. Clever and opportune innovations are seen in such costumes as "Hard Times," a fool's gown covered with newspaper headlines, worthless stock, tape from the ticker, etc.; "Mr. Old Year," wearing a long gray beard and carrying a scythe and an hour-glass, to be discarded at the stroke of 12; "Good Resolutions," a "professor" wearing blue glasses, a loose black robe, and carrying a huge roll of manuscript from which dangles an enormous pencil. The guests usually unmask at midnight.

The theatre party is also popular, and is becoming more and more so, particularly among people who entertain out-of-town guests. It is interesting to have dinner at one of the hotels in town, attend the theatre, join the revelling mobs after the play for a half-hour taste of street celebration, and return home just in time to crack nuts and roast apples around the fireplace while the New Year announces its arrival.

LINCOLN'S BIRTHDAY

The custom of celebrating birthdays of individuals appears to have originated in Egypt. The birthdays of kings and queens, of important persons and of the gods were celebrated with feasting and merrymaking. According to the Old Testament, Pharaoh, king of Egypt, celebrated his birthday with a feast; according to the New Testament, Herod did likewise.

The early followers of Christ, however, did not favour

the celebrating of birthdays. They conceived it no benefit to be born, and they saw no reason for making a festivity of the occasion. To them, birth was the entrance to a hostile world, the beginning of a life of oppression and persecution; death was the release from that life and the beginning of eternal peace and glory. Later, when Christianity swept the world, there was a reversal in this as in other things.

America has always remembered the birthdays of its great men—to honour them. February, a red-letter month, has two such famous birthdays.

There is February 12th, made glamorous with the romance of Lincoln's life, tinged with memories of one of the most powerful and pathetic figures American history has known. We need not eulogize Lincoln; every schoolchild knows his glory.

Lincoln's birthday has been observed ever since the great man was martyred. He was born on February 12, 1809, and was killed by an assassin on April 14, 1865. We remember him best as the genius who guided the country through four years of Civil War, keeping the union together when dissolution seemed inevitable; and for his Emancipation Proclamation which freed every Negro slave in the United States.

State action sometimes makes Lincoln's birthday a legal holiday, but whether legal or not we like to observe February 12th. Of course, whatever celebrations we have on this day are of a dignified and solemn character. Gay frivolities do no justice to the memory of our Lincoln.

Celebrating Lincoln's Birthday.—A tea or a dance or a musicale will do for any day of the week, but bring out the best china and the best silver in honour of Lincoln!

The Lincoln Dinner offers endless opportunities for cleverness in menu and in decoration. For the table centrepiece one might use a bust of Lincoln draped in the flag. Or one might use a miniature reproduction of Lincoln's birthplace—a decoration which was very popular on dinner

(Courtesy of Metropolitan Museum of Art)

The origin of our Santa Claus. The Bishop of Myra was said to have brought murdered children to life again—and he became their Saint Nicholas.

(Courtesy of Metropolitan Museum of Art)

Jazz in its native environment. African boys with native and European musical instruments.

tables toward the close of the last century. These miniatures can be purchased at stationery and novelty shops, or they can be made at home from cardboard, covered with brown crêpe paper and tinted with water colour to give the effect of logs.

Innovations in food, relevant to the occasion, may be introduced. There may be a cake, for instance, boasting twelve tiny silk flags, in honour of the twelfth. There may be ices shaped to simulate the forage caps of Civil War soldiers, the baskets used in cotton-picking. There may be little gingerbread cookies, baked and iced to look like pickaninnies.

When young people are entertained at a Lincoln Dinner, an interesting game with which to amuse them is called the "Emancipation Proclamation." It is nothing less than a glorified donkey game. A sketch of Lincoln is made with charcoal on a sheet and pinned against the wall. Several "proclamations" are made of paper, numbered, and distributed among the guests, who are then blindfolded and proceed, in the way of the game, to pin their "proclamations" all over Lincoln—every place but the right place. The person who pins the "proclamation" closest to Lincoln's outstretched hand receives a prize.

Readings from the boyhood of Lincoln are always interesting after a Lincoln Dinner. The early handicaps of poverty, the struggle for knowledge, the youth that will go down the vista of years as an inspiration to all generations of youth, the war-time trials, the murder at the theatre—all make fascinating reading.

VALENTINE'S DAY

Far back in folk and village customs the festival of February 14th originated. No one knows precisely how. No one knows its true significance. The Valentine festival appears to be a day of fun, dedicated to the little fellow with the bow and arrow whom we call Dan Cupid. To-day the holiday is almost obsolete, but at one time it ranked with Christmas and the New Year in importance.

Most authorities are agreed that the festival is named for St. Valentine, known as "the lovers' saint." Some writers, however, are inclined to believe that no such person as St. Valentine ever existed, although there appears to be ample proof that he was a Christian Bishop in the 3rd century after the death of Christ, and that he suffered martyrdom under the Emperor Claudius on February 14, 271 (A.D.).

The story is that Emperor Claudius, at Rome, issued a decree forbidding marriage. Married men were loath to leave their families for war, and they did not make good soldiers, according to the Emperor's notion. Since good soldiers were needed in warfare, he decided that marriage must be abolished.

The good priest Valentine heard, and was sad. He invited young lovers to come to him and secretly married them. The Emperor learned of this and had Valentine dragged to prison. There the "friend of lovers" languished and died, a martyr to love.

The Church was busy at that era replacing heathen divinities by ecclesiastical saints, and it is not surprising that they made a saint of Valentine, and allotted the day of his death, February 14th, to him. Nor is it surprising that the Roman youths and maidens for whom he gave his life set apart the day in which to do him honour. St. Valentine's Day came to be known as "the day for all true lovers."

A pretty origin, and one which is very possibly true. But there does not seem to be any way of definitely authenticating the story. We must accept the tale tentatively until someone can come forward and offer a true, proved origin. Valentine, and the day named in honour of his memory, are both shrouded in obscurity.

Origin of the Valentine Favour.—There is a quaint old tradition, prevalent still in some rural sections, that "birds choose their mates on St. Valentine's Day." Shakespeare alludes to this tradition in his "Midsummer Night's Dream."

In the Middle Ages it was customary in England, Scotland, and parts of France for the young people to assemble on the evening before Valentine's Day and draw names by chance. Each person drew a slip—a "valentine"—from an urn or bowl, on which was written the name of one of the young people present. The person whose name was on the slip became the holder's sweetheart for the year. Although this custom was at first confined solely to peasantry, it was later taken up by the upper classes and became very popular.

Bourne says:

> It is a ceremony never omitted among the vulgar to draw lots which they term Valentines on the evening before St. Valentine's Day. The names of a select number of one sex are, with an equal number of the other, put into some vessel and after that every one draws a name which, for the present, is called his Valentine.

Bourne, who wrote a long time ago, was among those who refused to believe in an actual person by the name of Valentine.

> Three Egyptian words will tell us more about the customs of Valentine's Day than all the falsehoods concerning the saint. *Va* (Egyptian) or *Fa* means "to bear." *Ren* is "the name" and "to name." *Ten* means "to determine." Thus the day of Va-len-tine is that of determining whose name shall be borne by each person in this mode of marriage by drawing lots. Valentine's Day is a day of coupling, and the custom points to the time when chance rather than choice was the law. Marriage is still said to be a lottery. The custom of sending caricatures on Valentine's Day is probably based on asserting the freedom of choice, and making a mock of chance.

Gradually the approach of Valentine's Day came to be heralded by the exchange of pretty sentiments, written with flourishes upon scented paper and profusely decorated with hearts, arrows, doves, and various other love tokens. Most of the valentines were written in verse. In 1797 a book of verses appeared called "The Young Man's Valentine Writer." It contained many verses suited to men and women and a collection of pretty and elaborate valentine sentiments. These were copied with painstaking care upon cards or sheets of paper and presented to "My Valentine."

Valentine's Day has very little significance to us and the holiday is rapidly falling into desuetude. But a few generations ago the very name of Valentine carried with it the breath of lavender, the scent of musk. Our great-great-grandmothers received the scraps of ornamented paper with trembling hands. They blushed as they read, and crumpled the love missives tenderly to their hearts. For the pretty verses, written carefully by hand, were not mere sentiments to them; they were actual declarations of love.

But presently the manufactured valentine came into vogue and took the place of the individual sentiments. Because it was very much less trouble, men purchased their valentine favours instead of writing them by hand. Consequently the valentine lost much of its dignity and much of its true significance. The gaudy prints and postcards were a popular fad for a while, but they were quickly discarded by people of better taste.

Entertaining on Valentine's Day.—In England, in the 15th century, it was customary for the upper classes to entertain on Valentine's Day. The custom of drawing for a valentine was at its height at about 1480, and when the gentry came together for the purpose of valentine-drawing, they usually concluded the sport with a dinner or party.

Because it lends itself so admirably to decorative schemes, and because of the wealth of tradition surrounding the very name, hostesses like to entertain on Valentine's Day even now, though the holiday is practically obsolete. We quote from the February issue of a fashionable magazine:

Mixing history and allegory, George Washington, the Father of

His Country, is honoured in the same month as Dan Cupid, who it is claimed makes the world go round.

But with all due honour to the noblest figure in our history, it must be confessed that it is the spirit of St. Valentine's Day that permeates through all the merrymaking of the month.

Entertainment on Valentine's Day is usually of a gay and frivolous nature. The "Lover's Luncheon" is a favourite; "Hearts and Showers," a special valentine shower for the bride-to-be, is becoming very popular; the valentine masquerade dance is particularly appropriate; and, of course, there is always the valentine dinner. Recently the Valentine bridge party has come into favour. The pretty conceits and favours displayed by stationers at this period make excellent bridge prizes.

A brilliant masquerade ball was held in New York recently on Valentine's Eve. The invitations were for couples only, and each couple was requested to come to the "Lovers' Pageant" as a pair of famous lovers. There were Romeo and Juliet, Jack and Jill, Tristan and Isolde, Cinderella and the Prince. The clever hostess supplied each guest, on arrival, with a lacy Valentine, upon which was written the name of his or her partner for the evening. And so, Jack went in to dinner with Juliet, and Romeo with Cinderella!

If one decides to entertain at a supper or dinner on Valentine's Day the decorations, favours, and even the food should be in the spirit of the day. Invitations are usually heart-shaped—a custom that originated with the first manufactured Valentines which were usually in the shape of hearts darted through with arrows. Decoration is a simple matter, thanks to the genius of the novelty maker.

An appropriate centrepiece for the Valentine dinner table is a satin-covered, heart-shaped box from which extend as many streamers as there are guests. Each streamer terminates in a tiny Cupid doll or a red pasteboard heart. At the proper moment the guests are advised to pull their streamers; the top of the box is jerked away and each guest pulls forth a favour.

There are many appropriate Valentine dishes for the menu. Here are some suggestions:

Oysters on heart-shaped toast
Chicken soup with heart-shaped croutons
Creamed chicken in heart ramekins
Twin soles
Jellied chicken in heart mould
Heart-shaped sandwiches
Valentine salad, with hearts of lettuce
Chocolate kisses
Ices in heart mould
Heart tarts

If you wish to serve sandwiches, you can avoid cutting them into heart shape by wrapping them in waxed paper and sealing with tiny red hearts. These can be made at home, or purchased by the dozen at stationers' shops.

For Valentine games, frolics, and entertainments we suggest two very helpful books, which contain also many suggestions for other holidays. They are: "The Book of Entertainments," by Mary Dawson, and "The Complete Hostess," by Clara E. Laughlin.

WASHINGTON'S BIRTHDAY

February 22d is dedicated to the memory of the great George Washington, one of the most noble and inspiring figures of history—unquestionably the most important and conspicuous in American history.

When Washington was born in Virginia, in 1732, there were no states, no union. There were but a few struggling colonies belonging to England. Through Washington's genius those colonies cut loose from the shackles that bound them to a land across the sea, lifted their faces proudly to the sky, and shouted their freedom to the world.

England's answer was swift and cruel—War! But Washington carried his people safely through the crisis, and a new nation marched forth from the battlefield. A child nation that might have floundered on the rocks that wrecked many another nation had not Washington sat at the helm. His example brought strength to the tottering nation.

It is but fitting that we, who gather the harvest, set aside one day a year to do reverence to the memory of the great man who planted the seeds. Washington was the first man so honoured by the new nation. His birthday is a legal holiday, made so by state action. On February 22d the wheels of industry cease while the nation pay homage to Washington—gentleman, soldier, statesman, writer, diplomat—America's pioneer president.

On Washington's Birthday.—Celebrations on February 22d are usually of a dignified character. The Colonial Ball was a favourite a century ago; it is still a favourite to-day. Its very nature seems to partake of the spirit of Washington and his times.

It is an old custom to issue the invitations on tiny paper flags. At a Colonial Ball given in Virginia nearly a hundred years ago in honour of Washington, the invitations were hand-painted flags, the message written in the white spaces, the flag rolled and tied with a bit of red-white-and-blue ribbon. These invitations were delivered personally by small boys dressed in the costume of Washington's boyhood.

That the hostess be Martha Washington and the host George Washington at a Colonial Ball is a long-established precedent. The guests may choose any other costumes they like.

Tradition has preserved the tale of the hatchet and the cherry tree. The story appeared for the first time in a book called "The Life of George Washington," a charming history written by M. L. Weems who was rector of the Mount Vernon Parish. The cherry-tree story, as related in his quaint little book, was communicated to him by "an aged lady who as a distant relative had spent a great deal of her time in the family when a girl."

The hatchet and the cherry tree, symbols of the boy

Washington's truthfulness, are invariably used in decoration. A new interpretation is to make a miniature tree of bare twigs, neatly peeled, upon which candied cherries have been impaled. This is used as a centrepiece, and after dinner the guests gather the fruit from the tree.

Another interpretation is to have a Colonial vase with a few sprays of Japanese cherry blossoms in the centre of the table, and at each cover a tiny pot with its own individual cherry tree. The guests keep the trees as souvenirs.

At a Colonial Ball, the Virginia Reel and old-fashioned waltz are favourite dance numbers. Prizes are sometimes offered for the best exhibitions of Colonial dancing, and also for the best songs or recitations concerning the life of George Washington. A decade or so ago it was customary to supply the men with long corncob pipes and good old Virginia tobacco, while the ladies were presented with small cherry-blossom vases as souvenirs.

A simple dinner in honour of Washington's birthday might consist of some such menu as this:

> Old-fashioned Southern Chicken Pie
> Maryland Biscuits, Candied Sweet Potatoes
> Cherry Pie, Southern Fruit Cake
> Eggnog or Coffee

At a large dinner Virginia fried chicken is usually served, as it was a favourite dish in Washington's day.

Here is a genuine old Virginia Colonial recipe for making "A Frickasie." It is quoted from a rare old book of Colonial recipes:

> Take ye fowls, cut them in pieces and clean them. Season with pepper and salt, a little mace, nutmeg, cloves, some parsley, a little bit of onion. Let them lay two hours, then flour them well, fry in sweet butter hott before you put them in. Fry a fine brown. Wash ye pan and put them in again with a pint of gravy. Let them swimyer in ye gravy. Take the yolks of three eggs with a little grated nutmeg and a little juice of lemon, and two spoonfuls of wine. Shake it over the fire until it is as thick as cream, pour over ye frickasie, and so serve it to ye table hott.

Perhaps some modern hostess would like to try this recipe—without the "two spoonfuls of wine."

ST. PATRICK'S DAY

St. Patrick, patron saint of Ireland, was not Irish himself, as many suppose. His birth is somewhat obscure. The French claim him, the Scotch and the Welsh claim him. His true birthplace is not known.

Jones ("Historical Account of the Welsh Bards") says:

> St. Patrick, the Apostle of Ireland, is said to be the son of Calphurnius and Concha. He was born in the Vale of Rhos, in Pembrokeshire, about the year 373.

But the very same writer later refers to St. Patrick as being of Caernarvonshire. Others say that France was his birthplace.

In 432 Pope Celestine sent St. Patrick to Ireland to convert the Irish to Christianity. Until then, his name had been Maewyn, but the Pope bestowed upon him the ecclesiastical name of Patricius.

St. Patrick landed near Wicklow, according to the tradition. The people were preparing to stone him for attempting to change the religion of their ancestors. But fearlessly he preached the gospel to the pagan Irish, and they listened to his eloquence. He illustrated the doctrine of the Trinity by showing them a trefoil—a three-leafed grass like the clover. The Irish were impressed, and they were solemnly baptized by St. Patrick.

It is because of this trefoil grass tradition that the Irish wear the shamrock and the green on St. Patrick's Day, which is simply an Irish jollification day in honour of the saint. There are usually parades and pageants on this day, and plenty of fun seasoned with feasting.

The hostess who entertains on March 17th carries out the old tradition by decorating her table in green and white and giving her guests souvenirs in the form of silk shamrocks, chocolate harps, or long clay pipes. Mary Dawson says:

> The hostess who must squeeze her occasional hospitality out of a bill of small dimensions should appreciate in full the possibilities of St. Patrick's Day—that feast of fun pure and simple.
>
> Here to her hand is a celebration where jokes and comic ingenuity take the place of expensive elaboration, and where anyone with some little knack of tricking out a table or making a special dish out of an everyday course can give a successful luncheon or dinner.

The stationers provide clever and attractive novelties with which to decorate the home and the table on St. Patrick's Day. It is a popular plan to carry out a green-and-yellow colour scheme in the menu—green and yellow being the colours of the Irish flag.

APRIL FOOLS' DAY

In nearly all parts of the earth there exists a day which corresponds to our April Fools' Day. It is a day consecrated to the playing of practical jokes on friends and neighbours, sending them on fools' errands, tricking them into doing ludicrous things.

The origin of this day of practical joking is much disputed. This rhyme, found in "Poor Robin's Almanac" for 1760, is as true to-day as it was then:

> The first of April, some do say
> Is set apart for All Fools' Day;
> But why the people call it so
> Nor I, nor they themselves, do know.

Among the many stories advanced concerning the origin of this "fools' festival" is one which goes back to Noah and the Ark. The London *Public Advertiser* of March 13, 1769, says that the April Fools' custom arose from

> the mistake of Noah sending the dove out of the ark before the water had abated, on the first day of the month among the Hebrews which answers to our first of April, and to perpetuate the memory of this deliverance it was thought proper, whoever forgot so remarkable a

circumstance, to punish by sending upon some sleeveless errand similar to that ineffectual message upon which the bird was sent by the patriarch.

We cannot accept this story as authentic, however, and we are obliged to search for other origins. It has been plausibly suggested by several writers that Europe derived its custom of April-fooling from the French. In France, the person fooled is known as the *poisson d'avril* which means "an April fish"—in other words, a young fish and therefore a fish easily caught.

France was the first nation to adopt the reformed calendar; Charles IX decreed in 1564 that the year should begin with the 1st of January. Until then, New Year's visits and the exchange of New Year's gifts had been associated with the 1st of April. After Charles's decree they became associated with the 1st of January. There were some who objected to the change—as there always are—and these became the butts of the others. Mock gifts were sent them, pretended calls of ceremony were made at their homes, they were invited to mock New Year's celebrations —all on the 1st of April.

Many writers are of the opinion that the French *poisson d'avril* is the survival of the old spring offering to Aphrodite, "under whose auspices the constellation of the Fishes was then in ascendant influence." According to these same writers Friday is the *dies Veneris,* and fish, her own symbol, is regarded consequently as an appropriate food for the day. We are still of the opinion that fish is the food for Friday!

April Fools' Day has also been traced to an old nature feast. Maurice, in his "Indian Antiquities" speaks of the first of April as the "ancient feast of the Vernal Equinox." It is very possible that the day of fooling is a relic of the festivities that were once practically universal at the Vernal Equinox which began March 25th and ended on the 1st of April. What seems most plausible to this writer is that the custom of joking and fooling originated when the new calendar changed the first of the year from April to January. Some would still have regarded the 1st of April as the first of the year, and according to the others, who celebrated the 1st of January, these April-firsters were being "fooled." Thence would arise the custom of deliberate fooling on that day.

In Great Britain, as in France, the 1st of April was anciently observed as a general festival. But it was not until the end of the 17th century that "April fooling" became a common custom. There is no doubt whatever that the English copied the custom from the French.

The Custom of Playing Jokes.—We have seen how the custom of tricking one's friends and neighbours, or playing practical jokes on them, seems to have originated. In some countries the April Fool idea became so strong that very few dared to start an enterprise on the 1st of April, and only the brave were married on that day. Napoleon evidently scoffed at the idea, for on the 1st of April, 1810, he married Maria Louisa. And promptly his Parisian friends called him *"un poisson d'avril."*

There is a popular French story concerning the 1st of April. It appears that a woman stole a gold watch from the home of an acquaintance and set the police a lively search all over the town. Finally they located it hidden in her home, and laughingly she cried, *"Poisson d'avril!"* Nevertheless, she was taken before the magistrate who, having just as great a sense of humour as she, informed her that she would have plenty of time to laugh over her good April Fools' joke, as she was going to jail until the ensuing April 1st. She had really attempted to steal the watch but had tried to pass it off as an April Fools' joke.

Another story, which has not been authenticated, concerns Francis, Duke of Lorraine, and his wife. They escaped from captivity at Nantes one April 1st, dressed as peasants. They started off boldly, but someone detected the disguise and ran ahead to warn the sentries. As it was the 1st of April, the sentries merely laughed and cried at their informant, *"Poisson d'avril!"* and the pretended peasants escaped.

The custom of sending people on "sleeveless errands" appears to have been popular in England in the 18th century. We find many such "errands" recorded in "Poor Robin's Almanac" as early as 1728. Friends or neighbours were sent to the village store to purchase the "History of Eve's Grandmother"; to the grocer's to purchase a pint of pigeon's milk; to the cobbler for some strap oil. And it appears that there was always someone simple enough to go on the errand, to the delight of the crowd that followed discreetly behind.

In 1860 practical joking was carried to extremes in England. In March of this year many people of prominence received an invitation, in all appearances portending to be official, to witness the "Annual Ceremony of Washing the White Lions, on Sunday, April 1st, 1860. Admitted only at the White Gate." All that Sunday morning hundreds of cabs rattled about Tower Hill in vain search of the White Gate. The perpetrator of this April Fools' joke was, fortunately for himself, never discovered.

The custom of April-fooling has remained, and in the United States it is quite customary to play practical jokes on one's friends on this day. Children particularly are fond of the day and make of it a fun festival.

The April Fool Party.—It has long been the custom to open spring entertainment with an April Fool party. The English are fond of entertaining on this day, and the French usually celebrate the "festival of fun" by giving a dinner or party. With us, April 1st is a fairly popular time for entertaining informally, usually at jolly home parties.

An old custom is to pen the invitation on foolscap folded into the shape of a fool's cap. Invitations are usually bits of verse, a custom very popular fifty years ago. This is the type of verse used generally to invite friends to an April Fool party:

If for fun you've any thirst,
Come to my party on April 1st;
There'll be tea and fun galore—
So put on your best, and come at four!

Daffodils and daisies are popular for decorative purposes on April 1st. But it is an old custom to decorate the home in an absurd and foolish manner for this occasion. The English appear to have originated this custom. The home is decorated as it would be for Christmas, New Year's, or any other holidays but the one being celebrated. Imitation holly and mistletoe are used, and guests are greeted with "Merry Christmas" or "Happy New Year" upon arrival. This corresponds to the "Topsy Turvey" parties which are so popular here and which are found described in almost all books on social entertaining.

The "Fish Dinner" is always good fun on April 1st. Invitations are issued on small coloured pasteboard fish, of the kind that can be purchased at novelty or stationery shops. The table is decorated in green and white. In the centre is a bowl of goldfish from which rises a sheaf of miniature fishing rods. At the end of each rod is a narrow green ribbon line which extends across the table—one to each plate. At the end of the line is a souvenir for the guest, usually a tiny celluloid fish or a small fishing basket filled with candy. The dinner, of course, includes fish in several varieties.

Concerning the April Fool party, "The Book of Entertainments" says:

> Begin the fun by passing among the company some delicious-looking bonbons and fruit. Most persons will decline, believing the goodies to be of the too-familiar April Fool class. In this they will be mistaken, as the dainties are genuine. No one who has previously declined is allowed to alter his decision when the goodies prove edible.

The custom of April Fool candy, which originated in France, gave rise to the custom of "camouflaging" food that is served at the April Fool party. Clara E. Laughlin gives a typical April Fool menu, made up entirely of "April Fools":

First, large green peppers, on lettuce leaves, looks like a salad, but when the top is lifted off an oyster cocktail is inside. Then baked potatoes, large and piled on a platter, are passed, and prove to be full of minced sweetbread and fresh mushrooms. Turnovers and deviled crabs turn out to be pieces of broiled or roasted chicken wrapped in pie crust. Tomato salad is found to be raspberry ice, moulded in tomato form, on leaves of paper lettuce. In each "tomato" lies a heaped spoonful of what appears to be mayonnaise, but is a soft custard. Pillboxes full of tiny candies, covered with cake batter, baked and iced like little pink and white cakes, are the last deception.

Miss Laughlin's book and that of Mary Dawson (see p. 410) both contain excellent suggestions for the April Fool party.

EASTER

Through religious, in a sense, and solemn in character rather than jolly and frivolous, Easter is a holiday that appeals to everyone. Somehow the whole world becomes more beautiful at Easter-time. Millions of buried seeds burst suddenly into bloom. Winter shivers—and is gone. And the earth makes its beautiful Easter offering of spring flowers.

Two theories are advanced concerning the origin of Easter. Wheatley says that Easter is in memory of the crucifixion and that the holiday is so called from the Saxon *oster,* "to rise." Easter, then, is in honour of Christ's resurrection. But he mentions also, as do various other authorities, that Easter may have been the name of an old Saxon goddess worshipped at the period which now corresponds with our Easter, usually in April.

One writer says:

The name *Easter* comes from an ancient Anglo-Saxon goddess of spring, *Eastre,* in whose honour a festival of spring is held in the month of April.

There appear to be many marked similarities between New Year and Easter festivities. Among the Persians, the New Year is looked upon as being the period of renewal in all things—the triumph of the sun, of nature, of man. They present one another with eggs, as typifying the beginning of a new life (see p. 396). This "Feast of Eggs," as it was called, was preserved in the Easter festivities of the Christians when they changed the New Year to January 1st. It is to be noted that the Jews, whose Passover is older than the Christian Easter, also use eggs in their feasting at this period.

Beginning of the Easter Festival.—As a time of feasting and celebration, Easter goes back into great antiquity. No one seems to know precisely when it began, although many are inclined to believe that it is a relic of the ancient celebration of the Vernal Equinox—the time of the original New Year.

The earliest Easter hymn of which we have record takes us back to the 4th century. It is a simple thing by St. Ambrose, and it was probably written about the year 340. About 500 years later Alfred the Great, King of England, decreed by law that the week following Easter be kept holy—a time of spiritual rejoicing. The people obeyed the decree, but rejoicing of any nature, spiritual or otherwise, ultimately assumes but one form—mass festivity.

A popular superstition in ancient England was that the sun danced on Easter Day. It became a common custom for the people to rise early to witness this dance of the sun. Wheatley says that there existed, at one time, an ingenious method of making an artificial sun-dance. A huge vessel of water was set out in the open and the rays of the sun permitted to play upon its trembling surface. The result, of course, was a dancing of the sun's reflection, which greatly impressed and delighted the masses.

The dancing of the sun, the blooming of the flowers, the beautiful awakening of the earth after the winter's slumber, seem to symbolize to the people the awakening of Christ and His Resurrection. Mr. Brand says that the people in the middle districts of Ireland still rise at about

(*Courtesy of Metropolitan Museum of Art*)

Dancing girls, by Korbel. American, 20th Century.

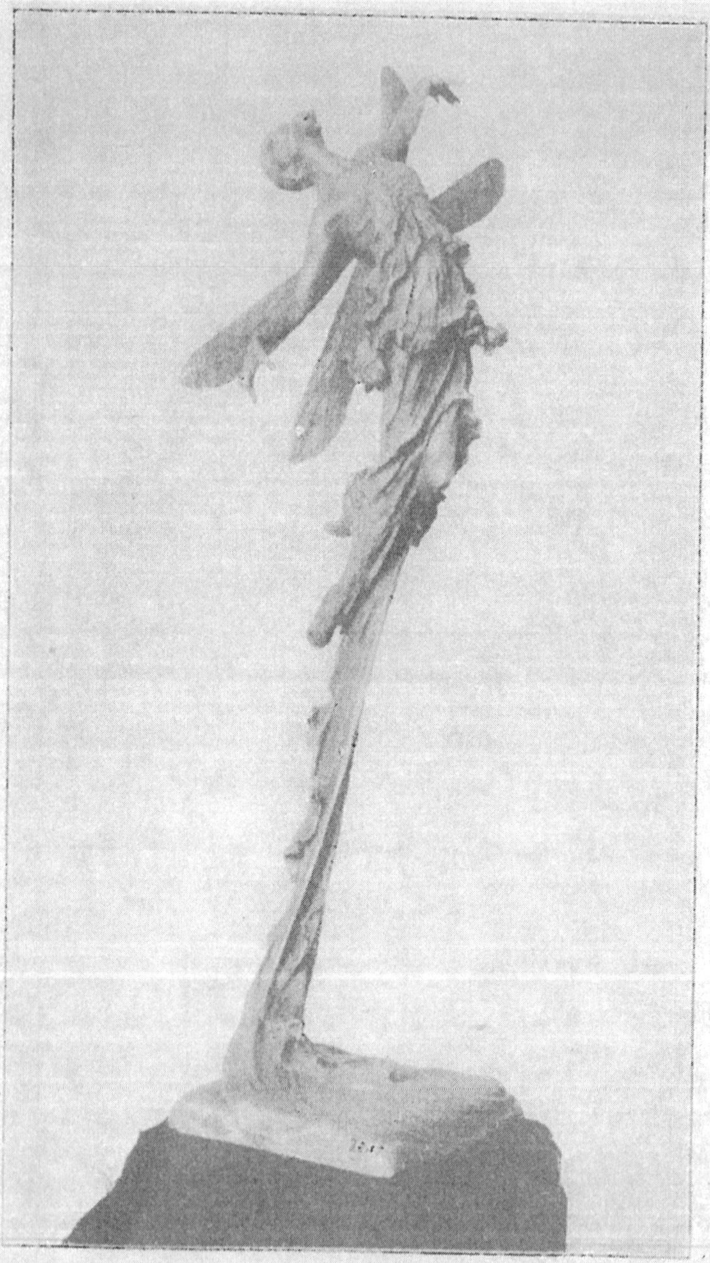

(Courtesy of Metropolitan Museum of Art)

An appreciation of Pavlowa by Lenz. American, 20th Century.

four o'clock on Easter morning to see the sun dance "in honour of Christ's rise from the darkness of the grave."

An ancient English custom was to put out all the fires and relight them on Easter Eve—typifying the beginning of a new life. We have seen how other peoples observed this very custom at the period of the New Year (pp. 393-394). In England it was customary to preserve consecrated flints in the churches for this special purpose. A popular superstition was that holy fire, obtained on Easter Eve with the consecrated flints, would afford protection from storms, draughts, famines, etc.

Concerning Easter Eggs.—Many peoples of antiquity regarded the egg as an emblem of life, of a beginning. The Egyptians, the Persians, the Greeks, Gauls, Romans, and others believed the secret of life to be within the egg, and they regarded it therefore as a token or symbol of creation. Easter was the time of the solar new year—as one writer calls it, the "incubation of nature." It was a time when all things were renewed, and the egg was regarded as a fitting emblem of the period.

The Christians borrowed the egg and made it part of their Easter festivities, but they made it emblematic of the Resurrection. To them the egg was regarded somewhat in the light of a prison or tomb, from which future life escaped. Thus, a writer in the *Gentleman's Magazine* for July, 1783, remarks that the egg at Easter is "an emblem of the rising up out of the grave, in the same manner as the chick, entombed, as it were in the egg, in due time is brought to life."

The custom of colouring eggs appears to be exceedingly ancient. The Jews boiled their eggs hard and decorated the shells. Le Brun says that the Persians always colour their eggs and have had the custom since ancient times. Father Carmeli, in his "History of Customs," tells us that coloured Easter eggs are to be found in Italy, Spain, and Provence, and that public sports with eggs are held during the Easter period.

It would seem that the original purpose in colouring eggs was to imitate the new colours of the earth, induced by the coming of spring and the blossoming of the flowers. But when the original custom was taken over by the Christian Church the eggs were decorated principally in red, to denote the blood of Christ.

In ancient England it was a popular custom to roll down Greenwich Hill at Easter—possibly to simulate ecstasy at the Resurrection, but more likely because of the natural ecstasy that the return of spring would incite. Later this custom was abandoned and eggs were rolled down the hill instead. This custom has survived, but now it is observed by children.

An old custom was to boil the eggs hard, paint them, and write mottoes on the shells. Boys and girls of the poorer classes sang in the streets and were given the coloured eggs. Then they gathered at the hill and rolled the eggs down to the base. One by one the eggs broke, and the child whose egg held out the longest won the "Egg Roll." He, or she, was entitled to all the eggs. The custom of rolling eggs down the green is observed at the White House in Washington at Easter-time—a quaint old custom in a modern setting.

The rabbit's part in Easter festivities originated with an old superstition that rabbits lay eggs on Easter Eve. This superstition is possibly Teutonic in origin, but no one knows precisely when it started or what was the original meaning or purpose behind it.

The Negroes of the South, through some quirk of fancy, believe that the "left hind foot of a graveyard rabbit killed in the dark of the moon" is a powerful talisman and will protect them from all evil. It is barely possible that this superstition grew out of the old Easter idea that rabbits are given supernatural powers on Easter Eve which enable them to lay eggs.

Dressing Up on Easter Day.—The Chinese, the Japanese, the North American Indians and many other peoples cast off all their old apparel at the period of the New Year and don everything new and fresh. The house is cleaned out, new fires are built—everything must be new and clean for the beginning of the New Year.

One sees a semblance to this idea in the custom of "dressing up" at Easter-time. Each little girl must have her new frock and shoes, each little boy his nice new suit. Men and women like to wear their "best." Just as the world dresses itself in its new spring flowers, mankind dresses itself in new, bright apparel. Psychologically, the custom originated solely in the desire to "spruce up" at the period in which all nature blooms with new life, at the period when Christ, it is said, rose from the earth and was resurrected. As a writer in the 18th century would have us believe, the flowers which we wear at Easter-time are simply emblems of the Resurrection.

But fundamentally, this custom of discarding old, worn clothes and appearing in attractive new apparel at Easter is part of our primitive instinct to place the old year behind and step forth, fresh and clean, into a new year (see p. 394).

Originally the ceremonies attending the observance of Easter were very simple. But a great change was brought about by Constantine in the early part of the 4th century. Constantine was fond of display, of gaudy ostentation. He caused Easter to be celebrated with pomp and extraordinary richness. He filled Easter Sunday with elaborate ceremonials.

It was during the time of Constantine that night watches lasting until midnight were instituted in churches. Finding the slender tapers which had been used until this time not sufficient to suit his pompous nature, he had huge pillars of wax made to be used instead. He found, in the Easter festivities, an excellent excuse to appear richly apparelled, wearing something so new and unusual that everyone else would seem poorly clad beside him.

But everyone else began to "dress up," too, and so was

established the custom of wearing new and bright apparel on Easter Sunday. The Easter bonnet originated in the popular superstition that to wear a new bonnet for the first time on Easter Sunday was to be assured happiness in love during the year.

Entertaining at Easter-time.—Dr. Drake, writing of Shakespeare and his times, tells us that Easter was a season of great social festivity. The English appear to be particularly fond of entertaining at the Easter period, and there are many dinners, parties, and other festivities. The custom of the Easter breakfast at high noon, Easter Sunday, originated in England and is now quite popular in the United States.

But by far the most popular form of Easter entertaining is a luncheon on Easter Sunday. It is usually quite elaborate and the invitations are engraved. Green, yellow, and white should be the colour scheme, pale yellow marigolds tied with green ribbon making excellent souvenir bouquets for the guests. The menu is the usual luncheon menu, with eggs used in salad and in garnishing to carry out the Easter idea.

A pretty feature for an Easter-time dance provided coloured Easter bonnets for each lady of the company. The bonnets were homemade millinery in crepe paper of different colours on the order of the universally becoming "poke." The bonnets were displayed on an old-time millinery "tree" and each lady selected one. The men in an adjoining room selected each a pair of strings. The man whose strings proved to match in colour a bonnet presented them to the wearer of it and claimed her as his partner for the cotillion.

The above refers to the popular type of dance given at Easter-time about fifteen years ago. To-day the costume dance is popular. The hostess issues the conventional dance invitation, adding only the word "Costume" in the lower left-hand corner. For this occasion appropriate costumes would be: a Humpty-dumpty costume, a rabbit costume, a chicken costume, an Easter-lily costume, a butterfly costume, etc.

MAY DAY

The May-day festival is one of the oldest of which we have record. Although we have only the children's May parties in the parks to remind us of this festival in the United States, May Day was at one time a prominent and popular holiday, observed with great festivity.

Most authorities maintain that the May-day festival originated with the ancient Druids. In their worship of the god Bel, the Druids made immense fires upon the cairns on May 1st and celebrated the occasion with song and dance. But the Romans also welcomed the 1st of May with joyful celebration, and the true origin of the May-day festival is still somewhat in doubt. Maurice contends that it can be traced back very much farther than we suspect, that "the May-day festival is identical with the Phallic festivals of India and Egypt, which in those countries took place upon the sun entering Taurus to celebrate Nature's renewed fertility."

Whatever its origin may be, May Day is unquestionably a form of nature worship. We are inclined to believe that it grew out of the natural joy and ecstasy of the masses welcoming spring and its bounties after a long winter. The very nature of the festival suggests this origin. The dance around the Maypole, which was originally a mass of green branches decorated with May flowers; the joyous feasting; the choosing of a King and Queen of the May—all suggest a people in ecstasy at the passing of winter and the promise of spring. The fact that May Day has always been the favourite festival of European peasantry, who would be the people to suffer most the hardships of winter, seems to bear out our contention.

In England the May feast was one of the greatest and most important events of the year. It was a time of great revelry and rejoicing. Green, being regarded as the symbol of re-birth, was used for decoration. There were sports, games, gay peasant dances. A King and Queen of the

May were selected and elaborately decorated for the occasion.

Before long the English May Day became a popular institution, like our Thanksgiving, and even royalty observed it. It became customary in the 15th century for the royal family to have May-day dinner served in the woods. For a long time it was the custom to wish one's friends "A Merry May!" as it is now the custom to wish one's friends "A Merry Christmas."

The Maypole.—The ancients believed that May 1st was the boundary day between summer and winter and that on this day a war took place between the two seasons to determine which would prevail. It became customary to stage a mock war between two people, one to represent winter, the other, summer. Summer always managed to win and was promptly crowned King of the May. In triumph he held aloft green branches decorated with beautiful May flowers and sang an old folk song, the thought of which seems to have been, "I have won, I bring you summer!"

The branches and flowers later were interpreted as the Maypole. At first a young tree was cut down and decorated with ribbons and flowers. This was set up triumphantly in the village and everyone danced around it. The Druids, incidentally, worshipped the tree, and it is very possible that the Maypole originated with them. But long before the time of Charles I in England the tree had given way to the pole. Huge poles were planted in the ground and decorated gaily with green and flowers. Long streamers were attached to the top, and each dancer held on proudly to his or her end of the ribbon.

May Day in America.—In America the May Day was never popular. A Puritan preacher is quoted as saying, "If Moses was angry when he saw the people dance around a golden calf, well may we be angry to see people dancing about a post."

Governor William Bradford wrote, under date of 1628:

They allso set up a May-pole, drinking and dancing about it many days together, inviting the Indean women for their consorts, dancing and frisking together. . . . Shortly after came over that worthy gentleman, Mr. John Indecott, who brought over a patent under the broad seal, for the governmente of Massachusets, who visiting those parts caused that May-pole to be cutte downe, and rebuked them for their profannes, and admonished them to look there should be better walking.

It seems that an old English custom was to seize a girl's gloves on May Day and demand a kiss in forfeit. This custom was brought across the ocean by the colonists and preserved in their lore. We are told that on May Day, 1660, Jacob Murline seized Sarah Tuttle's gloves and demanded the forfeit. Despite the law prohibiting love-making of any kind without the consent of the parents, they sat down together and kissed for a half-hour—much to the amusement of a group of onlookers who had gathered about them.

Sarah's father had Jacob dragged to court "on the charge of inveigling his daughter's affections." But the young lady calmly informed the court that the inveigling had been all on her part and that she had wanted to be kissed! She was fined and warned to mend her ways.

There is very little to remind us of May Day in this country, except, as has already been mentioned, the children's May parties in the parks. These May parties are held throughout the month of May, usually under the auspices of the neighbourhood school. The children decorate a Maypole with gay-coloured papers and ribbons, dress themselves in bright paper costumes, and march in proud parade to the park or the field. Here they dance around the Maypole, play games, compete for prizes, and feast on ice cream, cake, and candy. The only adults who attend May parties to-day are the teachers or the parents of the children.

A curious May-day superstition is that to bathe one's face in dew just before sunrise on May morning is to have a complexion of exquisite beauty. In England every girl at one time believed this tradition, and we are told that even Queen Catherine and her ladies-in-waiting "went out before sunrise to seek the Maydew bath."

An Irish superstition is that if you will go forth at sunrise on May Day and gaze down into a well, you will see the reflection of your lover; and if you make a wish at this well, the wish will come true. Scotland borrowed the superstition from Ireland and built miniature "wishing wells" to feature in their May Day festivities. These "wishing wells" are still to be found in rural sections.

MOTHER'S DAY

The second Sunday in May is set aside for honouring the nation's mothers. It is a day consecrated by suggestion of the late ex-President Wilson to the memory of mothers who are dead, to the thought of mothers who are alive.

It has become a general custom to send flowers to one's mother on this day, no matter where one may happen to be, and to wear a white carnation in her honour. Usually roses are sent, although other flowers are appropriate. Custom is making it a practice to send with the flowers a box of candy, an interesting book, a thoughtful remembrance.

While the holiday is not legal, it is observed almost universally in this country, and there has been some talk recently about establishing Mother's Day as a national legal holiday. There has also been some mention of a Father's Day, and it is very likely that both of these days will be set apart by the United States as official honour days for parents.

MEMORIAL DAY

During the Civil War a number of Southern women began the loving custom of decorating the soldiers' graves with flowers. They decorated not only the graves of their own soldiers, but also of the Northerners who had died in the South. For this noble work they were honoured by North and South alike.

Three years after the war, General A. Logan, then Commander-in-Chief of the Grand Army of the Republic, showed his admiration for what the Southern women were doing by issuing an order that the 30th day of May of that year (1868) be set apart for the purpose of strewing flowers on the graves of the soldiers. Various states in the Union took the cue, and soon Memorial Day, or as it is sometimes called, Decoration Day, was established and made legal by state action.

In the Northern states, Memorial Day is observed May 30th. In Southern states, however, the day is observed by some on April 26th, by some on June 10th. People visit the cemeteries with flowers and decorate the graves, usually the graves of their own loved ones. But wherever Civil War soldiers are buried, beautiful floral decorations from strangers are not uncommon.

Any entertainment on Memorial Day is of a solemn and dignified nature. Simple outdoor picnics are appropriate; the afternoon tea and the simple luncheon are acceptable. But anything of a gay frivolous nature is not in keeping with the spirit of the day.

ARBOUR DAY

One day a year is set aside for the purpose of tree-planting. The date varies in different localities, for spring comes to some parts much later than it does to others. Arbour Day is usually fixed by the governor.

The custom of tree-planting on a special day set apart for the purpose originated in 1872. A man by the name of Smith, governor of Nebraska, realized that for the future good of the country more trees would have to be planted. It occurred to him that if every child in school planted but one tree each year, there would always be plenty of trees.

Accordingly he set aside a certain day in April and called it Arbour Day. On this day the teachers took the children to the woods and taught them how to plant trees. Soon after Kansas copied the same idea, and set aside a day for the planting of trees. Other states quickly followed, and even Canada caught the idea.

To-day Arbour Day is made legal by state action, and each school has its own particular little rules, plans, and regulations as to what shall actually be done on that day. In most cases, however, the children are simply taken into the woods in holiday fashion and each child is required to take part in the tree-planting ceremonies. In some states the authorities supply whatever materials are needed; in others the children are required to do so.

Before leaving the subject of tree-planting and Arbour Day, it would be interesting to glance at some of the famous trees in this country. There is, for instance, the "Charter Oak" which, until 1855, stood on the northern slope of Wylly's Hill in Hartford, Conn. In that year it was blown down during a storm, and now a white marble slab marks the spot. The tree derived its name from the fact that in 1687 a charter from the King of England was hidden in it. The charter gave the people of Connecticut certain rights, and they wished to preserve it from Governor Andros, who would have destroyed it and ruled as he liked.

"Washington Elm" is the famous old tree under which George Washington took command of the Continental army in 1775. It is no longer standing.

"Burgoyne Elm" a favourite old historic tree is still alive and still standing. Burgoyne was an English officer who came to this country during the Revolution with an army of eight hundred men. He was forced to surrender his army on October 17, 1777, and he himself was taken to New York as prisoner of war. The citizens of New York planted a tree in honour of the victory, and named it for their prisoner.

The "Treaty Elm" is the tree under which William Penn made his famous treaty of good faith and friendship with the Indians. It stood, in Philadelphia, for several generations; when it was blown down in 1810 it was said to be at least two hundred and forty years old.

FLAG DAY

When the American Colonies decided to become a separate people, they decided also to have a flag of their own. The Continental Congress, which met in Philadelphia, appointed Franklin, Harrison, and Lynch a committee to arrange a flag. This was in 1775.

The committee decided upon a flag with thirteen stripes of red and white, with the "Union" in the corner. But the "Union" appeared also on the English flag, and on June 14, 1777, this resolution was adopted in Congress:

> *Resolved,* That the flag of the United States be thirteen stripes, alternate red and white, that the "Union" be thirteen stars, white, in a blue field, representing a new constellation.

Thus was originated the flag of the United States of America. A new star was added each time another state joined the union. The thirteen stripes, however, representing the thirteen original colonies, still remain.

Flag Day is a special day set aside by state action to honour the flag. June 14th is the day selected, because that was the day on which Congress adopted the resolution concerning the flag. The holiday is not legal in all states, but it is customary throughout the nation to display the flag on June 14th.

Any celebrations on this day are of a patriotic nature, with the flag very much in evidence.

INDEPENDENCE DAY

Independence Day, familiarly known as the Fourth of July, is in commemoration of the signing of the Declaration of Independence. It was on July 4th, 1776, that the old, cracked Liberty Bell rang for the first time for the independence of the new nation. This bell, made in Philadelphia, has hung in the building known as the "State House" since 1753.

State action has made of Independence Day a legal holiday, observed throughout the nation. On this day flags are hung from all the windows, industry temporarily ceases —and the nation celebrates all over again the triumph over oppression and the great note of freedom.

The custom of building huge bonfires, shooting off firecrackers, and making a great din, originated with the very first Fourth of July. In wild excitement at their victory, drunk with their new freedom, the people collected in the streets and celebrated as all mobs celebrate—with noise and fires and joyous shouting.

Since then it has been customary, on every recurring Independence Day, to commemorate the great occasion by shooting off firecrackers and making a great din, in the manner of those who first celebrated the triumph. Because of many accidents and disastrous fires, it has recently become customary for certain cities to forbid the sale of firecrackers on Independence Day, but as a general rule there is wild celebration throughout the country on that day.

A Fourth of July party may be as gay and jolly as one pleases. But the occasion should carry a note of patriotism. Of all the year's entertainments, the Independence Day celebration is undoubtedly the one most ideally spent in the country. Away from the noise and the heat and the madness of the city, one can reflect upon the hallowed memories of the day, and withal have a jolly good time.

The dinner table on Independence Day should carry a patriotic touch. The centrepiece might be blue and white flowers, in a red bowl. At each place there might be a Liberty Bell of hard chocolate, or perhaps of red-white-and-blue paper. Or the souvenir might take the form of a cracker, in the patriotic colours, containing a hat of tissue paper.

The menu sometimes carries out the patriotic colour scheme. The cakes are frosted with red-and-white striped icing and decorated with tiny silk flags. Bonbons are wrapped in red-white-and-blue tissue paper, as are also the sandwiches at a luncheon or tea. Vanilla and raspberry ice, sprinkled with tiny blue candies, makes an appropriate dessert.

A costume ball on Independence Day would require costumes of the Colonial period. Usually at evening entertainments on this day the electric bulbs are of red, blue, and plain glass, or the ordinary bulbs are covered with red and blue paper to carry out the patriotic note.

LABOUR DAY

The first Monday in September honours the dignity of labour. In a land of commercialism and great industry, sentiment sets apart one special day in which to honour labour.

This holiday, known as Labour Day, is made legal by state action. It is particularly popular in the industrial states, but not in agricultural territories, where its observance is likely to interfere with the harvesting.

There are no particular ceremonies or celebrations in connection with Labour Day. It is usually observed as a day of rest.

COLUMBUS DAY

Some states make the 12th of October a legal holiday in celebration of the discovery of America. It is called Columbus Day in honour of the discoverer, Columbus.

A tea party is regarded as the most appropriate type of entertaining on Columbus Day. Columbus suppers and Columbian dances are popular also. The home should be decorated with flags for the occasion, and any entertainment—such as music or recitation—should carry a patriotic tone.

It is interesting to entertain for children on Columbus Day. It has for generations been customary to observe the day at school with pageants and pantomimes, which can be introduced very easily into the home. The children can come to the party dressed as Indians, as sailors of the 15th century, as pirates, etc. There can be contests, prizes being offered for the best recitations or essays on Columbus and the discovery of America. The day lends itself more to the entertaining of children than of grown-ups.

HALLOWE'EN

There is probably no folk holiday which has taken a stronger hold upon the popular imagination than that celebrated on the eve of October 31st, the holiday known as Hallowe'en. The name means hallowed, or holy, evening.

Hallowe'en is really an Autumn festival, as May Day is a spring festival. But peasant superstition robbed the holiday of its original meaning and surrounded it with the delightful mystery of ghosts, witches, spirits, and hobgoblins. And because of these superstitious notions, Hallowe'en appeals to the public fancy and all its old customs and traditions have remained.

The ancient Druids had a great autumn festival which commenced at midnight, October 31st, and lasted throughout the following day, November 1st. Among other things, they believed that on this night the great lord of death, Saman, called together all the wicked souls that had been condemned, within the past twelve months, to inhabit the bodies of animals. Because of the wicked spirits that prowled about on this night, they lit huge bonfires and kept a sharp lookout. Thus it is unquestionably from the Druids that we derive the belief that witches and ghosts walk abroad on Hallowe'en—a belief still prevalent among rural peoples in Europe.

The Romans also had a festival about the 1st of November which was in honour of Pomona. Nuts and apples, as tokens of the winter store of fruits, were roasted before great bonfires. It appears that the Druidic ceremonies and the Roman ceremonies were grafted one upon the other, to become our Hallowe'en.

Originally the festival of Hallowe'en was simple and was

confined almost wholly to the church. But lower classes somehow took a peculiar interest in the festival, and weird tales of spirits and goblins were circulated among them. The tales took root. They spread. It became a general and widespread notion that ghosts and spirits walked abroad on Hallowe'en. Peasantry gathered together on the eve of October 31st, built great bonfires to keep the spooks away, and shudderingly told one another of queer noises, strange flutterings, trembling shadows.

And they tempered their fears with feasting. They brought out their winter stores of nuts and apples. In their hands the festival of Hallowe'en, meant to be simply a festival in honour of autumn, became perverted. Instead of being an evening hallowed to autumn and the winter stores, it became an evening hallowed to witches, to ghosts, to the supernatural. And young girls, suiting the holiday to their own hopes, decided that this was the one night of the year in which they were permitted to peer into the future and discover the names of their future husbands!

The roasting of nuts on Hallowe'en was very popular in mediæval England. Indeed, the roasting of nuts became so closely associated with this festival that it became known, in some localities, as "Nutcrack Night." The custom of "ducking" for apples is probably English in origin; it was widely prevalent among the English during the early period of mediævalism.

Customs and Superstitions of Hallowe'en.—It is customary for young people, throughout England, to dive or "duck" for apples. There are many superstitions connected with this custom. For instance, the maiden who is fortunate enough to win the apple is advised to sleep with it under her pillow, for she will surely dream of her lover. Another superstition is that if the young lady eats the apple while standing before her mirror, combing her hair, her future husband will look over her shoulder into the glass. She must under no circumstances turn around, or he will vanish.

One glimpses the almost childlike ingenuity of a superstition such as this. The apple is supposed to be eaten at midnight. The young lady, evidently very superstitious or she wouldn't be attempting the thing at all, peers into the mirror and actually imagines that she sees someone in the glass. She dares not turn around lest the vision disappear. She thinks of the person she would like to be her lover, stares wide-eyed and frightened into the mirror—*and sees him!* It is simply imagination tinged with fear and superstition, yet the next morning the young lady is quite positive that what happened at midnight was real, true. No one can convince her otherwise.

Most people avoid the churchyard and cemetery on Hallowe'en. The common notion is that the spirits of the dead walk abroad on that night. There is a superstition that if a man meet one of these spirits face to face, he will fall dead. Therefore, under no circumstances should one turn or look behind if one hears footsteps on Hallowe'en!

Young girls in England were for many generations in the habit of gathering milfoil on Hallowe'en and sleeping with it under their pillows. Like the apple, it caused them to dream of their future husbands.

Another old custom was to throw a skein or ball of yarn from the window, holding the end of the yarn in the hand. It was believed that an apparition of one's future husband would take the other end, rewind the ball, and leave it just beneath the window. Clever fellows, courting young ladies who would have none of them, watched for the ball of yarn to come hurtling through the window, and played at being "apparition." They knew that eager eyes watched behind the curtains!

The black cat, being the traditional companion of witches, is ever present at Hallowe'en. The pumpkin is simply a symbol of the harvest. Stealing gates, buggies, chairs, etc., a popular Hallowe'en prank until recently, was a relic of the time when gates and gate-posts disappeared and were said to have been stolen by the evil spirits. Ac-

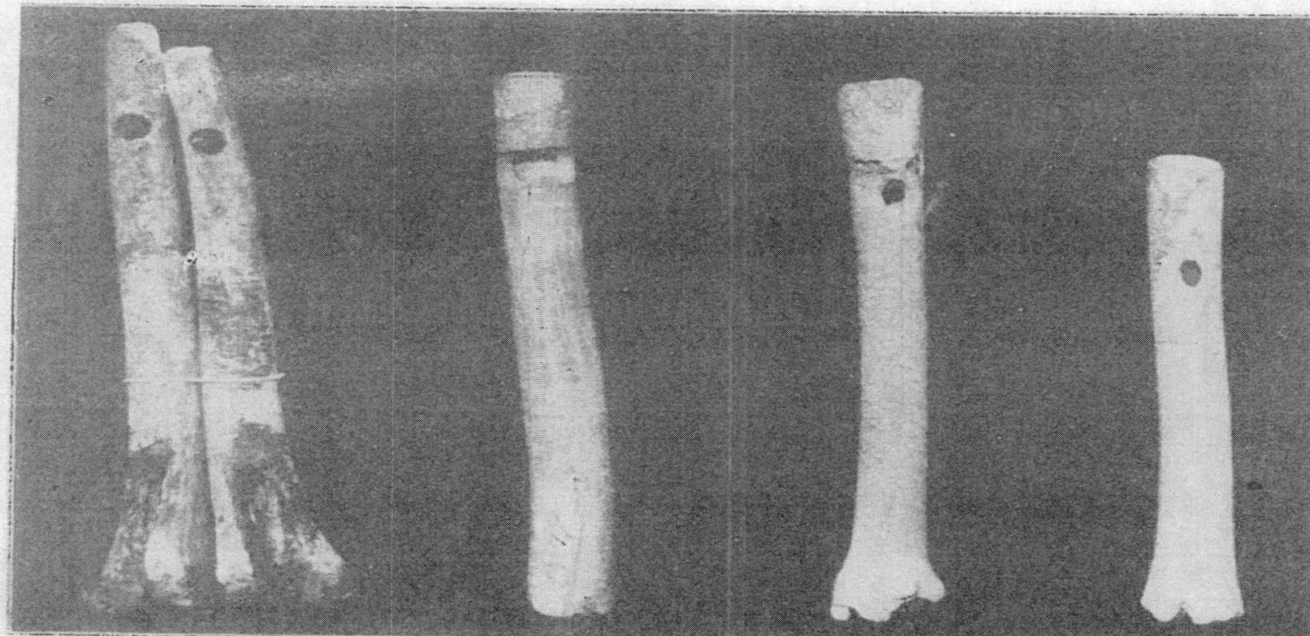

(Courtesy of Metropolitan Museum of Art)

A double whistle made from tibia of a deer. Also bone whistles, found in an ancient Indian grave at Santa Barbara, California.

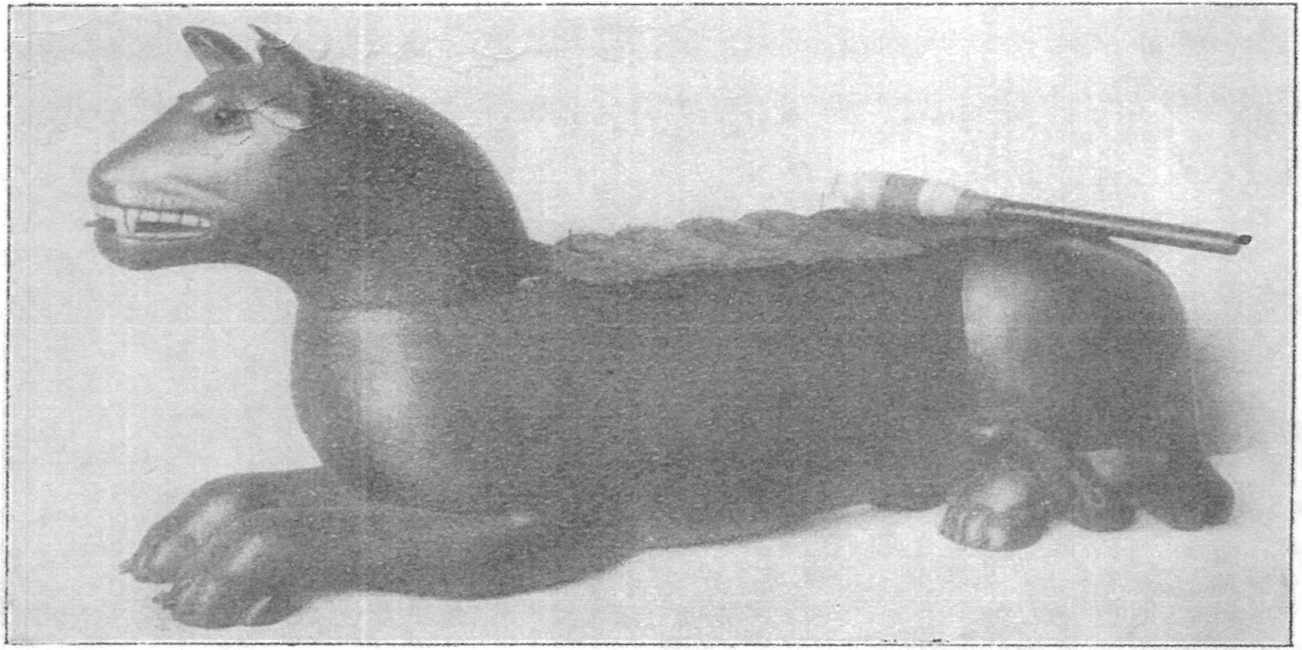

(Courtesy of Metropolitan Museum of Art)

The Javanese saron, an interesting musical instrument.

cording to tradition, everything connected with Hallowe'en smacks of the supernatural.

The white hare is more feared on Hallowe'en than any ghost. The superstition is that when a maiden, having loved not wisely but too well, dies of a broken heart, her spirit comes back in the shape of a white hare to haunt her deceiver. The phantom follows him eveywhere, and is invisible to all but him. Ultimately it causes his death—on some dark Hallowe'en. We see the white hare as a symbol of conscience. It is usually conscience that gives rise to fear, and fear, to superstition.

Chalking on Hallowe'en.—An old Hallowe'en custom, practised by street ruffians, is to chalk the backs of passers-by, shout "Hallowe'en!" and scamper off. This appears to be a very old custom practised in parts of England, and particularly at Diss, Norfolk.

For generations it has been customary, in this locality, for the children to keep "Chalk-back Day" on the Thursday before the fair day, which was held on the third Friday in September. It is at this period that the sun (the whitener) is supposed to enter "the hinder part of the circle and the children chalk the people's backs to indicate that the rule of the White God has ended."

Somehow the custom became connected with Hallowe'en, and even now the children of our own country find keen joy in chalking one another's clothes at this period.

Hallowe'en Festivities.—Tradition calls for feasting on Hallowe'en. The quaint old festival with its queer superstitions and fancies is becoming more and more an occasion for social entertaining. What, for instance, could be better fun than a Ghost Party?

From beginning to end the party must carry an element of mystery. The invitations, reading somewhat like the following, should be penned on cards in the form of witches, ghosts, or black cats:

FELLOW-SPOOK!

You are hereby notified to attend a Ghost Convention on the 31st

of October, otherwise known as Hallowe'en. Come at eight o'clock and park your troubles at the door. The password is "Fun." Full ghostly regalia of sheet and pillow case will be given each ghost on arrival. Be sure to come and see what happens at the stroke of twelve.
(Name of Hostess)
High Ghost.
(Address)

The home, of course, must be decorated for the occasion. Candlelight should be used, and only a few candles at that, so that everything is dim. Or if you are afraid of fire omit the candles and shroud all the lights in lavender paper. Drape the furniture, the dress form, the broom with sheets —for ghosts must have a ghostly atmosphere.

Strangely enough, ghosts eat, and no Hallowe'en party is a success without a properly planned menu. A long, narrow table is the best, for when there are spirits and witches in the air, the nearer to one another the guests are the better they will like it! At each place have a small black pasteboard cat filled with candy.

Hot bouillon should be served, as it helps dispel the shivery feeling of Hallowe'en. Pumpkin pie is, of course, a tradition. And there should by all means be deviled eggs, devil's cake, and sand-*witches*.

Barn parties are particularly appropriate at Hallowe'en. The barn offers many opportunities for clever decoration. Pumpkins lighted with candles can be wired around the barn; bats made of brown cheesecloth and whalebone can be suspended by threads from the ceiling; ghosts and skeletons, made of brownsticks and sheets, can be hidden behind bales of hay. The very environment lends itself to Hallowe'en fun.

In the 18th century a very popular Hallowe'en frolic called "Fire o' Love" was practised outdoors. The frolic is very appropriate for the barn party if one wishes to carry out the old custom.

A large tub of water is brought into the barn. Each girl writes her name on a separate piece of paper, twists it to keep it closed, and throws it upon the water. A candle end, attached to a flat cork, is placed on the water and floats this way and that among the slips. One by one it burns them up. In a few minutes the candle end sputters and dies, and there are always one or two slips left. These are taken out and opened. The unhappy young ladies whose names appear upon them will never marry, according to the old tradition. This method of divination was extremely popular about 1730 and was practised, and implicitly believed, by men and women alike.

Another time-honoured Hallowe'en custom is to bob or duck for apples. This, too, is appropriate at the barn party. The lucky person to win the apple pares it round and round in one piece and throws it over his or her head. It falls in some grotesque form, which the guests interpret as the letter it most closely resembles. This is regarded as the initial letter of the player's future mate.

The apple-paring method of divination appears to be American rather than English in origin. It was a favourite among Colonial maidens, who quoted this bit of old verse while casting the paring over the shoulder:

> By this paring let me discover
> The initial letter of my true lover.

The hostess who entertains at Hallowe'en should preserve all the old traditions and customs, no matter how silly and frivolous they may seem, for they add a certain quaintness which no one can fail to enjoy.

ARMISTICE DAY

On the eleventh day of the eleventh month at precisely eleven o'clock, 1918, America went mad. Armistice! The New York *Evening Sun*, dated Monday, November 11, 1918, carries this feature article:

HOLIDAY PROCLAIMED AS CITY WILDLY CELEBRATES ARMISTICE

Greater New York's millions, men, women, and children, went

wild with joy to-day over the news that Germany has been whipped to a frazzle, that the Kaiser has been chased out of Germany, and that the war is over. The delirious exultation that the city went through—and is still going through—would have been beyond all belief, if it had not actually been seen.

Early in the day the Mayor had proclaimed a public holiday, which was just a simple formality, for no one had the least intention of working anyway. Shops, factories, offices—all were deserted. The article continues:

Men and women, strangers, kissed each other in the streets. At twelve o'clock a huge parade of leaping, shouting, flag-waving men, women, and children surged northward from City Hall to encounter other riotous processions coming down Fifth Avenue, mingling one with another.

What was happening in New York was happening all over the country. Everyone went wild with rejoicing. The World War was over! Armistice!

And since that never-to-be-forgotten day in 1918 Armistice Day has been observed with celebration, and in some states with public ceremony. Though the day has not as yet been set aside legally as a holiday, everyone remembers Armistice Day and pauses, if but for a moment, to think kindly of the soldiers who lie buried "in Flanders fields," where "the poppies grow."

Poppies are worn on Armistice Day in memory of the soldiers and sailors who gave their lives in the World War. If a dinner, party, or celebration is given in honour of the signing of armistice, poppies should be the predominating note. Of course, any celebration on this day must carry with it a patriotic significance.

THANKSGIVING

Of all the holidays observed in this country, there is none so distinctively American as Thanksgiving. It is a legacy of the Puritans, cherished because of the romance and traditions that surrounded it.

Although Thanksgiving as we know it is an American institution, days of thanksgiving in recognition of special mercies or favours have been known since the earliest times, and have been common to almost all nations. We can only guess, but we can never know, what primitive people of a forgotten age first gave thanks in their crude way for rain after drought, for food after famine.

The Israelites appear to have been among the earliest people to observe a special day of thanksgiving. They observed faithfully, with great rejoicing and solemn ceremonies, their Feast of Tabernacles, a day of thanks not only for the bounties of the land, but for the escape from Egypt.

> The feast of tabernacles shalt thou hold for thyself seven days, when thou hast gathered in the produce of thy threshing-floor and of thy wine press. (Deuteronomy XVI, 13.)

The ancient Greeks had al a day of thanksgiving known as the Feast of Demeter. This nine-day feast was in honour of Demeter, goddess of the cornfield and harvests, and was meant, very obviously, as a day of gratitude for the richness and bounties of the harvest. Sacrifices of fruit, wine, honey, and milk were made. The Romans appear to have had a similar festival at harvest-time called Cerelia, a time of rejoicing and thanksgiving.

In England, as in other countries, it was customary to hold special days of fasting and prayer in times of peril, of famine, of pestilence. When the danger was past—when there was plenty of food, plenty of water, no ravaging diseases—feasts and celebrations would be given by the people. These celebrations were fundamentally thanksgiving festivals. A special day of thanksgiving was proclaimed by Oliver Cromwell at the time of the defeat of the Spanish Armada. Another day of thanksgiving was declared on the day that the famous Gunpowder Plot was discovered.

The Siamese have an old festival known as the "Swing Festival," which is like our Thanksgiving. Its purpose is to show gratitude for the richness of the land, the happiness of the people. It is in this festival that the much-quoted sacred white elephant of Siam takes conspicuous part.

But although there have been many days of thanksgiving and rejoicing, and although many festivals like our Thanksgiving exist in various parts of the world, America was the first nation definitely to set apart one day in each year for the sole purpose of rejoicing in the good things of life and "giving God thanks."

The First Thanksgiving.—We are all familiar with the appalling hardships that the first settlers in America were forced to endure. A handful of homesick men and women in a strange, bleak country, Indians everywhere, food scarce, and home across the ocean. No,—home here, for they could not return to the land from whose intolerance they had fled.

In the first year, forty-six of the one hundred and one white people who settled in Plymouth died and were buried on the bluff overlooking the landing. But in the Fall of 1621 the remaining men of Plymouth gathered in a wonderful crop from the twenty acres of corn and six acres of barley and peas they had planted. And the cold weather brought unexpectedly large quantities of game into the harbour. Plenty of food—and a great new hope in the hearts of the wanderers.

Governor Bradford gave directions that a day of thanksgiving be held on December 13, 1621, to give thanks for the great blessings that had been bestowed upon them. A feast was prepared including "as much fowle as with a little helpe beside, served the company almost a weeke." Friendly Massasoit with ninety of his Indian braves, was invited to the feast, and they came in all their holiday paint and feathers. Of white men and women there were only fifty-five at this First Thanksgiving.

Although Thanksgiving did not then become a regular yearly festival, our own Thanksgiving, which we observe every November, is a direct legacy of that historic feast with the Indians. It has not been definitely established just when Thanksgiving became a fixed annual observance in New England.

A great public Thanksgiving was held in Boston on February 22, 1630, by the Bay Colony. It was a celebration in gratitude for the safe arrival of the ships bringing food and friends from across the ocean.

From 1630 to 1680 there were about twenty Thanksgiving Days—one every two or three years. In 1675, when the Indians attacked the settlers and engaged them in various widely separated warfares, there was no Thanksgiving. In 1742 there were two such festivals.

It was not until after the Revolution, when Congress adopted the Constitution (1789), that Thanksgiving was definitely established as a yearly day of rejoicing and festivity. Just before the Congress adjourned, a man by the name of Boudinot moved that a day be recommended for universal thanksgiving. The motion was carried, and President Washington appointed Thursday, November 26th, as the "National Thanksgiving Day."

For a little while the holiday was observed faithfully, but somehow a break occurred, and one by one the states began to observe the day of Thanksgiving at different times. Just before the Civil War each state had a different day on which to observe Thanksgiving, but all these days were in November.

Carrying out Washington's first intention, Lincoln in 1860 appointed a national Thanksgiving Day to be observed by everyone alike. This day was the last Thursday in November, and so it has remained ever since.

The Puritan Distaste for Christmas Helped to Establish Thanksgiving.—The first Thanksgiving was unquestionably held in the winter of 1621 and was a simple, whole-souled expression of gratitude, voiced by a handful of people who found themselves suddenly saved from starvation. There are some writers, however, who attribute the establishing of Thanksgiving to an entirely different and unrelated cause.

It seems to be a common notion among writers on this subject that "To the mind of the Puritan, Christmas smelled to heaven of idolatry." They believe that the Puritans abolished Christmas as a hateful relic of popery, and that they established Thanksgiving as a purely Puritan festival to take its place.

Wanting a day to replace Christmas, says one writer, the Puritans "appointed every year some day in autumn, generally toward the end of November, as a day of solemn prayer and thanksgiving for the blessings of the year, and especially the bounties of the harvest."

According to this belief, Thanksgiving was simply a day of rejoicing and family reunion in November instead of December. The Puritans ate turkey, Indian pudding and pumpkin pie instead of the "superstitious meats and plum-pudding" of Christmas-time. But, we are told, the influx of Roman Catholics and Episcopalians brought Christmas and its customs into vogue again, and both holidays were accepted.

The distaste for Christmas among the Puritans may very possibly have helped to establish Thanksgiving as a national festival. There are even to-day certain people who regard Christmas as a strictly heathen holiday. But we can be absolutely certain that Thanksgiving had its true inception in 1621 when fifty-five grateful men and women, surrounded by ninety painted Indians, gave thanks for the corn and the fowl upon which they feasted.

Thanksgiving Customs.—On Thanksgiving Day children dress themselves in grotesque fashion, paint their faces, wear masks, and go about the streets singing or blowing on horns. This custom commemorates the presence of the Indians, in their gay paint and feathers, at the first Thanksgiving. The children preserve it because of the joy it affords them, little savages that they are. It delights the primitive personality to dress up in gay costume, paint the face, and parade around the streets.

The practice of disguise at times of festivity is very old.

In an ancient Argive festival held yearly like our Thanksgiving, the women dressed in men's garments and the men donned women's robes and veils. In the old Roman Saturnalia the slaves exchanged position and dress with their masters, and the men and women exchanged dress.

The custom of singing in the streets and of going from house to house begging for pennies is English in origin. It was an old custom for children, and even grown people, to sing carols in the street at Christmas-time, passersby throwing coins to them. A similar custom was for poor women to go from house to house, carrying images of the Virgin and Child or of Christ on the cross, receiving dole at each house visited. To-day the youngsters in the street at Thanksgiving-time shout, "Anything for Thanksgiving!" to all passersby, and even parade from one house to another.

Pumpkin pie and turkey are associated with the Thanksgiving feast because both appeared on the table of the first Thanksgiving. Corn, having played a large part in inspiring the Puritans to give thanks, usually appears in some form or other on the Thanksgiving table.

Cranberries have no definite significance. The fruit happens to ripen at the end of October, which makes it an opportune Thanksgiving "fixin'."

Thanksgiving is a time of great social activity, because the spirit of hospitality is woven eternally into this festival. The Puritans invited Massasoit and ninety of his men to their feast. The hostess to-day invites more friends and acquaintances to her dinner or party at Thanksgiving than she does ordinarily. Somehow one feels more strongly at this time of the year than any other the urge to give, to share, to be hospitable.

Before the Civil War it was a popular custom for families to hold great reunions on Thanksgiving. The children came home from school; the married sons and daughters came with their families; aunts, uncles, cousins, everyone came to the great Thanksgiving feast. During the war, and for a while afterward, this custom of family reunion at Thanksgiving ceased but was later revived. Many families still observe this old custom of reunion on Thanksgiving Day.

The custom of making up baskets of food for needy families originated in the early 18th century and was commenced by a group of young women who determined to set aside one period of each year to be devoted entirely to purposes of charity. They selected Thanksgiving as the most opportune time.

Accordingly, at Thanksgiving-time they packed baskets to brimming with all good things to eat and took them personally to the home of the needy. Word of what they were doing spread, and soon there were many people observing this worthy custom. Organizations were founded for the purpose of supplying food and clothing to the needy at Thanksgiving. The custom has survived, as good things do, and the charity-basket is one of our most gratifying Thanksgiving observances.

Thanksgiving Entertaining.—Thanksgiving and hospitality go hand-in-hand. There is probably no better time of the year to entertain.

Every hostess knows the old tradition that at Thanksgiving good food is as important as good fun, and that the games played hold but second place to the food served. Turkey, of course, is inevitable; and there is nothing like a great pumpkin pie for Thanksgiving atmosphere!

But remembering the background upon which this first of our purely American holidays is built, the hostess plans to have as much good cheer as good cooking. She starts off right by having the proper kind of setting. The table decorations, for instance, are simple fruits and vegetables, instead of the customary flowers. For the centrepiece a huge pumpkin may be used, banked around with polished apples, golden corn, autumn leaves, and nuts. At each place there may be a scooped-out apple filled with shelled nuts, or perhaps just slightly scooped out to hold a candle.

Sometimes a great yellow paper pumpkin is used for the centrepiece, and it is filled with favours for the guests. Green and orange ribbons attached to the favours reach out across the table and end under the service plate. Thanksgiving candles are usually shaded with yellow shades upon which tiny black turkeys have been pasted. The shades can be made of crêpe-paper; the turkeys can be purchased at any stationery shop.

True to the traditions of the day, the hostess uses all her finest and most cherished silver and chinaware. But she brings forth also her rare old pieces of Colonial chinaware, her curious pewter heirlooms; and if there is an old family spinning-wheel in the attic, it is tenderly carried downstairs, dusted, and given place of honour in the reception room.

The Thanksgiving dinner, by custom, is a jolly old-fashioned affair with no hint of formality. On any other occasion, the hostess may whisk her guests through several courses of dinner and hurry them into the drawing room, but not on Thanksgiving! It is the one time of the year when everyone likes to linger at the table, browsing in mellow lanes of memory, reminiscing fondly until the last candle has sputtered and died.

According to that delightful old authority, Mr. E. H. Arr, Thanksgiving is not Thanksgiving at all if the pie is lacking. It need not be pumpkin pie, says Mr. Arr, as he naïvely suggests his own favourite—mince pie. And he proceeds to inform us that:

> The true Thanksgiving mince pie should be an inch thick, with a thin flaky crust tinted by its imprisoned juices which threaten to break through. Around its edges must be a slight crinkle made by the tines of a fork, and in its top a hole here and there from the stroke of a knife to let the steam out. This steam, once known, can never be forgotten.

It typifies the joyous, generous Thanksgiving spirit, that steaming mince pie!

Some Popular Thanksgiving Games.—Memories of

wonderful games are entangled in our recollections of childhood Thanksgivings. Most of these old favourites have survived and are still a part of modern Thanksgiving festivity.

At the first Thanksgiving, the Indians entertained with weird dancing, pantomime, feats of skill. The others, according to Edward Winslow, "among other recreations . . . exercised our arms." For three days, they feasted and made merry, and somehow the spirit of jollity has hovered about the holiday ever since.

An old Thanksgiving game is called the Cranberry Contest. A large bowl of cranberries is placed on the floor and around it are seated from four to ten contestants. Each one is supplied with a spool of thread and a needle. At a given signal they thread the needle and begin to string the cranberries into a necklace. At the end of three minutes the one with the longest necklace receives the prize. A booby prize is usually awarded the person with the shortest necklace.

The Corn Game is very old but is always popular because it is in memory of the five grains of corn which tradition tells us were allotted to the Puritans. Five ears of corn are hidden in the room, and the guests begin a search for them. The five to find the ears of corn are the contestants in the game; the others are interested onlookers.

At a given signal, the five contestants begin to remove the kernels from the corn and drop them into a bowl which has been placed on the floor for the purpose. The one who removes all the kernels in the shortest time receives a prize.

Now all those who have not competed, gather around the bowl and guess how many kernels there are in it. A large box of popcorn is presented to the person whose guess comes closest.

In the old-fashioned Pumpkin Race, always a favourite, small pumpkins are rolled over a certain distance with small wooden spoons. The smaller the spoons the greater the fun! The pumpkins roll this way and that out of line, and must be coaxed back into line again, but the hands may not be used. The tiny spoons must do all the coaxing. Of course, there is a great deal of fun for the onlookers. The person whose pumpkin reaches the goal first receives a prize.

Games such as these help preserve the old Thankgiving traditions and add a certain jolly informality to the occasion, whether it be a Pumpkin party, a Mayflower luncheon, a Puritan tea, or just a good, old-fashioned Thanksgiving dinner.

CHRISTMAS

Out of the distant past comes a whispered greeting that warms the heart of humanity. Merry Christmas! It echoes and reëchoes back across the long ages. It throbs through the generations of life, while kingdoms rise and fall, while men and nations move like checkers on a checker-board.

Merry Christmas! It stirs the heart like some beautiful old memory. It quickens the pulse like a passionate violin. We forget to play at being grown-up, and in a moment we are all children again.

> Of all the old festivals [says Washington Irving], that of Christmas awakens the strongest and most heartfelt associations. There is a tone of solemn and sacred feeling that blends with our conviviality, and lifts the spirit to a state of hallowed and elevated enjoyment.

All yesterday is strewn with the embers of old Christmas fires. It is the festival of the nativity. From the early centuries of Christianity the anniversary of the birth of Christ has been celebrated. It is called "Christmas" because in early England the festival was called "Christes messe" which means "Christ's mass."

At first the time of the festival varied in different places.

Some churches observed it in December, others in January, April, May. There was no historical record as to the exact birth date of Christ. It seems possible that December 25th was established as the festival day—as Christmas—because it marked the beginning of the great winter festival when Britons, Germans, and Gauls made merry in pagan fashion. Christmas replaced these old pagan festivals, the customs and symbols of the one blending into the customs and the symbols of the other.

The celebration of December 25th, as Christmas, spread to various parts of the Christian world. By the 5th century it had become fairly well established. Later, as the festival spread, differences in date occurred owing to differences in calendar. But the general belief prevailed that Christ was born "at the hour of midnight on Christmas Eve."

Tracing the Christmas Festival.—Many of our popular holidays appear to have been nature festivals at one time. Easter and May Day were very likely spring festivals; Hallowe'en, an autumn festival.

Christmas was originally a festival of the winter solstice. At this period of the year it was customary to hold great feasts in honour of the heathen gods, to dance and make merry. But the early teachers of Christianity prohibited these primitive festivities as unsuited to the character of Christ.

Yet the old festival was not discarded entirely. Its symbols and customs were adapted to the new festival in celebration of the anniversary of Christ's nativity. And so we find Christmas patterned with many curious customs that are of pagan origin. The Yule log, the holly, and the mistletoe go much farther back into antiquity than we suspect.

It is said that the first Christmas-day festival held in Britain was celebrated by King Arthur in the city of York, A.D. 521. It lasted several days. The new customs were grafted upon the old, and the new symbols were adaptations of old ones. The festival appealed instantly to the masses; a tiny spark was fanned into flame and it has burned brightly throughout all these generations.

By the early Middle Ages, Christmas had become the greatest of popular festivals. Beggar and king observed the day. Churches were decorated and quaint plays concerning the nativity were enacted. Carols were sung in the streets and images of the Virgin and of Christ were carried about from house to house. And of course there were feasting and merrymaking, as there always are at a festival time.

In Shakespeare's time the Christmas festivities were extremely elaborate. Sometimes they lasted until Twelfth Day, or Epiphany—twelve days after Christmas. During this period there was no work of any kind. The people gave themselves over to feasting and gay celebration.

Then there was a reaction, as there generally is. The Puritans developed a keen distaste for the Christmas festivities, and prevailed upon Parliament to prohibit them. Christmas was declared a day of fast, and festivities were prohibited by law. After the Restoration, however, the old observances came back—somewhat subdued, but gay and festive as ever.

The observance of the Christmas festival spread all over the Christian world. The date is not everywhere the same, nor are the customs identical. January 6th is the date observed in the Armenian church. The Dutch watch for St. Nicholas on the eve of December 6th. The French have their own particular Christmas observances; the Germans have theirs. But wherever and whenever Christmas is celebrated, it is a day of rejoicing and good cheer.

CHRISTMAS CUSTOMS

At one time the customs and observances that we associate with Christmas had a very definite significance. Today they survive as part of our social scheme.

In America we have made of Christmas a period of great social activity. The old customs of other lands, combined with tender memories of the first Christmases in this country, make of the holiday a rare interval of joy and cheer which find expression in a semi-social, semi-religious celebration. Everybody wishes everybody else a merry Christmas, and even the echoes are glad!

The first Christmases in America were not the gay festivities to which we are accustomed. They were days like all the rest, devoted to work and prayer. Governor Bradford wrote, "Ye 25th day begane to erect ye first house for comone use to receive them and their goods." A few years after this was written the Church of England established Christmas services in Boston.

Our Christmas celebration carries threads from many lands. People coming here from France, England, Germany, Norway, Italy—all brought their own customs with them. Our Christmas tree and Santa Claus are imported. Our carols and our stocking superstition came from across the ocean. Even our "Merry Christmas" belongs to England.

Yet our Christmas festivities are individual, American. They are like those of no one country, but like a tapestry that has been patterned with many beautiful threads, our festivities reflect the customs, beliefs, and superstitions of many and widely separated lands.

Santa Claus.—Jolly old Santa Claus with his tinkling sleigh bells and pack of toys is very closely associated with the American Christmas. Our children hang up their stockings in high glee, fully believing that Santa will come down the chimney and fill them with good things, until, of course, they are old enough to separate fact from fancy, or until some cruel person shatters the beautiful belief.

Santa came to America by way of Holland. The old Dutch settlers of New York brought with them all the joyous and hospitable observances of their fatherland. They introduced to their neighbours in the New World St.

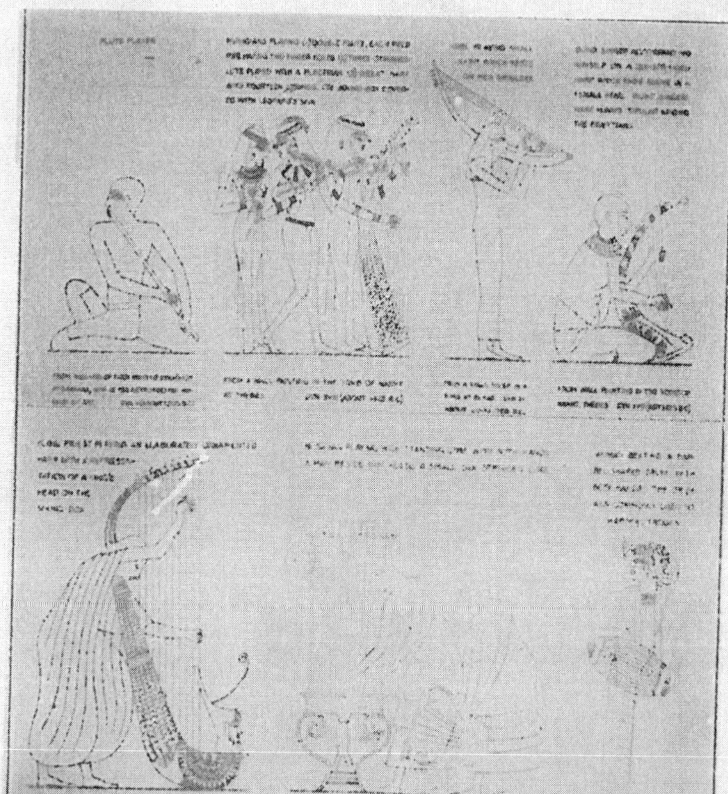

(Courtesy of Metropolitan Museum of Art.)

The paintings in their tombs indicate that the Egyptians were great lovers of music. They had drums, small bells, harps, tambourines, lyres, etc.

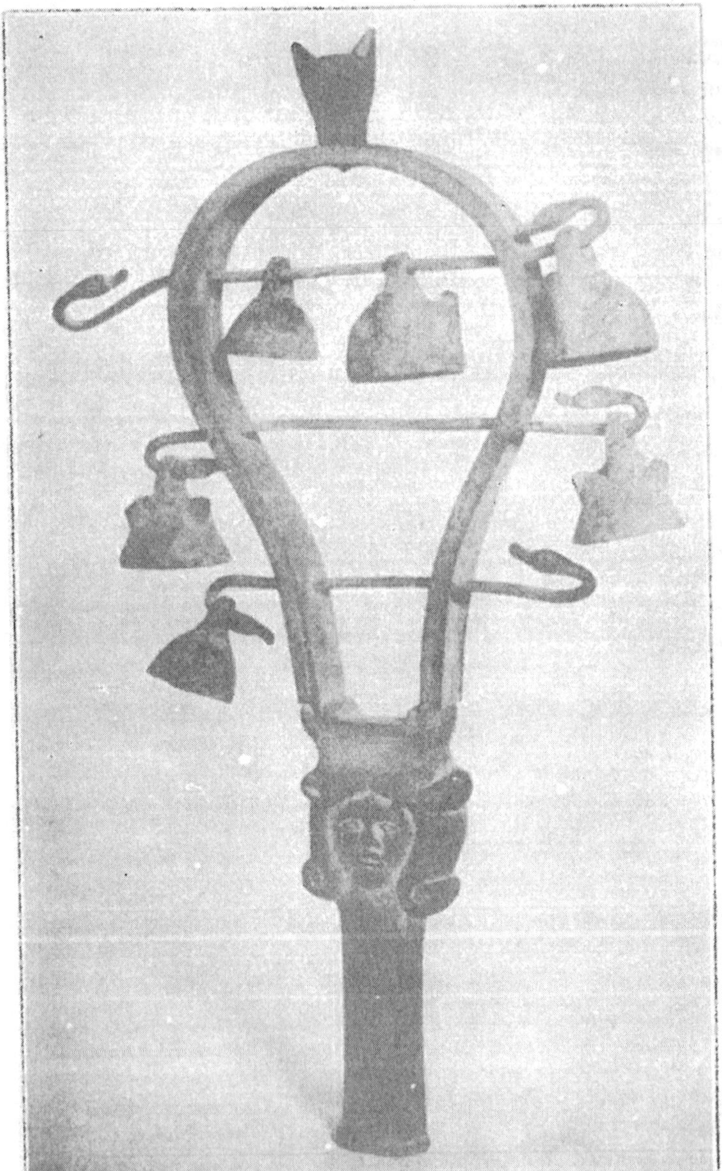

(Courtesy of Metropolitan Museum of Art)

Reproduction of Seshesh-Sistrum, a favourite musical instrument of other days.

Nicholas, or San Nicolaas, patron saint of children. And San Nicolaas promptly grew a long white beard, belted his jovial stoutness in a red coat, and made his bow to America as Santa Claus!

England, too, has its Santa Claus. The name appears to be derived in slurred interpretation from San Nicolaas, the English for which would be St. Nicholas. According to the popular myth, both here and in England, Santa Claus is supposed to sweep down from the north in a sleigh drawn by reindeer, come down the chimney, and fill the stockings hanging before the fireplace with gifts.

We have already seen how this myth might have originated. It seems to have developed from the custom, in old England, of cleaning out the chimney at the beginning of the New Year to enable good luck to enter the household (see p. 280).

An old myth, according to Hone's "Ancient Mysteries," accredits St. Nicholas with being the Bishop of Myra, a person of great virtue and piety. The old legend says that

> the sons of a rich Asiatic, on their way to Athens for education, were slain by a robber innkeeper, dismembered, and their parts hidden in a brine tub. In the morning came the Saint, whose visions had warned him of the crime, whose authority forced confession, and whose prayers restored the boys to life. . . .
>
> Ever since, St. Nicholas has been the special saint of the schoolboy, and certain of the customs of the montem day at Eton College are said to have originated in old festivals in his honour. ("The Book of Christmas.")

St. Nicholas became everywhere the child's saint, though his personality underwent some striking changes as he travelled from country to country. In Holland he remained St. Nicholas, but his personality was modified by memories of Woden, god of the elements and the harvest. He became the patron saint of the children of France, although it is Bonhomme Noël (Father Christmas, sometimes called Père Noël) who brings the good things for the children. In Germany the Christkindlein is the patron saint of the children. From this German phrase for Christ

Child comes our synonym for Santa Claus—Kriss Kringle.

Among the Norwegians, the toys are hidden away in unexpected places and the children search for them. In Italy the gifts are drawn from what is known as "The Urn of Fate." This custom originated with the ancient Romans who had also an "Urn of Fate" from which gifts were drawn. In Spain there are elaborate street festivals at which the children receive gifts.

This age-old custom of presenting the children with gifts makes Christmas one of our most enjoyable festivals. In "Elizabeth and her German Garden" the thought is beautifully expressed.

> For days beforehand, every time the three babies go into the garden they expect to meet the Christ Child with His arms full of gifts. They firmly believe that it is thus their presents are brought, and it is such a charming idea that Christmas would be worth celebrating for its sake alone.

Hanging up the Stocking.—There is an ancient tradition in Holland that St. Nicholas makes his rounds upon Woden's horse, Sleipner. This famous old horse of Dutch mythology is represented by the reindeer whose hoofs our children are supposed to hear on Christmas Eve.

According to the old tale, the children of Amsterdam set their little wooden shoes in the chimney corners because they believed Sleipner would pass by unless he saw them there. And St. Nicholas would leave no gifts unless he saw the little shoes all in a row by the chimneyplace and so knew that the children were tucked away in bed. Evidently some parents of long ago created the myth for their own convenience; it spread quickly, as such things do, and gradually became an established custom.

From Holland the custom spread to France, and children were taught to place their wooden shoes upon the hearth to receive the gifts of Bonhomme Noël. In Germany and Scandinavia the gifts are not placed in the shoe, but hidden in out-of-the-way places about the house.

The stockings that the children of England and the

United States hang up on Christmas Eve developed from the shoe. Shoes won't stretch, you know, and stockings are so much more roomy! Thus the shoe of Amsterdam became the stocking of New Amsterdam, and the custom was established.

There existed in the east of Russia, among the peasantry, an old custom whereby the young girl discovered through divination whom she would have as husband. The traditional formula, still prevalent, is, "Come and take my stockings off." Among the professional classes, and sometimes in the lesser nobility, parents placed money in the stockings of their child—boy or girl—at marriage as a gift for the other partner in the ceremony. Some writers, prominently among them Havelock Ellis, believe that the custom of hanging up the stocking at Christmas is a relic of these two customs from Russia.

The Christmas Tree.—The origin of the Christmas tree is much disputed. Many countries claim the honour of having given the custom to the world. There are scores of popular legends concerning its origin.

One popular tale describes Martin Luther as

> attempting to explain to his wife and children the beauty of a snow-covered forest under the glittering star-besprinkled sky. Suddenly an idea suggested itself. He went into the garden, cut off a little fir tree, dragged it into the nursery, put some candles on its branches and lighted them.

It appears that this happened on Christmas Eve, and the tale seeks to explain not only the origin of the tree, but the origin of the Christmas candles. One of the most popular of German engravings represents Luther and his family grouped about this first Christmas tree.

There is still an older German legend which makes St. Winfrid the originator of the idea. According to this legend the Saint, in the midst of a great crowd of converts, hewed down a giant oak which had been used in Druidic worship. When the tree was half hewn, a great wind passed over the forest and gripped the tree, sending it in a crashing heap backward. Everything in its path was ruined except a slender fir tree, which remained standing, its green spire pointing toward the sky. Because of the seeming miracle, Saint Winfrid decreed that the fir be known as the holy tree, the tree of the Christ Child.

An ancient Scandinavian myth speaks of a "service tree" which is supposed to have sprung

> from the blood-drenched soil where two lovers had been killed by violence. At certain nights in the Christmas season mysterious lights were seen flaming in its branches, that no wind could extinguish.

These "mysterious lights" seem to point to a possible origin for our bright-coloured globes which decorate the Christmas tree.

> It has been explained [says one authority of the tree] as being derived from the ancient Egyptian practice of decking houses at the time of the winter solstice with branches of the date palm—the symbol of life triumphant over death, and therefore of perennial life in the renewal of each bounteous year.

Among the Egyptians the date palm is also an emblem of the starlit firmament.

At about the time that the Egyptians were decking their houses with date-palm branches, the Jews were celebrating their Feast of Chanuckah, in which lighted candles are a feature. Some writers regard this as significant. It is equally interesting to note that the Greek festival at about this season is called the "Feast of Lights"; and the Chinese festival of a corresponding period is called "The Feast of the Lanterns."

The French also have a legend concerning the Christmas tree. They say that in the 13th century a gigantic tree was found, the branches of which were covered with candles, of which some stood erect, some upside down. On the top appeared a vision of a child with a halo around its head. The Pope was asked to explain this extraordinary tree. He said that the tree represented mankind, the child was the Saviour, and the candles were meant to indicate the good and bad human beings. Thenceforth, according to this myth, the Christmas tree was used at every Christmas-time to bring happiness and good cheer into the home.

Several writers trace the tree back to the Roman festival of Saturnalia. In this ancient festival the pine trees were decorated with images of Bacchus, and the Christmas tree is believed by some to be a survival or relic of this old custom.

All these vague traditions appear to have blended together, resulting finally in the permanent establishment of the Christmas tree. The development was most marked in Germany. An authentic German manuscript of 1608 refers to the tree as a regular feature of the Christmas season. For about two hundred years the custom of the tree was confined to the regions along the Rhine, then suddenly it spread all over Germany.

From Germany the custom of decorating the fir tree with candles and covering it with gifts spread everywhere. The marriage of Queen Victoria to the German prince introduced the custom into England as a regular Christmas institution. But the tree was known in England even before that period, for in the memoirs of Greville, under date of December 29, 1829, we read that at a Christmas fête given in honour of Henry VIII, "three trees, in great pots, were put upon a long table covered with pink linen." It was only with the marriage of Queen Victoria, however, that the Christmas tree became a regular English institution.

The French borrowed the custom of the Christmas tree from the Germans in 1870. It was during this year that the German Army celebrated Christmas in Notre Dame. The tree idea appealed to the French, and they adopted it. They usually plant the entire tree, root and all, in a tub.

The German emigrant brought the Christmas tree to America, and we borrowed it along with our other Christmas customs. With us, however, it is intended for the children; in Germany, gifts for all members of the family, from the youngest to the oldest, are on the tree.

The Exchange of Gifts.—Christmas gifts, according to most authorities, were invented to take the place of the pagan custom of exchanging gifts at the New Year. St. Augustine is reputed to have called New Year's gifts "diabolical" and Chrysostom preached that the customs of the New Year made it a "Satanic extravagance." These early divines suggested Christmas gifts as a substitute, for good will, generosity, and kindliness are part of the Christmas spirit. The new custom was adopted, but the old one survived in various places. We are unfortunate in having survivals of both!

In old England [says one writer], St. Stephen's Day was chiefly celebrated under the name of Boxing Day—not for pugilistic reasons, but because on that day it was the custom for persons in the humbler walks of life to go the rounds with a Christmas box and solicit money from patrons and employers. Hence the phrase Christmas box came to signify gifts made at this season to children or inferiors, even after the boxes themselves had gone out of use. This custom was of heathen origin and carries us back to the Roman Paganalia when earthen boxes in which money was slipped through a hole were hung up to receive contributions at these rural festivals.

The Romans had also what was known as the Priests' Box. This was placed upon all outgoing ships and the people were required to put money or gifts in it. At Christmas the box was opened, mass said, and the gifts distributed among the poor. The box received the name Priest's Box because the gifts were originally intended for the priest; but later it became known as the Christmas box, and the contents were distributed among the people. The custom was very popular.

The exchange of gifts, and particularly the presenting of gifts to children, became associated with Christmas at a very early period; and it has not only survived through all the generations, but has become more and more pronounced. Here in the United States Christmas is the great gift time of the year.

Origin of the Christmas Card.—The custom of calling "A Merry Christmas" to one's friends and neighbours originated with the English long ago. An old English custom was to shout this greeting from the window on Christmas morning.

Later it became the custom for the people to write one another congratulatory letters on religious and festival days. Bernard Picart mentions this custom in his "Ceremonies and Religious Customs" (vol. II, p. 4). The Christmas greeting was penned along with others.

W. S. Walsh, in his "Curiosities of Popular Customs," sums up the true origin and development of the Christmas card in an interesting fashion. He says:

> The Christmas card is the legitimate descendant of the "school pieces" or "Christmas pieces" which were popular from the beginning to the middle of the 19th century. These were sheets of writing-paper sometimes surrounded with those hideous and elaborate pen flourishes forming birds, scrolls, etc., so unnaturally dear to the hearts of writing masters, and sometimes headed with copper-plate engravings, plain or coloured. These were used by schoolboys at the approach of holidays for carefully written letters exploiting the progress they had made in composition and chirography. Charity boys were large purchasers of these pieces, says one writer, and at Christmas time used to take them around their parish to show and at the same time solicit a trifle.
>
> The Christmas card proper had its tentative origin in 1846. Mr. Joseph Cundall, a London artist, claims to have issued the first in that year. It was printed in lithography, coloured by hand, and was of the usual size of a lady's card.
>
> Not until 1862, however, did the custom obtain any foothold. Then experiments were made with cards of the size of an ordinary *carte de visite,* inscribed simply "A Merry Christmas" and "A Happy New Year." After that came to be added robins and holly branches, embossed figures and landscapes.

To-day of course, the exchange of greeting cards at Christmas-time is an established custom. Stock cards are printed and sold in the stationery shops. Some people have individual cards engraved. Millions of these greeting cards are mailed every year.

The Holly and the Mistletoe.—A century ago, William Hone, in his "Every-Day Book," wrote, "Girls, although they be ladies, are kissed under the mistletoe." This old

Druidic custom has survived many generations and is still popular.

Among the ancient Druids, the mistletoe was regarded with the utmost veneration. They cut sacred mistletoe with a golden knife and hung it over their doors to propitiate the woodland spirits. According to myth, only happiness could enter under the mistletoe. Hence our tradition of the kiss.

At the period of the winter solstice the Druids celebrated with a great festival. Ceremonies took place in the forest dedicated to the gods—so dedicated because of the mistletoe that grew there. Many of the rites and ceremonies observed at these ancient Druidic festivals were in connection with the mistletoe.

In ancient Scandinavian mythology it is noted that the mistletoe was gathered at the time of the winter festival and distributed in small quantities among the people. Each person hung up a bit of the mistletoe above the entrance to his or her dwelling-place, the purpose being to keep out the evil spirits. This corresponds with the custom of the ancient Druids, and similar rites in connection with the mistletoe are noted among other Celtic nations.

The ancient Romans used laurel as an emblem of peace, joy, and victory. Later the laurel was adopted by Christian people and used as decoration in the windows of the houses, to indicate that Christ had entered there. Ivy and holly replaced the laurel in old England, the reasons being given by this old English song:

The Holly and the Ivy,
Now both are full well grown;
Of all the trees that spring in wood,
The Holly bears the crown.
The Holly bears a blossom,
As white as lily flow'r;
And Mary bore sweet Jesus Christ,
To be our sweet Saviour,
To be our sweet Saviour.

The Holly bears a berry,
As red as any blood;
And Mary bore sweet Jesus Christ,
To do poor sinners good.
The Holly bears a prickle,
As sharp as any thorn;
And Mary bore sweet Jesus Christ,
On Christmas Day in the morn,
On Christmas Day in the morn.

The Holly bears a bark,
As bitter as any gall;
And Mary bore sweet Jesus Christ,
For to redeem us all.
The Holly and the Ivy,
Now both are full well grown;
Of all the trees that spring in wood,
The Holly bears the crown,
The Holly bears the crown.

The holly wreath appears to represent the crown of thorns which Christ wore on the cross, the little red berries symbolizing the drops of blood.

Some Popular Christmas Customs.—Burning the Yule log is an ancient Christmas custom which originated with the Scandinavians. At their feast of Juul, during the winter solstice, they kindled huge bonfires in honour of the god Thor. The ancient Goths and Saxons had winter festivals which they called Jul. Christmas is still frequently referred to as Yuletide.

In feudal times, the bringing in of the great yule log to the wide hearth in the baronial hall was one of the most joyous ceremonies connected with the festival. The men hewed down the greatest log—or clog, as it was called—singing merry yule songs while they dressed it and dragged it to the hearth.

Speaking of the clog, Hervey says:

> This huge block, which, in ancient times, and consistently with the capacity of its vast receptacle, was frequently the root of a large tree, it was the practice to introduce into the house with great ceremony, and to the sound of music.

According to Herrick, the yule clog "was to be lighted with the brand of the last year's log, which had been carefully laid aside for the purpose, and music was to be played during the ceremony of lighting." The burning of the yule log is now practically obsolete, although it is still a beloved and picturesque custom in various rural districts.

In this country it is a practice at Christmas-time to plant a great community tree, decorating it with coloured electric

Dragging the Yule-log to the castle-hearth—a joyous occasion during the feudal Christmas festivities.

bulbs and with a great star at the top. Huge crowds gather about the illuminated evergreen and sing Christmas songs. This custom had its origin in the elaborate street festivals of Italy and Spain. In these two countries there are fires and fireworks, and a great deal of street celebration. Some trace the origin to the old Scandinavian custom of placing a sheaf of grain on a tall pole in the dooryard "for the birds on Christmas morning."

The Christmas cakes, the iced cookies and gingerbread figures which are a part of our Christmas goodies are survivals of the confectionery gifts presented to the senators of Rome in early times. The cakes were in the form of figures of animals and people. Later the cakes became more elaborate, and were adopted as Christmas cakes. In early England these cakes were very popular. They were given to the poor women who sang carols in the street, or who went from house to house with images of the Virgin and of Christ.

The singing of carols originated in England. The word carol itself is said to be derived from *cantare,* to sing, and *rola,* an interjection of joy. The word was first applied to the bishops who carolled, or sang joyful hymns, at Christmas-time. Later it became more general.

We quote from Compton's "Pictured Encyclopedia" this paragraph concerning Christmas carols:

> Almost every land of Christendom has its own Christmas carols. In England "waits" sing under windows on Christmas Eve, as they have done for countless Christmases. In Russia the ancient Kolyada songs, once sung to pagan gods, now dedicated to Christian saints, are sung about the streets. The French Noël songs, and the famous German *Kristlieder* are heard wherever there is Christmas music. In our own land, choirboys and schoolchildren hold carol parties and go about singing these old-time songs for "shut-ins" and other unfortunates.

According to tradition, this is the very first Christmas carol ever sung:

> Fear not: for, behold I bring you good tidings of great joy, which shall be to all people. For unto you is born this day in the city of David a Saviour, which is Christ the Lord.
>
> And this shall be a sign unto you; ye shall find the babe wrapped in swaddling clothes lying in a manger.

Chorus

Glory to God in the highest, and on
earth peace, good will toward men.

The giving of charity and gifts to the poor at the Christmas season originated with the belief that the Christ Child sometimes came to the door in the guise of a beggar. Elise Traut relates the old legend that on Christmas Eve the Christ Child wanders all over the world, going from castle to hovel, up hills and down valleys, in search of the good and the deserving. He pleads for succour at the various homes he enters, usually appearing as a beggar or humble wanderer. Because of this legend beggars were rarely turned away on Christmas Eve, and aid rendered the beggar was, and is still, looked upon as hospitality shown to Christ. Following close upon this custom came the now universal one of bestowing charity to the poor at Christmas-time.

Christmas Entertaining.—That Christmas is a time of gaiety and feasting is traditional. This account, by some forgotten writer of long ago, brings to mind the Christmas of yesterday and how it was celebrated:

> Now capons and hens, besides turkeys, geese and ducks, with beef and mutton—must all die; for in twelve days a multitude of people will not be fed with little. Now plums and spice, sugar and honey, square it among pies and broth. Now or never must music be in tune, for the young must dance and sing to get them a heat, while the aged sit by the fire.

To put the "merry" into "Merry Christmas" to-day, the hostess must borrow a bit of old-fashioned foolishness, add to it the flavour of steaming plum pudding and popcorn, sprinkle it well with a measure of good cheer, and serve with a sprig of mistletoe! Whether the entertainment takes the form of an intimate family reunion, or a great jolly party, it must be imbued with the proper Christmas spirit.

Not so very long ago it was customary to have huge wreaths and laurel ropes drooping from every corner. Now a sprig of mistletoe and a bit of holly with "its berries like reddened pearls" are used for the Christmas decoration. A custom delightfully old-fashioned is to have an untrimmed evergreen flanking each side of the front door outside the house.

Another old-fashioned custom, which is said to have been originated in Colonial days, is to include a tiny bit of the mistletoe in the invitation. It is slipped into the envelope with the card "to carry the season's good tidings." It is really meant as a wish or omen for happiness and prosperity throughout the coming year.

Decorations for the Christmas table are not difficult to achieve. One may have a flat bowl of coloured glass piled high with fruit. Or one may have a slender silver vase with a cluster of holly in it, or perhaps a lower vase with cut winter flowers. An old custom is to have a miniature tree in the centre of the table bearing gifts or favours for the guests. Of course, candles are used for illumination at the Christmas dinner, whether it be formal or informal, because they carry out an old Christmas tradition.

There are many old superstitions that cling to the popular Christmas foods. To refuse a piece of mince pie at a Christmas dinner, for instance, means ill luck for the year. To eat apples at midnight on Christmas Eve is to enjoy great health during the year. If a loaf of bread is allowed to remain on the table after the Christmas Eve celebrations, there will be no lack of bread in the house for the next twelve months. According to the old tradition, "by all means you must have a plum pudding—a plum pudding grown rich and black and solid." Otherwise, it seems, you will lose a friend between this Christmas and next!

It is interesting to have an English Christmas party, observing all the many English customs which have contributed to our own Christmas observances. The invitations are printed in Old English text. The home is decorated with mistletoe, holly, ivy. Wax tapers, in brass, iron, or pewter candlesticks add the proper touch in illumination. For the centrepiece a boar's head, made of dough, should be used. If it is made large enough, it can be used to cover the little roast pig with the traditional apple in its mouth which constitutes one of the main courses of the dinner.

At an English dinner the wassail cup must be passed around. Drinking the wassail is an old English custom.

> They sat down by the huge fire of blazing logs to a substantial supper [says Charles Dickens], and a mighty bowl of wassail, something smaller than an ordinary wash-house copper, in which the hot apples were hissing and bubbling with a rich look, and a jolly sound that were perfectly irresistible.

Instead of containing the brew, ale, or steaming punch of the old-time wassail bowl, the cup at our modern English dinner may contain any mild punch or soft drink that the hostess likes. It is passed around just to carry out the old custom, and to "wish cheer with the brimming cup."

After dinner the guests repair to the drawing room, which is illumined solely with candles and is decorated with mistletoe suspended from unexpected places. The famous old English games are played, old Christmas carols are sung, and old Christmas traditions related. If possible there should be a glowing yule log in the fireplace.

Mary Dawson gives some interesting old English games appropriate for Christmas-time in her "Book of Entertainments."

Perhaps you would prefer a German dinner with all its pretty customs. Use as a centrepiece for the table a diminutive representation of the Nativity, and have a tiny Kriss Kringle or small, decorative Christmas tree at each place. Have gifts packed and marked with the names of the persons for whom they are intended, hidden everywhere throughout the house. After dinner the guests search for the gifts, which are exchanged among them as each new one is found, until every guest has his or her own gift. This is an old German custom, and is always good fun if the guests are young people.

The Druidic Christmas dinner would carry out all the traditions of the Druids. There would be a great fire crackling merrily in the fireplace. There would be mistletoe hanging everywhere. There would be a jolly feast, with nuts and apples and all good things to eat. And after the dinner there would be music, dancing, entertainment.

The Scandinavian Christmas dinner could be made most delightful. The menu may be the same as one would select for any ordinary Christmas dinner—turkey, roast meats, mince pie, fritters, nuts, raisins, apples, whatever one likes. But there would be a huge tree in the drawing room hung with coloured balls and made beautiful with tiny lighted candles. There would be gifts on the tree for each guest, and in each gift package a card bearing some delightful bit of wisdom or cheer from the old Scandinavian writings. And of course there would be a yule log, a great roaring fire, and perhaps the host, in the part of Thor, would quote interesting bits of Scandinavian mythology.

Whatever form the Christmas entertainment takes, it must be free from formality. There must be plenty of good cheer and fun; the day is one of rejoicing. For generations it has been customary to play favourite old games on this day and to make merry with one's family and friends. As Dickens has Mr. Wardle say to Mr. Pickwick:

> Everybody sits down with us on Christmas Eve, as you see them now—servants and all; and here we wait till the clock strikes twelve, to usher Christmas in, and while away the time with forfeits and old stories. Trundle, my boy, rake up the fire!

CHAPTER XV

THE DANCE

Civilization is a process of making life more complex and subtle. We have the piano, the violin, the orchestra. Yet we have also ragtime, which is a reaction from the nervous tension of American commercial life, a swinging back to the old days when man, though a brute, was free. There is a release and exhilaration in the barbaric, syncopated songs and in the animal-like motion of the jazz dances with their wild and passionate attitudes, their unrestrained rhythms, and their direct appeal to sex. These ragtime melodies, coming straight from the jungles of Africa through the Negro, call to impulses in man that are stifled in big cities, in factory and slum and the nerve-wearing struggle of business.

—FREDERICK O'BRIEN.

LIFE'S DANCE

LIFE is a clown, hiding a million hurts. A dancing, happy clown, born with the gift of laughter. This clown came to earth, one day, and danced naked through empty lands. Civilization clothed him, but he is dancing still.

On with this dance—of life!

The first is a shadowy dance while man emerges from the dawn of prehistory to rise with reason above the brute. A dance that is light and almost unreal, like sunlight dancing in patches through a tree. We have watched children dance so.

And now a weird dance, passionate, cruel. Black puppets with arms and legs jumping fiercely in circles, bathed in moonlight, clothed in beads. The savage beat of the drum. The pat-pat of naked feet on the ground. Faster! Faster!

But the moonlight fades, and man dances to the tune of progress. We see a classic dance, stately and beautiful, while infant civilizations lift their faces to the sky. Egypt —Greece—Rome——

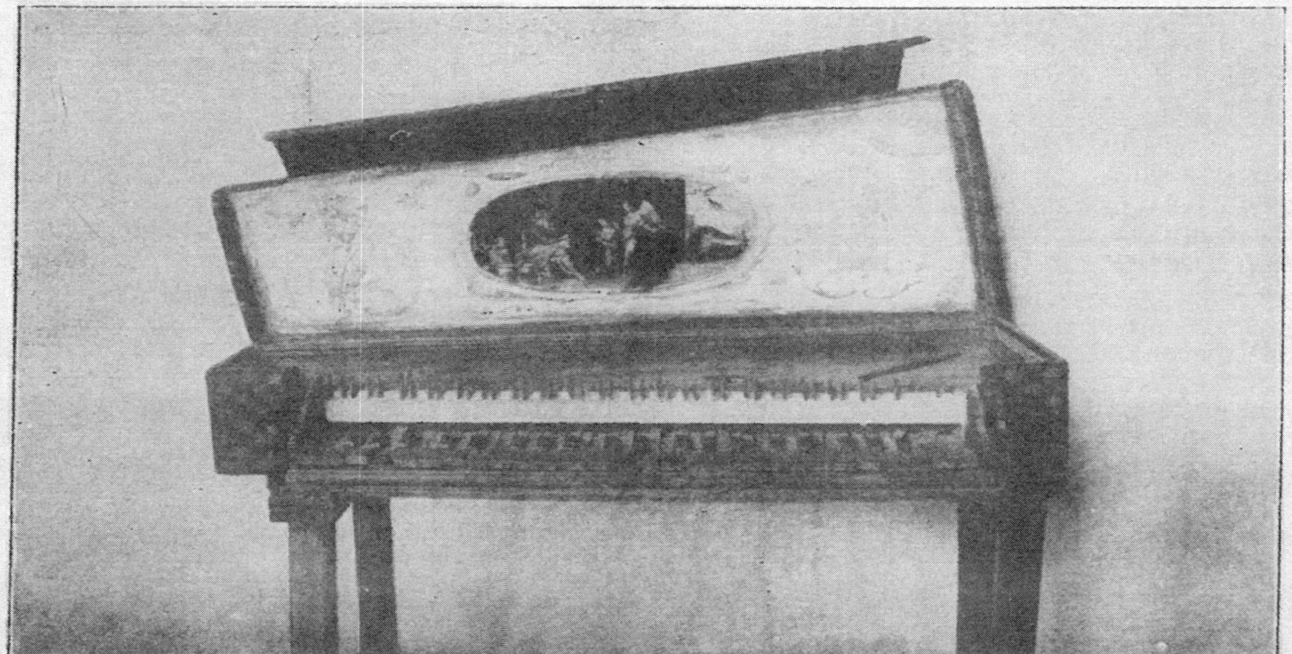

(Courtesy of Metropolitan Museum of Art)

Spinet or virginet—Italian, 1500.

(Courtesy of Metropolitan Museum of Art)

The clavichord—Italy, about 1600.

It does not last. The music changes. It becomes harsh, many-toned, like a hurdy-gurdy in narrow streets. And the dance is like a merry-go-round when the music stops. One does not walk when the clown called life cracks his whip.

The dance is solemn now, and one seems to hear, ever so faintly, the echo of cathedral bells. Religion, the church —— It makes a difference in the steps of the dance. They seem more sure, more skillful. And there is a subtleness that is new.

But the dance is mad again, frenzied! Man is jumping now about a burning witch, screaming curses with every step. He is whirling dizzily through wars and revolutions. With hysterical freedom he is chopping off heads, destroying those who led the band with their little batons. And the clown with his cap and bells laughs.

So has the whole world been a ballroom, and we the dancers. King and beggar, prince and peasant, artist and merchant, poet and politician—all dance in endless pageant through the ages.

The Early History of Dancing.—Long ago Lucian wrote:

> We are not to believe that saltation [dancing] is of modern invention, born recently, or even that our ancestors saw its beginning. Those who have spoken with truth of the origin of this art affirm that it takes its birth from the time of the creation of all things, and that it is as old as Love, the most ancient of the gods.

Pantomime was the first language of man, and pantomime is just a step removed from dancing. Undoubtedly the primitive peoples danced for pleasure, like children, as the Veddahs and many other savage races do to-day. These primitive dances would have been mere jumpings up and down, perhaps the first vague appearance of cadenced swinging. There was no music other than that in the dancer's heart.

The word dance itself is from the French *danse,* which is of obscure origin. It appears to be connected in some way with the old High German *danson,* meaning "to stretch."

Most authorities are of the opinion that dancing as an expressive art had its inception in Egypt. There are fragments of Egyptian frescoes on exhibition in the British Museum that show dancing figures. Hieratic dances have been traced as far back as 2545 B.C.

According to the old tradition, David danced before the Ark. The Hebrews have always held the dance in high honour, and they have an imposing dance at their Feast of the Tabernacles.

In Greece dancing became a veritable language, beautiful, expressive, interpreting the sentiments and the passions. The Greeks knew it as *Nomas* or *Orchesis,* the art of expressive gesture. They danced everywhere, in the temples, the woods, the fields. Every birth, marriage, and death was the occasion for dancing. According to Plato, relatives and friends took part in the funeral dances, although professionals were engaged for the occasion.

The virginal dances of early Greece were of great simplicity and beauty. The dancers decorated themselves with oak leaves and garlands of flowers. On the famous Borghese Vase in the Louvre are some graceful dancing figures like those of early Greece. But the Vase itself dates about 350 B.C.

It is interesting to note that in early Greece military dancing formed part of the education of youth. As an art it was held in high esteem, and it seems also to have been regarded as an excellent means of moulding the body into ways of strength and suppleness.

The Romans borrowed the art of dancing from Greece, adding a new kind of pantomimic dancing. It was among the Romans that theatrical dancing had its origin. We are told that the Gaditanas, famous dancing girls of Cadiz, created a great furore among the ancient Romans.

The Religious Aspect.—In primitive life, dancing is closely connected with prayer. As a natural expression of joy, of thankfulness for sun or shower, of gratitude for food, dancing came to be looked upon as a means to be used for the attainment of a desire. Thus sacred pageants and ceremonies, in which dancing makes a vague appearance, date back to the earliest times.

For a long time the only form of worship among the Indians was dancing, accompanied by singing and chanting. The Hopi Indians perform an extraordinary dance, with poisonous snakes held between their teeth, in appeal to the gods for rain. This is very possibly the strangest and most spectacular dance ceremony to be found in any part of the world. It would require a volume to do justice to the many religious ceremonies of the Indians in which dancing holds a conspicuous place.

The Devil Dance is one of the greatest festivals of the Lama Church (China). It takes place every spring, and its purpose is "to chase out the Spirit of Evil that hides in the land." Men and boys attired in rich costumes and wearing hideous animal masks go through the imposing steps and postures of the Devil Dance. It is purely a religious ceremony.

In India dancing is a religion. The Nautch dancers are connected with the temples in India and are known as the servants of god because they sing and dance before the idols. They dance also at banquets, weddings, and large public entertainments. These Nautch dancers are usually very graceful, and beautiful according to the standards of their people. When dancing they wear a jewel in the right nostril.

Christianity favoured religious dancing at the beginning. In the Church of St. Pancras at Rome there still exists a sort of stage, separated from the altar, on which priests and worshippers are said to have joined in dance measures led by their Bishop.

This secular dancing was extremely popular for a while, but the extremists gradually came to regard it as unsuited to the solemnity of the church. In 744 a papal decree abolished all dancing in churches and in cemeteries.

Mahomet, imitating the early Christian practice, instituted a sect of dancers known as the Dervishes. These Dervishes are religious dancers who twirl round and round with astonishing swiftness, sometimes continuing until they fall down in a swoon. This dance is said to be in honour of Menelaus who is supposed to have danced for four days to the sound of the flute and was rewarded by a divine ecstasy. (G. Vuillier.)

So did dancing find its way into the religious ceremonies of early peoples. The Indians danced to the sun and the moon, at their rising and setting. The Greeks danced to Pan, to Apollo, to Diana, to the harvest and to the vintage. The early Egyptians and Hebrews had dancing ceremonies. In old England, dances at May-time were in honour of Spring. As it found its way into religion, so did dancing find its way into the popular festivals and celebrations of the people, weaving itself eternally into the pattern of life.

Imitative Dancing.—There is a form of dancing which corresponds to the imitative magic which we studied in an earlier chapter (see p. 34). It is both ceremonious and religious in aspect.

It has been definitely established by authorities that savage peoples had definite dances for definite purposes. As in imitative magic water is poured from a treetop to make rain come, so in dancing there is a phase in which the thing desired is imitated to bring about its happening. To this type of dancing we have applied the term imitative dancing.

An old Motu-Motu man once said, "No drums are beaten uselessly, there are no dances that are merely useless." Every savage dance has its significance. It is no mere amusement, but rather a ceremony. As Robertson expresses it:

> The dance [among savages] is a serious and important occupation which mingles in every occurrence of private or public life. If war is announced against an enemy, it is by a dance, expressive of the resentment which they feel. If the wrath of their gods is to be appeased, or their beneficence celebrated; if they rejoice at the birth of a child or mourn the death of a friend, they have dances appro-

priate for each of these situations. If a person is indisposed, a dance is prescribed as the most effectual means to restore him to health. If he cannot stand the fatigue, a physician or conjurer performs it in his name.

The war dance is an excellent example of this imitative, or sympathetic, dancing. The Indians believe that by imitating or pantomiming the warfare and their success, imitating also the complete destruction of their enemy, they are assured of victory. They believe that the war dance weakens the enemy through magic influence.

The war dance of the Chippewa Indians imitates the actions of surprising the enemy, tomahawking and scalping the foe, drinking his blood. In the Algonquin war dance, each man in turn brandishes his tomahawk and furiously strikes the post around which they are dancing. Each blow is supposed to weaken one of the enemy warriors. The dancers then fictitiously scalp the enemy in characteristic mimic action. The war dance of the Navajos of New Mexico is very picturesque and ceremonious. Of course, besides being a mode of inviting victory by imitating it, the war dance is also a sort of training for the actual wars.

Among the Indians in Mexico the dance has always been ceremonious, and regarded not only as a favourite amusement but as a serious occupation. Robertson says:

> If an Indian came with an emblem of peace, he had to approach with a solemn dance, while the caciques [chiefs] received him in the same manner. If war was denounced against an enemy, a dance expressed their resentment.

Imitative dancing is used by savages in preparation for the hunt. In Africa, for instance, on the eve of a gorilla hunt there is a gorilla dance. The natives dance to a drum, and closely imitate all the attitudes and movements of the gorilla. Those who are to hunt imitate the act of stealing unseen upon the gorilla, capturing and killing it. All present join in the chorus, which imitates the triumphant march home.

For several days before starting on a bear hunt, the Sioux Indians used to hold their bear dance. The whole tribe joined in a song or chant to the Bear Spirit. Here again the dance imitated the capture and killing of the beast.

At one time every Mandan Indian was compelled to keep his buffalo mask in his lodge, ready to put on and wear at the Buffalo Dance whenever necessary. This mask was made of the skin and horns of the buffalo's head. Whenever a long absence of the buffalo from the prairies made meat scarce, the Mandans had a great Buffalo Dance "for the purpose of inducing the herds to change the direction of their wanderings and bend their course towards the Mandan villages." In the dance one or two of the men, dressed to imitate buffalo, are slain in pantomime, skinned, cut up and eaten.

In Vancouver there is a seal dance for which the natives, stripping naked, enter the water and imitate the manners and motions of the seal. The dancers enter the water regardless of the cold or the night, and emerge dragging their bodies along the sand as a seal does. They enter the houses and crawl about the fires, finally jumping up and dancing in mad ecstasy. The dance is partly religious, partly imitative for purposes of inviting the seal to come to the locality.

The imitative dance undoubtedly grew out of the primitive belief in imitative magic, but we are inclined to believe that the love of pantomime had something to do with it. Pantomime is a form of play, of make-believe, and it is one of man's oldest instincts. The warrior likes to play at being chief; the chief likes to play at being king; the king likes to play at being god. It is inevitable that this instinct for make-believe should have found its way into the dance, which is a free and unrestrained expression of desires.

We find this love of pantomime, of make-believe, interwoven with all manifestations of popular life in early times.

In South Australia, for instance, boys upon reaching puberty undergo the ceremony of having their front teeth knocked out. At the same time they join in what is known as the Kangaroo Dance. A kangaroo of grass is deposited at the feet of the boys who are being initiated. The actors, adults of the tribe, fit themselves with long tails of grass and set off "as a herd of kangaroos, now jumping, now basking in the sun." Two armed men follow to steal upon and spear them. This Kangaroo Dance serves two purposes: it *pretends* that the boys are present at a kangaroo hunt and thus admits them to the state of manhood; and it imitates the various stages of the hunt, thus showing the boys how it should be done.

Even in modern Europe we find instances of make-believe practised in popular ceremonies. In Servia, to mention one example, the peasants cover a girl with grass and flowers and pour water over her, in pantomimic petition for rain. This is followed by a dance in which the falling of the rain and its blessings to the earth are imitated.

DEVELOPMENT OF THE SOCIAL DANCE

It is interesting to note what famous men of other days thought of dancing. Aristotle says that the dance is valuable because it mirrors the manners and actions of the men of various periods. Homer held the dance in high esteem and mentions it as a favourite form of social entertainment. But evidently Cicero had little use for dancing of any kind, religious or social, for he says:

> No man who is sober dances, unless he is out of his mind, either when alone or in any decent society; for dancing is the companion of wanton conviviality, dissoluteness and luxury.

We wonder what Cicero would say if he glimpsed our modern ballroom!

It was in Greece that dancing had its greatest development as a social amusement. In the time of Aristophanes there was dancing at all the banquets and festivities.

From the eighth book of the Odyssey we learn that dancing lent its charms to all the important banquets of ancient Greece. Both Socrates and Plato mention the art with apparent esteem.

As a social art, dancing existed in Egypt at least four thousand years ago. We know that dinner guests were entertained with dancing; for there are in existence Egyptian dinner scenes of 2000 B.C., showing dancing figures. Most of them are on fragments of old Egyptian frescoes which are now in the British Museum.

Dancing has existed as a social art in India for many generations. Since the earliest times it has been customary in certain sections of India to entertain callers with elaborate dancing festivities, although these dances are more or less religious in import.

Spanish dancing is of great antiquity, and has always been associated with social life. Many of the steps familiarized to us through Spanish dancing are of old Arab origin.

In Italy, Ireland, Scotland, England, Germany, France, Russia—everywhere we find the dance making its social appearance.

Development of Popular Dances.—France may be said to be the nursery of the social dance. Although the dances were born or originated in other countries, they were invariably brought to France to be nurtured and developed.

At the court of France, the origin of social dancing is associated with the rise of chivalry. This old proverb would seem to indicate that it was customary to dance after a feast or banquet: *"Après la panse, vient la danse"* (After good cheer comes dancing).

Catherine de' Medici brought to France not only new splendour in court functions, but a taste for social dancing. The taste spread and found its way into private homes. Catherine was particularly fond of the masked ball and did much to encourage its development.

In the rural districts of France there were many popular

festivals which were celebrated with feasting and dancing. These festivals came to take on the nature of neighbourhood dances, and they became extremely popular as a form of entertainment. The dancing was gay, unrestrained, wild.

But at the Court the dance was dignified and ceremonious. Masquerade dancing was in particular favour. At Versailles, under Louis XIV, ballets were organized with great magnificence of costume and of decoration. Lulli, famous composer of the period, devoted a large part of his time to composing music expressly for the dances at the court.

The dances in vogue at the court of France in the 16th century were the *pavane* and the *courante*. The *pavane* was a grave, solemn dance and was in high favour until about 1530. Louis XIV preferred the *courante*, a livelier dance. Some refer the origin of this dance to Spain, others to Padua. Because it was the popular dance at the court of Louis XIV it became well known throughout Europe. But for a long time the *pavane* was the popular dance of all Europe's princely caste.

The Minuet.—Perhaps the dance for which France is best known is the beautiful and graceful minuet. Although the minuet is not French in origin, the dance was brought to its highest point of perfection at the French court. Most people regard it as a French dance.

The minuet is of unknown origin and very antique. It came to France in 1650 and was first set to music by Lulli for Louis XIV. Beauchamps, who flourished in the reign of Louis XIV, and who is sometimes called the father of dancing masters, mentions the minuet affectionately. But it was not until the time of Louis XV that the minuet became the special court dance.

Louis XV was delighted with the minuet and he preferred it to any other dance. At first it was gay and lively, but upon being made the special dance of the court it became grave and dignified, and it was developed to a high degree of grace and beauty. The minuet is always closely associated with chivalry, courtesy, grace.

During the reigns of Louis XV and XVI the gavotte was almost as popular as the minuet. A coquettish and

Our grandfathers danced a graceful waltz to the tune of "The Beautiful Blue Danube." Though danced now to livelier melodies, the waltz is still a ballroom favourite.

lively dance, it quickly became a favourite with the people outside of the court, and for a long time it was almost the French national dance. But it gradually disappeared, while the minuet remained and became more and more elaborate, more and more beautiful.

In Colonial days the minuet was brought to America and became a favourite here. It was danced in every ballroom, at every festive occasion in the home. To-day it is a favourite on the stage but has disappeared entirely from the ballroom.

The Waltz.—The volte, known later as the valse or waltz, is regarded by some authorities as being of French origin. Henry III is said to have danced the waltz *"à trois temps"* under the name of volte, but whether it was originated in France or borrowed from the national dance of another country is not definitely known.

The first German waltz tune is dated 1770 and is known as "Ach! du lieber Augustin." It was danced for the first time at the Paris opera in 1793. In 1812 it was introduced to English ballrooms and instantly aroused a storm of protest. But in 1816 Emperor Alexander danced it at Almack's (a famous old dancing place) and it became popular.

From France, where it was developed to exquisite perfection, the waltz spread everywhere. It found its way across the ocean and ranked second to the minuet in Colonial America. As the minuet slowly faded into the background, the waltz became the most popular dance in this country, and although newer and livelier dances have replaced it, the waltz is still an old favourite.

A dance of great antiquity is the quadrille. It was brought from Normandy to England by William the Conqueror, and was slowly developed from its original simple form to a dance measure of great beauty and charm. It was popular all over Europe in the 16th and 17th centuries.

The dances of the 18th century, as we have seen, were the minuet, the gavotte, the waltz. The cotillion also was danced in the 18th century—a dance which derives its name from the short skirts worn by the ladies who danced it. It is French in origin and was at one time extremely fashionable.

At the end of the 18th century there came the spark

that set France ablaze—the Revolution. Yet the dancing went on, but it was the mad dancing of red-capped Carmagnoles to the tune of *"Ca ira."* With bloodstained feet the liberty-crazed men and women danced around the guillotine.

The first social dance to become popular after the Revolution was the cotillion. Waltzing and galoping (a dance introduced from Hungary) were favourite also. Until about 1830 balls had been confined almost entirely to the aristocracy, but now the middle classes were beginning to

In the shadow of the guillotine Paris danced in frenzied madness to the tune of Ca ira. The dress and the dance reflect the trend of the times.

make of the dance a social institution. By 1840 the passion for dancing was general.

The Polka and Mazurka.—Authorities are agreed that the polka came originally from Bohemia. It appeared first at Vienna, then at Baden. It was adopted by society at Prague in 1835.

Cellaruius, the famous dancing-master, introduced the polka to Paris. He achieved what is frequently referred to as a social *coup d'état.* He opened a school for the purpose of teaching dancing, and social dances took place at this school several evenings a week. He gave great dancing fêtes, and he inaugurated artists' balls to which admission could be obtained only by means of invitation.

So popular did the polka become that it invaded the very saloons and shops. It was danced on street corners,

During the latter half of the 19th century the polka was so popular that it was danced on street corners, in private homes, at balls—everywhere.

in private homes, everywhere. Boots, frocks, hats, materials were named after the dance. Our "polka dot" is a relic of this period.

The schottische, also Bohemian in origin, was introduced to France in 1844 by Markowski, the originator. Markowski is sometimes credited with having originated the quadrille, but he merely improved it. The quadrille in its original form was introduced, as we have seen, by William the Conqueror. It was popular for a while, was forgotten, was revived during the 16th and 17th centuries, and again in the 19th century.

But Markowski is best remembered for his mazurka. This lively and graceful dance he introduced to Paris about 1840. It became popular instantly and was danced by everyone. It spread even to England, where it was fashionable for a little while.

It was at the Austrian Embassy that the famous *déjeuners dansants* were inaugurated in the 18th century. These delightful dinner dances are still a popular form of social entertaining. There is dancing between the courses and after the dinner. The popular dances at that time were the polka, mazurka, and waltz.

The Lancers, a novelty dance, is said to have been originated by Laborde in Paris in 1836. In 1850 it was introduced to England and became very fashionable there.

Concerning Jazz.—It would be fascinating to tread our way through the various countries, searching out the farthermost corners of the globe, studying the types of dancing we find among the people. We would see the brisk jigs of Ireland and Scotland; the slow, melancholy dances of the South Seas. We would see the lively dances of Russia, and the formal dances of old England. We would see how climatic conditions and conditions within the country influenced the dance and made it slow or brisk, solemn or impassioned.

But the history of dancing is worthy of a volume in itself, and we can barely touch upon it here. We must resist the temptation to wander with fancy in faraway lands, and concern ourselves solely with dancing as it applies to the modern ballroom.

Jazz, for instance, though it belongs to a savage race on the other side of the globe, concerns us vitally—for it is to be found in our own polished ballroom. Beneath syncopation and ragtime we catch the faint echo of tom-toms, of bare feet pat-patting against the ground, of naked bodies swaying in wild exaltation.

There is no doubt whatever that jazz comes to us direct from the jungles of Africa. The jazz rhythms quicken the blood, wake wild and primitive instincts, stir barbaric memories sleeping in our souls for ages. The band plays; we dance. Faster! Wilder! We are savages dancing in the moonlight. We are primitives throwing our spears. We are free, unrestrained. Jazz!

As O'Brien says, rag-time melodies and jazz "call to impulses in man that are stifled in big cities, in factory and slum and the nerve-wearing struggle of business." Jazz is a reaction from civilization, a stripping off of the veneer of culture and cultivation. It is a temporary freedom, "a swinging back to the old days when man, though a brute, was free."

The Negro, of course, brought jazz to America. Popular tradition has it that a Southern darky, performing the wild dance of his native land to the clapping and chanting of his fellows, was quickly surrounded by a fascinated audience. After the dance a theatrical man approached the darky and said:

"What kind of a dance was that, my good fellow?"

"Jes' jazz, sah—jes' jazz!" the darky answered. And "jazz" that type of dancing has remained ever since.

There is a direct sex appeal in jazz which is found also in the dances of South Sea Islanders. The Marquesans, for instance, have a sexual dance known as the *haka*—more formal and melancholy than jazz, but with the same rhythmic motion and the same unrestrained attitudes. O'Brien tells us of the dance:

A gruesome cannibal chant followed, accompanied by the booming of the drum, and then, warmed by the liquor that fired their brains, the dancers began the *haka,* the sexual dance. Inflamed by the rum, they flung themselves into it with such abandon as I have never seen, and I saw a *kamaaina* in Hawaii and have seen Caroline, Miri, and Mamoe, most skilled dancers of the Hawaiian Islands. With the continued passing of the cup, the *hurahura* soon became general. The men and women who had begun dancing in rows, in an organized way, now broke ranks and danced freely all over the lawn. Men sought out the women they liked, and women the men, challenging each other in frenzied and startling exposition of the ancient ways.

Origin of the Public Dance Hall.—The first public dance hall was opened in 1788 by an Englishman called Tinkson. A little rare old book describes how Tinkson raised thatched sheds near the Observatory and organized periodic balls and dances. The novelty and originality of this rustic idea drew the crowd; on occasions of dancing, the little thatched sheds were filled to capacity.

Later, when his sheds proved inadequate and his dances became more and more popular, Tinkson built a large and ostentatious hall known as the Grande Chaumière. It was the first large and public dance hall opened to the public. So popular did the idea become that scores of similar dance halls were opened. There are thousands of such halls now in existence.

The idea for the Winter Garden is said to have originated with a Frenchman by the name of Victor Bohan. M. Bohan, who died at Batignolles in 1856, was a great lover of flowers. He despised winter because the flowers died, and the great desire of his life was to build a great winter garden where flowers would bloom all year through.

And so M. Bohan built a great glass conservatory which he heated and in which flowers were able to blossom no matter how cold it might be outside. He cultivated the most exquisite and delicate flowers, and his conservatory was a place of consummate beauty.

To earn the money to keep his conservatory, M. Bohan gave concerts and masquerades in his "Winter Garden." It became very popular, and people of the better classes came regularly to the "fairy palace" to be entertained. The entertainment was invariably in the form of dancing and singing.

(Courtesy of Metropolitan Museum of Art)

Piano of Carl Lang, Nuremburg, Germany, 18th Century.

(Courtesy of Metropolitan Museum of Art)

A rare old book organ.
France, 17th Century.

The Winter Garden in New York seems to be a modern interpretation of this old idea. We are able to step out of the winter into a theatre of great beauty, and be entertained with singing and dancing.

The Masquerade Ball.—The custom of masking is very old. We have already commented upon the love of make-believe, of pantomime. Associated with this, of course, is the love of "dressing up" of wearing masks and strange or beautiful costumes.

Primitive peoples disguised themselves as a protection from the evil spirits. Savages even to-day wear masks to scare away their enemies and the evil spirits that are supposed to cause all their trouble and misfortune. In imitative dances, masks are worn and the dancers disguised.

The New Caledonians, before murdering a man or committing an act of violence, always put on grotesque masks so as not to be recognized. Our burglar and highwayman wear black masks for the same reason.

In Tonga the natives change their war costume at every battle, by way of disguise. In Zanzibar parents "paint the faces of their children to look like little devils so as to preserve them from the evil eye." In many savage tribes the medicine man or the wizard—he who is supposed to have communication with the god or gods of the people—wears a terrifying mask during tribal ceremonies, to show his kinship with the god. Since gods are fearful creatures to the primitive mind, the medicine man who conveys messages from the god must, perforce, be fearful too. Thus he dons the grotesque mask.

The ancient Greeks wore masks at the feast of Bacchus, and later on the stage to represent different ages and types of characters. The Romans always used masks in their theatrical dances. One writer says, "The custom of wearing the mask had its origin in the classical theatre and formed an essential part of the ballet from the Renaissance onwards."

In the 16th century Italy used masks for comedy, and

it was during this century that masks were worn on the street. Frank A. Parsons says:

> All great ladies wore masks "à la Venise" in the streets and in public places. People carried mirrors in their hands, and sometimes hung two or three about their persons, while other toilet articles were found in bags suspended from the waist.

From Italy the mask was introduced to England and took entertainment form. Catherine de' Medici was very fond of masked balls and introduced them in France. The custom of mask disguise became popular everywhere.

Coryat, the English traveller in the 17th century, records that until he went to Venice he had never seen a woman on the stage. And even in Venice most of the female parts were taken by men and there were few women in the audience. The women in the audience, he records, were courtesans, who wore masks and never permitted their features to be seen.

For generations it was customary for men to take women's parts in plays and theatrical dances, wearing masks and costumes for the purpose. Even as late as the 17th century there were no women actors. To act before an audience on a stage was regarded as degrading and immoral for a woman.

But even after women had appeared on the stage and established themselves as excellent actors, the mask remained. In 1772 Rameau's opera, "Castor and Pollux," was given in Paris. The part of Apollo was taken by Gaetano Vestris, who appeared, in accordance with the fashion of the time, in a mask with an enormous full black wig. One night Vestris was unable to perform, and Gardel, who was one of the leading dancers of the day, was asked to substitute. He agreed, on the condition that he be permitted to discard the mask and wig and appear precisely as he was. At the last minute permission was granted him, and he appeared in the character of Apollo without the customary mask. This innovation so pleased the public that the fashion of masking was doomed.

Its disappearance from the stage made mask disguise more popular than ever at social functions. The court balls during the 17th and 18th centuries were almost invariably masquerade affairs, gorgeous costumes and masks being worn by men and women alike. So popular, indeed, did the mask become that an elaborate and complicated etiquette grew up around it. For instance, in France no woman, whatever her rank, might wear a mask in the presence of a distinguished person. Men and women Loth were required to remove masks when bowing to royalty.

During the reign of Charles VI, Duchesse de Berri gave an elaborate ball to which the whole court was invited. This ball has since become celebrated under the name of "Ballet des Ardents." At the time the court was passionately fond of masks and of masquerading and everyone came disguised. The King came disguised as a savage, wearing a costume of tow held together by pitch. The Duke of Orleans, coming close to examine the costume, touched it with his torch and it flamed instantly into fire. The King was saved but became insane, and two of his companions, who were attired as he, caught fire and lost their lives when they attempted to save him.

Despite this, and many other similar misfortunes, like the assassination of Gustavus III, King of Sweden, at a masquerade ball in 1792, the masquerade ball flourished and became increasingly popular. To-day it is known as the costume ball and is a popular form of entertainment at New Year's and Thanksgiving. We quote from "The Book of Etiquette":

> The costume ball is conducted very much on the same order as the formal ball. The invitations are issued two or three weeks before the date set for the dance. The words "Costumes of the Twelfth Century" or "Shakespearean Costumes," or whatever may be decided upon, are printed in the lower left-hand corner of usual "at home" cards.
>
> In selecting a fancy costume, one must be careful to choose only what is *individually* becoming. It must be in perfect harmony with one's personality. A sedate, quiet young miss should not choose a Folly Costume. Nor should a jolly, vivacious young lady elect to

emulate Martha Washington. And furthermore, a character must not be merely dressed—it must be *lived.* The successful costume ball must be realistic.

And from another book on etiquette:

> Vouchers or tickets of admission like those sent with invitations to assembly or public balls should be enclosed in invitations to a masquerade; it would be too easy otherwise for dishonest or other undesirable persons to gain admittance. If vouchers are not sent with the invitations, or better yet, mailed afterwards to all those who have accepted, it is necessary that the hostess receive her guests singly in a small private room and request each to unmask before her.

ETIQUETTE OF THE BALLROOM

We have by no means, in the pages preceding, made a thorough study of dancing. We have merely touched upon, in a rudimentary way, the dances with which we in this country are familiar. We have not even mentioned the fandango, the Sir Roger de Coverley, the morris dance, the cakewalk, the bolero, the hornpipe, the rigadoon, the shindig—the dozens of dances that had their moment of popularity and faded for ever into oblivion.

Nor have we mentioned the barn dance, the Virginia reel, the delightful old country dances "where partners separated, by the length of high-held arms, for several steps and then joined together again." These were the dances that were enjoyed by young and old alike, and that are even to-day popular in rural sections. They are gay, picturesque old dances and will never entirely be forgotten.

Following the period of barn and country dances, there were waltzes, two-steps, one-steps. Then came the period of the tango and maxixe, and elaborate variations of the waltz and one-step. The fox-trot replaced the tango, but now—"even the fox-trot is no more, and people totter and toddle, and jig and jazz, each according to the manner of his liking."

The manners of the ballroom have not changed as have the dances. Although there is a greater freedom and a lesser restraint in the modern ballroom, the old courtesies are observed and the old politenesses prevail.

The programme, or as it is more familiarly known, the "dance card," and its companion, the chaperon, have disappeared from the modern ballroom. The "dance card" is still in vogue, however, at large public balls and at college and Army and Navy dances.

"A lady never asks a gentleman to dance" the books on etiquette assure us. Why? Because in an age of mistaken chivalry the lady was simply a beautiful flower to be plucked by him who admired her fragrance and colouring best. So came the expression "wallflower," referring to those who were perhaps withered a little, or, like the daisy and marigold, unable to compete with the rose and the lily.

The dancing position introduced by the German waltz still prevails.

> In guiding a lady across the polished floor to the tune of a simple waltz or a gay fox-trot, the gentleman encircles her waist halfway with his right arm, placing the palm of his hand lightly just above the waistline. With his left hand he holds her right at arm's length in the position most comfortable for both of them. His face is always turned slightly to the left, while hers usually faces front or slightly to the right. The girl should place her left arm on her partner's right arm. She must follow him and not try to lead the dance herself.

There was a time when, to enter a room correctly, was regarded as the greatest test of good breeding. Emily Post still finds it necessary to write on "How to Walk Across a Ballroom." She says:

> When the late Ward McAllister classified New York society as having four hundred people who were "at ease in a ballroom," he indicated that the ballroom was the test of the best manners. He also said at a dinner—after his book was published and the country had already made New York's "Four Hundred" a theme for cartoons and jests—that among the "Four hundred who were at ease" not more than ten could gracefully cross a ballroom floor alone. If his ghost is haunting the ballrooms of our time, it is certain that the number is still further reduced. The athletic young woman of to-day strides across the ballroom floor as though she were on the

golf course; the happy-go-lucky one ambles—shoulders stooped, arms swinging, hips and head in advance of chest; others trot, others shuffle, others make a rush for it. The young girl who could walk across a room with the consummate grace of Mrs. Oldname (who as a girl of eighteen was one of Mr. McAllister's ten) would have to be very assiduously sought for.

How does Mrs. Oldname walk? One might answer by describing how Pavlowa dances. Her body is perfectly balanced, she holds herself straight, and yet in nothing suggests a ramrod. She takes steps of medium length, and, like all people who move and dance well, walks from the hip, not the knee. On no account does she swing her arms, nor does she rest a hand on her hip. Nor when walking, does she wave her hands about in gesticulation.

The custom of "cutting in" originated in crowded ballrooms and somehow found its way even into polite society, where it is even to-day regarded as good form. Through this custom, established by general usage, while a dance is in progress, a young man may "cut in" and ask the lady to finish the dance with him. Although quite generally accepted here in America, it is regarded as far from polite behaviour in Europe.

Perhaps this custom of "cutting in" carries with it the merest suggestion of discourtesy [says "The Book of Etiquette"], but when we consider the informal gaiety of the ballroom, the keen and wholehearted love of dancing, we can understand why the privilege is extended. But like many another privilege, it becomes distasteful when it is abused.

The dinner dance originated in the 18th century, being introduced by the Austrian Embassy as an excellent mode of social entertainment. At the dinner dance to-day,

the hostess issues two sets of invitations, one for those whom she wishes to invite for dinner and dance both, and one for those whom she wishes to invite to the dance only. . . . Often the hostess has a buffet supper instead of a dinner, and all guests partake of this refreshment. On a long table, decorated with flowers, are salads, sandwiches, ices, jellies, and fruits of which the guests may partake throughout the evening.

The débutante dance, or début dance as it is frequently

called, originated in savage life long ago, as we have already seen (pp. 167-168). The "coming out" of the fashionable young lady of to-day is reminiscent of the "coming out" of the savage young lady from her hut where she was confined for years.

At the début dance

> the hostess receives and welcomes each guest. She may be assisted by several of her friends who are well-known in society. Her daughter stands beside her and is introduced to those of her mother's guests whom she has not already met. The débutante has her first partner selected for her by her mother. She may not dance with one man more than once on the occasion of her introduction to society. But she is expected to dance every dance, returning to receive guests during the intervals.

So does custom dictate what one must and must not do!

Originally dancing was confined to the courts and to the palaces of aristocracy. It was not until about 1840 that dancing had become at all general. After the Revolution in France the middle classes developed a passion for social dancing, and the custom of the social dance spread quickly among the masses everywhere. But because of the original courtly significance of the dance, it became customary to wear always at these social functions one's most elaborate gowns and costly jewels.

Our "Book of Etiquette" says:

> Of course one wears one's most important jewels to the ball, and indulges in a headdress that is a trifle more elaborate than usual. The event is a brilliant one, and if gaudiness and ostentation are avoided, one may dress as elaborately as one pleases.

And again:

> Hats are never worn to the ball. A shawl or scarf of fine lace may be thrown over the hair and shoulders.

One recalls that hats were not worn to the old court functions, but that elaborate headdresses, like those seen at fashionable balls to-day, were the vogue.

MUSIC AND MUSICAL INSTRUMENTS

Music is as old as man. It was one of the very first languages of man. To the primitive it was a spontaneous means of expression, like the dance. We can imagine him squatting under the stars, singing his happiness to the moon. Perhaps there is no music in his song—as there is no music in the howling of a dog at night—but it is song, nevertheless.

Taken in its fullest and truest sense, music is even older than man. What music is more beautiful than a tiny stream singing its way to the open sea? What music more subtle than the whisper of breezes playing in the treetops? What music more mournful than rain pit-patting on a sodden earth; more gentle than waves that lap softly against a beach?

When man came to earth he found music already here. Birds sang for him, and the sea moaned an endless dirge. His heart caught the tuneful echoes, to hold them imprisoned for ever.

We can be reasonably certain that man felt music long before he was able to express it. A sudden happiness surging through his heart and clutching at his throat. An irrepressible urge to shout and jump and sing, as children do. The miracle of a sunset behind a purple mountain; the thrill of sexual awakening; the discovery of a clear, sparkling cascade of water after a sun-parched day—all these would have brought to primitive man the feeling of music.

The first man-made music was song. There can be little doubt that the first songs ever sung were those of love and of fear. In other words, the first songs were love songs and dirges. We can see a brutish cave fellow pencilled sharply against the gray of dawn, his head thrown back, his muscles tense as he makes music of the madness that pounds through his veins. Inside a bright-eyed woman, frightened, awed. He is singing partly to impress her with the greatness of his voice, partly to keep pace with the

Delighted with the minuet, Louis XV made it the special dance of the court—and it was at court that the dance acquired its exquisite grace and beauty.

sexual excitement that pulses through him. Crude music, toneless and guttural, but bred in the heart and born of the voice. And therefore—song.

Now we cross to another corner of the world, in a latter era, and come upon a handful of savages grouped about the body of their dead chief. They are chanting "magic music," performing curious ceremonies to keep the evil spirits away. These savage chants, intended as magic to ward off the evil influences of the dead and so protect the living, were the original funeral dirges.

It is interesting to meditate upon the preponderance of love and grief songs in modern life. The primitive personality expresses itself subtly and in unexpected ways.

The love songs and dirges of primitive life developed into the folksongs with which we are even yet familiar. Then came the songs of secular life, like the carols of old England. And finally the song entered social life and took on a wholly new significance.

But we are here concerned more with music as it concerns the dance than we are with song and its development. Dancing rarely takes place without accompaniment of some sort. In savage life the accompaniment is a rude chant emphasized by the drum beat or the cymbal. In Tonga there is cracking of the fingers; in Tahiti stamping of the earth with bare feet. In New Caledonia the savages whistle, in Altuona they clap their hands. In modern life we have the piano, the violin, the orchestra.

The First Musical Instruments.—

> Since Neolithic man had the bow [says Wells], he probably also had stringed instruments, for the rhythmic twanging of a bow-string seems almost inevitably to lead to that. He also had earthenware drums across which skins were stretched; perhaps also he made drums by stretching skins over hollow tree stems.

The drum is unquestionably one of the oldest man-made instruments intended to produce sound. No one knows precisely how the drum originated or when it first was used, but drums of many different kinds have been found all over the world—relics of primitive races long forgotten.

It would appear that the drum was first intended as a means whereby the scattered members of the tribe could be called together for warfare. The boom-boom of the war drum is profound, ominous, like the roar of a jungle lion before it springs. It quickens the blood, stirs memories as old as mankind, calls to the primitive instincts. A writer who has lived long in the South Sea Islands heard the savage beat of the drums, and he says:

> The air thrummed with the resonance of the drums. The sound carried one back to the days when men first tied the skins of animals about hollow tree trunks and thumped them to call the naked tribes together under the oaks of England. They made one want to be a savage, to throw a spear, to dance in the moonlight.

We can see how the drum would quickly have found its way into the magic music that primitive peoples used to charm away the evil spirits. And from that it would be just a step to the use of the drum as an accompaniment to the savage dances. The rhythmic boom of the drum inspires a rhythmic swaying and stamping and stepping—such as we know in our jazz—such as the savage knows in his dancing.

Frederick O'Brien says:

> We who have become refined and diverse in our musical expression, using a dozen or scores of instruments to interpret our subtle emotions, cannot know the primitive and savage exaltation that surges through the veins when the war-drum beats. . . . It has ever been a summons to action, the call of the war-gods, the frenzy of the dance. Born of the thunder, speaking with the voice of the storm and the cataract, it rouses in man the beast with quivering nostrils and lashing tail who was part of the forest and the night.

The primitives used drums of various kinds. Some were hollow tree trunks over which animal skins had been stretched. Others were bamboo drums, long sections of the hollow reed, slit and beaten with sticks, like the drum which is used by the Marquesans to-day. Some primitive people beat their own bodies to produce the rhythmic sound; others beat the ground.

Both the Egyptians and the Hebrews are known to have used drums in ancient times. The Egyptians were extremely fond of music, as is indicated by the paintings in their tombs, and in addition to the drum they had small bells, harps, tambourines, lyres. The Egyptian drum was small and carried in the hand. The Hebrew drum seems to have been a sort of tambourine which was beaten sometimes with the hand, sometimes with a stick.

The Chinese and Japanese have had drums since early times. The Chinese drum was always, even in antiquity, large and powerful in sound, like our bass drum. The Japanese drum was smaller, though no less powerful in sound.

Cymbals are also extremely old, having been used by the ancient Assyrians. They had cymbals that were plate-shaped, but there have also been found recently Assyrian cymbals that are distinctly cup-shaped. The ancient Egyptians used cymbals that closely resembled our own, as also the Japanese. Of course, many savage peoples knew and used cymbals.

The castanets of modern Spain were the *crotalia* of the ancient Romans. In ancient Rome, as in modern Spain, the popular dances were cadenced by the clink of castanets (Spanish, *castanuelas*). These are twin hollow portions which give out sharp resonant sounds. The Romans generally used bronze for their *crotalia*.

Reed pipes and whistles are of great antiquity. Bone whistles, belonging to the Palæolithic age are in existence. The ancient Maoris had a reed-pipe instrument which they called *vivo*. In ancient Greece the *aulos* were a class of woodwind instruments with double or single reed mouthpiece, and with conical or cylindrical bore. Most authorities regard the *aulos* as the earliest prototype of the organ. The bagpipe, which is of great antiquity, is a complex reed instrument.

Wind Instruments.—The whistle and reed pipe represent, or course, the earliest wind instruments. There must have been many variations of the reed pipe, traces of which have been lost for ever. And there certainly must have been many kinds of whistles—bone, wood and clay.

Among the remains of the old Inca civilization, destroyed by Pizarro, have been found many bone and clay flutes, and some trumpets of shells. The Incas evidently made great progress in music, for they had also bells of many different tones, some of bronze and some of pure copper. The flute was known not only to the Incas, but to the ancient Egyptians and to others.

The first horns used in music, it seems, were ram's horns. These natural hollow tubes were the pattern from which tubes of brass were later made. In time these hollow brass tubes were improved by the addition of valves, worked by keys, and so were our popular brass instruments originated.

There is an interesting story behind each instrument. The saxophone, for instance, is named for a Belgian by the name of Adolphe Sax who devoted a lifetime to the perfection of saxhorns—a new kind of wind instrument named for him. This volume is not big enough to hold the story of each instrument; but you can read here the origin of each type.

Stringed Instruments.—Tradition tells us that the first stringed instrument was a shell across which a string had been stretched to give forth sound. However true this may be, we know that stringed instruments are very old, for the Bible mentions them:

> And his brother's name was Jubal; he was the father of all such as play on the harp and guitar. (Genesis IV, 21.)

The ancient Africans had many crude stringed instruments, most of them either made of or decorated with, human skulls. The Phœnicians and Egyptians both had stringed instruments, the lyre being among the best known. The harp, of course, is very old and was known and used by many of the ancients.

The Japanese are credited with having given us about a dozen stringed instruments, besides many wind and cymbal instruments. The traditions of the Japanese give to music a divine origin. They believed that the sun goddess, to show her resentment of the violence directed against her by her brother, hid in a cave and left the world in darkness. In order to lure her from the cave and give light to the world again, the gods invented music.

The first stringed instrument played with a bow, like our violin, is said to have been invented by a king of Ceylon about 5000 B.C. We do not know how true this tradition is, but we know that there are in India to this day wandering minstrels who play a strange, two-stringed instrument which they call the *rebek*. This instrument found its way to Europe about the 9th century A.D. and became popular in Italy. It was in Italy that the violin was perfected, and in the 16th century it took approximately the form we know to-day. Antonio Stradivari (1644-1737) is regarded as having been the finest violin-maker of all times.

The ukulele, a small guitar-shaped instrument, is not of Hawaiian origin as is generally supposed. A white man in Hawaii designed the instrument, using the Portuguese taro-patch violin as his model. He simply made the instrument one half the size and gave it one half as many strings as the Portuguese instrument, and the result was a twanging, tuneful sound that offered an excellent accompaniment to singing. The Hawaiians adopted the instrument and used it at their festivities, as an accompaniment to their weird songs. Travellers who saw the Hawaiians use the ukulele associated it with them, and gradually it came to be looked upon as a Hawaiian instrument. They have been using it now for more than a century.

The stringed instrument which is most familiar to all of us is the piano. The cithara, an ancient stringed instrument which has been traced back to 1700 B.C. and which was used by the Semitic races in Egypt, Assyria, Asia Minor, Greece, and Rome, is regarded by some as being a primitive prototype of what was later to be the piano. But most authorities are of the opinion that the mediæval clavichord was the true forerunner of the piano.

The clavichord was simply a box-shaped instrument made sometimes with legs, sometimes without. It had many interesting variations. The strings of this instrument were set in vibration by a blow from a brass tangent, instead of a hammer as in the modern instrument.

After the clavichord there were the harpsichord and the spinet. The first genuine piano was built in the city of Florence, 1709, by an Italian named Bartolomeo Cristofori. He gave his instrument the name pianoforte because it could be played with either a soft or a loud tone. The word for soft in Italian is *piano;* the word for loud is *forte.* Thus by combining the two words for soft and loud, Cristofori had the name for his new instrument—pianoforte.

In 1760 the square piano was invented. In 1800 the first upright piano made its appearance. The accordion was invented in 1820 by Damian in Vienna. The accordion is a small, portable reed instrument with a keyboard, and is the smallest representative of the organ family. The barrel organ made its appearance about 1860, and for the first time in that year there appeared in the streets the spectacle of a travelling organ with children dancing after it.

In a recent article on the "Evolution of the Piano" Mr. Henry T. Finck says:

> Even William Jennings Bryan could be persuaded of the truth of the evolutionary doctrine if he spent an hour or two looking at the collections of primitive and obsolete musical instruments in the Metropolitan Museum. Here are the ancestors of the instruments we now hear at home and in concert halls and some of them look as funny and "preliminary" when compared with ours as monkeys do compared with humans.

We have looked over this collection of primitive and obsolete musical instruments, and as it is impossible to tell you about them all in a book limited to origins of the things that intimately concern us, we have selected those which seem most interesting and most closely associated with our own instruments, and have pictured them here for you to see.

CHAPTER XVI

Dress Through The Centuries

More snow fell on the mountains, snow and again snow, and in the valleys it rained unceasingly. The Ice Age was coming on in earnest. . . . One frosty night when he [Carl, myth man of the Ice Age] felt he would never see another morning, as he lay naked and worn out under an ice-clad rock, he got up half delirious and made for the warm lair of a bear that he had scented near by. . . . He killed the bear and slobbered up its blood; afterwards he made a hole in its body and crept into the dead beast. He slept until the bear's carcass was cold, but did not leave the place until he had got the skin flayed off. The next night he slept under a rock with the skin on, and afterwards he always dragged it with him on his wanderings. Now he could stand the nights fairly well, and it was not long before he learned to wrap himself in the bearskin in the daytime too.

—Johannes V. Jensen (in "The Long Journey")

THE HABIT OF DRESS

MAN originally came into the world fully clothed. He had all that nature ever intended him to have—a coat of coarse hair from head to feet. It was never planned that he have any other "dress" than this.

Cradled in the tropical regions of the earth, man, for the first long age of his existence, was quite comfortable in his hairy coat. But as he wandered slowly toward the poles, and the temperature became lower, his natural clothing seemed inadequate protection against the cold, the rain, the wind.

And so man stood upon the brink of a cold prehistory, and shivered. Other creatures, dressed like man in natural coats of fur or hair, shivered too. Some died of the cold, became extinct. Some migrated to warmer regions. Some grew heavier coats of hair, became hardened, acclimated, like the polar bear.

(Courtesy of Metropolitan Museum of Art)

Barrel organ with figures—Italian, early 19th Century.

(Courtesy of Metropolitan Museum of Art)

A Japanese dance band, showing the popular shoulder drum. Recent photograph.

Though he was the last creature to come to earth, man was the first creature to reason. Finding himself in a cold and uncomfortable world, this thinking creature called man ripped the warm skins from lesser animals and wrapped them about his own body. Here were warmth and comfort! Here was protection from wind and rain! So man in the very earliest times acquired the habit of dress.

Many elements entered into the cultivation of dress as a custom, as we shall presently see. But principally and fundamentally dress was intended as an added protection against climatic conditions. Man found his natural coat of hair inadequate. Reason taught him to add another coat of his own making.

In the cold regions, where man wrapped himself continuously, day and night, in warm skins, the need for hair on the body gradually diminished. Instead of man's natural hairy coat becoming thicker and heavier, as is the case of animals in cold regions, it became thinner, finer. The more man wrapped himself in skins and furs, the less of a protection his own coat became. Civilization, with its custom of dress, refined the hairy coat to a thin down on the surface of the skin.

In the tropical regions the sun and the air gradually made the body of man smooth, refining the useless hair and causing it to disappear. Among these people the habit of dress assumed another form. The skin was tattooed, the body painted and mutilated, for purposes of self-adornment. This we will discuss later.

Dress, then, is a custom. In savage life it is a custom imposed by climate, by vanity—and by missionaries. In civilized life it is a custom so closely woven into the fabric of modesty and man-made standards of decency, that it is accepted as the only natural and proper state of man.

The popular notion that hairy men are strong is simply an association of hair with the great brute men who roamed the earth unclothed in primitive days. The modern man with his carefully tailored clothes, and his body covered only with a fine down, is a comparative weakling; while the ape-like men of primitive times, unclothed except for the hair that covered their bodies, were veritable giants in strength.

What Is Modesty?—Man alone of all earthly creatures clothes himself. The bear never knows other dress than his shaggy coat. The leopard wears from birth to death his spotted mantle. The gorilla, closer to man than any other animal, finds sufficient warmth and comfort in the hairy coat provided by nature.

Though man comes into the world fully clothed, according to nature's original intentions, he takes the wool from sheep, the flax and hemp from the fields, the silk from the silkworm, and makes for himself garments of great usefulness and beauty. Why?

We have seen how climate conditions inspired man, in his ingenuity, to form the habit of dress. But what about those regions where even man's natural dress was a burden? Why did the habit of dress follow man everywhere, keeping pace with his progress through the ages, until with civilization the original order of things is reversed, dress rather than undress being regarded as the only natural and proper state of man?

Many writers advance the theory of modesty. Man, they say, clothes himself to conceal his nakedness. But we agree with M. Wiener ("Le Pérou") who says:

> Clothing does not result from modesty. On the contrary, modesty appears as a result of clothing; that is to say, the clothing which conceals any part of the human body makes the nakedness of the parts which we are accustomed to see covered, appear indecent.

The element of shame does, of course, enter into dress. But the feeling of shame came comparatively late, when civilization had already reached a fairly advanced stage. We must regard it as a result, rather than a cause, of dress.

Modesty is, after all, highly conventional. The standards of modesty vary among different people. Mohammedan women, surprised in bathing, will cover their faces; Chinese women will hide their artificially compressed feet. In Sumatra and Celebes the wild tribes regard exposure of the knee as highly immodest; in Central Asia the fingertips are concealed. Nudity is not regarded as immodest among the Tahitians and Tongans if the body is tattooed.

Tacitus relates that chastity was "a controlling virtue among the Teutons, ranking among women as bravery among men; yet all Teutons bathed in the streams together." The Japanese also bathe together, men and women, in natural hot pools. While they regard nudity with indifference, they wear loose garments to conceal the contour of the figure. It is interesting to notice by contrast that we who consider nakedness among the sexes horrifying, nevertheless emphasize the difference of form in our dress. Clothing in civilized life tends to accentuate rather than to conceal the difference between the sexes.

In his "Studies in the Psychology of Sex" Havelock Ellis cites many instances of savage or uncivilized people in various parts of the world who wear only short loincloths or aprons, yet among whom "the feeling of modesty is greatly developed." There are, indeed, some people so accustomed to nudity that when made to wear clothing for the first time, they exhibit great confusion and embarrassment. O' Brien relates, for instance:

> Missionaries bewilder the savage mind by imposing their standards of the moment and calling them modesty. The African Negro, struggling to harmonize these two ideas, wore a tall silk hat and a pair of slippers as his only garments when he obeyed Livingstone's exhortations to clothe himself in the presence of white women.

According to the sacred narrative, clothing was introduced through sin. Adam and Eve partook of the forbidden fruit and

> the eyes of both of them were opened, and they felt that they were naked; and they sewed fig-leaves together and made themselves aprons. (Genesis III, 7.)

Many writers, like Swedenborg, taught that in heaven all would be naked, for clothing was a punishment for the sin of man. But others, like Erasmus, the devout theologian, taught that "angels abhor nakedness" and that in heaven men and women both would wear clothes of great richness and beauty.

So from age to age, from country to country, have the standards of dress and of modesty varied, always according with the customs of the people. It is a custom of civilized life to dress, therefore the state of undress is regarded as immodest. In matters of dress, as in all other matters concerning man, everything is relative.

Primitive Dress.—Man made himself a covering because he was cold. In regions of low temperature, therefore, the development of dress was rapid. But in the tropical latitudes the development of dress was slow, and for a long age it was interpreted only in terms of beads, shells, paint, and tattooing.

The first dress of man, in the colder regions, was the skin of some beast. We can be reasonably certain that animal skins were used for dress as early as the Palæolithic Age, for the intelligence, the reason, that enabled man to kill a beast many times his own size and strength would also have taught the value of the warm, furry skins. These skins were probably separated from the flesh with flint knives or sharpened bits of stone, and either pounded or rubbed until all adhering flesh had been removed.

And so was created man's first dress—a raw, ugly, blood-stained skin.

Neolithic man dressed chiefly in skins. But we know that he had also a rough cloth of flax, for fragments of flaxen cloth have been found with other Neolithic relics and are still in existence. Neolithic man is also credited with pins and ornaments of bronze.

According to the biblical story the first dress of man was the fig leaf. "And they sewed fig-leaves together, and made themselves aprons." But evidently this dress displeased the Lord, for the Bible tells us, "And the Lord God made unto Adam and to his wife coats of skins, and clothed them."

Superstition, like climate, exerted a powerful influence upon dress. Primitive man wore all sorts of trophies to protect and benefit him. He strung the claws and teeth of the animals he killed and wore them around his neck, partly as decoration, partly to protect him from other beasts. His body was a mystery to him, and he pampered it with his treasures—his shells and claws, his curious bits of stone, his trophies. These were the first talismans, the first "good luck" charms. The Africans and Australians, both highly superstitious, covered their bodies with talismans of every description. An African of the central regions even to-day will pick up a curiously shaped stone and wear it around his neck for years, fully confident that it protects him from harm.

The simplest of all clothing or coverings is the loincloth. It is characteristic of the warmer climates where dress developed slowly. In ancient Egypt the loincloth was a plain, short linen cloth which was wrapped around the loins and tied in front. In the early dynasties it was worn by everyone, even men of rank. Later, the men of importance wore loincloths of matting or leather, and later still the fringed girdle became the mark of distinction.

The Semites who visited Egypt wore larger loincloths, usually of coloured cloth. They were ornamented with parallel strips of the cloth, and sometimes bordered with fringe. Apparently the Semites wore close-fitting tunics, or skirts, also, for on the famous Beni-Hasan tombs (20th century B.C.) the Semites wear richly decorated cloth tunics "while the leader is arrayed in a magnificent wrapper in blue, red and white and fringed edges and a neck-ribbon to keep it in position." (Encyclopædia Britannica.)

The Savage Love of Ornament.

The desire for self-decoration, although a specifically human quality, is exceedingly old. There are peoples destitute of almost everything which we regard as necessities of life, but there is no people so rude as not to take pleasure in ornaments.

The ancient barbarians who inhabited the south of Europe at the same time as the reindeer and the mammoth, brought to their caves brilliant and ornamental objects. The women of the utterly wretched Veddahs in Ceylon decorate themselves with necklaces of brass beads. The Australians, without taking the slightest pride in their appearance so far as neatness or cleanliness is concerned, are yet very vain of their own rude decorations. The Tasmanians are never eager to obtain useful articles but always wish the ornamental.

Writers who tell us of savage races never fail to impress upon us this love of ornament and decoration. To the savage mind nothing is more fascinating than a bright and colourful bauble to hang upon his body. Feathers, beads, bone, rings, flowers, anklets, bracelets, shells—all are used by savage man to adorn and decorate his body.

Among many savage races the women are strangely unadorned, while the men are laden with ornaments of every conceivable kind. The reason for this is, simply, that the men are so passionately fond of self-adornment that they monopolize all the beads and shells and decorations for themselves. Thus, for instance, among the aborigines of the New Hebrides, New Hanover, New Ireland, and Australia, the men and boys appropriate all the ornaments. But as a general rule, men and women alike are gaily decorated in savage life.

There are some savage races who leave much or all of their skin uncovered, yet delight in painting themselves with brilliant colours. This love of bright colours is one of the prime characteristics of the savage. Children, little savages that they are, love the coloured cartoons in the newspapers because the colours attract and fascinate them.

Throughout the entire Australian continent we find natives staining their naked bodies with black, red, yellow, and white paint. Red ochre is a particular favourite and is regarded as the finest and most important embellishment.

Although perfectly naked, the Australians of Botany Bay were by no means without ornaments. They painted themselves with red ochre, white clay and charcoal; the red was laid on in broad patches, the white generally in stripes or on the face in spots, often with a circle around each eye. Through the septum of the nose they wore a bone, thick as a finger and five or six inches long. Though this was awkward and interfered with breathing, they submitted freely to the inconvenience for the sake of appearance.

Among the Guaycurus, the men paint their bodies half red and half white. In New Zealand the lips of both sexes are generally dyed blue. Many savage peoples paint the body on occasions of importance, as for instance the ancient Patagonians, who painted their bodies black whenever there was a death.

Decoration and self-adornment take many curious forms in savage life. In Eastern Central Africa there is scarcely a woman who is without her lip ring—an ugly, grotesque affair which is sometimes so enormous that the mouth can hardly be opened. Yet the larger the ring, the more handsome the woman is supposed to be!

Many tribes pierce, enlarge, and mutilate the ear lobes. Cases have been known where the ear lobes were so mutilated that they reached down almost to the shoulders. The hole is pierced in childhood and a small disc placed within it. Later a larger disc is placed in the opening, then a still larger one, until finally the hole in the ear lobe accommodates a disc as large as a saucer! Earrings are, of course, worn by savage peoples everywhere; somehow the earring appeals strongly to the savage taste. In modern life the earring is a last relic of this taste, and it is quickly vanishing.

Teeth, like the ear lobes, are subject to mutilation. In the Malay Archipelago the teeth are filed to points and blackened. Various tribes in New Guinea also file the teeth. In Australia it is customary, among various tribes, to knock out the two front teeth in the upper jaw of the boys of the tribe as soon as they reach maturity.

Nose mutilations have always been practised by savages. The Shulis bore a hole sometimes in the septum of the nose, sometimes in the underlip. The Papuans perforate the septum of the nose and insert sticks—a most fashionable decoration among these people. There are many tribes scattered throughout Australia, and some in Africa, who pierce the septum of the nose and wear either a ring or a bone thrust through it.

There have been many other kinds of decoration and self-adornment. In some parts of the world it has been the practice to modify the human form. The most familiar form of body modification is the compressed feet of the Chinese women. The ancient Peruvians and many Indian tribes of Northwest America practised head deformation. Deforming of the head was practised to some extent also in Africa and among the Eskimo. Waist compression was widely practised in civilized Europe until twenty-five years ago.

Still another form of decoration is to suspend foreign bodies from the arms, ears, legs, neck, and other convenient parts of the body.

A savage begins by painting or tattooing himself for ornament. Then he adopts a movable appendage, which he hangs on his body, and on which he puts the ornamentation which he formerly marked more or less indelibly on his skin. In this way he is able to gratify his taste for change.

These movable appendages include ear, nose, and lip ornaments, necklaces, armlets, and wristlets, anklets, finger, and toe rings, etc.

The Custom of Tattooing.—One of the most widely practised forms of decoration is the application of extraneous matter to the body, as in tattooing. Darwin says:

Not one great country can be named from the Polar regions in the north of New Zealand in the south in which the aborigines do not tattoo themselves.

Tattooing is a form of skin decoration achieved by pricking a design into the skin with an awl or needle dipped into colouring matter. The ancient Assyrians, Britons, and Thracians practised it. Most savage races had the custom. It is still widely prevalent throughout Africa and Australia. Sometimes we find it in civilized life, as among sailors.

Many theories have been advanced as to the origin of tattooing. The word for tattoo in Egyptian is *Tattu* which means "The Eternal," and some authorities are of the opinion that the custom of tattooing was meant originally, not as a decoration, but as a means of preserving significant facts eternally. Thus a chief would have his special totem animal tattooed upon his chest as a reminder to others in this world, and to himself in the next world, that the particular animal belonged to him.

Mr. Frazer suggests that tattooing may have been originated for the purpose of placing the savage more fully under the protection of his totem. The clansman represented his totem on his body so that no matter how far from home he wandered, he was always under his totem's protection.

Among certain tribes in Africa, tattooing is done as a mark of courage in war. Frequently warriors are tattooed in order to present a more terrifying aspect before the enemy. Sometimes the tattooing has a religious significance; sometimes it is a mark of mourning. Among some savage races the tattooing has become merely a form of decoration and no particular pattern is followed; but among others each clan has a special identifying pattern. Tattooing makes it easier for savages to distinguish their own clansmen from enemies.

Tattooing can be very beautiful, especially when patterned by an expert. The process is very painful but usually endured without a murmur, for it is regarded as a mark of extreme cowardice to wince or cry in pain when being tattooed. The New Zealanders tattoo on the lips, a torture which few civilized people could endure.

The New Zealanders, incidentally, boast the most beautiful tattooing in the world. It is generally in curved or spiral lines, elaborately and artistically patterned.

To some extent, tattooing destroys the appearance of nakedness. The South Sea Islander in the familiar *pareu* has a greater appearance of nakedness than the unclothed but tattooed New Zealander. Laird says that in West Africa the tattooing "in the absence of clothing gives a finish to the skin."

Despite all the social and "magic-religious purposes of tattooing" there can be no doubt whatever that men and women mutilated and tattooed themselves partly, if not chiefly, in order to make themselves attractive to the opposite sex. In New Guinea the women tattoo themselves solely to please the men. In some tribes no girl is considered eligible for marriage until she has been tattooed. The Makalaka girls, for instance, had to submit to horrible torture before they could marry. About four thousand stitches were made in the skin of the chest and stomach, a black fluid being rubbed into the wounds to colour the design.

Among the Abipones, a tribe of South American Indians now practically extinct, the faces, breasts, and arms of the women were covered with black figures of various designs. No woman was considered pretty or attractive without these figures on her body. They were made with sharp thorns, the tattooing paint being a mixture of ashes and blood. A painful process, but one gladly endured for the sake of beauty!

Cicatrization, which is practised by many savage peoples, is a form of scar tattooing. It is achieved by repeatedly cutting the skin in the same place so that when it finally heals a raised scar remains. The natives of Botany Bay consider these scars highly ornamental. The Australians are partial to this type of scar tattooing, employing it as a form of decoration. It conveys no idea of tribal connection, as does the patterned tattooing.

Many African tribes mark their boys with cicatrices, rubbing wood ashes in the wounds on the face and body. This causes them to swell and heal in a purple colour which is regarded as a mark of distinction. Men so marked are more attractive to the women than those whose scars are uncoloured.

In the Fijis the women make themselves attractive to the men by having wart-like spots burned along their arms and backs. The men consider these burns ornamental.

The Beginning of Fashion.—Jensen places the origin of fashion in the Ice Age. What he says is purely imaginative, of course, but we quote it here for its romantic interest, for its rare whimsies of thought:

> When the women were not at their dainty arts by the fire, they wove themselves clothes, each finer and more extravagant than the last, but always in the strictest conformity with the general taste. One century it was absolutely necessary to wear nothing but a polar bear's skin which had to be open all down the front; the polar bears were almost exterminated and the women never went out, because the fashion was such a chilly one; but what were they to do? What made it indispensable to dress in this particular way was that nobody on any account might have the smallest glimpse of a woman's back. A later and more sober age found it difficult to understand that people of the olden time could be such unfortunate victims of a one-sided modesty.
>
> Naturally the women of the icefield were always collecting things for their adornment. A necklace of wolves' teeth bored through and strung was very effective in setting off a frail creature who was only a woman. A bone stuck through the cartilage of the nose was one of those ornaments that were within the reach of all and therefore went out of fashion comparatively quickly. A great deal was thought of a fine complexion, which the women tried to achieve by treating their skin with ochre, obtained from springs on the island. This blooming tint soon spread from the face over the whole body, and here it must be said that the men caught the fashion; they too loved to smear themselves with ochre and fat till they looked like fiery red men and could be seen a long way off in their glory.

We can be no more definite concerning the origin of fashion than is Jensen. No one knows precisely how fashion was created, when it began—indeed, whether it originated with women or with men. It is a mistaken notion, as we shall presently see, that women are more vain than men.

It is difficult to believe that any sort of fashion existed as early as Jensen indicates, although we cannot, of course, be certain about it. The extreme conditions of the Ice Age would have obviated any possibility of man, or woman, giving up a nice, warm, polar bear's skin because some other kind of skin was being worn. These early people unquestionably wore whatever warm skins they could obtain, throwing them over their shoulders in the most comfortable and convenient manner.

But fashion is intrinsically imitative, and it is possible that even when bearskins were the only dress, one tribe of people would copy another's method of wearing them. Perhaps some clever fellow conceived the notion of fastening his bearskin on the left shoulder with a thong or wooden skewer. This kept the skin from slipping down and left the right arm, the weapon arm, free for action. Instantly the people of his tribe would copy this convenient method. And as this tribe wandered here and there, meeting others, the "fashion" of wearing the bearskin in this particular way would spread.

Fashion evidences itself more clearly in ornamentation than it does in the dress intended for warmth and comfort. For instance, even among savages closely associated there were various kinds of body mutilation, various methods of wearing trophies and adornments. One tribe had the "fashion" of wearing a bone thrust through the cartilage of the nose; another had this "fashion" of piercing the nose but wearing sticks through it instead of bone. And still another tribe, in the same vicinity, spared the nose but had the "fashion" of mutilating the ear lobes by piercing them and gradually enlarging the holes with discs. Each tribe in early life appears to have had some mode of body adornment peculiar to itself. Even in tattooing, a fairly general custom, there were various tribal fashions. We are inclined to regard this as the first crude manifestation of fashion.

The Development.—Only yesterday dress was a covering, a protection, with no apparent beauty. When "Adam delved and Eve span" the fig leaf vied with the more modest skin, but still fashion was undeveloped.

To-day Fifth Avenue is heralding a new season. The shop windows are showing gowns from Lanvin and Poiret. Brilliant colours flash in the sun. Graceful women, faultlessly gowned, brush by in a rustle of silks and satins. Laces stir and jewels tremble. A limousine draws up to the curb and a buckled slipper finds the running board. One catches ever so faintly the breath of a perfume from the Orient.

The development of dress from the first raw skin to the silks and sables of Fifth Avenue is one of the most fascinating phases in the study of man. Like some inseparable shadow, fashion has kept pace with man through the long ages of his development. To study dress and fashion, therefore, is to study man, for the one parallels the other.

> Long years have rolled between the woman who sat huddled in the prehistoric cave and the strutting mannequin who symbolizes our own complex civilization [writes Katherine M. Kelly]. The art of dressing the woman has developed with her own development through the centuries. . . . Each generation from the earliest time has contributed something to this art.

It is a common notion that women are by nature vainer than men, and "more addicted to dressing and decorating themselves." This certainly does not hold true among savage peoples in general. Among the Uaupes the men and boys appropriate all ornaments for themselves. In New Hebrides and various parts of Australia the men alone wear body adornments. There are several African tribes in which tattooing as a form of body adornment is confined solely to the men.

A prominent New York photographer, who prefers to have his name remain a secret, says that men sitters are invariably more vain than women. "The woman who comes to be photographed," he said to the author recently, "seems to realize her shortcomings. If she is stout she asks to be placed in the position that would make her appear most slender. She has a wave put in her hair, and uses rouge to make her lips prettier. That is not vanity, as I see it. She is merely trying to make the most of her personal appearance. She wants the photograph to be flattering.

"The man, on the other hand, resents any advice or suggestions. He wants to appear in the photograph precisely as he is in life. He is indignant if it is suggested that a bit of rouge be applied to the lips for photographic purposes. The truer the likeness to himself the more he is pleased. In other words, he is satisfied and vain; his appearance pleases him and he will not make any attempt to improve it."

However true this may be, it seems certain that men and women both have an equal share of vanity. The man may not be more vain than the woman, but it is doubtful that he is any less vain. Why, then, does woman give so much more thought and attention to matters of dress than the man? Why is woman's dress so very much more elaborate than man's?

The general belief is that women adorn themselves to attract the opposite sex. This is true, but only in a very limited sense. Many fashions are ridiculed by men, yet women persist in wearing them. And women continue to adorn themselves long after they have won the men of their desires.

Arnold Bennett says:

> The truth is that the competition among women for men is chiefly a legend—not wholly. There are more women than men, but not many more. Women want marriage more than men want marriage, but not much more. Competition is by no means so fierce that women have to perform prodigies of self-ornamentation in order to inveigle a fellow-creature so simple that he worries about the tint of his own necktie and socks; and the idea of such a phenomenon is derogatory to women. After all, nature has the business of sex-attraction in hand, and she is not dependent on fashions. Long before fashions had been evolved she managed it precisely as well as she manages it to-day. She relies not on textile stuffs, but upon the stuff that dreams are made of.

Another general belief, fostered by the masculine world,

is that women are like sheep who follow one another, slaves to fashion. Which is absolutely untrue as can readily be proved. But let us quote from Arnold Bennett again, for his is a *man's* opinion:

> This argument is more than insincere; it is impudent. For women show much wider originality and variations in attire among themselves than men do among themselves. Half a dozen average well-dressed women will be as different from one another as half a dozen flowers of different species; you could distinguish them half a mile off. But half a dozen well-dressed men would be indistinguishably alike if you decapitated them. It is notorious that men are the slaves of fashion. . . . They have a perfect passion for being exactly like other men—not merely in clothes, but in everything. So much so that they cannot bear to think that there are men unlike themselves.

We are all familiar with this state of affairs, if we will only recognize it. The man is the slave of fashion, not the woman. Let one man dare to dress a little differently, a little more daintily than his fellows, and he is immediately dubbed a "sissy." Let him take a trifle more care of his personal appearance than men usually do, and he is labelled a "dude." It is the men who are like sheep, slavishly following the fashion of dress that has been originated for them. How the present mode of masculine attire was originated we shall presently see.

The women of to-day give more care and attention to their dress, and wear more elaborate garments than men, because it is the long-established custom for them to do so. They are expected to wear attractive clothes. In bird life and animal life it is the male who wears the gayest feathers, the brightest coat. We shall see why this has been reversed in human life.

Why Women Dress More Elaborately Than Men.—In the earliest times, men monopolized all ornaments. The prettiest shells, the sharpest sabre teeth, the most highly polished stones belonged to them. They plastered their hair with mud and weighted their bodies with trophies and decorations.

The chief and the medicine man were particularly resplendent in their ornaments and decorations. They were painted and greased; they wore skulls and image idols; their heads ached with the weight of the ornaments they carried. They even made for themselves bracelets of the human hair cut from war victims.

When man became a hunter and a clansman, giving up the life of the nomad to become the head of a family, he found that many decorations and body adornments were a hindrance to him. He could not steal upon an animal silently when his body was laden with bracelets and shells and other cumbersome ornaments. He could not climb a tree as quickly, could not fight as easily.

Warriors, too, found the ornaments a hindrance. They could swing the stone ax and wield the great spear much more easily when their bodies were free from heavy ornaments. They gave up everything except the trophy—the "good-luck charm"—which they believed would protect them on the battlefield.

And so the dress of man became simpler and simpler as man developed and found new duties, new responsibilities. Only the dress of the chief and the medicine man—both of whom remained at a safe distance on the battlefield, and who led but had little participation in the hunt—continued to be highly elaborate and ornamental, a hindrance to every movement.

Yet man retained all his innate love of ornamentation and display, and in savage life there are always festivities in which the men wear grotesque masks or paint themselves in gay colours, festivities in which the men have an orgy of body decoration to satisfy the hunger for display. Many African and Australian tribes have such festivities. We find them also in China and Japan. American and Mexican Indians have the custom. It prevails, in a modified form, even in civilized life, the masquerade ball being the most familiar example.

It was when man began to find elaborate dress and

(Courtesy of Metropolitan Museum of Art)

An interesting study in costume and interior—model of the Narthex of the Church of S. Sophia, Constantinople. Byzantine, 532–537 A. D.

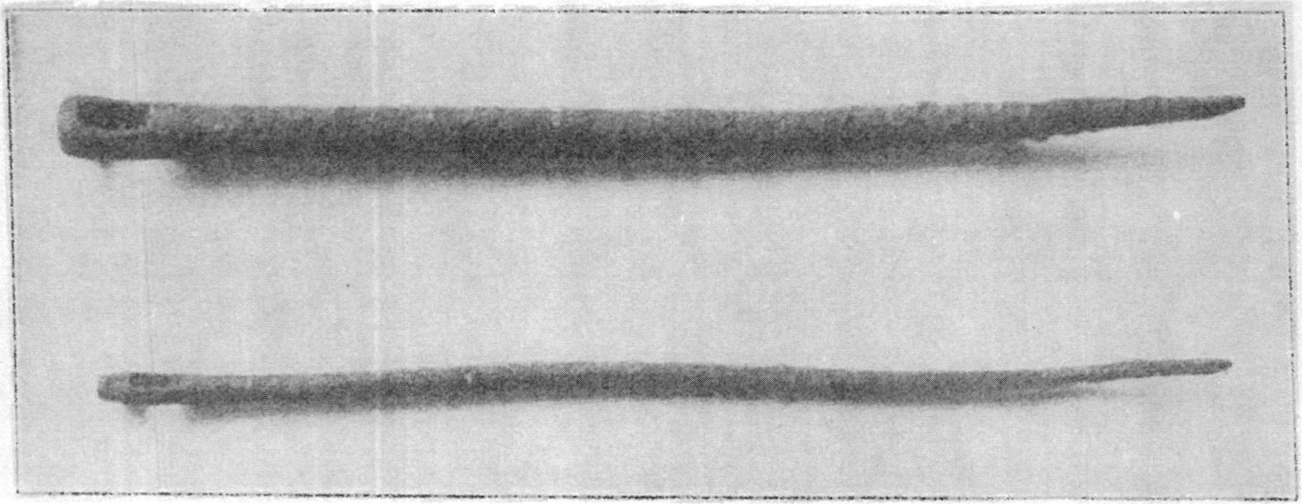

(Courtesy of Metropolitan Museum of Art)

Ancient iron needles unearthed in Egypt.

decoration a hindrance that he forced woman to decorate herself, for *his pleasure*. Since he could not very well wear with ease the shells he brought from the sea, the stones he polished until they shone like gems, the little images he carved from bone and wood, the woman was obliged to wear them for him.

And woman was nothing loath to pamper her body. She found it a pleasant diversion to sit by the fire and string teeth on a cord-like fibre to wear around her neck. She liked to make ornaments that she knew would delight her master, and perhaps make the other women a little envious. She had leisure while the man was away on the hunt to make things for herself, and she began to enjoy the occupation.

Thus while man hunted and fished and warred with his neighbours, woman sat before the fire and kept the food in readiness for his return; and while the food cooked to softness in the big iron pot, she made new things for herself to wear. She must look attractive when the man returned. She must please him. She learned to adorn herself for his pleasure rather than her own. But habit quickly become custom, and custom is usually pleasant. Woman gradually began to dress for her own pleasure, as she still does to a very great extent.

It would seem, then, strangely enough, that woman adorned herself originally because of man's vanity rather than her own. The more ornaments, the rarer shells and beads she wore, the wealthier the man. As Bennett says, "Man employed the lady to be expensive in his behalf." He advances the theory that the fashionable Chinese male kept his fingernails so long that the hands could not be used, and maimed the feet of his females so that they could not walk, for the purpose of publicly demonstrating that he was wealthy and had plenty of servants to do all necessary work.

As we trace the development of dress through the ages we find almost everywhere the tendency to make the woman look "expensive." Nevertheless, we find also a tendency for the man to dress elaborately and display his wealth whenever leisure gives him the chance to do so.

In savage life, for instance, it is the chief and the medicine man who dress in rich skins and gaudy decorations, while the huntsmen and the warriors wear little or nothing. In civilized life, the king and his courtiers, the noblemen and their associates, always wore silks, satins, and velvets every whit as elaborate as those worn by their ladies, while the men who worked in the fields and on the roads wore only what was absolutely plain and comfortable.

Story of Man's Dress.—In cold regions, man's clothing began with the animal skin. In warm regions it began with the loincloth.

The loincloth in ancient Egypt, as we have seen, was simply a short linen cloth which was wrapped around the loins and tied. Later it was made of matting, and sometimes of leather. During one period it took the form of a narrow fringed girdle.

The loincloth of Egypt developed into a skirt which fell below the knee—possibly inspired by the close-fitting tunics worn by the Semites of this period (20th century B.C.). In Babylonia there was a similar tunic, or skirt, covering the lower half of the body.

The costume changed perceptibly during the XVIIIth and XIXth dynasties. Now we find the Egyptians covering the upper part of the body with a tunic fastening over a girdle. The fashionable material is linen. But again the fashion changes, and again—many times in quick succession. Evidently the Egyptians copied from everyone who visited them. By the time of Herodotus woollen mantles trimmed with fringe were being worn by the men. And those of high rank wore finer materials and mantles of a different cut to distinguish them from the slaves.

In Greece, man wore a loose-girdled mantle like the chiton worn by the woman. Usually it was short but musicians and charioteers wore long, trailing garments which were drawn up in front through a girdle to permit them to walk.

The Roman costume of the classic period was the toga. This was simply a piece of cloth in the form of a segment of a circle. One end was thrown over the left shoulder and allowed to hang down in front. The remainder was drawn around the body. Ordinary citizens or plebs wore the plain white toga. People of rank or patricians wore one entirely of purple, or with a purple border, and on

Primitive. Early Christian. Greek. 15th Century European.

occasions of importance added a gold-embroidered tunic. A long robe was usually worn over the toga at dinner parties.

In early Britain the men wore tunics which opened at the side and fell to the knees. The tunics had sleeves which were generally loose above the elbow and tight-fitting below. With the tunic dark hose was worn, or breeches which were cross-bandaged below the knee. This type of costume appears to have prevailed from the 2d or 3d century A.D. until the 8th century.

The year 785 marked an era of great splendour in men's

attire among the Anglo-Saxons. The Council of Cloveshoe found it necessary to denounce the extravagance of the people in general, the clergy in particular. But according to all accounts, the Danish dandies of this era completely eclipsed the Saxons. The men of rank wore rich and elaborate clothes and were fond of jewels and decorations.

The Norman Conquest marked no great change in English costume, except that a French influence was introduced. A general luxury prevailed among men and women alike.

At the end of the eleventh century began the Crusades, and men began to see life from another angle, began to make new associations, see new phases of life. The Crusaders acquired a new appreciation of art and beauty, and they brought back with them cloths of rich, gorgeous patterns, precious jewels, ornaments and garments of great beauty. The 12th century saw a rapid development in dress and in the manufacture of materials.

Though costume was elaborate and beautiful during the 12th century the workmen were obliged, as always, to wear what was comfortable and convenient. The usual costume for those employed in daily labour was a simple tunic with close sleeves and a hat with a brim. The men of rank wore gorgeous tunics of silks, elaborated with jewels and ornaments.

Writing of mediæval Europe, Parsons says:

> During the reign of Philippe (Philip II, 1180–1223) tournaments were often given. Not only were the guests of noble origin, but there were crowds of troubadours with their instruments, minstrels, fools, jugglers, dancers, and other strange and amusing people. Booths and tents were raised around the castle gate and merchants of all sorts hastened thither with their wares of cloth-of-gold and silver, velvets and silks, stuffs of all kinds, ermine and other furs, silver cups, gold clasps, ornaments of great variety for lords and ladies, cutlery, armour, and embroidered articles of personal adornment, as well as trifles for amusement. Flags, banners, pennants, and lovely tapestries hung and fluttered from the windows and balconies of the *châteaux*. These tournaments persisted, growing in number and gorgeous sumptuousness throughout the twelfth and thirteenth centuries.

There was great elaboration of dress in the 13th century. Nobles were regally clothed in silk tunics trimmed with gold, stockings and sandals, and embroidered gloves with jewelled backs. They curled their hair with irons and bound them in ribbons.

The size of the cloak and robe, breadth of the trimming, and the number of stuffs each person was permitted to possess were regulated by law. The higher the rank, the greater the variety allowed, the larger the cloak and robe, and the broader their trimmings. Hoods were universal, but their size and shape was not left to the caprice

16th Century European. *17th Century French.* *18th Century European.* *19th Century European.*

of their owners. The nobles wore large hoods hanging to their heels, the common people little sugar-loafed cowls.

During the 14th century the custom of wearing long hose, drawn up the legs to join a short breech, became popular. The hood and robe of the previous century disappeared and men began to wear short, tight-fitting jackets. Dress became more practical than it had been before, and for the first time fashion began to change very distinctly from season to season. Sleeves, skirts, and head-dresses ran through various interesting fashions. Belts and buttons came into general use.

It was during this period that a new soul was being born in Italy—a soul which was to make its influence felt throughout Europe. We refer to the great Renaissance which was born, nurtured, and developed in Italy, and which found its way into France and England, leaving in its wake a new appreciation of the classic ideals. Social, political, and religious life responded to the new influence. And of course dress reflected the change.

Parsons says:

By 1400 the hour of mediæval life had struck, and consequently of mediæval art. Its shadow lingered for near a century in the west, but the expression was abnormal, for it was insincere. The spirit was dead and the body, robbed of its soul, refused to function and began slowly to crumble away.

During the 15th century costume was simple in line but rich and luxurious in materials. We find both an ecclesiastic and a classic influence, with memories of a mediæval idealism. There seems also to be a new feeling, a decorative effect wholly lacking before. Toward the middle of the century one senses an Eastern influence in turban-like headdresses worn by the men and women.

Parsons tells us that at this time in England "the male sex appears to have been first to show pride in brilliant plumage and to have succeeded in exploiting it." And France, he tells us, "was true to form and sought to convey the impression of decorative appearance whatever the conditions might be under the surface."

In England in the 16th century the men of the court and nobility were great dandies. Sir Walter Raleigh wore a corset, as did all fashionable noblemen. Velvet caps and plumes were worn, doublets of satin, coats of cloth-of-gold or silver, trimmed with ermine. Jewels were hung about the neck and monstrous ruffs, introduced by Queen Elizabeth, were worn. In France the same ostentation in costume prevailed. But in Italy the costume of the men was simpler, carrying still a suggestion of the dignity and classic influence of the Renaissance.

The 17th century saw a return to simplicity after the gorgeous artificiality of the Elizabethan times. With the accession of James I, dress took on a saner note. We see a new interest in line, and in men's costume a tendency to follow the lines of the figure. The dandy is beginning to flourish, and there is a vague suggestion of the uniform which is to become later man's general attire.

In this century the ruff disappeared, giving way to wide, flat collars, laces, and ribbons. The doublet, ancestor of the coat, became longer; the breeches became smaller and were fastened below the knee. Charles I introduced the Vandyke beard, and it was during his reign that the fashionable noblemen wore the notorious "love-locks" and roses in their ears.

The magnificent court of Louis XIV introduced many new and striking style notes, all of them as capricious as the King himself, and lasting but a moment. It was during Louis's long reign that the mode in France reached the climax of its richness and splendour, influencing all the rest of Europe. One of the important fashions of the period was the petticoat breeches, strangely effeminate with their cascades of lace and ribbon below the knee. Louis XIV also began the custom of wearing curled wigs, and he is reputed to have had forty wigs for his own use.

The dandyism which began to manifest itself in the 17th century became paramount with the beginning of the 18th century. In France, Louis XV followed, or tried to follow, the pace set by his magnificent predecessor. Fashions were introduced, had a moment of popularity, and gave way to something new again. In two years the fashion for hats changed about twenty times. One week there was a mania for Greek robes; the next week a rural peasant idea was adopted by everyone at Versailles. Great luxury prevailed. Then, in 1789 came the crash and "each step of the Revolution was followed by its own peculiar response in fashion which expressed the dominant idea of the particular part of the convulsion which it represented."

The young Englishman of the 18th century tried to emulate the French dandy, with little success. He succeeded only in making himself ludicrous, the butt of the wits and satirists. We quote from "The History of English Costume":

> Everywhere the beaux. He rides the world like a cockhorse or like Og the giant rode the Ark of Noah steering it with his feet, getting his washing for nothing and his meals passed up to him out of the chimney. Here the beaux, the everlasting beaux in gold lace, wide cuffs, full skirts, swinging cane, a scarf of flashing colour, the coats embroidered with flowers and butterflies, the cuffs a mass of fine sewing, the three cornered hats cocked at a jaunty angle, the stockings rolled above the knees, lacquer hilted swords, paste buckles, gold and silver snuffboxes flashing in the sun.

But the "beaux" passed and toward the end of the century a new dignity entered English dress. There were still fops, however, who carried muffs in winter, wore velvet bows and lace cravats, and were never without their snuffboxes. Toward the close of the century there stepped upon the stage of fashion the master dandy of all times, the man whose influence is most strongly felt in modern dress.

Beau Brummell.—Throughout the 18th and 19th centuries, there were many dandies who flourished for a moment and were forgotten, but Brummell remained the "sublime dandy" of all time.

He was born George Bryan Brummell. He is said to have been of low birth and with no wealth other than his astonishing personality. His manner gained him wide popularity, and at Eton and Oxford he won many influential friends. He entered society as a young man and was instantly accepted.

Brummell had a wonderful personality. He was witty and charming; there was a magnetism about him that few could resist. And he had the most amazing insolence one can imagine. Roger Boutet de Monvel has written an excellent work on "Beau Brummell and His Times." In it he relates that on one occasion Brummell ordered a duchess to leave the ball backward, because her back offended his

Portrait-drawing of Beau Brummell, master dandy of the early 19th Century. His influence is expressed in the present mode of dress for men.

tastes! At the theatre, when he wanted to speak to a lord or a lady he would simply beckon, and they would come to him instantly.

Unlike most of his contemporaries, Brummell had exquisite taste. He frequented the best clubs, the most exclusive homes, the most fashionable amusement places, and he became a connoisseur of good living. He decided to dress not as others did, but as he himself saw fit.

And so Brummell, in the limelight, began a new era in dress. He changed the prevailing fashions to suit himself, without fear of criticism. He wore his hair short and without powder. He avoided bright colours and appeared almost invariably in black or dark blue. He distinguished himself not by gay colours or elaborate jewels, but by the superb fit of his garments, the meticulous neatness of his attire.

Eventually Brummell, now known as Beau Brummell, the best-dressed man in London, selected one definite style of dress to which he adhered. He wore a dark blue or black coat, a buff-coloured waistcoat, and black, close-fitting trousers. With this costume he wore light pumps or lace boots, according to whether he was going to a ball or merely taking a walk. His manner was perfect, his bearing was delightful. Others emulated this distinguished-looking man, and soon it became the custom for men to wear inconspicuous but well-fitting clothes. The modern dress coat originated with Brummell, as well as the idea of a uniform type of dress for men.

With all his exquisite taste and perfect manner, Brummell was conceited. He devoted three and four hours to his toilet in the morning, sometimes deliberating for an hour before selecting his cravat. On one occasion a young man, fascinated by the brilliance of Brummell's boots, inquired the manner of keeping them so and begged the recipe for his own use. "Blacking, my dear sir?" said Brummell. "Well, you know, for blacking I never use anything but the froth of champagne!"

After a life of great influence and power, Brummell died in an insane asylum—in poverty and without friends. The story of his life is fascinating and well worth reading.

Colonial Costume.—What was happening in America all this while? Let us see how men were dressing here, what they were wearing, what fashions they were following.

The Southern colonists were in constant communication with England and followed closely the ideals, customs, and practices of the mother country. Their fashions came from England, as well as the materials with which to interpret those fashions. The early Southern colonists, therefore, were wearing practically the same type of dress as was being worn in England of the corresponding period.

The Northern colonists followed some of the fashions of England, but adopted also new ones of their own. The Dutch settlers made their influence felt in large flat collars, bright kerchiefs, and small caps. With the coming of a national consciousness, fashions changed and the new influence made itself definitely felt.

The presence of French officers inspired the colonists to emulate to some extent the fashions prevalent at the court of Versailles. By the time George Washington was being inaugurated as the first president of the United States, the dress of men and women was an interesting combination of French, English, and Colonial ideals.

> Great stress was laid on the cleanliness and attention which was paid to details of dress, by all foreign visitors, while the unheard of neatness of American women was the subject of much discussion abroad.

In 1784 John Adams was sent to London as the first ambassador from the United States to the court of St. James. Writing at this period his wife says:

> I am not a little surprised to find dress, unless on public occasions, so little regarded here. The gentlemen are very plainly dressed, the ladies much less so than us.

The 19th century ushered in many curious and ugly

fashions in women's dress, but the tendency to dress simply and in good taste, like the Londoners under the influence of Beau Brummell, prevailed among men. While women worried about "mutton-leg" sleeves, wasp waists, towering headdress, bustles, and the absurdities of the Victorian Era, men were learning to enjoy simpler and more dignified dress than any to which they had previously been accustomed. It is curious to note that while woman's dress became more elaborate, man's dress became simpler. While woman's dress became more cumbersome, more uncomfortable, man's dress became more comfortable and convenient than ever before.

We have studied man's dress in its development because it represents more clearly the periodic changes to which fashion has been subjected. Woman's dress changed with every season, sometimes several times within one season. While man's costume for a generation, or for the period of a king's life, represented some definite influence, woman's costume borrowed from the whims and fancies of other countries and changed incessantly. Therefore, the study of man's dress is of interest to the historian; the study of woman's dress is of interest to the costume designer, the fashion artist.

The more pronounced style notes in woman's dress during the most prolific periods of fashion development are shown in the Parade of the Dolls. (See pp. 540). These dolls, dressed in accurate reproductions of historic costume, have been photographed and permission to use them in this book has been given by the Metropolitan Museum of Art.

How Fashions Are Made.—During its development through the ages, dress has submitted to various external influences. Architecture, sculpture, the stage, climate, wars —all have left their mark on dress and on the creation of fashions.

Climate influenced fashion to a great extent during the formative periods. In ancient Egypt, for instance, dress was designed to be cool, simple, and comfortable. The wealthy women wore costly, veil-like draperies which were a protection against gnats and flies but had no warmth. Women slaves wore coarse cotton garments, and slave girls trained as dancers wore nothing at all.

In the South Sea Islands and other tropical regions natives went unclothed as nature intended. Missionaries, visiting these islands, forced clothes upon the natives, with disastrous results. Unaccustomed for ages to be without covering, these uncivilized people lost their resistance through dress and became subject to pneumonia and other fatal diseases. As O'Brien points out, the natives of the South Sea Islands are not the tall, straight, strong specimens of humanity the white men found when they visited the Islands for the first time, but weakened men and women striving to understand the standards of civilization which have been imposed upon them.

Civilization, accepting dress as the natural state and undress as the improper and unnatural state, devised special clothes for winter and special clothes for summer. This idea appears to have originated with late Neolithic man, who wore his bear skin when the weather was cold but made himself coverings of a flaxen cloth when the weather became warmer. In civilized life, wherever there is winter and summer there are also winter dress and summer dress.

But besides inspiring two types of dress, climatic conditions have originated many little peculiarities of style which we still retain. The V-shaped nick on the lapel of the coat, for instance, takes us back to the time when a collar was needed for protection against the bad weather, and the nick was made so that the collar could more easily be turned up around the neck. Modern tailors retain this nick and it is seen on all coats of the present day, although cut frequently in a manner that would quite prevent its earlier use.

Among the marauding nomads of the western Sahara, called by the Arabs the *Tawarek* (God Forsaken), every man wears a cloth across his face. It is never removed.

Originally these cloths were worn to protect the face from the driving sand and the glare of the desert. But so ingrained has become the habit or custom of wearing the "litham," as it is called, that a *Tawarek* will not show his face even to a member of his own family, regarding it the height of immodesty to do so. In this manner are fashions made.

The ancient Egyptians had the custom of wearing a band around the head, when travelling, to keep the hair in place. This custom created the fashion for wearing a band around the head, and to-day we retain the fashion but place the band on the outside of the hat instead of around the head. All men's hats have this band. The streamers around the crown of a child's hat is a remnant of an old Greek custom. To protect the head from the sun the Greeks wore a flat, broad-brimmed hat which had long streamers. When the sun was strong, the streamers were tied under the chin to hold the hat in place. When there was no sun and the hat was burdensome on the head, the streamers were loosened and the hat permitted to hang down the back, in the manner of our sunbonnet.

Of course, fashion is largely imitative. There are two distinct reasons for imitation in matters of dress. The first is a desire to be like everyone else, to avoid being thought strange or queer by one's fellows. The second is a desire to assert quality with the others, to show them that one is able to have the things they have. Then, too, imitation may be prompted by a reverence for the person or persons imitated.

The story is told of a Fijian chief who was on one occasion going over a mountain path followed by a long string of his people. He stumbled and fell. Instantly all his people fell down upon the ground, except one man at the end of the procession. The others set upon this man at once. Did he consider himself better than the chief? Had he no reverence for the great chief who led the procession?

A story, similar in idea, is told of Duke Philip of Burgundy who, in 1461, suffered a severe illness during which his hair was completely shorn. More than five hundred nobles of the time sacrificed their hair that the Duke might not feel conspicuous. What was a necessity with the Duke became a fashion among the nobles.

We are told that in 1775

> the queen [Marie Antoinette of France] adopted a chestnut brown colour for her gown. This colour pleased the king and it is written that every lady in court had on a dress of that colour the following day.

There has always been quick aping of the clothes and manners of favourites. Madame du Barry, the inimitable Ninon de Lenclos, Nell Gwynn, the orange girl of Drury Lane, Mme. de Montespan, the magnificent Pompadour—all the long list of historic beauties in whose boudoirs plots were hatched, in whose perfumed palms kingdoms rested—swayed for a moment the pendulum of fashion according to their own whims and tastes. And among the men there were fashion satellites, too—Louis XIV, Beau Brummell, Napoleon.

Beau Brummell appeared one morning, about a hundred years ago, in tight-fitting black trousers which a contemporary describes as "shocking." Yet instantly the London smart set adopted Brummell's fashion, and pretty soon everyone was wearing the tight-fitting black trousers. But knee breeches were not given up without a struggle. It is said that the Duke of Wellington was refused admission to a ball because he presented himself in these long, tight trousers introduced by the dandy of the age.

Many fashions were created by law. There is, for instance, a distinct order or edict concerning the shape of pocket handkerchiefs. It is dated June 2, 1785, and was issued by Louis XVI, supposedly at the request of Marie Antoinette. Up to her time, it would appear, handkerchiefs had been of all sizes and shapes. Some had been oblong, some round, some triangular, some square. The Queen believed that if the square form only were used the handkerchief would be very much more convenient. Consequently it was decreed that, "The length of handkerchiefs shall equal their width, throughout my entire kingdom." Handkerchiefs have remained square since that day, and what the edict in 1785 made the fashion then is still the fashion with us.

Parsons says:

> The Queen, Catherine de' Medici, was always partial to crimson, particularly to crimson velvet. This colour became so universally admired that a law was passed forbidding any woman not a princess to wear a gown wholly of crimson. No man might wear more than one article of dress of this colour. . . . The bourgeoisie rebelled at the magnificence of the court, and the lord gave them permission to wear gold bands on their heads with jewelled belts and necklaces of gold. They were apparently appeased, for a year later we find the lower classes clamouring to be allowed to wear the same, including lace and silk petticoats. This was refused them but they were instead given leave to edge their robes with lace and to participate otherwise in the orgy of "being fashionable."

In Puritan New England, in the 17th century, the size of one's fortune, and the amount contributed to the church, determined the material of which one's clothes might be made. Laws were passed concerning the kind and amount of lace permitted individuals in decoration. History abounds with rules and regulations concerning fashion, and it would be tiresome to mention even a small part of them.

There have been times when the court was the birthplace of fashion, and the bourgeoisie feverishly imitated every little whim and fancy. During the seventy-five years of Louis XIV's reign, for instance, all that was new and fashionable originated at Versailles, quickly seeped through the cities and became the fashion of the bourgeoisie. And the lower classes imitated, as far as they were able, these copied fashions of the bourgeoisie.

But there have been reversals, as during the era of Louis XV when, for novelty, the court adopted the rural peasant idea in dress. There was recently in America a wave of peasant idealism when every shop displayed gowns and blouses and even underthings of peasant inspiration.

We who have lived through the great World War know the influence of war and political upheavals upon fashion and dress. Every war of history has had some influence upon the dress of the masses. The war with which we are acquainted by virtue of having lived through it brought a tendency to wear simple, inconspicuous garments—*while the war was in progress;* but the moment armistice was declared there was a great reaction and the pendulum swung to the other extreme. For a period of two years extreme fashions were the vogue, only the brightest and most vivid colours were popular, and every week saw a new fad or fancy.

The French Revolution, and the period of the *Directoire* following close upon it, exerted a powerful influence upon fashion. Play-life in France suddenly ceased, and the cloud of the guillotine hung over the gay gardens and palaces where nobility idled in silks, satins, and velvets. The crash came—and the day belonged to the people. Laces and jewels were replaced by bloodstained cloths. Luxury in dress was changed to eloquent simplicity. The hair was cut short. Comfort and freedom was the keynote of dress rather than richness and decoration.

Writing of the period, Parsons says:

> To annihilate not only the old monarchic ideas and practices, but every vestige of its externalized forms, was the aim of this period, and in no other one is a clearer psychological response of materials to the power of ideas traceable than in that of the French Revolution. Fashion responded as readily and as completely to human desires and instincts as they expressed themselves in this period, as they had in any other, and strange and wonderful were some of the things she did.

The influences which have been moulding and shaping fashion through the ages are many and varied. A sudden wave of "daring," a brief reversal to classic dignity, a season of mediæval gaudiness and display, a year of great extremes and then again a year of great simplicity—definite external influences inspire such fashions. Sometimes it is the aftermath of a war; sometimes the influence of a pow-

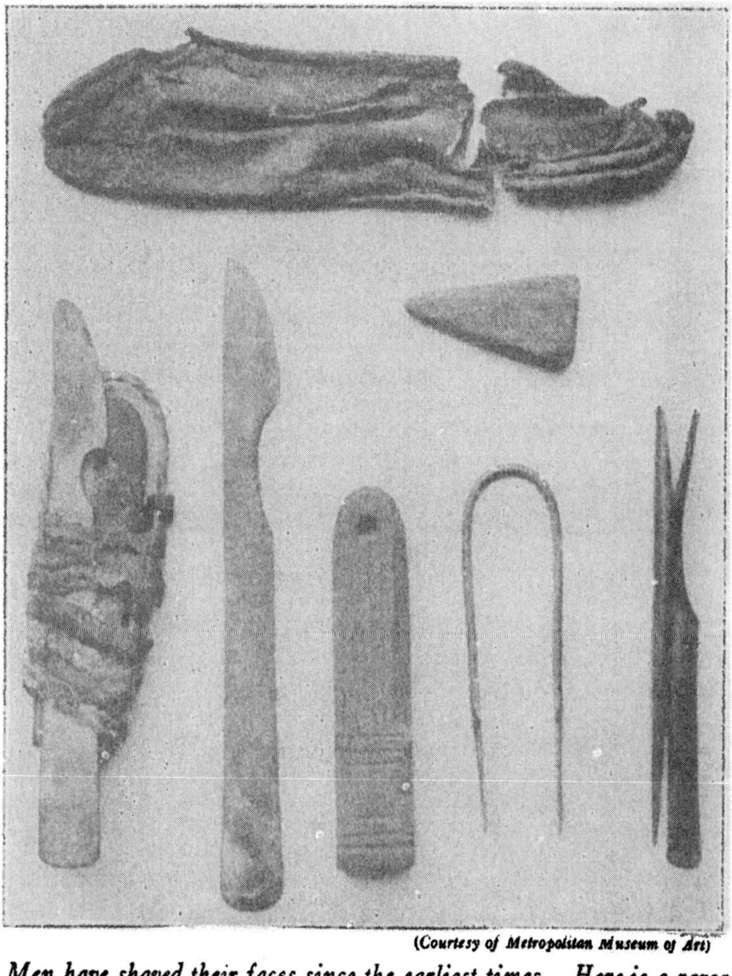

(Courtesy of Metropolitan Museum of Art)

Men have shaved their faces since the earliest times. Here is a razor set of the 18th Dynasty, Egypt.

(Courtesy of Metropolitan Museum of Art)

The gold signet ring of King Tut-ankh-amen, Egyptian, 18th Dynasty.

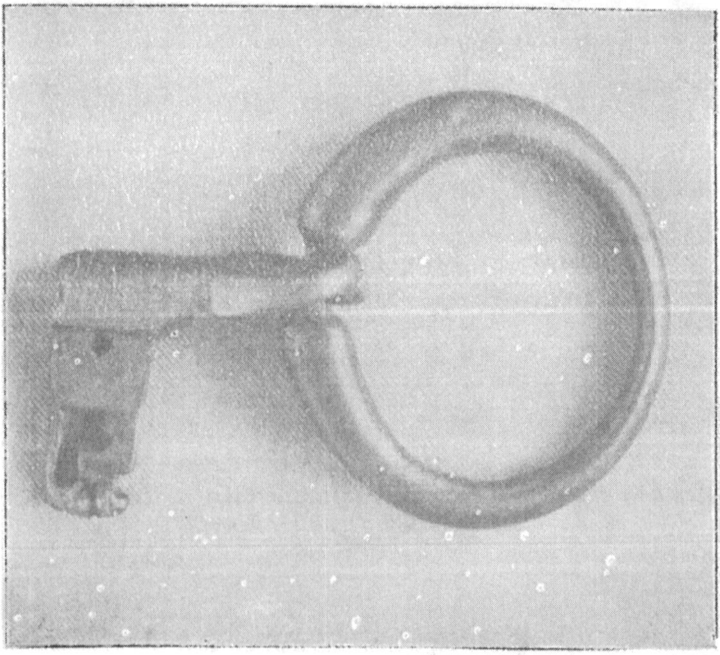

(Courtesy of Metropolitan Museum of Art)

Brass key on ring. Egypt, 5th Dynasty.

erful national character. Sometimes it is the plan of a crafty costumer, for purposes of commercial gain, sometimes the whim of a prima donna or the famous actress. The stage has always swayed the mode.

This story of the origin of a single fashion during the times of Louis XIV reveals the gay bubble that fashion is, permitting itself to be wafted here and there by every passing breath of fancy—a bright and beautiful bubble but short-lived like those that children blow from clay pipes:

> An amusing instance of the derivation of a single fashion is given in the description of a hunting party at which the king and one of his mistresses, the Duchesse de Fontanges, were present. A sudden gust of wind blew aside her elaborate headdress. She immediately tied it in place with her garters, allowing the ribbon ends to fall over her forehead. The king was delighted with this device and the court is said to have adopted the fashion immediately, as did the entire bourgeoisie, naming it "coiffure à la Fontanges." This fashion was taken up by the gentry in England also, and it persisted there for some time under its French name.[1]

Ancient and mediæval dress have a distinct influence upon modern fashions, as was clearly indicated during the recent excavations in Egypt. A West End court dressmaker is quoted as having remarked:

> Every well-dressed woman will be wearing evening gowns designed after the ancient Egyptian models. Lord Carnarvon's discoveries in Egypt have had a tremendous effect upon the styles which will be in vogue next season, and already we have been flooded with requests from society women for gowns designed on lines that found favour in the Egyptian court 1300 years before Christ.

Though the Egyptian excavations aroused world-wide interest, it is notable that the Egyptian influence in dress lasted but one brief season—flourished and died while the printers' ink was still damp with the news.

MATERIALS AND ACCESSORIES

The tale of textiles reads like a page from the "Arabian

[1] From "The Psychology of Dress," by Frank Alvah Parsons.

Nights." Even before man inhabited the earth, spiders wove intricate silken webs, patterning with infinite pains the filmy threads that unwound from the spools of their bodies. Birds interlaced grass and bits of twig into cozy little nests. Even some types of trees and plants grew inner fibres so closely interwoven that they formed a sort of natural cloth.

One of the most primitive of human arts is weaving. The museums exhibit beautiful examples of this primitive weaving—rushes and grass cleverly interlaced to form little mats. Some are decorated with leaf and flower designs. In ancient Egypt the papyrus plant furnished material for some of the shorter coverings, like the early loincloths of papyrus matting.

The first actual cloth made by man was derived from the bark of trees. The bark was soaked in water until soft and pulpy, then beaten with rough wooden mallets to felt the fibres together. This crude cloth was permitted to dry and bleach in the sun, and was then decorated with coloured designs produced through the use of vegetable dyes.

Flax was one of the first materials that man utilized for purposes of cloth-making. Neolithic man about 10,000 years ago was already making mats and cloths of flax, and was wearing flaxen coverings in addition to the skins which constituted his chief attire. The ancient Egyptians, however, were evidently the first fully to realize the value of flax as a source of linen.

"Purple and fine linen was the raiment of princes in biblical days," says the historian. And "Pharaoh arrayed Joseph in vestures of fine linen," says the Bible. (Genesis XLI, 41, 42.) Picture writing on the walls of tombs indicates that the industry of weaving linen from the fibres of the flax plant flourished 4000 or more years ago, and that the flax plant was used as the symbol of a favourite deity.

But the linen industry was not confined to Egypt for any very great length of time. It spread to Babylon, to

Greece, and to Rome. By the beginning of mediævalism the use of linen was prevalent throughout all of Europe.

Woollen fabrics are almost as old as those of linen. The Greeks of Homer's time produced woollen fabrics of great beauty and firmness. Woollen shawls were made in India long before the Christian Era. Cotton is also of great antiquity, having been known to the ancient Egyptians and Greeks. But of all materials used by early man in clothes-making there is probably none with so romantic and interesting a background as silk.

Tradition says that silk was discovered 4500 years ago in China by the Empress Si-Ling-Shi. It is related that the Empress watched the caterpillars as they drew their shining threads across a leaf or bit of twig. She cultivated the silkworms, collected the silk and made from it a gorgeous, shimmering material which amazed and delighted everyone who saw it.

Then began the culture of silkworms in China and the manufacture of silken fabrics. For 2000 years China is said to have manufactured silk, selling to Japan, India, Persia, and keeping the secret faithfully hidden.

About 330 B.C. the great Alexander swept through Asia into India. When he returned to the Mediterranean lands he brought back with him the first raw silk Europe had ever seen. And Europe was fascinated. Where did it come from? How was it made?

But it was not until the 4th century after the Christian Era that the secret of the silkworm was finally disclosed. Four Chinese girls, kidnapped from a silk-weaving village, carried the secret to Japan, and from Japan the industry spread slowly to France, to England. In France the industry began to flourish in the 13th century, but in England all attempts to breed silkworms have failed. Attempts have failed in the United States also, so that China and Japan are still the centres of silk manufacture.

We have seen that weaving was one of the oldest of human arts. Egypt carried this art to a singularly high level, and developed also the art of spinning. No one knows how thread was first invented. Possibly wool torn from sheep while passing through the bushes or brambles suggested the idea to the alert mind of man. Historians tell us that early nomadic tribes used threads to fasten together the skins or other garments they wore.

As early as 2000 B.C. the Egyptians were winding thread on sticks and spinning fabrics by hand. This original stick later became the spindle.

> Women soon found that if a piece of wood was attached to the lower end of the stick, or spindle, it could be whirled around at a much greater speed. This weight at the end of the spindle came to be known as the whorl. And as a subsequent development, the need of something to fasten the wool to so that it would not become ravelled brought the distaff. At first, it was simply a piece of twig or wood around which the wool was wrapped. It was held in the hand or tucked in the belt, as most convenient.

Spinning by hand was a tedious and slow process, but the Egyptians made fabrics of extraordinary fineness. Some of the linen mummy cloths brought from the heart of Egyptian tombs are extremely fine of thread and even of weave. It was not until the beginning of the 16th century that a one-thread machine was invented to replace the old hand method perfected by the ancient Egyptians.

Arthur Weigall, present at the excavation and opening of the tomb of King Tutankhamen, says:

> Among the clothes found in the tomb was a garment belonging to a king. It is of white linen, covered with 3700 sequins. It is a soft flowing robe, much like a nightgown. . . . One of the Queen's gowns is of deep blue, trimmed with blue fringe. It is made in cloak fashion, very loose. We also found sandals. These are like the strap pumps worn by women of to-day.

The Art of Dyeing.—One of the most primitive forms of dyeing fabrics or woven mats was to place a leaf or flower on the material which has been covered with the dye extract from vegetables, and place the whole in the sun. The sun transferred the outline of the leaf or flower to the material, and then a small rounded twig was used to press in the design more firmly and fix it in place.

Various methods of dyeing existed in remote times among the Persians, and in India and China. The Arabs also had a method of dyeing fabrics, and the ancient Egyptians used rich dyes.

The Phœnicians carried the art to a high degree of perfection. They dyed fabrics with the juice of the *Murex trunculus* and *Buccinum lapillus* (shellfish) and produced various tints through different methods of manipulating the dye. Metallic and vegetable agents were also employed, but the use of the shellfish predominated.

To-day the dyeing of fabrics is a highly developed industry and one of the most fascinating phases of textile study.

Pins and Needles.—The origin of the needle is lost in antiquity. Embroidery, apparently achieved with needle and thread, has been found on ancient Egyptian garments, and we know that embroidery was known to the Greeks and Romans. Iron needles have been found in Egypt and in Rome. (A pair of Egyptian needles are illustrated.) Nevertheless, it was not until the 16th century that the manufacture of pins and needles was introduced in England.

Though bronze pins were known to Neolithic man, and pins of bone were used by savage races, women used wooden skewers to keep their clothes together until the end of the 15th century. It was then that the manufacture of pins began, and during the 16th century the most appropriate New Year's gift was a collection of these pins. Sometimes the money equivalent was given, from whence comes our term "pin money."

The safety pin, or its ancestor, appears to have been originated in central Europe about the close of the Bronze Age (1000 B.C.). A pin has been found which is of bronze, very slender, and bent in such manner that its point is caught against the head. Various modifications of this type of pin are found, some highly decorative, among the people of early Europe. It seems that the pin was used for ornamentation, like our brooch, rather than to serve any useful purpose. It is surprising, since early man actually had pins of various kinds, that he did not use them for fastening clothes, that they did not come into general use until the 16th century.

Besides pins and needles, the Romans were well equipped with crude scissors and with thimbles. The word thimble is from "thumb bell," as the small, bell-like contrivance was originally worn on the thumb. The use of the thimble did not become general until 1675 when John Softing introduced it into England from Holland.

For keeping articles of dress, ornaments, etc., drawers and boxes were used resembling old-fashioned trunks. They were attractive, ornate—like the treasure chests of fiction. Most of them were fitted with bolts and locks. Small rings have been discovered fastened to miniature keys which would have been too small for a door, and were undoubtedly made for clothes or treasure boxes (see illustration).

Queen Elizabeth, who had 3000 separate dresses, found chests wholly inadequate for her wardrobe. Nor were cupboards or closets convenient, since the frocks and gowns were of gaudy crinolines. Therefore a special room was set aside for the Queen's gowns, and each one was hung on a separate wooden peg. This clothes room with its wooden pegs developed into the modern clothes closet with its separate hangers.

Some Popular Accessories.—The walking stick, or cane, has a history that reaches back to biblical times. The Hebrews carried long, crutched sticks like those of the shepherds who tended the flocks.

The young Athenian dandies also carried walking sticks while Greece was still an infant civilization. Some were tall like those of the Hebrews; some were short like the modern riding-crop.

In Europe the walking stick probably took the place of the sword when it began to disappear after the age of chivalry. Apparently, however, its use did not become general until the time of Queen Elizabeth, when everyone carried a cane or stick to be fashionable. The celebrated portrait of Charles I shows the King with his left arm akimbo, with his right hand resting on a long walking stick.

Under Louis XIV the custom of the walking stick was introduced to the French court. It became fashionable for men and women alike to carry the long, slender sticks. The women's walking sticks were invariably decorated with love knots.

Gloves are very old and were invented for purposes of protection. We find them particularly prevalent among early peoples in cold regions.

The ancient Persians and Romans wore gloves. In Homer Laërtes is described as wearing gloves while walking in his garden. (Odyssey, XXIV, 230.) Gloves of leather were worn at a very early period in war and in the chase to protect the hands. In the 8th and 9th centuries the custom of wearing gloves was almost universal in Germany and in Scandinavian countries.

From the 10th to the 13th century gloves showed a remarkable development. Gauntlets of leather were worn by men; those in military costume wore gloves the backs of which were covered by overlapping plates. During the 13th century women began to wear gloves for purposes of ornament, most of them being made of linen and reaching to the elbow. In the 16th century Queen Elizabeth set the fashion for wearing jewelled and embroidered gloves. In France, under Louis XIV, gloves of kid made their appearance. The women wore gloves of netted silk.

The cravat was originally a scarf. The word is from the French *cravate,* a corruption of *Croat.* This was the name given by the French of Louis XIV's time to the scarfs worn by the Croatian soldiers in the royal regiment. The scarfs were usually of linen or muslin, with broad edges of lace. They became fashionable throughout France and travelled to England where they were known as *cravates*. When various forms of neckwear for men were introduced, the name for the scarf was applied to them, and it has survived in our word cravat.

The first handkerchief was a jackal's tail mounted on a stick. These "handkerchiefs" were used by the Bushmen in primitive times and served the double purpose of handkerchief and fan. Other savage races wove little mats of rush to wear on their heads, and used them also to mop away the perspiration from their foreheads,—a crude ancestor of the handkerchief.

The Greeks and Romans had both napkins and handkerchiefs. The napkins were used to dry the hands at the table; the handkerchiefs were small squares of linen which were sometimes tucked beneath the girdle when the Greek started on a trip.

The development of the handkerchief was rapid and in France particularly it reached an elegance scarcely conceivable. In the 17th century the handkerchief was made of exquisite hand-wrought laces, sometimes even ornamented with gems. In the 18th century when the taking of snuff became an established custom, women began to use coloured handkerchiefs. Louis XVI, inspired by Marie Antoinette, issued an edict during this century causing handkerchiefs to be made square rather than oval, round, or oblong, as individual taste saw fit.

Fans have an interesting history. The first fan was probably a palm leaf or some other natural device appropriated by man to keep away flies and gnats, perhaps even to cool the fevered brow in tropical climates. We know that in Egypt, 2000 years ago, fashionable hosts had special servants to stand behind dinner guests and fan them with huge papyrus fans.

Both men and women carry fans in China. Many carry with them also a pair of chopsticks tucked into the girdle. In Japan the woman does not consider herself well dressed unless her fan harmonizes with the rest of her costume.

PARADE OF THE DOLLS

(Courtesy of Metropolitan Museum of Art)

French, 1430. Period of Charles VII.

Italian. End of 14th Century.

(Courtesy of Metropolitan Museum of Art)

Burgundian, 1480. Period of Maximilian I.

French. Early 15th Century. Period of Charles VI.

(Courtesy of Metropolitan Museum of Art)

Italian, Venetian, 1560.

German, Early 16th Century. Period of Maximilian I.

(Courtesy of Metropolitan Museum of Art)

English, 1536. Period of Henry VIII.

Burgundian, 16th Century.

French, 1690. Period of Louis XIV.

(Courtesy of Metropolitan Museum of Art)

French, 1646. Period of Louis XIV.

French, 1605. Period of Henry IV.

(Courtesy of Metropolitan Museum of Art.)

English, 1649.

(Courtesy of Metropolitan Museum of Art)

1740. Period of Louis XV

1775. Period of Louis XVI.

(Courtesy of Metropolitan Museum of Art)

1795.

1780. Period of Louis XVI.

(Courtesy of Metropolitan Museum of Art)

Italian Venetian costumes of the 18th Century.

(Courtesy of Metropolitan Museum of Art)

Italian Venetian costumes of the 18th Century.

(Courtesy of Metropolitan Museum of Art)

American, about 1860.

English, 1858. Mid-Victorian.

(Courtesy of Metropolitan Museum of Art)

French. Period of Louis XVIII

American, 1874.

In France the fan reached the height of its development under Louis XIV. We read that

> Fans are an invariable accompaniment of feminine costume, and they are of rare beauty, exquisitely painted and mounted on sticks of carved or painted wood, mother-of-pearl, carved ivory, or gold. There are over five hundred makers of fans in Paris, and they enjoy special privileges accorded by the King.

The fan is still a popular accessory and we find it the "accomplishment of feminine costume" in the ballroom. Ostrich fans, to match or harmonize with the costume, are fashionable to-day as they have been for a century.

The first mirror was a quiet pool in which one caught a fleeting reflection. But the early Greeks had mirrors which were made of circular pieces of polished bronze, sometimes with richly adorned handles, sometimes without. The early Egyptians also had bronze mirrors, highly polished dishes, usually with graceful and decorative handles.

It was not until 1688, however, that glass mirrors were invented. A Frenchman, Louis Lucas, in the year mentioned, invented plate glass which, backed with the proper alloy, formed a mirror that for the first time gave woman a true reflection of her appearance, of herself.

The veil, like the glove and the walking stick, belongs to antiquity. In ancient Greece veils were worn to distinguish the different ranks, to indicate the free women from the slaves. The Bible makes definite mention of veils, as for instance:

> And the servant said, This is my master; therefore she took a veil and covered herself. (Genesis, XXIV, 65.)

As we have seen in an earlier chapter, veils have been used in marriage ceremonies from earliest times, and by various widely separated peoples. Among the Turkish people a law forbids unmarried girls to unveil before any men, and married women may unveil only before their husbands and relatives. A Turk, therefore, does not see his bride until he has married her, and he knows nothing of her beauty save from the reports smuggled to him by women who have seen her.

An amusing tale is related of a man who, as is the custom,

> Not having seen his wife until after his marriage and finding her far from handsome, was wholly disappointed in her. Two days after the nuptials, when she desired him to name the persons who were to have the privilege of *Namaharem* (the privilege of entering the harem, generally accorded to father, uncle, and brothers of the married woman) he said, "I give you my free permission to show yourself to all the men in the world except myself!"

Mohammedan women and Arabian women also veil themselves. But there is one tribe, the Tuaregs, nomads of the Desert, among whom the men veil and not the women. At the age of thirteen the Tuareg boy is veiled, and he does not show his face to anyone throughout life. The veil is not even removed for meals, but the food is brought up under it.

Women adopted the veil as a fashion to enhance their beauty during early mediævalism. We read that women—girls, young ladies, married women, widows, matrons—wear veils of linen and silk, shot with a gold thread, in which they appear ten times better-looking. In England all women wore the wimple and the veil because it was regarded as modest and fashionable to do so. Toward the close of mediævalism women in France and in England wore long veils which sometimes reached the ground.

To-day the veil is an important accessory to the fashionable costume and is worn without thought of modesty or custom, but for the sole purpose of improving the appearance.

Hats were intended originally as a protection from the sun, the cold. Later they became largely ornamental and decorative. The Egyptians wore simply a band around the hair. The ancient Greeks protected their heads with a flat, broad-brimmed hat which tied under the chin. Throughout the ages of dress development, hats for men and women assumed many striking and curious forms—

sometimes mere caps, sometimes great horned headdresses, sometimes hoods. During the Louis XIV age of elegance, hats were jewelled and plumed.

Until a short time ago hats were made in only a few popular sizes, but were fitted inside with a lining on a drawstring so that they could be tightened or loosened to fit the head. The little bow inside a man's hat is a relic of the old drawstring.

The Corset.—The story is told of a young woman who tried to engage Tennyson in a conversation. She could elicit only an occasional "humph" from him, until in embarrassment she began to fidget.

"You are like all the rest of them!" the great man then exclaimed. "You are laced too tightly. I can hear your stays creak."

Mortified and humiliated the young woman withdrew. A little later in the afternoon Tennyson came behind her, placed his hand on her shoulder, and said kindly:

"I was wrong, young lady. It wasn't your stays I heard creaking, but my braces; they are hitched up too tightly."

Long before Tennyson's day men and women both wore corset-like contrivances to make the waist appear slender and shapely. There are in existence Cretan frescoes 3500 years old, which show women in low-necked bodices and with wasp-like waists. Men and women on this fresco appear to be wearing something in the nature of a corset. Joseph McCabe tells how a Frenchman, examining these frescoes, was so amazed he exclaimed that they weren't Cretans at all but Parisians.

The North American Indians had a form of belt which was worn during the hunt. It was usually made of buffalo hide and had various methods of fastening. The purpose was not to keep the waist slender but to protect the stomach from the hoofs of animals.

As early as the 10th century corsets were being worn pretty generally by women everywhere. They were long and tight, mercilessly compressing the waist. Throughout the Middle Ages these "stays" remained, varying with each new generation but becoming always more and more torturous. The tightly laced bodice also made its appearance, and the familiar stomacher. In the 16th century the stomachers were peaked and jewelled.

During the Elizabethan era fashion ran to remarkable extremes. Fashionable men were never uncorseted and women wore corset covers of steel. In 1628 Harvey made the discovery of the circulation of the blood, and his theory seems to have aroused considerable discussion concerning the corset. People began to think that the corset stopped the natural circulation of the blood, and therefore was the cause of all the little pains and aches and ills they had been suffering. It is notable that from this period the corset became gradually simpler and less hampering, although there have been several periods of reversal when it became more of a nuisance than ever, as, for instance, during the Victorian Era.

The corset has survived, but it is to-day modelled on lines that follow the lines of the figure. It is pliant, comfortable, with elastic and silk where whalebone was yesterday.

Shoes and Stockings.—In rocky districts it was necessary to give attention to the feet. The first sandals or coverings to protect the feet were mats of woven grass, strips of hide, flat pieces of wood. These were fastened to the bottom or soles of the feet with thongs that were sometimes brought between the toes and bound around the ankles. This was the original sandal. In colder regions more material was added to protect the foot, and the sandal became the shoe.

The man of rank, in early Egypt, was followed by a servant who carried a pair of sandals—evidently in case of need. These sandals, which later became general in use, were simply pads of leather or papyrus bound to the foot by two straps, one passing over the instep and the other between the toes. Sometimes the front of the sandal was turned up to protect the toes.

The Egyptians were among the first to make shoes. Their warriors wore a sort of elaborated sandal, turned up around the foot and bound around the legs with thongs—the first type of crude shoe. They were being worn 4000 years ago.

The Greeks and Romans had decorative sandals, some of the Roman varieties approaching the shoe. For every-day purposes the Romans wore a light sandal, but when in full dress (toga) the *calceus* was worn—a shoe with slits at the side and straps knotted in front. The *calceus* had various forms by which the different classes were distinguished.

In Greece sandals were worn, but for hunting the men wore high boots that laced in the front. At first they wore only sandals which were fastened to the feet with straps around the ankle. These straps gradually developed into solid leather, attached to the sandal base. So was the boot originated.

Roman and Greek sandals are apparently as popular to-day as they were in ancient times. A recent advertisement featured sandal pumps of the type worn by the ancients, advising that "Roman and Grecian sandals are as popular as ever. These always give a line of grace to the foot and when developed in beautiful brocades are especially welcome."

In the cold regions some of the first shoes were bags padded with grass and tied around the feet. These clumsy foot coverings gradually developed into the moccasins and soft skin boots of the Indian and the Eskimo. Among the Eskimo it is regarded as the height of immodesty for a woman to show her feet, as it is also among the Chinese.

There has been much speculation as to the origin of bandaging the feet of female infants in China. An old tradition is that a Chinese Empress, noted for her vice, had a congenital club foot. Unwilling to have different feet from the women of the empire, and desiring to conceal her own deformity, she decreed that every female infant have her feet bound immediately upon birth. Thus the custom of compressing the feet arose. But this is only tradition and has by no means been authenticated.

Many theories have been advanced concerning the nature and purpose of this custom. Havelock Ellis says that the foot was at one time "the focus of sexual attraction" and that the foot binding found among Southern Chinese is a relic of foot-fetishism. He points out that the husband would much prefer seeing his wife's compressed feet than her face—evidently because the foot to the Chinese is a sex symbol. This would account to some extent for the modesty of the young Chinese woman in concealing her feet.

It has also been suggested that the practice of foot compression had its origin in the wish to keep women indoors. This hardly seems true, for the compression of the feet does not render the woman unable to walk, nor are women secluded to any great extent in China. Another theory is that foot compression distinguished the lady from the menial, that the feet of wealthy infants were compressed and deformed to indicate publicly that they were helpless and dependent upon the bounty of their elders.

But whatever the origin and meaning of foot compression, it is interesting to note that the old custom is passing. Societies are being formed in China for the sole purpose of preventing the binding of women's feet.

To return to the evolution of the shoe, modern footwear had its beginning about the time that the Crusades started. The Crusaders and those who took long pilgrimages needed protection for their feet, and durable shoes began to make their appearance. In Holland the peasantry were wearing shoes cut from solid blocks of wood. Leather shoes and sandals of great beauty made their appearance in Italy, in France, in England.

When James I came to the throne of England,

High heels and immense roses distinguish the shoes of the day, and the high boots with turned-back tops win increased favour. Sharing the general tendency to softness, these are made of leather so limp that the weight of the wide top presses them down in creases above the broad strap which crosses the instep, while the width of the flaring top makes it not a little difficult for the wearer to walk, thereby adding, no doubt, to the famous cavalier swagger.

Long-toed shoes enjoyed a vogue before the appearance of the high heel. The shoes were extremely narrow, with toes five and six inches long, terminating usually in a point. The higher the rank, the longer the toes. The sacrifice of the long toes, because of their discomfort, brought about the popularity of the high heel. Fashion must be served!

Shoemaking as an industry was introduced into America in 1629. Thomas Beard arrived under contract to make shoes for the pilgrim colony. It was not until 1785 that right and left lasts were introduced in England; until then all shoes were made on one last. The use of machinery in shoemaking was introduced in the early half of the 19th century.

The first leg coverings or stockings were of leather. When they were originated is not definitely known, although it is fairly certain that man did not begin to cover his legs as a general practice until after the Christmas Era. The French were the first to attempt to make a stocking of any kind, and in the 7th century their men were wearing leather encasings, solely for purposes of protection and warmth.

But the decorative idea quickly entered the stocking, as it entered all other wearing apparel. From the 7th to the 13th century fabric stockings were worn, some of them of velvet decorated with gold embroidery, some of them pieces of cloth, silk or velvet sewn together. An authority tells us that during the 12th century "nobles wore stockings with sandals of purple trimmed with gold, and they bandaged their legs."

Chaucer makes frequent allusion to hose. From him we learn that in England in the 13th century long cloth or velvet hose were worn by the fashionable, and that blue and white and red and white were the favourite colour combinations. He assures us that ladies wore "straite y-teyed stockings." Those who could not afford velvet were satisfied with blanket cloth.

Knitted worsted stockings were first made about 1565 in London by an apprentice named William Ryder. It was about this time that Queen Elizabeth received as a gift a pair of silk knitted hose which so delighted her that henceforth she wore stockings made only of the finest silk. These silk stockings were made in Italy and were very rare and costly in the beginning—"worth only a king's acceptance." But by the close of the 17th century every dandy and coquette had a supply of the shimmering hose—although it was not until twenty-five years ago that real silk hose came into general and common use.

Concerning the Hair.—As far back as we have record men and women have dressed and decorated their hair. Women have had combs from earliest times. The Iroquois Indians made combs from the antlers of deer. Primitive races made combs of bone, wood, even bronze.

Savage races have always given a great deal of attention and care to their hair. The Fijians, for instance, arrange their hair in a huge knot or mop, sometimes three feet in circumference, and dye it black, white, or red. The natives of the Belgian Congo in Africa use the oil from the castor bean for dressing the hair. Many African tribes have the custom of plastering the hair with mud.

Originally the Chinese permitted the hair to grow and wore it in a knot at the top of the head. But when the country was conquered by the Manchu, they were compelled to adopt the queue or pigtail. This was intended as a mark of bondage, but eventually it became a popular fashion and the pigtails were frequently lengthened by use of silk thread.

The ancient Greek women used long hairpins ornamented with sculpture. On festive occasions they adorned

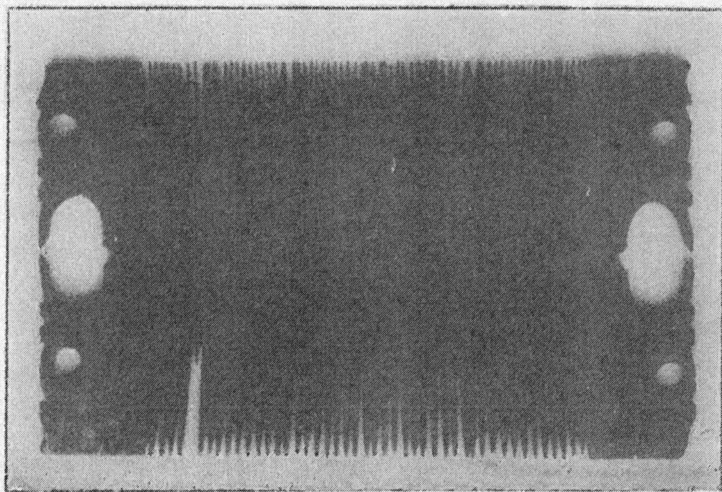

(Courtesy of Metropolitan Museum of Art)

An ebony comb used by an Egyptian lady thousands of years ago.

(Courtesy of Metropolitan Museum of Art)

A comb found at Lisht, North Pyramid, Egypt, 20th Dynasty.

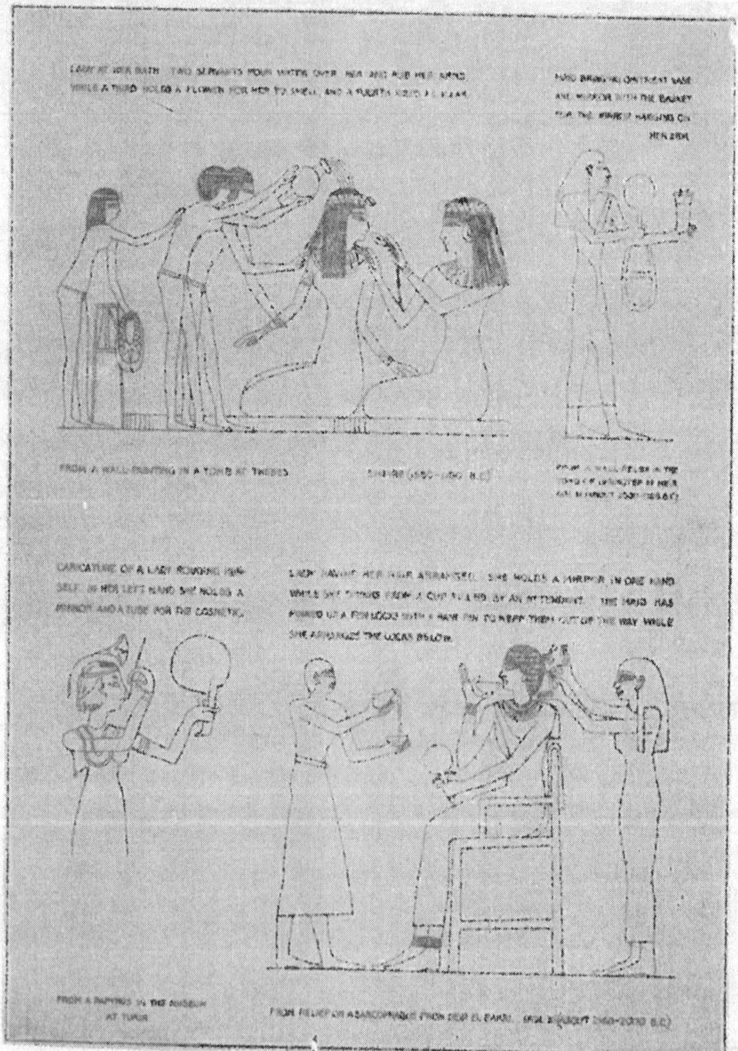

(*Courtesy of Metropolitan Museum of Art*)

Ladies at their toilets.

their hair with garlands and wreaths of flowers. They used also ribbon decorations which later developed into the net and the kerchief.

Methods of arranging the hair in primitive times were so varied, and changed so constantly, that it would be tiresome to discuss them all. Apparently curled hair was considered more attractive than straight, even in ancient times, for in archaic figures we frequently see the hair arranged over the brow and temples in parallel rows of small curls which must have been made and kept in place by artificial means. Men and women alike curled their hair, and men also curled their beards.

Poppea Sabina, Empress of Rome (A.D. 65), Queen of half the world and enslaver of the boy king Nero, is pictured sometimes with her hair hanging straight, sometimes with her head a mass of tiny flat ringlets. Pomades and unguents were used to keep the curls in place, and sometimes they were plastered in position with a sort of mud.

With the coming of civilization methods of arranging and dressing the hair varied more than ever. No two people had the same type of headdress. In some places we find the hair brushed straight back from the forehead and allowed to hang loosely in back. Elsewhere at the same period we find the hair brushed high on the head and falling loosely around the temples. Sometimes the hair is straight; sometimes curled. Sometimes it is decorated with ribbons, pins, and ornaments; sometimes it is devoid of all ornament save a band or cap to keep it in place.

Our custom of short hair for men, long hair for women, is comparatively modern. Until mediævalism had been left well behind, men wore their hair long and flowing and devoted to it as much care and attention as the women. Writing of the nobles of the 12th century, one authority says:

> Under the cap of velvet on their heads their hair, curled with crisping irons, hung, bound with ribbons, yet they wore beards and moustaches.

During the 13th and 14th centuries men wore their hair long and were particularly proud of their decorated beards. The Renaissance brought many interesting changes and we read that in Venice

> the hair was for the most part false, bought from the country folks. It was combed in various ways, curled, plaited, dressed like a crescent moon with its horns turned up, or twisted into the form of a pyramid. In the middle of the 16th century a towering toupe came into vogue. Great pains were taken to achieve the blonde type and all sorts of hair bleaches were invented for that purpose.

Curling irons, henna for dyeing and silk floss wigs were popular throughout Europe during the period of the Renaissance. A fad widely prevalent in Italy in the 15th century was to "bask in the rays of the moon to thread the hair with beauty." Fashionable young ladies slept during the day that they might wander through their gardens at night, while their lovers told them how pretty the moon made their hair. Modernism, for purposes of its own, has attributed these hair-beautifying powers to the sun.

It was during the Renaissance also that "the King (Henry VIII of England) condemned all men to wear short hair, but gave them permission to make their beards as fierce as they chose, and to curl their moustaches in which, it is written, they took great solace." We have already seen how, in 1461, the Duke Philip of Burgundy caused 500 nobles to sacrifice their hair because he lost his through illness (see p. 530).

But with James I on the throne of England (1603) man again "aspires to length of locks and one sees them grow, deftly aided no doubt by the wig-maker, through the Dutch cut of James I to the rippling curls of the cavaliers, to mark their distinction, in the later Puritan period, from the more closely shorn 'Roundheads.'"

With the accession of Charles I to the throne we become familiar for the first time with the Vandyke beard. In France Louis XIV, with forty wigmakers permanently busy in his employ, is establishing the fashion of long dyed wigs beautifully curled. In Venice "beards are large, waxed and ugly" and the Venetian nun, Arcangela Tarabotti, hotly rebukes those who "curl their beards and moustaches with curling tongs and paste them shiny with citron." But another writer of the period comes to the rescue of his sex and declares that "a man without a beard is hardly worthy of the name of man, his beard being the greatest proof of his manhood.

Nevertheless, in 1657, a man called Foscari was denounced as an ancient and a boor because he persisted in wearing a beard and cutting his hair. People divided themselves into factions: those who believed the hair should be cut and the beard permitted to grow; and those who believed the beard should be cut and the hair permitted to grow. For a while, toward the end of the century, custom and fashion favoured the clean-shaven face; but the fashion did not become a permanent one, for men still preserve for themselves the privilege of wearing the beard when it pleases their fancy to do so.

Toward the beginning of the 18th century, the tendency to wear short hair became evident among men. However, it did not manifest itself strongly, and we find the mode changing constantly. Sometimes the hair is worn short, sometimes long. Those whose hair is short wear wigs when the fashion decrees long locks. Not until the 19th century did the custom of short hair for men become definitely established. And even now, England, faithful to the old custom, insists upon wigs being worn in the law courts.

Through the centuries women wore their hair long because they were always taught to believe that the hair is the "crowning glory" of their appearance. It is interesting to note, however, the tendency of bobbing to remain among American women. Bobbing the hair was a fad at the court of Louis XIV and the "Dutch cut," a form of bob, was popular at the court of James I. But the bob of to-day, which originated during the war, is by no means a fad. It has become a custom. Women may have cut the hair originally because it was the fashion to do so, because it improved the appearance. But bobbing has become a custom because women find it comfortable and convenient and are loath to return to the old-time methods of pins and combs and elaborate coifs.

The theory has been advanced that the bob which originated during the war, when women stepped into men's places and did their work while they were at the front, is a symbol of freedom. We read in a scientific journal that

> The style of hair has played a conspicuous rôle throughout the ages in distinguishing slave from freeman. The Manchu conquerors imposed the queue upon the Chinese as a mark of their subjection. . . . The shaved head of the convict is the symbol of penal captivity. The tonsure of the priest is the symbol of his special (if voluntary) subjection to the Church.

Perhaps bobbing the hair *is* a reaction from the long ages of enforced adherence to the fashion of long hair. Perhaps woman is expressing freedom by extending to herself the privilege which man created for his own comfort and convenience—the privilege of cutting the hair. It is significant that men, as a whole, are opposed to the bob. They declare, as the Bible did more than 2000 years ago, that "If a woman have long hair, it is a glory to her." Is woman, in defiance, attempting to prove that short hair can be a glory too?

Or will the bob, riding on the wave of feminism, prove but another whim to be swallowed eventually in the vast ocean of changing fashion?

THE CAREER OF COSMETICS

The paint pot and the lipstick belong to another age than ours. We are the lucky heirs who have inherited beauty methods of 4000 years or more in the making.

> Beauty is no quality in things themselves [says Hume]. It exists

merely in the mind which contemplates them; and each mind perceives a different beauty.

The savage lady in the heart of Africa cuts her skin with sharp shells and rubs black paint into the wounds. The wounds heal in glorious purple scars which mark the woman a great beauty, according to African standards. The Eskimo lady rubs her skin with grease and fat—a complexion secret handed down from mother to daughter. Every Guiana lady knows that she must be fat to be attractive; and the lady who lives in the northern parts of the Chinese empire knows that she is hopelessly plain if her ears are not enormous.

Standards of beauty are as varied as the flowers of nature. But among civilized peoples there are certain definite standards of beauty universally acknowledged. The ancient Egyptians appear to have judged beauty according to these standards, and they had methods for coaxing and camouflaging nature to give the desired effect. These methods are singularly like our own.

The Egyptians, for instance, believed that lustrous, healthy hair was a great beauty. They approved of well-shaped lips and well-defined brows and lashes. They regarded a good complexion as absolutely indispensable to beauty, and they admired a slim, graceful figure even as we do.

On the occasion of the opening of Tutankhamen's tomb recently, the New York newspapers carried lengthy reports on the daily life of the Egyptians 4000 years ago. From the most authoritative of these reports we quote:

> It was the custom of the Egyptian lady to make generous use of cosmetics, and her beautifully carved and ivory inlaid dressing table was always well supplied with appurtenances to beauty which have not changed much even to the present day. She had silver and bronze highly polished into hand mirrors, and alabaster pots filled with black and green eyebrow paint. And she carried abroad a rouge with which she generously dabbed her cheeks as soon as the bustling feet on the city streets had raised sufficient dust to take away the first bloom of her morning beautifying art.

The eyebrow pencil and the lipstick were quite familiar to the Egyptian lady. She painted her lips, her cheeks, her eyelids; she shaped her brows and tipped her lashes with a black pomade to make them look longer. We use the word "paint" advisedly, for even in pre-dynastic times the Egyptian ladies had alabaster palettes on which they mixed to a just-right hue the slate and paints with which they beautified themselves.

The Egyptians were extremely fond of perfumes. We read that

> Exquisites of the day had as many as fifteen different kinds of perfume scattering their odours from their false wigs, while it was customary for the women to conceal little glass globules containing their favourite perfume within the tightly plaited tresses.

Costly perfumes were kept in alabaster jars and bottles. Perfume bottles, taken from the heart of old tombs, still have a lingering suggestion of the perfumes they once contained.

The use of perfumes is very ancient and is found among widely separated peoples. The Hottentot woman, for instance, has since the earliest times rubbed her body with butter, soot, and buchu leaves. Ancient writers identify Cleopatra with "the utmost luxury in the use of perfumery and flowers." Hawaiian women, and indeed almost all women of the South Sea Islands, decorate themselves with wreaths and garlands of fragrant flowers. Lucullus (Rome, 75 B.C.) always had fountains of perfumed water at his famous feasts.

In biblical times perfumed oils and ointments were used for purposes of enhancing bodily attractiveness. O. A. Wall says:

> The Bible contains many references to perfume as of sexual importance, as when Ruth anointed herself to be attractive to Boaz; or when the bride in Solomon's Song says of her lover, "Who is it that cometh, perfumed with myrrh, frankincense and all the powders of the merchants?" When Judith prepared herself to captivate Holofernes, "She washed herself all over with water, and anointed herself with precious ointment."

Many of the ancients were fond of fragrant perfumes and ointments. We are told that

> The aim of the ancients was to find some perfume so fully in accord with their bodies that the odour might seem as a real emanation from their own bodies.

Lucian, an ancient writer, tells us that the Athenians used different perfumes for different parts of the body, as for instance:

> Egyptian essences for the hands and feet, Phœnician perfumes for the cheeks and bosom, marjoram for the hair, and the spirit of wild thyme for the thighs.

It is notable that while the ancients were fond of perfumes they regarded men who used them as effeminate. They admired fragrance only as emanating from the woman. It is related that Zeno, a Greek who lived about 350 B.C., upon meeting a man who was fragrant with many perfumes said, "Who is this, who smells like a woman?"

There are at the museums many rare old vases which show ancient Athenian maidens bathing and adorning themselves. On one such vase we see a slave pouring in the contents of a hydria over her nude mistress. On another we see a woman applying paint to her lips with a long, slender stick. Still another shows a young girl drying her hair in the sun. The Greeks had great faith in the sun as a beautifying agent for the hair and thousands of years ago the poet Menander wrote:

> The rays of the sun are the best aid in making the hair fair. And our own men know it. For after they have bathed their heads copiously in the special ointment they make here in Athens, they sit in the sun, their heads uncovered, and wait there for hours for the hair to turn. And it does. Their hair gradually becomes a lovely golden.

When the Romans swept down upon Greece they captured "beauty doctors" who knew all the secrets of the golden ointment for the hair, face washes and skin foods for clear complexions, dyes for the fingernails, all the arts of beauty in which Athens had excelled. They carried their captives westward with them—and the beauty secrets that had belonged to Greece became the property of Rome. The fashion of dyeing and waving the hair became popular among the conquerors. Men and women used special ointments and washes for their complexions, and used rouges and dyes to enhance their appearance. Special jars and pots for rouge, for perfumes and powders were made.

> Old-fashioned Romans grumbled; they were shocked. Ancient Rome, which reared Romulus and conquered the world, was getting soft. Young men actually had their hair waved, like the slaves brought from Greece.

The toilet of the Roman lady of this period involved an elaborate and costly process. At night the face was covered with a poultice composed of boiled or moistened flour spread on with the fingers. It dried and hardened into a fragrant mask, like our much advertised beauty clays, and like our clays was supposed to clear the complexion of blemishes, make it smooth and attractive.

Poppea Sabina, Empress of Rome, was true to the arts of her ancestors. She

> employed a hundred slaves to paint her face; to roll up the tight little curls of her coiffure, and then to right properly "pack" them with gum arabic that they might put to shame the ringlets of the goat's own hair. . . . Then her milk bath must be ready when she awoke each morn, and for this bath no milk but that of the she-ass must be used, for in this milk, her oracles had assured her, lurked a magic that would dispel all disease and blights from her beauty.

Milk baths have been popular at various intervals during the ages. Many famous French beauties are reputed to have bathed daily in milk. The bath of Poppea was made fragrant with a vial of precious Arabian scent, and we read of a beauty in Louis XIV's time that "her milk bath, warm and steaming, was rich with the fragrance of roses and lilies."

Not only the ladies of Egypt, Greece, and Rome were attentive to their toilet. Laird tells us that even savages

(Courtesy of Metropolitan Museum of Art)

"The Dying Meleager."
Relief from an ancient Roman sarcophagus. The first man carries a helmet.

(Courtesy of Metropolitan Museum of Art)

Photographic view of the site of the tomb of Perneb. Party of excavators in foreground.

in the heart of the jungle have special paints and dyes which they use for beautifying purposes. In his "Expedition into the Interior of Africa" (vol. II), he tells us that the Felatah ladies in Central Africa are accustomed to devote several hours a day to their personal appearance. At night, he says, they wrap their fingers and toes in henna leaves so that by morning they are a beautiful purple. The eyelids are pencilled with sulphuret of antimony. The hair is coloured carefully with indigo. What Mr. Laird tells us of the Felatah ladies other authorities tell us of other savages who live in widely separated parts of the world. Even the most crude and primitive peoples have methods of beautifying themselves according to their own particular standards.

After the Christian Era the use of cosmetics was for several centuries more pronounced in Italy than elsewhere. Indeed, so extreme did the use of paints and powders and special ointments become that the Italian monks were moved to complain that "the ladies of Italy are immodest and dishonest for they try to cheat Nature herself, spending hours in the sunshine, after anointing their hair with some secret ointment." This "secret ointment" by the way, has been discovered:

> Take dried cauls, from the Orient, grind them to powder, and mix in equal proportions with the yolks of eggs that have been boiled; then mix with wild honey. Rub on the hair in the evening, wrap the head in a kerchief and wash in the morning with olive oil soap and fresh water.

The user is further advised to sit in the sun all day after using the ointment, "being careful not to get sunstroke."

The custom of powdering the hair originated in Venice. In Venice too, about 1500, the custom of wearing beauty patches came into style. False hair of all kinds was worn, and a sort of gum pomade was used to keep it in place.

The 17th century in France saw an extravagant use of cosmetics of all kinds. Rouges and powders were used to such extremes that La Bruyère says:

If their wish is to be pleasing to men, if it is for the men's sake that they lay on their white and red paint, I have inquired into the matter and I can tell them that in the opinion of men the use of white paint and rouge makes them hideous and disgusting; and that rouge by itself, both ages and disguises them.

La Bruyere does not stand alone. In every generation there have been men, and sometimes women, who condemned the beauty methods of the "younger generation." It was true thousands of years ago in Athens. It was true when oatmeal paste and lemon juice were applied to freckles, when dragon's blood and the fat of sheep made a pomade for the fingernails and toenails, when eyelashes were dyed and faces whitened. It is true to-day, and it will continue to be true as long as young people introduce unusual methods of beautifying themselves. The world resents anything that suggests a change in the old order of things.

At all stages of civilization people like a slight variety, but deviations from what they are accustomed to provoke a disagreeable association of ideas.

Which explains the appearance each season of old complexion washes and hair bleaches in new guise, and the ever-present protest of the reformer.

CHAPTER XVII

Funeral Customs

All that tread
The globe are but a handful to the tribes
That slumber in its bosom.

—Bryant, "Thanatopsis."

The world will turn when we are earth,
As though we had not come nor gone;
There was no lack before our birth,
When we are gone there will be none.

—Omar Khayyam.

What man is he that liveth, and shall not see death? Shall he deliver his soul from the hand of the grave? —Psalm LXXXIX, 48.

FEAR OF THE DEAD

LIFE is a prelude to death. The one lasts but a moment; the other is an eternity.

For man there is no life—without death. Fate breathes upon a handful of dust, and a soul comes tumbling down to earth. And at the same moment a life-spent soul crumbles comfortably into dust again. The pendulum of life swings everlastingly to the tune of *life—death; life—death.*

While the arc of life swings with the pendulum across time, man lives, and plays, and eats, and reproduces his own kind. He divides his gift of life into little cubes called years, and each cube is a bit of lifetime cut from the whole. Then comes death and the long silence.

Where does man go? What does he do and see when he vanishes into the great unknown? Does he live again? Can he return to earth again? Or is he just—gone?

Man puzzled the problem on prehistoric plains when one of his fellows dropped dead on the march. He could not solve it then. He cannot solve it now, though he has created religions to comfort him.

And it is because man does not understand the mystery of death that he fears it. To-day the fear of death and of the dead is tempered with faith and hope and with an understanding of life's eternal cycle. But when man was young he had neither faith nor hope nor understanding. His little world was shrouded in superstition; he regarded his very shadow with ignorant fear.

It is interesting to meditate upon man's earliest experiences with death: A cave fellow lying cold and silent. A savage who was but yesterday drunk with life, now flat and still on the ground. A cautious hand reaches out to touch the body. It is clammy. Glazy eyes stare unseeing into the sky. Those who look upon this mystery are filled with a sudden terror. An evil spirit must have claimed their comrade. Some unseen enemy must have killed him. Perhaps an enemy that still lurks in the vicinity! And so they flee from the spot in panic, leaving the body to be ravaged by the beasts.

Primitive man did not accept death as due to natural causes. He believed that death was the result of violence, either at the hands of human or animal enemies, or caused by evil and unseen demons. To the primitive mind man should continue to live until old age wore out the body or until some beast crushed out the breath. For a man or woman still young, without wound or injury, to fall silently asleep and never awaken was inconceivable, uncanny.

Consequently there existed in early times a universal dread of the "long sleep"—the death which came without tangible cause. Man refused to accept this mysterious "sleep" as the end of life. Surely he who slept so had been bewitched! He who lay so stiff and cold must be the victim of malevolent spirits!

And there grew up many word-by-mouth myths concerning this terrible demon who struck silently and without warning. There were, indeed, some fellows more imaginative than others who claimed actually to have seen this demon—a great bird-like creature with huge black wings and a tongue of fire.

The familiar Reaper and Death-angel are relics of these old, old myths. The Bible speaks of the Death-angel who

> stretched out his hand upon Jerusalem to destroy it, the Lord repented him of the evil, and said to the angel that destroyed the people, It is enough: stay now thy hand. (II Samuel, XXIV, 16.)

And again:

> I looked, and behold, a pale horse; and his name that sat on him was Death . . . And power was given . . . to kill with sword, and with hunger, and with death. (Revelations, VI, 8.)

Even the poet Longfellow was faithful to the old superstitious notion that attributed death to a grim and unseen Reaper. He tells us:

> There is a Reaper whose name is Death
> And with his sickle keen
> He reaps the bearded grain at a breath
> And the flowers that grow between.

Among the ancients, death was the great Evil before which the strongest tribesman quailed. Our savage ancestors were fully convinced that when death claimed one of their number an evil spirit entered the body and dwelt there. Thus they feared not only the unknown Evil which caused death, but the dead body in which this Evil was supposed to linger.

O'Brien says:

> Afraid of no living enemy, nor of the sea, meeting the shark in his own element and worsting him, fearlessly enduring the thrust of the fatal spear when an accident of battle left him defenseless, the Marquesan warrior, as much as the youngest child, had an unutterable horror of their own dead and of burial places, and of the demons who hovered about them.

The Veddahs desert their homes whenever any one dies, returning only when they feel that the demon or demons have gone. Sometimes they do not return at all. The Australian Blackfellows show their fear of the dead by burning all his property and running away. Evidently they believe that the demon resides not only in the dead body, but in the property belonging to the dead man.

At Batta funerals natives march behind the body brandishing swords, to drive away the demons. The members of a Zulu *kraal* eat "medicine" in time of death to protect themselves from the evil influences. The Greenlanders throw out of the house everything belonging to the dead man. The Galibis of Guiana dance on the newly covered grave to "stamp down the spirits."

Since the earliest times the corpse has been an object of superstitious dread. As Elsie Parsons indicates, "The dead have become alien to the living, and hence formidable." Even we are encumbered with fear of the dead. Who will with perfect ease spend a night in the cemetery? Who will sit at night beside a dead body without being conscious of a vague and disquieting nervousness?

To avoid the evil influences of the dead, primitive man developed a system of precautions; and upon these precautions are modern burial customs based.

Disposing of the Body.—In the beginning man did not bury his dead. If a tribe were on the march and one of their number died, they deserted the body—left it to rot or be devoured by animals where it fell. Or if a tribe were squatting at the foot of a mountain and one of their number died, they moved on a little, found another squatting place a little way off, and the body was left to bleach its bones in the sun.

Jensen tells us in "The Long Journey" of the life and death of the Man—he who was strong of body and of voice, he who marched at the head of the tribe, leader of his little band. Brutal and powerful was the Man in youth, wise and cruel in age. Then feebleness overtook him and he became weaker, weaker.

Finally the Man lay down all the time and had people brought to him, felt his way with closed eyes until he found a fleshy spot and then dug his fingers in. Ah, at one time he had had such strength in his thumbs that he could pluck a piece of flesh out of a man's body, but now his claws scarcely left a blue mark.

And thus he lay one morning, with scarcely a sign of change, but without movement and without breath, white-haired, long and thin, with stupid eyes open to the sky. He was cold; they brought a child to his hand, but he pinched no more. It was he and yet not he—in silent wonder and fear the tribe stood around him. . . .

When they realized that he would move no more, one of the men stretched out his hand and took the staff, swung it above his head with a roar, and instinctively all the rest fell on their knees—now *he* was the Man.

For years afterwards, when the tribe passed the spot where the Old Man had lain down, he was still there; they reverently turned aside, but stole a glance and saw him lying in the same position, a long whitened skeleton in the grass and the dreaded head turned to the sky with gaping teeth and great empty eye-sockets.

It was fear of the dead body that led early man to dispose of it. Since demons and evil spirits caused the "long sleep" they must still be lurking about the victim, and man was afraid of falling into the "long sleep" himself. The thing to do, consequently, was to dispose of the body, demons and all. This originated customs of burning, burying, and otherwise disposing of the dead.

Burying would appeal particularly to the primitive mind seeking to shake off a superstitious fear. A body buried five or six feet below the ground could do no harm. But a body lying on the surface of the ground could shed its evil influence upon the living.

The custom of burying the dead can be traced back even to the Neanderthal men. Wells says:

The later Neanderthal men seem to have buried their dead, and apparently with food and weapons.

Writing later of Neolithic man, Wells says:

They buried their dead, but before they buried them they cut up the bodies and apparently ate portions of the flesh. They seem to have done this out of a feeling of reverence for the departed; the dead were "eaten with honour" according to the phrase of Mr.

Flinders Petrie. It may have been that the survivors hoped to retain thereby some vestige of the strength and virtue that had died. Traces of similar savage customs have been found in the long barrows that were scattered over western Europe before the spreading of the Aryan peoples, and they have pervaded Negro Africa, where they are only dying out at the present time.

It is difficult to decide just when man began to bury his dead. We have record of the custom as far back as it is possible for us to have definite record of anything concerning man. Recent discoveries in South France indicate that man not only buried his dead 15,000 years ago, but actually had tombstones to indicate the graves. In reporting the discoveries, the New York *World* published a cable from France, part of which we quote here:

> Dean Charles Deperet of the Faculte des Sciences at Lyons has been excavating in the famous prehistoric deposits at Solutre in South France and has uncovered two carefully buried skeletons, in quaternary layers, judged to be at least 15,000 years old.
>
> Above the head of each skeleton Dean Deperet found a cut stone placed vertically, so it would have been above ground, in the epoch when the Cro-Magnon hunters buried these two with their feet toward the rising ground and their heads toward the setting sun. It is considered the first authentic palæolithic sepulchre.

Customs of Burial.—At first the burial of a dead body was very crude. A hole was dug in the ground and the body dropped into it and covered with earth. Or if there happened to be a handy ravine or crater in which to drop the body, so much the better. It obviated the need for digging a hole.

But gradually death came to be looked upon as the last great event in man's life, and like all great events was duly celebrated. The breaking of the earth and preparing of the grave became a cermony. The body was lowered carefully and with a certain reverence. And when the hole was filled with earth again, there were dancing and feasting—inevitable accompaniments of primitive ceremony.

The natives of Guiana dance upon graves even to-day. The Congo Kaffirs bury their dead amid elaborate cere-

(Courtesy of Metropolitan Museum of Art)

Coffin of the baby prince Amenem-hat, as found in the tomb. Egyptian, 18th Dynasty, Thebes.

(Courtesy of Metropolitan Museum of Art)

Coffin from Lisht, South Pyramid, Egypt, 12th Dynasty.

monies, and keep fires burning over the graves for a month. Among the Samoyeds there is considerable ceremony while the sorcerer goes through the sacred rites of soothing the departed. The Bushmen not only dance upon the graves but cover them with stones.

Ceremony was apparently a part of the burial customs of primitive man. In the third interglacial period, about 100,000 years ago, man buried the important dead—the leaders and the "strong men"—with elaborate ceremonial, and with evident respect. One of the famous skeletons of this period

> is that of a youth who apparently had been deliberately interred. He had been placed in a sleeping posture, head on the right forearm. The head lay on a number of flint fragments carefully piled together "pillow fashion." A big hand-axe lay near his head and around him were numerous charred and split ox bones, as though there had been a feast or an offering.

Our fancy lingers for a moment with these people. We see a circle of naked men, dancing and chanting in the moonlight. There is a youth lying stiff and silent in the centre of the circle—dead. His head rests on a flint "pillow." His favourite axe is at his side. Nearby the sacrificial fire sends its thin gray coil of smoke into the sky. All the night long there are dancing and stamping to frighten away evil spirits that may be lurking about the body; and there is feasting in honour of the departed. Sacrifices and ceremonies take place, while the moon looks on in solemn wonder. And when the moon fades slowly from the heavens and the first golden ray of the sun greets the morning, the body is lowered into the grave prepared to receive it—buried—with more chanting and more feasting.

Thousands of years later, in the Palæolithic age, man is burying his dead with greater ceremony. The body is painted and decorated. There are great feasting and celebration. And with the body are buried weapons, food, ornaments. The significance of these gifts to the dead will presently be discussed.

The European Neolithic people buried their dead but ate part of the bodies before burial, as we have already seen. Wells informs us, however, that

> They buried some of their dead, but not the common herd, with great care and distinction, and made huge heaps of earth over their sepulchres; these heaps are the barrows. . . . In connection with these mounds, or independently of them, they set up great stones (megaliths) either singly or in groups, of which Stonehenge in Wiltshire and Carnac in Brittany are among the best-known examples.

The Iberian race, distributed over Greece, Asia Minor, Great Britain, Ireland, France, Spain, North Africa, and Italy, before the Aryans spread over those lands, made of burial a great ceremony—elaborate and impressive. The important people were buried in chambers made of huge stones, covered over with earth. These great mounds of earth, concealing Iberian graves, are known as the long barrows because they are considerably longer than they are broad. The bodies were placed in these "megalithic chambers" in a sitting posture.

The Aryans, who followed the Iberians, burned their dead and placed the ashes in urns shaped like houses. Most of them are like rounded huts with thatched roofs. Some of these little houses, containing the ashes of human bodies, have been found in ancient Aryan burial mounds, known as round barrows.

The making of a prehistoric barrow is very interestingly described in the concluding passage of the Iliad. The following, re-quoted from the "Outline of History," is from Chapman's rhymed translation:

> . . . Then they brought the bravest of his kind
> Forth to be burned. Troy swam in tears. Upon the pile's most height
> They laid the body, and gave fire. All day it burn'd, all night.
> But when the elev'nth morn let on earth her rosy fingers shine,
> The people flock'd about the pile, and first with gleaming wine

Quench'd all the flames. His brothers then, and friends, the snowy bones
Gather'd into an urn of gold, still pouring out their moans.
Then wrapt they in soft purple veils the rich urn, digg'd a pit,
Grav'd it, built up the grave with stones, and quickly piled on it
A barrow. . . .
The barrow heap'd once, all the town
In Jove-nurs'd Priam's Court partook a sumptuous funeral feast,
And so horse-taming Hector's rites gave up his soul to rest.

Burning the dead was simply another way of destroying the body—and the demons supposed to dwell within it. The Aryan peoples, the North American Indians, and many savage peoples burned or cremated their dead—a phase of funeral customs that we will consider in a moment.

The ancient Vikings buried their kings and queens in their ships. One of these ancient ships which served as the sepulchral chamber of a Viking queen and her handmaiden was discovered accidentally a short time ago by an Oseberg farmer while he was digging a barrow.

In the early civilizations we find burials of a more pronounced ceremonial nature than ever before. In Egypt we find anointing and embalming. We find pyramids, which are huge tombs; and mummifying, which is a method of preserving the body. The burial ceremonies are elaborate and impressive and vast treasures are buried with the important dead. Recently a unique cemetery was discovered in Egypt in which a number of black cats were unearthed—mummies of cats sacred to Egyptians who lived four or five thousand years ago.

The passage from the Iliad on the preceding page gives us a fairly good idea of the burial, or rather cremation customs, of the ancient Greeks. In Greece only suicides, unteethed children, and persons struck by lightning were denied the privilege of cremation and were buried. The ceremonies attending the disposal of the body, however, were always elaborate and solemn.

With the catacombs of Rome we are all familiar. These

famous underground cemeteries represent one of the most amazing wonders of antiquity. The catacombs are about from fifty to seventy-five feet below the surface of the earth, and so intricate and extensive are they in their corridors, passages, and windings that they form an endless labyrinth. One authority has calculated that about seven million human beings are buried in these ancient catacombs!

The Assyrians dug huge excavations into which they cast the bodies of their dead, one upon the other. Even when they began to use coffins they piled them one above the other in a great excavation which reached sometimes to a depth of sixty feet.

The ancient Hebrews buried their dead, and used stone pillars to mark the graves. The Bible tells us that "Rachel died, and was buried in the way of Ephrath, which is Bethlehem. And Jacob set a pillar upon her grave." (Genesis, XXXV, 19, 20.) Many references to burials are made in the Bible, which give us excellent verbal pictures not only of the burial customs of the Hebrews but of their neighbours.

It would be useless to attempt a discussion of all the burial customs of ancient and of savage life. There is a wide variation in custom with regard to death—the inevitable climax. Every savage tribe has its own peculiar ceremony, its own distinctive customs. There are some who think very little of the corpse and dispose of it in an unceremonious manner. There are others who fear the mystery of death and dispose of the body amid great ceremonies and rites. A thorough discussion of the burial customs of mankind would fill a volume.

Then, of course, there are the savage races that do not bury their dead, even to-day. The Veddahs, for instance, do not bury their dead but throw the bodies into the jungle. Many Australian tribes run away from the dead bodies, leaving them to rot where they fall—a custom which goes back to dim antiquity—or else they destroy the body by burning. The Mongolians throw dead bodies to horrible wild dogs that live on nothing but human flesh. These dogs are of the mastiff type and are said to be the most vicious and dangerous beasts in the world.

The Coffin and the Tomb.—In its long development through the ages, the coffin has taken many shapes and forms. One of the earliest types of coffin was the tree, cut down and hollowed to accommodate the body. These tree coffins bearing the dead were sometimes set adrift in the river, sometimes left upon the ground, sometimes buried—depending entirely upon the people and the conditions in which they found themselves.

The custom of burying the dead in a tree-trunk is symbolical. The tree represents the Great Mother, the tree of life that bore the child as the branch. Use was therefore made of the scooped-out tree in death and in burial. This is simply another version of the dust-to-dust theory.

The presence of the tree in the churchyard or cemetery is due to ancient notions concerning the tree as a dwelling place for the spirits of the dead. The Dieri tribe of South Australia, for instance, regards certain trees as sacred, believing them to be ancient ancestors transformed. In other sections of Australia it is believed that the great bat which causes death lives in a tree, and that when a man is killed by this bat—in other words, when he dies of no apparent cause—his soul goes to join it in the treetop. Some of the natives of New Guinea think that the spirits of their ancestors live in the trees; a belief found also in Corea.

To be buried "in the shade of a tree," therefore, came to be looked upon as a man's natural right. If there were no tree in the vicinity, where would his spirit dwell?

The first actual coffins, as we know them, probably originated in Egypt. There is no doubt whatever that the use of coffins originated in the desire to preserve the body, rather than destroy it. The Egyptians believed that the spirit would return to the body some time in the future, and that consequently "the body must be kept habitable for the soul when it should return to earth from its celestial wanderings." It was believed that resurrection would take place from 3000 to 10,000 years in the future.

At first burial in Egypt was in stone compartments, and all were buried in this manner, some in more elaborate compartments than others. The people had an intense belief in and concern about their life after death, and they made every provision for the comfort of the spirit in the next world. The richer Egyptians were buried with all their precious ornaments and furniture, with beautiful clothes and food. In the natural sequence of events, the rifling of graves became a common crime, and not even the graves of the mighty were spared.

To protect their remains from desecration, the kings built great stone structures to house their bodies and their valuables, tremendous coffins in which to preserve their mummified bodies until such time, thousands of years hence, as the spirit should see fit to return. These great stone structures are known as the pyramids; they are the tombs of the kings of the early dynasties.

The Sphinx, generally associated with the pyramids, is believed by most authorities to be a sort of guardian of the royal cemetery it overlooks, frightening away evil spirits that might seek to enter this abode of the important dead. But no one knows definitely when the Sphinx was carved, by whom, or precisely what is its significance. The lips of the Sphinx are still sealed; its secret still baffles the world. What seems possible to this author is that the Sphinx may have been carved by some vain king who desired his tomb to be different from the others, and who kept thousands of slaves busy a lifetime building this impressive monster to house his body. The Sphinx faces east; could it not have been placed so as to be ready to welcome the spirit when it should come with the sun from the east, and reënter the body of the king?

It is only in Lower Egypt that we find the pyramids.

The Theban kings and their subjects never erected these great stone structures, but cut their tombs from living rocks. It appears to have been the custom with the kings, as soon as they ascended the throne, to begin the preparation of their tombs and "the excavation seems to have gone on uninterruptedly, year by year, until the hand of death ended the king's reign and simultaneously the work on his tomb. The tomb thus became an index of the length of the king's reign, as well as his magnificence." These tombs, cut from the rock in the mountains of Thebaid, are still to be seen in Upper Egypt.

Not every one who died in Egypt was buried in a tomb. Although they believed firmly in an after life, the Egyptians were of the opinion that only those who were powerful and important in this life would be important in the next; while those who had no importance here would have none in after life. Thus the great were buried in magnificent tombs; ordinary people were buried in rude stone compartments.

The Egyptian word for "coffin" is from *Kas* which means "to embalm," "to bury." The word, elaborated into *Kast,* means the enclosure of the body, the receptacle into which the body is placed—hence, the coffin.

In Babylonia great boxes of clay were baked to form coffins. We find clay coffins also among the neighbours of Babylonians, who doubtless copied the custom from the originators.

The Greeks, as we have seen, cremated their dead. Like the Egyptians, however, they believed in an after-life for the great and gradually it became customary to bury the important people. When cremation was practised, the ashes were placed in urns of burned clay and buried. When burial became the custom, the body was enclosed in an elaborate stone casket, like the Roman sarcophagus.

The Chinese have buried their dead since the earliest times. Custom dictates that no matter where a Chinese may die, he must be brought back to his place of birth for burial. The coffin which the Chinese uses is ornate and elaborate, and it is regarded as an appropriate present for an aged or ailing relative. Many wealthy Chinese own their coffins long before they die; some even carry their coffins with them when they travel.

Nor is this custom confined solely to the Chinese. It is well known that Sarah Bernhardt provided in her lifetime for her coffin, and carried it with her wherever she went. Darwin, too, ordered his coffin in his lifetime for the purpose, it is said, of giving work in the slack season to the carpenter who made boxes for his natural science collection.

There have been many kinds of coffins, just as there have been many customs of burial. Clay, stone, wood, even iron coffins have been used. And just as there have been many kinds of coffins, there have been many laws, regulations and customs concerning the manner of placing the body in the coffin.

The Bushmen, for instance, believe that the sun will begin to rise late in the morning if the dead are not buried with their faces to the west. The Samoans and Fijians bury their dead with feet and faces toward the west, whither their souls are supposed to have preceded them. The Guarayos, on the other hand, bury their dead with the head turned to the east, because their god Tamoi is said to have his happy hunting grounds in that quarter.

Recent excavations in Queens, under the direction of Dr. Thomas H. Evans of the American Museum of Natural History, disclosed more than a dozen skeletons. According to the report, all the skeletons when found were so placed that their heads turned to the west—an old Indian burial custom.

In "Gulliver's Travels" we read that the Lilliputians "buried their dead with the head downward because of the belief that in eleven thousand moons the earth would turn upside down and the dead would rise again." Evidently by this means of burial the Lilliputians planned to be on their feet when they came to life again.

There is an old legend that Christ was buried with His face toward the west; but the Church follows the custom of burying the dead looking east, because of a custom older than itself of facing the east when in attitude of prayer.

The savages have many customs concerning the method of placing the dead in the ground. Some bury their dead in a sitting posture, some with the faces toward the ground. Some bury the dead with the knees drawn up under the chin, others with the body curved in the position it takes in the womb before birth—a custom which indicates an early understanding of impregnation. The ancient Peruvians, for instance, always placed their dead in the position of a fœtus for burial.

Among many savages—indeed, even with us—the body is carried away feet foremost. Savages believe that if the dead body "sees" the house while it is being carried away for burial or for burning, it will cast its evil influence upon it and cause either illness or other deaths to enter. Hence, the carrying away of the body feet foremost.

It was a custom in Egypt to cast sand three times upon the remains of the deceased—a custom observed with great ceremonial. This survives with us to-day in our "ashes to ashes, dust to dust," and a handful of earth cast three times upon the coffin lid.

Marking the Grave.—The first gravestones were those used by the Bushmen and other savages to keep the evil spirits from rising and causing damage. The Bushmen believed that unless heavy stones were placed upon the grave mounds, the evil spirits supposed to dwell in the dead bodies would not remain in the earth, but would rise to claim more lives.

The marking of graves goes back into remote antiquity. Evidently primitive man placed stones or other markings on graves not only to keep the evil spirits from rising, but to mark the spot so that he could avoid it. The custom originated for the purpose of warning people away from a grave has become a custom for distinguishing one grave from another, and so enabling mourners to recognize the particular mound for which they search.

We have already seen that Palœolithic man, thousands of years ago, used headpieces of cut stone to mark the graves of his dead. Whether these stones were used for purposes of avoidance or purposes of recognition we cannot be certain.

Neolithic man set up great stone megaliths above the mounds which hid the dead. Sometimes these stones were put up singly, sometimes in groups. Stonehenge is an excellent example. It is known as "the finest megalithic ruin in Europe." The name Stonehenge means "hanging stones"—the stones being partly suspended. Stones of huge size were used, and the marvel is that they could have been lifted to be placed in their cross-wise position. The stone cross placed on the modern grave is like a pinpoint in comparison with the great, cross-like stones at Stonehenge.

We know that the Greeks used gravestones, for relics have been found. The stones were usually ornamented with sculpture. The Hebrews marked the graves of the dead with stone pillars (see p. 486). The tombs and the pyramids of ancient Egypt mark the places where dead are buried. Some peoples built vaults for their dead, others erected tall pillars of ornamented stone. Some marked their graves with simple slabs of wood or stone; others built magnificent shrines and mausoleums.

Even among the savages we find customs of marking the graves. Among the Congo Kaffirs we find that the grave of the man was marked with a staff; the grave of the woman, with a simple basket. The Kaffirs mark the graves so that they can be identified.

With the coming of Christianity the marking of graves became common. The ring cross which primitive peoples used on their graves to represent the sun was adopted as an appropriate headpiece, but after the crucifixion the simple cross was used, for religious as well as reverential purposes. The cross is even to-day the popular grave mark among Christians.

Decorating graves with flowers and wreaths is an old custom, handed down to us through many generations. Wreaths made of thin gold have been found in Athenian graves. The Egyptians adorned their mummies with flowers, and the mourners carried flowers in their hands.

In a recent article concerning the opening of Tutankhamen's tomb, we read:

> Opening one of the gold and jewelled boxes a romantic touch was added to the sombre silence of the tomb. It was filled with roses, still preserved through the 3000 years or more which separate us from Tutankhamen's funeral. As the explorers gently lifted the lid from these old flowers of the Nile's bank, plucked thousands of years ago, a slight perfume greeted them, which had remained in the flowers in their sealed boxes down through the centuries.

A custom of early Christianity, still observed in various rural sections of Europe, was to make wreaths of flowers from ribbon and paper and give them to the church as a memento of the departed one. These artificial wreaths were hung in garlands around the walls of the church where they remained until so old and dusty that they were no longer recognizable. Then they were removed to make room for the new wreaths. These artificial wreaths of long ago have evolved into our mourning wreath of living flowers, usually sent by friends or relatives of the departed and placed upon the grave.

The Custom of Cremation.—Since the evil spirits that cause death are supposed to dwell in the body, according to the primitive notion, it is not surprising that cremation should have become one of the earliest methods of disposing of the dead. Cremation, or burning of the body, appears to have been practised universally in the ancient world, except in Egypt, in China, and among the Hebrews.

The Greenlanders, who cremate their dead to-day as they have done for centuries, believe that there is danger of pollution from the evil spirits until the smell of the corpse has passed away. They burn the dead body almost before it has become cold and try to avoid inhaling any of the fumes. They burn also everything in the house that belonged to the dead person.

We find this custom of burning the belongings of the dead among many savage tribes. The Zulus always burn the property of the dead to prevent the evil spirits from hovering in the vicinity. Many Australian and African tribes observe this custom. It is found also in certain Indian tribes—indeed, exists even among civilized peoples. We frequently hear of clothes or other belongings being burned after a funeral.

In Burma, "the more important the person the longer he is kept lying in state after death previous to cremation." One writer tells of an archbishop who was kept embalmed and on public exhibition for a period of two years before the funeral ceremony finally took place and the body was cremated.

The Iberian and Aryan races practised cremation, and the custom in India is a relic of the Aryan practice. In India the body is cremated on the funeral pyre, and until recently widows were sacrificed alive on the burning pyres with their husbands.

At one time the practice of cremation was widespread and seemed likely to become a universal custom. However, the Christian doctrine of the resurrection of the body discouraged the custom. If the body were to be resurrected, why burn it? *Could* it be resurrected if it were burned? The early followers of Christianity pondered this problem, and it is pondered still. Many clergymen, however, have from time to time debated the advisability of cremation, declaring that the power able to resurrect the body decomposed in the grave could resurrect the body cremated and reduced to ashes. Mr. Haweis, for instance, in his *Ashes to Ashes* (London, 1874) proclaims himself an advocate of cremation. Discussions on this subject come up even to-day.

Belief in an After Life.—The first thought of another life after death possibly occurred to primitive man when he saw some dead friend or relative in a dream. Waking from his sleep he recalls that he saw the person they had burned or buried. He lived after all! Life did not end on this earth, then. There was another life, another existence. Man must have made much of this important discovery.

It was not a sudden discovery, of course, nor did the thought occur to all men at once. It came as all other great truths came, dawning slowly but surely upon the consciousness of primitive man as he emerged from the darkness.

The savage's conception of the soul, or the spirit, is a miniature man—an exact reproduction of the person. The Hurons, for instance, believed that the spirit had arms, legs, head, body just like the person it represented. The Nootkas (British Columbia) believed the soul to be a tiny man living within the head.

There are, however, savages who think of the soul as a bird which can fly from the body at will. The Bororos (Brazil) have the notion that the soul is a bird which leaves the body occasionally, during which time the person sleeps. When the bird returns, the sleeper awakens. Should the bird forget to return, the sleeper enters the "long sleep," or death. The Bohemians also regard the soul as a bird, as do various Indian tribes.

The shadow, or reflection, is another form of soul, in the savage sense. The Basutos thoroughly believed that a crocodile can cause a man's death by snapping at his reflection in the water. Other savages believe that to see one's own face in a mirror or a pool of water is to insult the soul and thus invite disaster.

To most peoples who believe in a spirit and in an after

life, the land to which the spirits go and where they dwell in everlasting happiness is a fixed and definite place. In the ancient Egyptian "Book of the Dead," for instance, a ship is figured carrying the dead to another world. The Greeks thought that the dead were ferried over the river Styx by Charon—the river being composed of all the tears that had been shed in the world. Charon was supposed to charge a fee for his services as ferryman; therefore, when the Greeks buried any one they provided him with a small coin which they placed in his hand.

The same idea is found among the Chinese who furnish the dead with paper money and passports. We will consider this more thoroughly in our talk on gifts to the dead.

The ghost land or spirit land of primitive peoples, the happy hunting ground of the Indians, the Elysian Fields of the ancients, the Valhalla of the Vikings—all are equivalents of our heaven. The idea of a purgatory seems to have originated with the Greeks. They believed that if their dead did not have the fee for Charon they would be detained for a hundred years before being permitted to proceed. The belief in purgatory was adopted from the Greeks and made "an article of faith for Catholics by Pope Gregory the Great, about 500 A.D." The masses which are said in Catholic churches are intended to expedite the journey of the dead from purgatory to paradise.

Since the spirit was to continue in another life, and might some day return to the body, it occurred to the awakening mind of man that it was necessary to protect and preserve the body. The Marquesans, for instance, who locate the soul below the belt and the spirit world below the surface of the earth, take every precaution to protect their dead from being desecrated either by man or by animal. O'Brien says:

> In the very old days the Marquesans interred the dead secretly in the night at the foot of great trees. Or they carried the bodies to the mountains and in a rocky hole shaded by trees covered them

over and made the grave as much as possible like the surrounding soil. The secret of the burial place was kept inviolate.

And O'Brien continues to tell us of a man of more recent times who

in the darkest night climbed a supposedly inaccessible precipice carrying the body of his young wife lashed to his back, to place it carefully on a lofty shelf and descend safely.

These precautions undoubtedly came from a fear of profanation of the dead. Among the Marquesans the belief was strong that if the body were injured the soul that fled from it would be injured, too. Therefore it was a custom among the tribes in early days, when invading the vicinity of a foe, to devastate the cemeteries. They believed that mutilating the corpse hurt the souls, and one of their first acts of violence in warfare was hurting the dead—even before hurting the living.

Primitive man must at first have groped pathetically with the thought of a "double," of another life, of a soul or spirit within him. Many interesting customs, born of the first crude notions concerning the soul, have come under our observation. Among the Ojibwas, for instance, "when a child dies they cut some of its hair and make a little doll which they call the doll of sorrow. This lifeless object takes the place of the deceased child. The mother carries it with her everywhere for a year." The belief is that the soul, or the spirit, of the child is transferred through the hair from the dead body to the doll.

The Chavante mother, on the Uruguay, believed that to eat her dead child was to regain the tiny soul. Therefore, among the Chavantes we find from earliest times a tendency to devour the dead children, either partially or entirely. The notion was that to bury the child without eating of it was to lose the little soul and never be able to retrieve it. We find this same custom, in modified form, existing among many of the savage races of Australia and of Africa—a bit of everyone being eaten, not only the children. Among these people, however, the thought behind the eating of the bodies is to regain the strength, the power, or the knowledge of the person who has died. Cannibalistic warriors always fatten themselves upon their enemy, to gain some of the strength of the opposing tribe (see p. 51).

The ancient Scotch, Australians, Hebrews, French, and Aztecs—widely separated peoples—all appear to have had the custom of spreading dust around the body of a dead man to discover the footsteps of the ghost in the morning. It seems to have been a widespread notion that the ghost itself was invisible, but that it left traces if the wary were wise enough to find them. Thus was the dust left around a corpse, and if the merest suggestion of a footprint were found in the dust the following morning—well, there was proof that the soul had left the body, was there not?

The common notion that ghosts cast no shadow evidently originated in the belief that the soul was the shadow. This belief in the shadow soul is widely prevalent among savage peoples even to-day.

Another widespread belief, one which originated in antiquity, is that those who die a violent death become malignant spirits, endangering the lives of those who come near the spot. We speak of such a spot as "haunted." The mourners in the Andaman Islands shoot arrows into the jungle to frighten away these evil spirits. The Ahts burn everything that belonged to the one who died by violence, believing that the evil spirits dwelt therein. The fear of the evil spirits gave rise to the belief, which at one time became almost universal, that it is dangerous to venture near the spot where the dead are buried. Our fear of cemeteries, or rather our superstitious notion that cemeteries are sometimes haunted, no doubt traces its origin to the primitive fear of evil spirits.

The Chinese have always believed that the spirit of the dead leaves the body and travels to other lands. The

(Courtesy of Metropolitan Museum of Art)

Cypriote: A massive sarcophagus found at Golgoi. Of the period of 500–450 B. C.

(Courtesy of Metropolitan Museum of Art)

Cypriote: Sarcophagus found at Amaultius. Period of about 600 B. C. Elaborate and ornate.

spirit of the man who has been murdered, however, is supposed to remain in the body until it has been avenged. Therefore it was the custom in China, and also among other peoples, to fasten the body of the dead man to the murderer, compelling him to go about thus encumbered for a stated period. They believed this a greater punishment than any other they could inflict.

Among the North American Indians we find a tendency to believe in a spirit which lurks for a while around the body, but finally goes to a paradise of happy hunting grounds where everything is provided without toil. There are handsome wigwams, fruitful fields, winding rivers, and fair weather all the time. We are told that in the ancient Ohio tribes it was customary to bore holes in the coffin to let the spirit pass in and out. The Iroquois left small holes in the grave for the same purpose.

The Mandans had an interesting method of burial. They wrapped the dead bodies in buffalo skins and exposed them on crossbeams or scaffolds, suspended at a height of about ten feet. There they were allowed to remain, safe from animals, until entirely decomposed. Then there was a wholesale burial—ten or twelve skeletons being buried in a single grave. Judging from their customs, the Mandans did not fear the dead as did other peoples, but evidently they had some belief in a spirit and in an after life.

In ancient Ireland it was believed that the souls of those who died abroad greatly desired to come back to rest in Ireland. It was therefore deemed the duty of relatives to bring back the body and lay it to rest in its native earth. And even then the soul will not be at rest unless the body is laid with its forefathers, not among strangers. Writers who tell of the manners and customs of ancient Ireland like to tell this story:

A young girl died of a fever while away on a visit to some friends, and her father thought it safer not to bring her home but have her buried in the nearest churchyard. A few nights after his return home, however, he was awakened by a mournful wail at the window and a voice cried, "I am alone! I am alone!" The father knew at once what it meant, and prayed that the spirit of his dead child might rest in peace until the morning. And when the day broke he arose and set off to the strange burial ground, and there he drew the coffin from the earth and had it carried all the way back from Cork to Mayo; and after he had laid the dead in the old graveyard beside his people and his kindred, the spirit of his child had rest. And the mournful cry was no more heard in the night.

Preserving the Body.—The belief in a spirit which might some day desire to return to its earthly body inspired early man to make efforts to preserve the body. Thus burial, at first intended solely as a means of disposing of the dead, came in time to be a method of preserving the dead for the return of the spirit.

In Africa, for instance, the Loango people smoke their corpses to preserve them. The Congo Kaffirs bury their dead, build fires above the graves, and keep these fires burning for a month. Then the bodies are unearthed, smoked, and amid great ceremonies wound in cloth. The smoked corpse is placed upright, in the hut where the man died, and is left there for years. If a man happens to die while visiting a friend, his smoked corpse is brought to the friend's house and not taken to his own. The belief is that the spirit will return to the very spot where the man died, and that the body must be there to welcome it.

Embalming, for purposes of preserving the body, is very old. It was practised in ancient Egypt where the warm, dry climate assured its success. As one writer says, "Embalming would probably not succeed in climates less warm and dry than Egypt." The Egyptians were pre-eminent as anointers, and greased the bodies of the living and the dead. The custom of "glorifying by means of grease" is essentially African—and we find it prevalent to-day among many African tribes. Even the statues of gods were anointed by the Egyptians.

The Egyptians practised the custom of mummifying the body. The purpose of mummifying, of course, is to preserve the body as a home for the spirit when it should return to take up its abode in its rightful place again.

To mummify, the Egyptians extracted the brain and the intestines, cleaned out the body through an incision in the side, and filled the cavities with spices. The body was then sewn up and permitted to lie in salt for a period of 70 days. Then it was placed in gummed mummy cloth and fastened into its ornamental case. Sometimes instead of making incisions they injected cedar oil into the body by means of syringes. The poorer classes were not mummified but merely salted.

When cremation was introduced, the Egyptians made a substitute body from the ashes of the dead, or to hold them, thus creating a suitable habitation for the spirit when it should return. The Egyptians were not partial to cremating, however, and soon abandoned the custom. They buried their dead, anointed and embalmed the bodies, and made mummies of the men and women of importance. Even the bodies of sacred animals, like the black cat, were preserved and mummified.

Sometimes instances of natural mummification are brought to light, as during some very recent excavations in South Dakota. In the graves of the Arikara Indians, on the banks of the Missouri River, a mummified infant was found, evidently the child of some mighty chief who lived long ago. Mr. Stirling, who led and directed the expedition, says:

> On no single adult that we found was there anything like the elaborate decorations with which this tiny body was weighed down. In his grave were two pieces of pottery that had probably been filled with food. Around his neck were a couple of elk's teeth. . . . He was further ornamented with a number of beads of stone, shell and copper, but it was the copper trinkets that accomplished the mummification. Copper is a natural preservative, though it turned the little red body green. Although the baby's flesh is somewhat desiccated, it is a striking example of a case of natural mummification—something that has never come to my notice before.

We find even in civilized life a desire to preserve the body after death. Coffins are advertised as being of "enduring granite" and vaults are built "to preserve the bodies of those who once lived and breathed, who loved and were loved." The dead are still embalmed and every effort is made to preserve the body as long as possible.

Gifts to the Dead.—The general belief in early times was that man went on into the next world with as little break as possible, that his life resembled very closely the life in the tribe, and that therefore he would need his property, his valuables. Therefore, it was customary to bury material things with the body.

The religious aspect of funerals possibly originated in the belief that death is but a journey to another world, and that the dying expect to have ceremonies performed for them to expedite their travels and lessen the dangers of the journey. Among most savages, therefore, we find it customary to dance and feast at time of death for purposes of pleasing the spirit of the departed; to stamp upon the ground and frighten away evil spirits; to build sacrificial fires and so satisfy the fearful One who causes death. Religion made of these savage observances a ceremonial; and Christianity gave the ceremonial a new note of solemnity.

It was customary, besides preparing the soul for its wanderings by feasting, dancing, and chanting, to bury with the dead whatever would be needed to secure admission to the new world. We have already mentioned the fee of Charon, ferryman of the Styx. Buried with the Chinese are miniature sedan chairs of bamboo or paper (so that the soul may rest every now and then throughout its wearisome journey!) and also paper money to furnish *Lû-in,* or a passport, for travelling from this life to the next.

The firm belief in an after life is indicated by the custom of the religious Hebrews of the Near East who entrust the dying with messages to carry to the patriarchs and the prophets. Distinguished rabbis are given letters to carry to deceased friends. A similar custom is noticed among the chiefs and head tribesmen of Africa. It is customary among these people to give messages or news intended for dead friends to slaves, and to kill them so that they will be able to carry the news to the other world.

Since the dead live again in another world they must be provided with food and necessities of life until they become accustomed to their new surroundings. Thus, among the Papuans, Tahitians, Sandwich Islanders, Malanans, Karens, ancient Peruvians, Brazilians, and countless others, it was customary to leave food and drink with the corpse. In Patagonia it was the custom annually to open the sepulchral chambers and reclothe the dead. This same custom is found among the Eskimo who, every year, take clothes as a gift to the dead.

Among the Kukis, the widow is compelled to remain for a year beside the tomb of her deceased husband, the family bringing food daily for her and for the spirit of the dead man. In the Mosquito tribe the widow is obligated to supply the grave of her husband with provisions for a year. Many of the North American Indians buried wampum, food, bows and arrows, useful utensils, and trinkets with the dead.

The Egyptians entombed with the dead everything that might be needed in the next life. Arms, ornaments, decorations, furniture, food—all go into the tomb where the mummy in its double coffin is to rest throughout the centuries. The wealthy Egyptians were buried with their slaves, that they might be certain of services in the next life. Frequently a child was buried alive with a dead parent, so that the parent would not be alone and a stranger in the future state. Slaves were placed in the great tombs of Egyptian kings before they were sealed for ever, and the legs of these slaves were cut off so that they could not possibly escape.

The Dyak head-hunters believe that every head they add to their collection means another slave in the next world. When one of their own people dies, they set about to secure a man's head, thereby sending a slave to serve the deceased. The more powerful and important the person who dies, the more slaves are sent to join him.

In Russia it was formerly a general custom to place a pair of new shoes upon the feet of the dead, in anticipation of the long journey to be taken. The Ahts bury blankets with the dead that they may not be cold. At Reichenbach, in Germany, a man's umbrella and goloshes are placed in his grave even to-day. Until recently, in certain parts of Sweden, a man's pipe and tobacco pouch and a little money were buried with him.

During the early period of Christianity, the priest used to place upon a man's breast, as he lay in his coffin, a pass to the next world. This pass gave the man's Christian name, the dates of his birth and death, and was also "a certificate of his baptism, of the piety of his life, and of his having taken of the communion before his death."

The Chinese bury their dead with many gifts. They place in the coffin the "seat of the soul" called *Ling-tso-tze* (the ghost's slab). This is merely a paper tablet, like a large rectangular red envelope and it is supposed to contain the soul of the departed. The name of the person is written in great letters upon it. Beside this tablet, to the left, is placed a bowl of rice, in the centre of which is placed a hard-boiled egg with a hole pierced in its upper part. Two chopsticks are stuck into the rice or into the hole in the egg.

Many early peoples took wives with them into the next world. Among the Comanches, for instance, it was once customary to kill a man's favourite wife to accompany him on his journey. In the Congo region, and throughout practically all of Africa, wives were sacrificed at the death of men. In Polynesia and Melanesia widows were always killed. To-day the Polynesian widows are not killed, but they are obliged to mutilate themselves by making gashes on the face and the body. The Melanesians also mutilate themselves, and similar customs are found throughout Africa and Australia.

In certain tribes of New Zealand, the widow strangled herself when her husband died. Among the Crees the widow was usually sacrificed upon the pyre with her husband. We are familiar with the age-old custom in India of burning widows at the funeral of the deceased husband,—a custom which prevailed until very recently. In 1803 there were 275 women sacrificed on funeral pyres within thirty miles around Calcutta. In six months of 1804 in the same area the number was 115. (C. Buchanan, "Christian Researches in India.")

Among the Tartars, on the occasion of a man's death one of his favourite wives hanged herself. In Darien it was customary to inter with a chief all his concubines. In equatorial Africa, at Yourriba, four of the king's wives poison themselves when he dies; but the Hottentot women of Africa do not kill themselves, merely cutting off one finger to indicate loss and mourning.

In both China and Japan the custom of killing people to accompany the dead prevailed. The Japanese burned servants to accompany their masters. But later they substituted effigies for the real servants and burned these, permitting the men to live. It is interesting to note that on November 11, 1918, a band of people from Little Italy in New York marched to the Battery where they burned the Kaiser in effigy. This custom of burning in effigy originated with the primitives of antiquity who practised imitative magic and believed that they could injure their enemies by burning or destroying images of them (see p. 34).

Centuries ago the Chinese believed that the widow ought to kill herself at her husband's funeral. They regarded it as the only wifely thing to do, but made no provisions for the husband burning *himself* when the wife died. So accustomed did the Chinese women become to sacrificing themselves at their husband's funerals that they began to do it of their own accord, and it was no longer necessary to enforce the custom.

As late as 1857 the Pekin *Gazette* published the report of a decree which accorded a tablet to the memory of the wife of a prominent mandarin. Reporting the story, the *Gazette* told how the widow had poisoned herself upon hearing of the death of her husband in a battle against rebels, and asserted that the magnificent tablet was a fitting tribute to the memory of so noble a woman.

In January, 1861, two widows committed suicide at Fou-Chow in the presence of thousands of spectators. Not one person attempted to prevent the women from destroying themselves because of an age-old custom.

The natives of Dutch New Guinea have an interesting custom. They always place upon the grave, instead of a stone, a spade, so that if the corpse regains its soul and comes to life it can dig itself out.

In modern life, we still make gifts to the dead. We decorate the graves with beautiful flowers. We frequently inter with the body a favourite old jewel, a cherished trinket, a bridal gown or flower, excusing the deed as an act of sentiment. What we are really doing is instinctively observing the custom almost as old as death itself of burying food and belongings with the dead that they will not want in the future state.

Only the other day the newspapers carried a headline "Cash Put on Gypsy's Bier to Pay Debts in Heaven." The story was of the death of the King of the Gypsies, who drank muriatic acid by mistake and died. His relatives and friends, believing that his soul would presently leave the body and go to heaven, dropped coins upon the bier with a silent request that the money be used to pay whatever debts they might have in the other world. According to this report a considerable amount of money was buried with the dead king.

Mourning Customs.—Doctor Frazer, in an article in the *Journal of the Anthropological Institute*, calls mourning a disguise because it is the reverse of ordinary wear. It seems very possible that the ancients, fearing the return of the spirit that caused death, disguised themselves.

(Courtesy of Metropolitan Museum of Art)

A gravestone of the 4th Century, B. C., Greek. The handclasp is probably symbolic of a farewell.

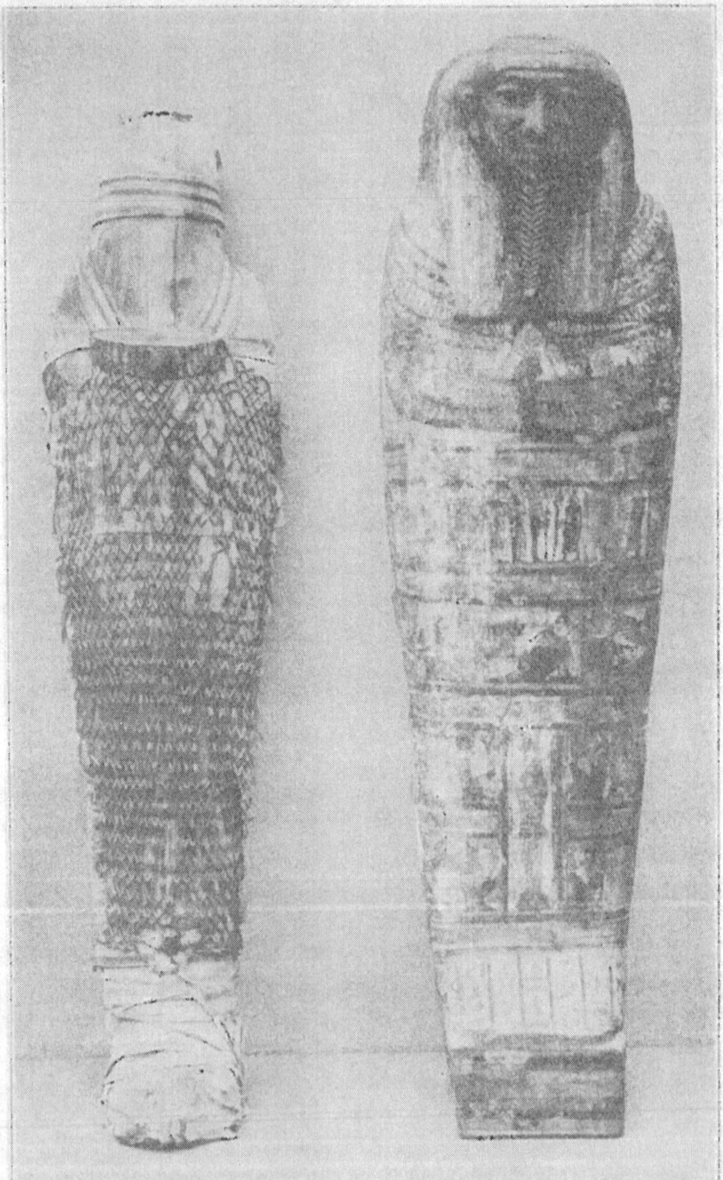

(Courtesy of Metropolitan Museum of Art)

Coffin and mummy of Khor. Egypt, 23rd Dynasty.

Among the Blackfellows the man smears his body with pipeclay when a death occurs and goes about furtively, looking always over his shoulder. Evidently he fears that if he is recognized as belonging to the same family as the deceased, the evil spirits will claim him, too. The women do not cover their bodies with the pipeclay, but they hang a chaplet of bones over the face. Most writers are of the opinion that:

> Whatever may be the reason for wearing crêpe veils or clothes of special cut or colour during mourning, the pipeclay of the mourning Blackfellow or the chaplet of bones his widow hangs over her face look very much like disguises from the ghost.

In Melanesia the widow smears her body with mud and wears a costume of grass. This grass mourning costume covers her whole body, her face and head—a perfect disguise if there ever was one. In Gaima the men and women alike wear veils which cover them completely. It is more of a net than a veil, and is in the shape of a hood which is drawn over the head.

Women of the upper Congo have smeared their bodies with white clay upon the death of their husbands for countless centuries. Perhaps this was originated as a method of disguise from the spirit of the husband if it should return to claim her.

The Congo Kaffirs assume a mourning costume of black, achieved in this manner. A certain species of oily ground nut is roasted and then ground into a black paste. This paste is smeared over the whole surface of the body, giving to the naked Kaffirs a mourning costume of black. This, too, is regarded by most authorities as a form of disguise. Are we, who wear black in time of mourning, really observing a primitive custom originated for the purpose of frightening away spirits or concealing ourselves from them?

The Encyclopædia Britannica says that "originally special garb for mourning seems to have been intended to warn the general public that persons so attired were unclean." This was true among certain people and to a limited extent, whereas most early peoples practised the custom of disguise.

In ancient Rome, men in time of death remained at home and avoided all feasts and amusements. They cut neither the hair nor the beard. For a stated period they were "retired"—that is, they did not mingle with their friends and relatives, remaining only with the immediate family. We find this true of many other people of antiquity.

The Hebrews, for instance, believed that any one who touched a corpse was unclean and definite periods were stipulated during which that person was prohibited from mingling with others. It is even to-day customary with the Hebrews to wash the hands immediately upon the return from a funeral.

It is very possible that mourning was intended as a warning, as the Encyclopædia Britannica suggests. Savage peoples were strongly of the notion that death was contagious—that to remain in the vicinity of death was to be threatened with like fate. Therefore, those who were dangerous, by virtue of having been present at the time of death (the family, in other words) donned special clothes or in some way marked themselves tabu.

Thus, when death occurs in a family of Kaffirs, the family becomes unclean and unable to mix with others for a definite period. Among many savages who practise cremation, the ashes of the dead are carried around by the widow for two or three years, during which time she is avoided by everyone. In Melanesia visible signs of mourning are worn; among various tribes of equatorial Africa tattooing and mutilating of the body are practised for purposes of indicating proximity with death; the Andamanese disinter the body after it has been buried a certain time and wear the bones of the dead to indicate mourning, and while they wear these bones they are avoided by the others. Savage life abounds with countless customs of this nature, and it would be monotonous to consider them all.

But it is important to note that our custom of retiring from social life originated with these old savage customs of warning against mingling with those who have been present at death, and therefore liable to contaminate those with whom they come in contact. There was a very definite tabu upon mourners, and upon mention of the dead. Therefore, mourners went into temporary retirement—a custom irretrievably a part of our modern social life.

In India it was customary until recently for the widow to sacrifice herself upon her deceased husband's pyre. Now the widow shaves her head, gives away her jewels and valuables, retires from social life, and spends the rest of her life performing menial duties for the family of her dead husband.

The Egyptians shaved their heads in time of death and for a certain period abstained from mixing with their fellows. The Hebrews were "unclean" for a certain period during which they kept to themselves. There are countless examples of this same custom not only in savage life, but among the early civilizations.

There were many methods of determining the period of retirement, particularly of widowhood, since women were expected to mourn more than men. Among the Tacullies the widow is compelled to carry around the ashes of her husband for two years, during which time she may not marry. Among the Kutchin Indians, the widow takes all decorations from her body, and for a period of a year is obliged to remain near the body of her husband to protect it from animals. When the body is quite decayed and only bones remain, she may put on beads, ornaments, etc., and attract another suitor.

Among some Indian tribes of North America it was customary to cut the hair of widows and forbid them to remarry until the hair had grown again to its original length. Among the Chickasaws the widow was obliged to live a single life for three years. Other Indian tribes sacrificed the wife when the husband died; still others shut her into a grave with him for a period of a year during which time her family was permitted to bring her food. At the end of a year she was allowed to mingle again with the others. The Navajo Indians protected their bodies with tar in time of death, believing that the evil spirits could not enter beneath the tar; and to protect themselves still further they caused the widow to live in retirement for a certain period. The woman was regarded as the exclusive property of the dead man, and his property was supposed to be influenced by the evil which had caused his death.

These periods of retirement and of widowhood, these countless prohibitions after death, were not meant solely to protect the others. They served also the purpose of removing all doubts concerning pregnancy and paternity.

We still practise retirement during mourning, and we still have very definite regulations concerning periods of widowhood and widowerhood. "The Book of Etiquette" says:

> For three weeks after a bereavement, women seclude themselves and receive no visitors except their most intimate friends. After this they are expected to be sufficiently resigned to receive the calls of condolence of their friends and acquaintances. They themselves make no visits until six months after the death.

And later:

> The length of the mourning period depends upon the tie which existed between the deceased and the bereaved. Except for an elderly woman whose husband has died and who never intends taking off black, the longest period is usually two years, the first in deep mourning, the next in "second mourning" during which time gray, lavender, purple, and white may be worn. This may be shortened to six months of deep mourning followed by six months of semi-mourning.

Black is to-day almost the universal mourning colour, because of its sombreness and because of the age-old traditions behind it. But in Japan and in China pure white is worn when mourning. In some sections of Africa red is the mourning colour, red paint being applied to the naked body. At one time yellow was the mourning colour of queens, and we are told that "Anne Boleyn paid her respects to the memory of Catherine by putting on yellow mourning." This was only a fad, however, inspired by the French.

Parsons says:

> The universality of human desire for symbolic signs of private emotions is ever astounding. The emotion of grief at the loss of relatives and friends by death has found in dress a fertile field for expressing this desire. Black, death's particular emblem, has been used for this purpose certainly since the early part of the 14th century. Chaucer and Shakespeare give occasional allusions to its use, particularly in the case of the widow.

He tells us also of a curious custom of giving away black gloves to be worn "in memoriam." In 1736 at the funeral of Governor Belcher of Boston more than a thousand pairs of mourning gloves were distributed. At the funeral of Andrew Faneuil three thousand pairs were given away.

> But [he says] nothing seems more incongruous and amazing than the fashion of mourning rings, which were often of great cost. At one Boston funeral more than two hundred were bestowed upon friends. . . . All kinds of mourning jewelry was fashionable, particularly such as exposed a design made from the hair of the departed and where black enamel could also be used.

Concerning the mourning customs of the present day, "The Book of Etiquette" says:

> Grief turns instinctively to the sombre garments of mourning for the slight measure of comfort they give. . . . Black fabrics for mourning should not have a shiny finish, nor should they be trimmed except in the simplest way. . . . A woman in mourning does not wear jewellery aside from the wedding and engagement rings. Dull bar pins when needed may be used. Handkerchiefs may have a black border or they may be pure white.

The Irish Wake.—A story is told of a rogue who, upon being led to the gallows on a Monday and seeing the sun begin to rise, remarked, "Yes, this week is beginning well!"

There seems always, in time of death, a tendency to relieve the tension in some way. The savages feast and dance and sing in the face of the great mystery called death. In ancient Abyssinia it was customary, at about the time of Queen Sheba, to have "mourning bees." These were held every time a person of prominence died. The people would gather in a great circle in the village and from a low moan work themselves up into frantic exhibitions of grief. Yet this was a form of relaxation, a method of relieving the tension caused by fear and superstitious dread of the great unknown.

The Irish have their well-known "wake."

There is an old popular tradition that when St. Patrick was dying he requested his weeping and lamenting friends "to forego their grief and rejoice at his comfortable exit, for the better furtherance of which, he advised each one to take a drop of something to drink." This last injunction of the saint is in reverence complied with at every Irish wake!

The Irish wake was intended originally to prevent the dead man's soul from prowling around the homes of survivors—a relic of the primitive custom. It was found to relieve the tension of the relatives and friends who gathered in the midst of death, and the custom became a popular one. There is eating and drinking, dancing and music at the old-time wake. The name probably originated in the idea of being awake to watch the body and keeping the soul from doing mischief.

There is indeed no better way to judge a man's character or his personality than to be present at his death. Does he cringe? Does he meet the Unknown bravely, with a smile of farewell and faint smile of welcome? Does he regret his life? Does he die fully satisfied with his achievements? What does he say? What are his last words?

Compare, for instance, the dying words of two queens—Cleopatra and the great Elizabeth. Cleopatra's last sentence was addressed to the asp which she drew from a basket of figs and applied to her bosom. "Here thou art, then!" she cried. But Elizabeth met death with no such fortitude. "All my possessions for one moment of time!" was her last sentence.

The Dying Words of Famous Men.—"I want for nothing but to die in the correct way," said Confucius, sage of China. And generations later Montaigne says, "There is nothing of which I am so inquisitive, and delight so to inform myself, as the manner of men's deaths, their words, looks and bearing. . . ."

The Roman consul under Claudius was condemned to die by his own hand. He hesitated, and Arria, his wife, was embarrassed by the hesitation. She seized the dagger from his hand and before he could stop her plunged it into her own breast. Calmly she withdrew the dagger, held it out to her husband and said, "It is not painful, Paetus." An instant later she fell dead at his feet.

It is related that Reverend Patrick Brontë, father of the famous Brontë sisters, determined to die standing on his feet. Although so weak that he could hardly see or hear anything going on around him, he managed to get to his feet, uttering his dying words, "While there is life there is will."

Anne Boleyn was condemned to be beheaded. As she stood before the headsman she clasped her fingers around her neck and said bravely, "It is small, very small indeed." Then she knelt quickly, and paid the penalty to Henry VIII.

George Miller Beard, distinguished American doctor and scientist, was eager to serve to the very end. His last words were, "I should like to record the thoughts of a dying man for the benefit of science, but it is impossible."

Lord Chesterfield, ever the polished gentleman and faultless host, closed his inspiring career with a typical sentence. "Give Day Rolles a chair," he said.

As Aaron Burr breathed his last, the one word "Madame" escaped from his lips. Whom was he greeting? Whom did he see? What last picture did he carry in his mind into eternity?

The great Beethoven was deaf for a period of more than twenty years before his death. His last sentence is pathetic, and one wishes with all one's heart that his dream has come true. "I shall hear in heaven," he whispered.

Rabelais, the dramatist, died with this sentence upon his lips: "Let down the curtain, the farce is over."

John Keats knew that he was dying, and he expressed his last thought in poetry—"I feel the daisies growing over me."

One is interested in the dying words of the glorious Louis XIV. Was he magnificent in life only, or could he be magnificent too when that life ebbed away? Was he brave, or was he cowardly? Louis died when he was close to eighty years of age, and he appears to have been spirited to the very end. Seeing everyone around him weeping, he exclaimed, "Why weep ye? Did you think I should live for ever? I thought dying had been harder."

The great Napoleon died in a fit of delirium during his exile. A thunderstorm burst over St. Helena and he jumped up crying, "Mon Dieu! The French Nation! Head of the Army!"

Would that some writer had been present at the guillotine during the reign of terror to jot down the dying words of those whose heads tumbled into blood-soaked bags! What eloquent sentences must have been uttered; what pathetic appeals from the women, what haughty sneers from the men—what bravery, and cowardice, and tenderness, and brutality, all blurred into one horrible massacre! There was the powerful Danton, standing before his executioner, thundering his defiance for all to hear: "You will show my head to the people; it will be worth the display."

Another kind of pathos in the dying words of Byron. Weary of life and of war, wasted with fever and with fasting, he breathed his last words at Missolonghi, and the echo has travelled all around the world. "Now I shall go to sleep," he said. And his eyes closed.

George Washington was the efficient executive to the

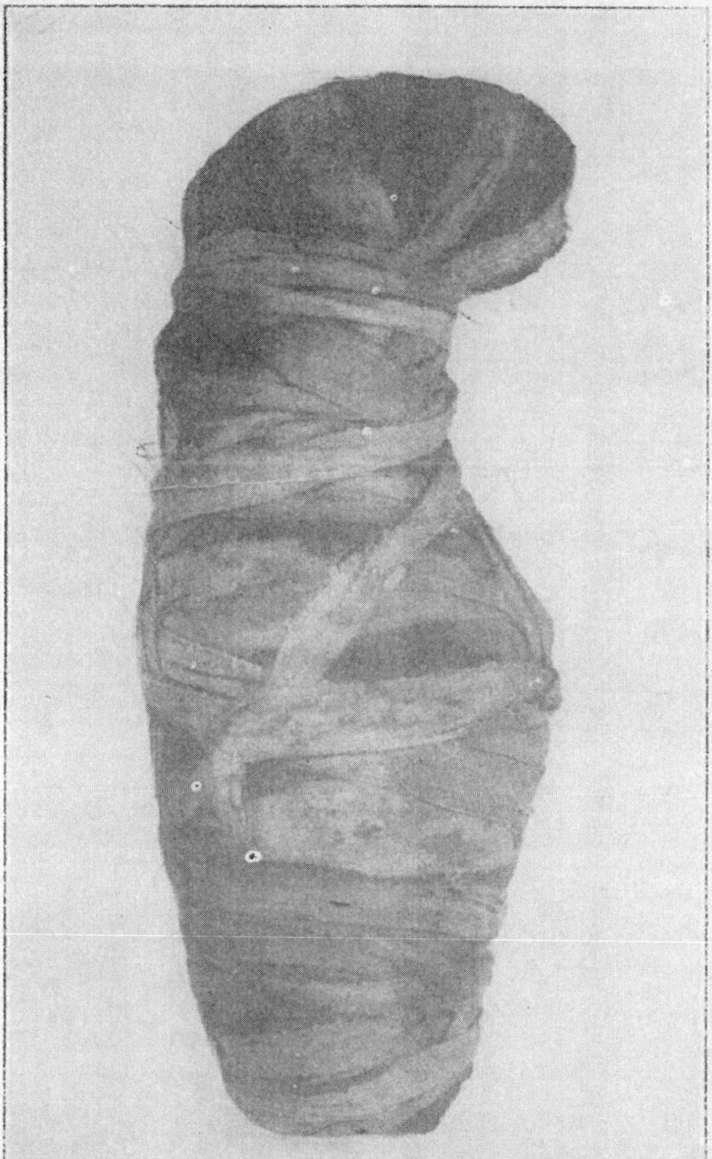

(Courtesy of Metropolitan Museum of Art)

Egyptian, Ptolemaic. Mummy of a black cat, sacred animal of ancient Egypt.

(Courtesy of Metropolitan Museum of Art)

"Bacchante."
MacMonnies, 19th Century.

last. The remarkable poise which characterized his life career did not desert him at the end, and he was self-possessed as he said to his secretary, "I am just going. Have me decently buried, but do not let my body be put into the vault in less than two days after I am dead. Do you understand? It is well."

When John Quincy Adams was informed of his approaching death, he said, simply and calmly, "Thomas Jefferson still survives."

Like Napoleon, the famous "Stonewall" Jackson died in delirium. He had been shot accidentally by his own soldiers. His last words were, "Let us go over the river and sit under the refreshing shadow of the trees."

One reads with interest of the end of the gallant and handsome Sir Walter Raleigh, condemned to death by beheading. With complete ease of manner, showing neither fear nor resentment, but rather a faint amusement, he ran his jewelled finger along the headsman's axe and said, "This is a sharp medicine, but a sure remedy for all evils." A moment later his lips could speak no more.

The last words of Theodore Roosevelt are significant. A fitting conclusion to a life gloriously spent. "Put out the light, please," he said to his attendant, and as the room darkened a great light left the world.

The whole world is familiar with President Harding's last words, uttered to his wife who sat at his bedside and read to him. "That's good; go on, read some more."

And the last words of Woodrow Wilson will be immortal: "I am ready."

CHAPTER XVIII

CONCERNING CHILDREN

The primary end of marriage is to beget and bear offspring, and to rear them until they are able to take care of themselves. On that basis Man is at one with all the mammals and most of the birds.

—HAVELOCK ELLIS.

Man is like God in this, that he has the power of creating human beings.

—O. A. WALL.

Search through the Bible from end to end,
You will find no verse so great as this:
"Male and female created he them"!

—EDGAR LEE MASTERS.

"BE FRUITFUL AND MULTIPLY"

THE first law of the Bible is also the first law of life. Every instinct and impulse cries, "Be fruitful and multiply!" Sex itself is a device for the propagation of the species; and sexual gratification is Nature's great scheme for attracting man and woman to each other.

The instinct for reproduction is present in all mankind, from the savages who live promiscuously in the heart of the jungle, to the men and women who belong to a highly refined and subtle civilization. Havelock Ellis says:

> Sex gradually becomes interwined with all the highest and subtlest human emotions and activities, with the refinements of social intercourse, with high adventure in every sphere, with art, with religion.

But slumbering always beneath sex and the sexual instinct is the animal urge which has procreation as its sole end—the age-old urge to reproduce, to give life.

Far back in the dawn of life, the brute man wandered prehistoric wastes concerned solely with the grim business of keeping life in his body. The beasts of the jungles and the elements of the heavens conspired against him. Sometimes there was food; more often, not. Sometimes there were warmth and comfort; more often there were rain, and cold, and an overwhelming dread of the unknown.

Then one day this brute man awoke and felt the warm sun bathing through every pore of his body. His tribesmen were already breakfasting on some sorry beast of the trail—a huge, hairy creature from whose side they tore great chunks of flesh. The brute man stirred in the sun and felt overpowered with a strange lassitude. Something spoke within him. He stretched his limbs. And suddenly, without warning, the blood began to pound through his veins at a terrific speed. His head swam. Reproduce! Reproduce! And almost without his realizing it he turned to look at the woman who sat beside him in the sun.

This primitive urge to reproduce sent its call across the universe, and its thundering echo vibrates still. The savage hears it as he dances wildly to the boom-boom of his tomtoms. The man of civilization hears it, but he chokes back his natural instinct to shout an answering challenge and soberly goes through the customary stages of courtship, love, marriage.

The sexual instinct is but a by-product of the great fundamental instinct of procreation. Man was attracted to woman because nature urged him to reproduce his own kind. Woman was attracted to man because every fibre of her body cried out for the child sleeping within her. Ellis says:

> The erotic idea in its deeper sense, that is to say the element of love, arose very slowly in mankind.

Jensen tells us of a group of prehistoric men and women caught in the trap of a great forest fire. They escaped the flaming demon, which they knew through bitter experience they could not fight with their flint axes, by jumping into a swamp and sitting in it up to their nostrils while the fire burned itself out. And then they emerged to begin their wanderings in search of another forest.

> But meanwhile [says Jensen], their number had increased, for one of the women had had a baby, from fright and before its time, while they sat in the pool given over to death—no easy birth. Amid all the thundering noise of the fire and the doomed beasts, a dismal note asserted itself, the cry of a woman in birth-pangs, and soon after the feeble whimperings of a new-born babe announcing its entry into the world with wailing.
>
> The little one came into the world half-drowned, the smoke of a disaster was his first breath, howls and heat his first sensations. . . . Happy was the mother to have got this little wretch, that was uglier than death, toothless as a senile but hungry as a leech; she made a nest for it of her arms and breast, hid it from the Man and kept it quiet with her mouth against its mouth, lest he should hate it and in an access of rage fall upon this new whining thing in his company. Weakened and devoted she stumbled on when they had to go, the last of the herd.

"Be fruitful and multiply!"

Early Love of Children.—The child was the tie that bound man and woman together. The love of offspring is inherent and instinctive in almost all living creatures. Nature has implanted in all mammals the desire to care for the young until they are able to care for themselves, provide them with food and the necessities of life, protect them from enemies and from dangers.

The infant whose birth Jensen describes on the preceding page grew into a straight little lad called Fyr. In childhood he played with a bear cub, had wrestling matches with a baby jackal. During one of these wrestling matches, we are informed that

> The muzzle and eyes of an elderly serious mother jackal were watching a little way off in the long grass, and on the other side Fyr's mother stood on guard, equally anxious and wrapped up in her young one.

Love of the young—in the jackal and in the human An instinct as old as life but new to every new generation that steps upon the shoulders of those who have gone before.

Prehistoric man welcomed children because "numbers were a consideration, especially at night, and for other reasons. Many yell louder than one, the greater the chorus the stronger their rights." Boy children were particularly welcome, for they grew into tall, straight, strong young men who could help in the hunt, who could wield battle axes when they were attacked.

Among savages in early life children were regarded as the chief wealth of the family. The more children a man had, the greater was his power. No savage young man was satisfied until he had a son of his own, for a direct heir greatly strengthened his position in the tribe, made him more important among his fellows.

The African Negro regards childlessness as the greatest disaster—an opinion he has had for many centuries. Among the Mayas disappointed couples prayed earnestly before their gods and made offerings to propitiate them. If their hopes for children were still deferred, they made sacrifices; and if again refused, they sometimes killed themselves. Among many savages we find the pronounced belief that to be childless is a disgrace. In Madagascar, to die without posterity is looked upon as the greatest misfortune that can befall a man.

An old Japanese proverb says, "Honest people have many children," and the Japanese always tried to live up to this maxim. The Chinese, too, believe in large families and in absolute filial devotion.

The Indian races are noted for the love and attention lavished upon offspring. The Crees, Chippewas, and various other Indians have a century-old desire for numerous children, and there are never gayer celebrations than when twins are born.

We find love of children existing among savages known for their brutality, as the Fijians, for instance, who are cannibals yet who seem to be greatly attached to their children, and the children to the parents. The young are carefully taken care of among the Tongans, although occasionally an infant is sacrificed cruelly for the purpose of bringing about some important person's recovery.

The New Zealanders are not entirely guiltless of infanticide, but they take noticeably good care of the children whose lives they spare. One writer tells us that the fathers especially seem fond of their children. Among the Bushmen, love for their children unites the family throughout life. And among the Greenlanders, a people untouched by the influence of higher civilization, barbarous and cruel in many ways, we find bonds of filial and parental love as strong as any to be found among us.

The savage is a better man than he is usually painted, and we find the love of children and the realization of marital responsibilities even among peoples so crude that they still go unclothed and still believe the thunder and lightning to be demons crashing and thundering above their heads.

Despite the love of children, which seems to be inherent and natural in most peoples, there come to us out of the past tales so cruel and barbarous that they make us wonder whether the perpetrators were humans at all or beasts parading in the guise of man. There have been savages with fiery, child-eating idols—beast-men who fed infants to the furnace burning within their monstrous iron gods. There have been ignorant and superstitious barbarians who sacrificed children as peace offerings whenever it rained or thundered. There have been cannibals who lived on their own young, or upon the young of their enemies. And even in early civilizations we find appalling numbers of children sacrificed in infanticide.

The Egyptians, advanced though they were in many things, fond of their children if we read rightly the records they have left behind them, nevertheless were guilty of several cruel practices toward children. It was customary, for instance, to bury alive a child or two with a parent that had died, the reason being that the parent would need someone to wait on him, or her, in the next world. Others took their children along for companionship—poor, helpless little tots walled into stone compartments alive with the dead body!

But luckily for civilization, love of the young and an instinctive desire to cherish and protect them, has characterized human nature from the very beginning, and became more and more pronounced with the development of man through the ages. The great mass mother loved her child in the beginning, fought bears and other beasts to protect it, starved herself no doubt to give it food, sat all day by the fire tending it, making clothes for it from the skins of animals, watching it as it crawled clumsily about like a little bear cub, kept always a careful eye on the jungle and the tiger that might at any moment spring from nowhere. The mass mother loves her child to-day, and the care and solicitude which characterized the primitive mother are still evident, though disguised by the niceties of modern life. There are now no bears to kill, no tigers to watch—only the social evils against which one must guard.

Across the great gulf of time which separates prehistoric savagery from glorified civilization two women clasp hands: the mother of yesterday and the mother of to-day. A golden thread stretches out across the ages and links their mother hearts together.

The Child and Marriage.—Many races do not consider marriage a true marriage until a child has been born. The child seals the marriage pact—makes the tie inviolable. We find this custom prevalent throughout Africa, Australia, and to a lesser extent among certain tribes of North American Indians.

It is apparent that in early life marriages were contracted for the sole purpose of bearing children. The earlier Greek poets spoke less of love and more of the glory of bearing children. The Romans of the Republic regarded marriage as the means for propagating the species and omitted love entirely from its significance. Among both the Greeks and the Romans marriages were sometimes contracted for a year, but if they proved fruitful at the end of that period they were renewed and made permanent.

We recall that one of the chief blessings which Moses, in the name of God, promised the Israelites, was "a numerous progeny." The Israelites were very eager to have many children and it was a great unhappiness to Rachel that she was unable to bear a child.

And when Rachel saw that she bore Jacob no children, she said unto him, Give me children, and if not, I die. (Genesis XXX, 1, 2.)

There is an elaborate mythological tale, borrowed from the Scandinavians and now existing in fragments of German folklore, which likens a marriage without offspring to a world without sun. This thought is found not only among the Germans, but among many Aryan peoples.

Marriage is intimately connected with the child, for it is almost wholly for the benefit of the young that the male and the female continue to live together. This refers, of course, to primitive and savage life where there are no legal or religious ties to bind men and women together. We have seen in a previous chapter how the child influenced early customs of marriage—how monogamy was established because of the child (p. 206).

Even among the lower animals the natural instinct to protect the young, and supply food for the subsistence of the young, is strong. In primitive life it must have been the tie which bound man to one cave, one woman, one home.

In primitive life, men lived in tribes or hordes. Connected with each tribe were several women who lived promiscuously with the men. No individual marriage existed, and the children were apparently the common property of the tribe. This was in the very beginning while man was still wandering from place to place—a bewildered and humble nomad in a terrifying world.

There were no real kinship ties at first, other than the fundamental kinship between mother and child. A group of children, growing into young manhood and young womanhood, traced their kinship through descent from a common ancestor, or claimed kinship through relationship to a common totem. This is known as artificial kinship.

In a later development kinship was traced through the father. When individual marriage became customary it was not difficult to regulate relationship, but in tribal or horde organization with no family ties, it was, of course, impossible to determine the paternal ancestry.

The father right in the child is interesting because it is the basis of the modern social system. It originated in early life when the father asserted his right over the right of the mother. The system of kinship, based upon male descent, introduced a more compact and permanent family organization. But we must not make the mistake of thinking that the father right existed universally or that it has prevailed uninterruptedly throughout the centuries. Throughout all Australia, Melanesia, and America in primitive times the mother right prevailed, and the children followed the mother, "taking their name from her and inheriting her property."

Mr. Dealey, in his "Sociology," says:

> While the family is usually considered the unit, or fundamental group of society, the term family has had a different significance at different times. When mankind was emerging from animal conditions the family group probably consisted simply of mother and child holding closely together merely during the helpless period of infancy. The mother herself persumably provided for and protected her children, who as they matured would feel a sympathetic connection because of their descent from a common mother. This furnishes the type of so-called matriarchal, or metronymic, family made up of a mother, her children and her daughter's children, forming a natural kin.

The patriarchal family, which traces its natural kin through the father, is so familiar to our minds that it seems to-day almost the only natural social system. It has existed since the earliest times among the Caucasians, but developed gradually among most other races. By the beginning of the Christian Era it was already an established custom or rule among civilized peoples.

The Child in Early Life.—Among the primitives children romped and played even as they do to-day. Indeed, the first two or three years of the child's life was similar to that of a child of corresponding age to-day, except, of course, that everything was relatively crude. The child was entirely dependent upon the mother for food and protection. It cried when it was hungry, slept when it was tired, crawled on all fours to catch shadows in the sun, blinked up at the clouds, cooed for hours at its fingers, its shell plaything, gazed out upon a strange and wonderful world. Omit the trained nurse and the inevitable "Care and Feeding of Children" and the life of the modern infant is not so far removed from this early existence.

There has never been an age so dark, or a people so barbarous, as to leave its children without toys. The first toys were probably polished stones, shells from the sea, beads strung on a bit of deerskin cut in a slender strip. An infant can be quite as happy with a rude stone as with a delicate ivory rattle. The rattle, by the way, is older than you would suspect and is said to have been invented by Archytas. He made painted clay puppets, representing human beings or animals, and put small stones inside of them to cause a rattling noise.

The Egyptians appear to have been particularly partial to dolls. They made dolls of wood with flat painted bodies, and made clever wigs for them of clay beads strung on thread. Examples of Egyptian dolls, in the British Museum, are more than three thousand years old.

The Eskimo baby has a doll, too. She dangles a lovely carved whalebone doll—the envy of any little pickaninny of far-away Africa who has only a doll of carved wood. In Mexico little girls have had funny little dolls of baked clay since the earliest times, and prefer them even to-day to the "pale dolls" sent by the United States.

The dolls of ancient Greece and Rome had well-shaped

heads and jointed arms and legs which moved by means of strings. Some interesting dolls were discovered in the catacombs and are now in the Museum Carpegna.

Besides dolls, small wooden carts, houses, ships, and other toys made of wood, leather, and bronze have been found. The fact that they have been found on children's graves and are absolutely absent from the graves of adults proves that they were toys.

Among the Indians of North America the baby was placed in a cradle and suspended near its mother from a tree bough. Cradles existed not only among the early Indians, but are found among primitives in widely separated localities. Most of these antique cradles consist of a flat board with buckskin or basketwork at the bottom and a strip of the buckskin or other material at the top to go around the mother's shoulders. While on the march, the cradle is carried suspended down the back. There have been many kinds of cradles, some of which are illustrated.

The Indian mother sang lullabies to her infant—another custom prevalent among most of the ancients. The child was taught that he must not cry; each time he began to do so his mother's hand was placed over his mouth. In early times it was dangerous to permit the child to cry, for it might attract enemies or animals. Almost from the day of its birth its whimperings were stifled, so that when the child grew up it could bear almost any pain without complaining.

Being bound constantly as an infant to a flat piece of wood or birch bark, the Indian boy grew up tall and straight. He learned to help his father in the hunt. He wrestled with other youths, ran races, tested his skill in imitating the sounds of the birds and beasts of the forests.

The Indian girl was taught all the arts of her mother—cooking, tending the fire, making baskets, weaving, painting pottery. She went to the stream for water, carried wood for the fire. She was prepared almost from infancy to become the drudge her mother was before her.

Among the Africans, and indeed among most savages in early times, the boy was trained from an early age to hunt, fish, tend the fire, make implements. At the age of fifteen or sixteen he was initiated, amid great ceremonies, to the secrets and traditions of the tribe. He was entrusted with the tribe's most cherished myths, magical rites, and traditions, and informed concerning his duties as a man. Then two or three of his teeth were knocked out, or he was tattooed, or he was obliged to take part in some weird dance, and he was accepted as a man.

Many peoples all over the world practise the custom of knocking out the teeth of young children. When asked why he knocked out the two front teeth of his children, the Australian Dieyerie replied that Muramura, a good spirit, disfigured the first child in this manner and was pleased with the result. Therefore he commanded all of his people thereafter to do the same to their children. The custom may have had a religious origin, but more possibly it originated in the primitive notion that to sacrifice a part of the body insured the safety of the rest.

In Rhodesia, for instance, if a baby's first tooth happens to show its tiny white tip in the infant's lower jaw, that tooth is instantly drawn out by the parents. They believe it to be an indication that the spirits for some unknown reason are displeased with the child, and they draw out the tooth to avoid injury to the infant.

The girl in primitive life always remained with the mother, helping prepare the food and the skins, until such time as she was old enough to be sold or exchanged in marriage. Sometimes she was stolen when still a child and sold either into slavery or into marriage.

A study of the child in early civilizations is interesting, and the subject offers opportunity for much fascinating discussion. But we can barely touch upon it here. In Egypt children of five and six years tended the sheep. All children, boys and girls, were expected to wait on their parents, and absolute obedience was required.

The Greeks and Romans practised infanticide to a startling degree. Female children were particularly undesirable. Yet both the Greeks and Romans are known to have practised adoption accompanied by a ceremony of mock birth. These adoptions appear to have been very frequent.

One authority says:

> The Spartan government was founded on the principle that the life of every individual from the moment of birth belonged absolutely to the state. The elders of the city inspected the newly born infants and ordered the weak and unhealthy to be carried to a nearby chasm and left to die. By this inhuman practice Sparta made sure that those who were physically fit should survive.
>
> Children who were allowed to grow up were brought up under an iron rule. At the age of seven the boys were removed from their parents and organized into small bands over which the strongest and most courageous were made captains. They slept in public dormitories, on hard beds of rushes. They ate of black broth and coarse, meagre fare. They were drilled each day in gymnastic and military exercises. Their muscles became like iron and they learned great endurance.

The Japanese have always been very fond of children. They have a "Dolls' Festival" for the girls, and a special "Boys' Festival," both being of great antiquity. The "Dolls' Festival" takes place on the third day of the third month of the year, and it is observed in every home where there is a little girl who loves dolls. The girls bring out all their dolls—some representing knights, some dancers and clowns, some boys and girls—and place them in a great heap on a row of shelves arranged like a miniature grandstand. They invite one another to come in and see their dolls, and there is much merrymaking.

On the fifth day of the fifth month, the Japanese boy has his particular holiday. Instead of dolls, pieces of armour and figures of warriors appear on the shelves. In the garden before the house a pole is set up at the top of which flutters a huge cloth carp—that fish being the symbol of the boys' festival.

The Chinese, like the Japanese, are extremely fond of

children, but they demand the utmost respect and absolute obedience in all things. Confucius taught that a disrespectful or disobedient child was a disgrace and misfortune to its parents.

Race progress, of course, is intimately involved with the quality and nature of child-training. Civilization has always received its greatest impetus in those localities where children were taught the wisdom of their elders, where they were carefully trained for manhood and womanhood.

The Jewish religion, being sustained through literature, inspired the first efforts to provide elementary education generally for all the children in the community. In his "Ancient Israel From Earliest Times to A.D. 70" Fletcher H. Swift gives an interesting and instructive account of these first efforts, and of how the literature-sustained religion of the Jews supplied the impetus.

By way of contrast, it is interesting to meditate upon the modern community kindergarten. Friedrich Wilhelm August Froebel (1782–1852) believed that it made a tremendous difference in the life of an individual if he were taught the wrong things before the sixth year. So important did he believe the teaching of young children that he opened a school in a little village called Blankenburg, which is in Germany. This was in 1837. Two years later he named this institution "Kindergarten" (garden for children). His educational theories proved epoch-making, for in a short time all England, France, and the United States knew of his methods. To-day there is scarcely a corner of the civilized world that does not have its Kindergarten for the youngsters.

Primitive Notions Concerning Birth.—The source of life must have been as puzzling to early man as the mystery of death. How did the children come? What gave them life? Did some good spirit breathe the spark of life into their tiny bodies? Or did they just awaken, as man awakens from sleep?

As Robinson points out:

In the beginning man did not know how children came, for it was not easy to connect a common impulsive act with the event of birth so far removed in time.

It is doubtful whether prehistoric man realized in the beginning that he had anything to do at all with the miracle of birth.

Jensen's story of the birth of Fyr, part of which is quoted at the beginning of this chapter, gives an excellent picture of the birth customs of those early times. The child came into the world unannounced, unexpected. Only the mother knew of the tiny voice that whispered to her, but even she did not know what was happening.

One day the woman would feel tired, and heavy, and suddenly the pangs of birth would grip her. Dropping back behind the horde on the march, she would deliver a child to life. The cry of the woman in birth-pangs, the whimper of a new little life—and the horde realizes that another has joined their numbers. But how did the child come? What was the mystery? Who sent it? They do not know, but they accept the little parcel of life as only a few days ago they accepted the grim visit of death.

Out of the early speculations of savage man to solve the mystery of birth, there evolved many mythical explanations, survivals of which are seen in the nursery tales told to children. Most familiar of these tales is that which concerns the stork.

An old tradition, so old that its origin is buried in dim antiquity, is that the stork brings good luck. An old belief also is that the coming of children is good luck. Somehow the two ideas were united—possibly because storks were frequently seen at times of birth and the superstitious believed that the bird was the good-luck omen which presaged the infant's arrival. Thus would evolve the custom of explaining the mystery of birth by advancing the mythological explanation that the stork brought the children. When man realized that this was untrue, the tale was retained in folklore and tradition, and gradually became a universal nursery explanation of birth.

Some writers advance other theories concerning the origin of the stork fable. One of our authorities, for instance, says that the stork symbolizes "filial piety" by reason of the care and solicitude it exercises toward aged storks. As defined by Confucius, "filial piety" means, fundamentally, the carrying on of the aims of one's forefathers. "It is not improbable that this notion of doing as our fathers have done is the explanation of the nursery lore that it is the stork who brings the babies."

Still another theory is that the bennu, a sort of heron, regarded as the emblem of Regeneration among the ancient Egyptians, gradually came to be mistaken for the stork. Among the Egyptians, the bennu was supposed to symbolize or betoken the re-arising of the sun, a thought easily connected with birth. The stork may have been substituted for the bennu in later interpretations of the tradition.

The Minnetarrees of North America have the curious old myth that there was no earth at all, in the beginning, only water. The "Never-Dying-One" sent a great red-eyed bird into the waters to bring up the earth in its beak. The stork bringing a new little life may in some way be connected with this fabulous bird carrying the earth—all of life—in it bleak. (See p. 18)

The evolution of the stork myth from an actual explanation to a nursery fable would have been expedited by the fact that the stork lives on roofs and chimneytops—a thought which would suggest itself to the mother when a child asks where the new baby came from. "The stork brought it, my dear! Brought it in a nice little bundle and dropped it down the chimney!"

When man had advanced sufficiently to have acquired the ability to reason logically, he began to connect birth with the sexual act. The generative organs, being the obvious physical basis for procreation, were venerated.

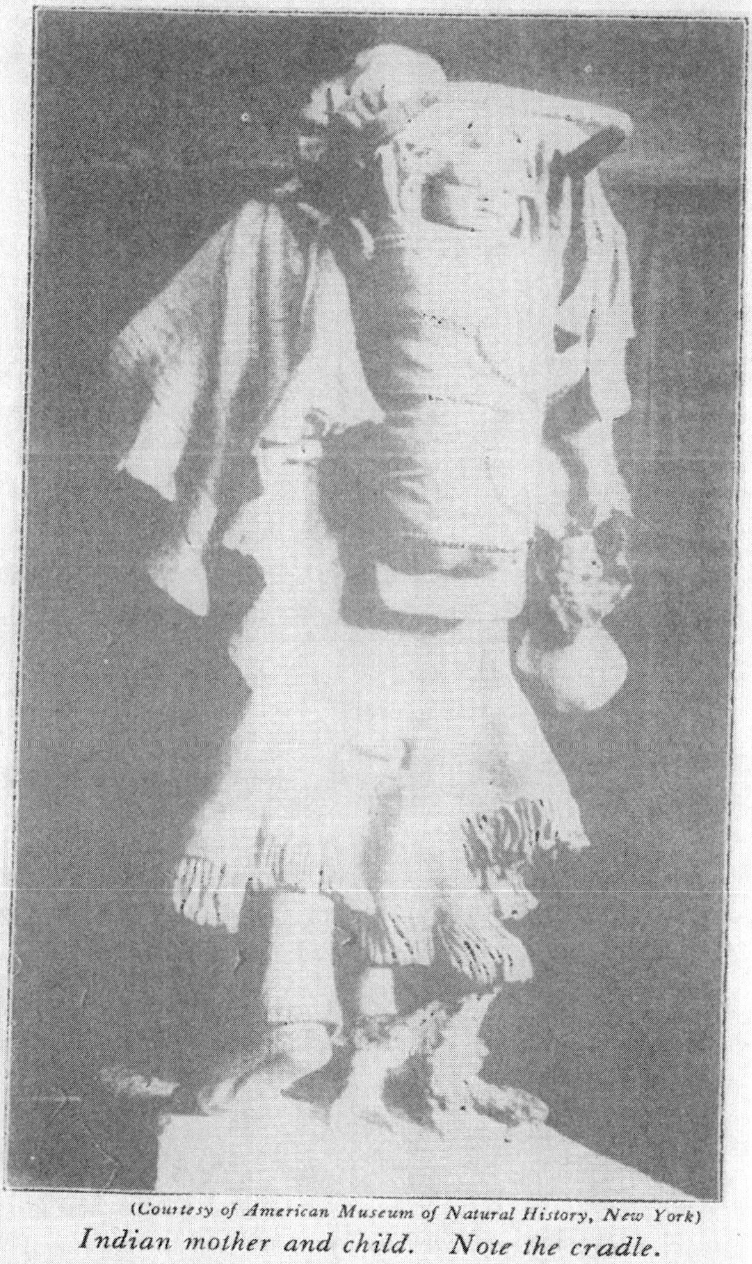

(Courtesy of American Museum of Natural History, New York)

Indian mother and child. Note the cradle.

(Courtesy of Metropolitan Museum of Art)

Photograph of a modern African mother and her child.

Thus originated the Phallic religion—a primitive religion based wholly upon sex and sex worship.

But man was for many centuries afterward wholly in ignorance of gestation, of the mystery and the processes of begetting and conceiving. When he discovered his own importance in the matter, his ego became inflated and he decided that he alone was responsible for the new life. The woman had no soul; he had. Therefore it was he who created the life, originated the new little soul, and the woman's body was merely the shell through which the infant entered the world. This gave rise to the custom of La Couvade, which we shall presently discuss.

Three thousand years ago the nature of gestation and the process of birth appear to have been fairly well understood. We find ample proof in the Bible that the ancient Hebrews, Egyptians, and their neighbours knew and understood the natural phenomenon, the miracle of birth. We read in the Bible, for instance, that

> God said unto Jacob, Israel shall be thy name. . . . *Kings shall come out of thy loins.* (Genesis XXXV, 11, about 1732 B.C.)

(O. A. Wall explains that "loins" in this connection is a translation from the Hebrew word meaning phallus or genitals.)

Anaxagoras, a Greek philosopher who lived about 475 B.C., taught that

> the embryo was formed entirely from the "seed" of the father and that the mother merely furnished the soil in which it grew and developed. This theory was not new. Anaxagoras merely gave it more definite expression and made it generally known and popular among the Greeks and the successors to Greek science.

Pythagoras, Democritus, Aristotle, Diogenes, Mohammed, Athenæus, Galen, and many others whose names are familiar, advanced theories during their lifetimes concerning the process of gestation and birth. Each had a different theory, each another twist of thought. It was not until a fairly recent time that science and medicine accepted any definite views concerning the subject.

It is interesting to note that the Chinese have for a long time regarded the child as one year old at birth, and two at what we call the first birthday. The period of gestation is counted as one year.

La Couvade.—Among many savage peoples it was believed that the child emanated from the body of the father, and that the mother merely nurtured it. From this belief came the custom of La Couvade. It is prevalent in Africa, Australia, and was at one time widely prevalent in Europe and among the North American Indians.

The custom of La Couvade requires that the father, at the time of birth, retire to bed as though it were he, and not the woman, who was delivering the child. Dobritzhoffer tells us that among a certain savage people of South America:

> No sooner do you hear that a woman has borne a child, than you see the husband lying in bed, huddled up with mats and skins, fasting, kept in private, and for a number of days abstaining religiously from certain viands; you would swear it was he who had the child. . . . I had read about this in old times, and laughed at it, never thinking I could believe such madness, and I used to suspect that this barbarian custom was related more in jest than in earnest, but at last I saw it with my own eyes among the Abipones.

Brett, in his "Indian Tribes of Guiana," says:

> "On the birth of a child, the ancient Indian etiquette requires the father to take to his hammock, where he remains some days as if he were sick, and receives the condolence and congratulations of his friends. An instance of this custom came under my own observation where the man, in robust health and excellent condition, without a single bodily ailment, was lying in his hammock in a most provoking manner, and carefully and respectfully attended by the women, while the mother of the new-born infant was cooking—none apparently regarding her.

The name La Couvade has been given to this peculiar custom by Professor Tylor. One authority, Bachofen, compares this custom with the symbolic pretense of birth practised in Greece and Rome as rites of adoption. He says that among various tribes La Couvade is the legal form by which the father recognizes a child as his. In other words, it is a symbolic custom through which the father acknowledges his paternity. This explanation of the custom is supported by Professor Tylor.

Isn't it barely possible, in primitive life, that man in his egotism believed that it was his own flesh and blood, his own bit of life that was being born through the woman? After all, it was a pretty widespread notion that woman was only the shell through which the child was born. It seems a plausible explanation of the curious custom of La Couvade.

The Miaos explain the custom in a manner of their own. Recognizing the husband's duty, they explain that "the husband goes to bed for forty days because of the principle that he should bear the same hardships as his wife." Others explain the custom as one intended to protect and preserve the infant—in other words, fooling the evil spirits who lurk in the home.

There are some who connect this custom of La Couvade with the world-wide belief that the conduct of the mothers before and after birth affects the child. For instance, the Hottentots believe that if a pregnant woman eat lion flesh or leopard flesh, the child will have the characteristics of the animal eaten. In European folklore there is an old superstitious notion that if a pregnant woman step over a grave her child will die.

The custom of La Couvade is still observed in Guiana and elsewhere in the savage world. Even in rural England there seems to be an obstinate belief that the birth of the child affects the husband. There is no trace of this custom, however, among educated and civilized peoples.

The Practice of Infanticide.—A great blot upon the history of the two early civilizations, Greece and Rome, is the practice of infanticide which they carried to extremes. Vast numbers of infants were sacrificed to this inhuman custom.

Female children were undesirable to the Greeks, therefore they killed many of them in infancy. Boy infants were deserted, left to perish, if they were weak or sickly. The Romans permitted only strong and healthy children to grow up. For more time than we like to think the custom of destroying undesirable children existed among the Greeks and Romans, but under the Republic the abuses of paternal authority were checked. With the coming of Constantine infanticide was checked even more, for the father who killed his child was declared a murderer.

Infanticide was practised also by many savage peoples. It was particularly prevalent among the Asiatics, and was at one time common in China. In ancient times it was customary to show a new-born baby to the father, who decided whether or not it would be permitted to live. Wall says,

> Especially were girls thus killed, because they were as expensive and troublesome to raise as boys, and when they were old enough to repay for this trouble by labour, the labour went to a stranger, the husband.

But other writers assure us that there was a widespread prejudice in favour of killing boy infants rather than girls. The Abipone mothers, for instance, spared girls oftener than boys "because their sons when grown up would want wherewithal to purchase a wife, and so tend to impoverish them, while their daughters would bring them in money by their sale in that capacity."

Among the Australian natives are many tribes accustomed to destroy infants born malformed or weakly. They also kill one child when twins are born—usually the smaller or weaker one.

The excuses offered for killing burdensome children are many and varied. Some savages offered children to their gods, to propitiate them—and incidently reduce the economic burden. Deformed and imperfect infants were almost invariably put to death. Among the prolific races, cannibalism existed no doubt because the population was a menace to existence itself. The Maoris who practised infanticide offered the excuse that they killed children to avoid the murder of men. In other words, they practised infanticide in preference to cannibalism.

One writer says:

> Infanticide was in some cases a device forced upon a group of men to adjust their numbers to the available food, or for security against enemies. The first infanticides were probably practised on the march. The mother, unable to keep up with the march and her burden, would be ordered to throw the child away or remain behind herself.

In modern life, the custom of leaving an undesirable child on a doorstep or in the vestry of a church has replaced the savage custom of infanticide.

There are, however, many savage tribes absolutely guiltless of this cruel practice. The Aleuts, for instance, regard child murder with horror, and believe that to practise it will bring disaster upon the whole village. The Blackfeet believe that women who have been guilty of infanticide will never reach the "happy mountain" after death. The story is told of a Bakundu woman in Africa condemned to death for the murder of her infant. It seems strange that in barbaric Africa there is not one district noted for the destruction of infants.

Baptism and Christening Customs.—Christening as we know it had its origin in the rite of John the Baptist. He belonged to a sect that believed that immersion in water would "wash away all sins and prepare the neophyte for the kingdom of God."

Mr. Picart, in his "Ceremonies and Religious Customs" says that baptism is

> a sacrament instituted to wash away original sin, and all those actual ones we may have committed; to communicate to mankind the spiritual regeneration and the grace of Christ Jesus; and to unite them to Him as the Living Members to their Head.

There are two methods of baptizing—by immersion and by ablution. Immersion only was used until the time of St. Gregory, and then ablution became the custom.

To-day in most cases just a few drops of the water are sprinkled upon the child's head.

The customs of baptism are based upon various ancient rites and ceremonies. Purification by water, for instance, forms "an integral part of Malay customs at birth, adolescence, marriage, sickness, death and in fact at every critical period of the life of a Malay." In the Congo the natives sprinkle water upon a new-born child—a custom they have observed for ages. Everyone who wishes to indicate a friendliness toward the child casts a drop of water upon it. The custom of immersion for purposes of purification exists among many savages to-day and can be traced far back into antiquity.

The practice of giving a name to the person baptized is very old. The ancient Greeks appear to have had both baptizing and naming customs, as we have this detailed information concerning the ceremony.

> On the fifth or seventh day the infant went through the ceremony of purification; the midwife holding him in her arms, walked several times around a burning altar. A festive meal on this day was given to the family. The door was decorated with an olive crown for a boy, with wool for a girl. On the tenth day after its birth the child was named and another feast took place. This ceremony implied the acknowledgment, on the part of the father, of the child's legitimacy. Friends and relatives presented the infant with toys of metal or clay, while the mother received painted vases.

Name-giving has always been regarded as a serious and important business. Throughout almost all grades of culture name-giving is achieved with ceremony and solemnity, with rites and impressive observances. The Red Indians, for instance, hold name-giving in such importance that they always consult the medicine man concerning the correct procedure. Usually the child is not named until some feat of strength in early childhood, some accident or some personal peculiarity, determines the name for him.

A Zuni boy is "initiated" any time after his fourth birthday. Before this time he had answered simply to the name of "baby." Now he is given a name. At the ceremonies there is a "godfather" who breathes upon a wand which is then extended to the child's mouth. The authority who tells us of this Zuni custom refers to it as a prototype of baptism.

In Nias, men take new names at marriage. A Haida youth changes his name four times during his lifetime. The Iroquois receives a new name at puberty. Among the Quojas and Guinea when a boy is named the father parades the village armed with bow and arrows and sings constantly, to frighten away evil spirits and to drown the sound of the boy's name so that the spirits cannot overhear and use it.

This fear of having the name heard and used injuriously is widespread among savages. The Gillsland blacks object strongly to let any one outside the tribe know their names, lest their enemies, learning them, make them "vehicles of incantation and so charm their lives away." This is on the principle of imitative magic.

In Abyssinia the child has two names given him, one for common use and the other to remain a secret. This is true among various savage peoples, and was true also in ancient times. The child was supposed to be known by one name to the supernatural powers in the other world, and if the enemy knew this name he could harm the child. In savage life one is rarely addressed by one's real name, for to do so is to invite danger. Among the Barea not even a wife may mention her husband's name. We still find a reluctance to reveal the name among children in modern Europe, sometimes even here in the United States.

There is an interesting method of securing safety by spreading a newborn child's identity over a number of children. In the Kei Islands, after naming, the parents entertain all children of the vicinity. The same custom is found in Ceramlaut. In Amboina, shortly after birth, three to five children are brought into the birth chamber and there feasted.

It seems to this author that customs such as these would have originated the practice of giving birthday parties.

Another interesting custom is observed in New Zealand. It appears that after baptizing an infant the New Zealanders forced it to swallow pebbles, "so that its heart might become hard and incapable of pity."

The godfather and godmothers, in Christianity, were intended originally to represent the church which offered the child to Christ to baptize. But godparents are found also in primitive ceremonies and among savage peoples.

"Parential anxiety for the child's safety, combined with the primitive impulse to shift responsibility, as the best way of meeting it, is the *raison d'être* of godparents." The godparents in primitive thought are proxies for the real parents, and both sets of parents are supposed to represent the children. The underlying principle of the custom is that a set of "artificial parents" lessens the responsibilities of the real parents. Many savages believe that the child acquires its characteristics from the godparents. Even in European folklore there is a common belief that the child is affected by the appearance and characteristics of its godparents, and also of those whose names its bears.

We find the custom of godparents among the Mayas, the Caribs, and the Japanese. In savage tribes scattered throughout Africa we find the peculiar custom of pretending that another man and woman had the child, not those to whom it has really been born. This other couple dance, shout, and pretend to be extremely happy. They receive gifts and act for all the world as though there were a new little life in their hut. The purpose of this custom is to confuse the evil spirits who may have come to do injury to the child.

In Altmark godparents are given bread and cheese to divide between themselves. This custom of making the godparents a gift of some sort is widely practised in Europe. In early times the gift usually took the form of

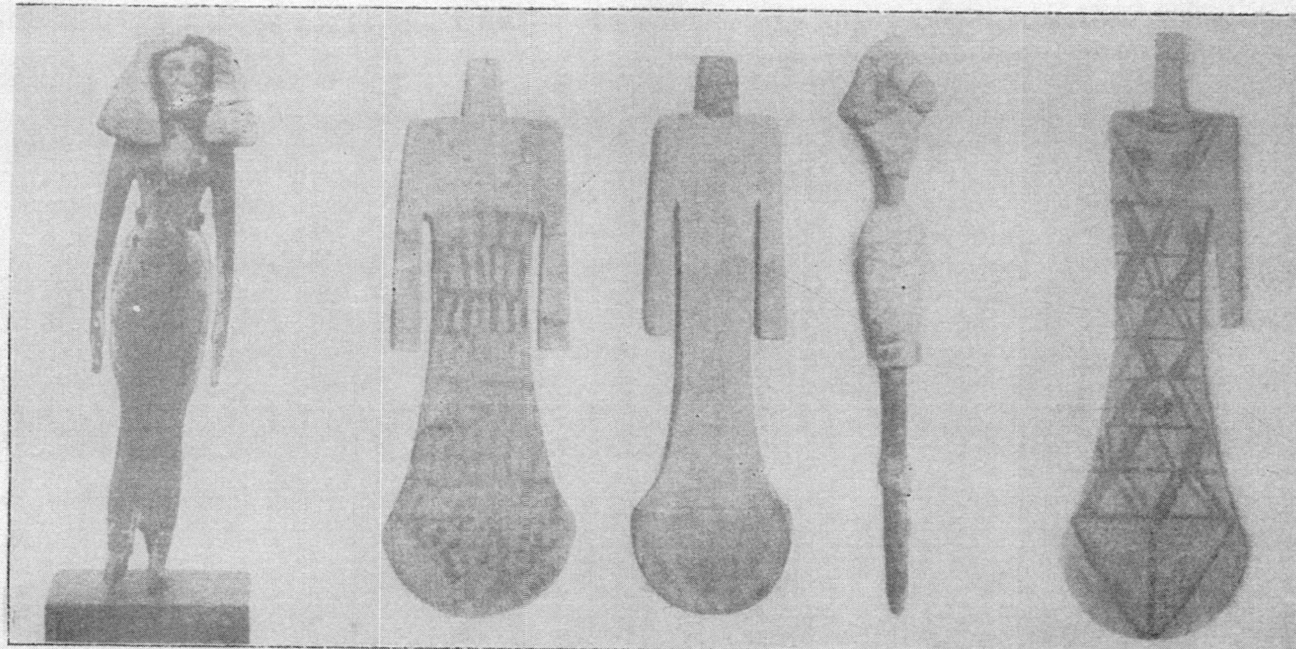

(Courtesy of Metropolitan Museum of Art)

A child's doll of wood, discovered in Egypt.

Ancient Egyptian dolls of wood.

A wooden doll from Sheik Abd-el-Kurng

(Courtesy of Metropolitan Museum of Art)

Latona and her children, Apollo and Diana. William Henry Rinehart, 19th Century, American.

food, but later the food gifts were replaced by trinkets, and later still, by jewels.

The custom of gifting the child is more prevalent and survives with us. Among many savage tribes we find the tendency to present the child with something, even if it is just a beast's claw, said to ward off sickness. In early Europe it was customary to present the child with small pieces of money, salt, bread, and cheese. We suspect that the bread and cheese gifts were for their own consumption! These gifts, according to an old superstition, were to insure the child money and food throughout life.

The familiar gift of a coral with bells has its origin in an ancient superstition. According to Pliny, coral was anciently regarded as an amulet against fascination, and therefore it would keep the evil spirits from bewitching the child. It was also thought an excellent device for preserving the teeth. The bells on the coral were intended to frighten away the spirits, and during the early stages of Christianity it was customary to have these bells blessed by the priest.

In mediæval times the custom of presenting the child with "Apostle Spoons" was practised. These spoons were usually presented by the godparents. They were of silver gilt, the handles terminating in figures of the apostles, each with his distinctive emblem. Sometimes single spoons were given, bearing the figure of the patron or name saint of the child. But more frequently the spoons were presented in sets. The complete set included twelve spoons, but the wealthy included an extra one, larger than the others, with a figure of Christ on it. Complete sets of the thirteen Apostle spoons are very rare.

At about 1665 the custom of presenting the child with these spoons began to die out. But by that time the phrase "born with a silver spoon in its mouth" had become a familiar metaphor for children born to wealthy parents. The child of poor parents was "born with a wooden spoon in its mouth."

Names and Their Meaning.—One of the oldest methods of name-giving is from some event taking place at the time of birth, or some striking characteristic of the child displayed a little while after birth. For instance, in the Bible we find that Rachel, dying in childbed, called her child Ben-oni, meaning "a son of sorrow." Later the father changed the name to Benjamin, "son of the right hand."

Among the Indians of North America, among the Mordvines of the Caucasus, and among many savage peoples, the name was determined by accident or by whim. A thunderstorm at the time of birth, a tiger lurking in the vicinity, any peculiarity of weather or of season was adapted into a name for the child.

We are to-day born with at least one name all ready and waiting for us, but this is a fairly recent custom. Until about the 10th century A.D. names were given after birth and there was no so-called "family name" by which all members of the family were known. It was between the 11th and 16th centuries that "our modern nomenclature established itself in the more populous and civilized European societies."

The custom began with the nobility. Toward the close of the 10th century, members of nobility began to call themselves after their ancestral seats. For two centuries the custom persisted, and then we find citizens patterning themselves after nobility—proudly adopting the names of their trades. These names were handed down from father to son.

An investigation into the personal names of people would be exhaustless; but it will be interesting to the reader to give here just a few examples to indicate how names were originated.

The custom of adopting the name of the trade was prevalent in England during the 12th and 13th centuries. There is a family in Sussex, for instance, which has carried on the trade of weaving as far back as the traditions of the family extend. The family name is Webb.

Our most common surname, Smith, is a trade appellation. During the Middle Ages the smith supplied many of the mechanical needs ordinarily required by the people. He was everywhere. Almost every little community had its smith. Therefore the smith has left a great impression upon our nomenclature, and we find a vast number of Smiths in England and the United States.

The name Johnson indicates a man who had no distinguishing characteristics of his own, no definite trade, nothing to provide him with a name. He was simply the colourless *son of John*. But he who bore the proud name of Smith was somebody. He was *the smith* of the locality.

The origins of such names as Tailor or Taylor, Cooper, Barber, Baker, Carpenter, Clerk (Clark), etc., are obvious. Like Smith, they suggest the trade of the person they represent.

The relationship of son was variously expressed. Johnson is but one example. Thomson, Jackson, Wilson are names of the same type. The original forms were Tom-his-son, William-his-son, etc. Among the Anglo-Saxons and Scandinavians, the suffix *ing* also indicates sonship, giving us some names as *Willing*, son of William, *Godding*, son of Godwin, *Henning*, son of Henry.

In Ireland the O' before a name, and the Mac or Mc before a name in Ireland and Scotland, are equivalent to the *ing* among the Scandinavians. Thus O'Brien is the son of Brien; MacCarthy meant originally the son of Arthur. Sometimes the name was derived from the trade or profession, and the prefix added, as for instance MacPherson means the son of the parson; MacNab indicates the son of the abbot.

The Norman French express sonship through the use of Fitz. Thus Fitzroy is the son of Roy; Fitzsimmons is the son of Simon.

Such names as Marshall, Stuart, Cleaver, etc. are derived from the occupation of the man to whom the name was first given. For instance, the Stuarts at one time had an ancestor who was a steward. The Marshalls had an ancestor who was a marshal. The people whose surname is Cleaver or Claver have for their forefather the clavinger, or keeper of the keys.

Then, of course, there are the many place or country names. A Scotchman coming to live in England would be known as the Scot. Hence, in time, the surname Scott applied to him and to his family. Wallace originally indicated a Welshman—he who came from Wales. In early times, newcomers to the golden land called America discarded the old, hard-to-pronounce names which they brought with them and adopted such names as Strange, Newcomb or Newcome, Travellers or Travers, etc.

Every name has its own story, and every story its different, fascinating. One picks up the thread of a name and follows it back over the centuries to its source. Sometimes there is a knight at the end of the thread, holding his banner high. Sometimes there is a wanderer at the end of the thread, crossing a great, wide ocean to reach an unknown land. Always there is some one person who has given the name it significance.

To-day cannot forget yesterday, for the one is linked eternally to the other.

CHAPTER XIX

Popular Superstitions with some Curious Customs and Many Miscellaneous Origins

The savage is very close to us indeed, both in his physical and mental make-up and in the forms of his social life. Tribal society is virtually delayed civilization, and the savages are a sort of contemporaneous ancestry.

—William I. Thomas.

Few of us take the pains to study the origin of our cherished convictions; indeed, we have a natural repugnance to so doing. We like to continue to believe what we have been accustomed to accept as true, and the resentment aroused when doubt is cast upon any of our assumptions leads us to seek every manner of excuse for clinging to them.

—James H. Robinson.

THE BIRTH OF SUPERSTITION

ONE of the oldest of human instincts is fear. Man was cradled in a world of bewildering hostility, and he saw danger lurking everywhere around him. Smouldering craters belched fire before his frightened gaze. The thunder crashed in terrific bolts above his head. The night sky winked at him with thousands of silver eyes. And man was afraid. In this primitive chaos his very shadow seemed a grim spectre that stalked by his side. The whole world was peopled with fiendish creatures of his own imagining.

For man felt long before he reasoned. The thunder sent him cowering to the fartherst corner of the cave. The stars filled him with a vague unease. The gnarled, twisted trees in the forest, and the grotesque, sun-patterned shadows that they cast upon the ground bewildered and terrified him. He could not explain them; he did not know what they were. Be he *felt* weak, and powerless—and afraid.

Primitive man groped about in a world of bewildering hostility. The very shadows trembling upon the ground filled him with terror.

Out of this fear came the germ called superstition. The germ grew, and multiplied, and spread. It eased the fear-stricken primitive mind. It founded the first crude religions. It moulded mass thought into strange ways of custom and belief. It swept out across the whole of humanity, seeped through the barriers of civilization, found its way even into advanced thought and advanced religions, became a definite part of man's personality.

William J. Fielding says: "Before we have the power to love or hate or comprehend, we are *able to be afraid.*" The observant notice that the first emotions a child has are those of fear and surprise. And so it was with man in early life. What he did not understand he feared—and there was much that he did not understand (see pp. 21-22).

Thousands upon thousands of magic practices and superstitions have been evolved since the first dawn of superstitious fear, all with the idea of warding off danger, of propitiating angry deities, of inviting better fortune. Like a brand of fire these magic practices and superstitions sent sparks in all directions, and the sparks were fanned into flame by fear and ignorance. Thus did superstition spread quickly. It was as contagious as any infectious disease. Witch doctors, medicine men, magicians, sorcerers rode in upon the crest of the superstitious wave to begin their march across the ages.

These witches and wizards, medicine men and magicians made their appearance wherever the belief in magic prevailed. They were regarded with awe and fearful respect, and the general notion was that they were in direct communication with the spirit world. Therefore, it was believed that they could foretell the future or read the past; that they could prevent thunderstorms or invite rain in time of drought; that they could propitiate angry deities and so save the people from impending punishment. Hence, the witch doctor received gifts—the best that the tribe could procure. And as a consequence, everyone who was able to do so posed as a witch doctor.

Magic practices were divided into two definite kinds—black magic and white magic. The term "black magic" applied to all those practices which caused evil and harm to others, as, for instance, the age-old practice of burning a wooden image of an enemy for the purpose of causing his destruction—still practiced in Africa and among other savage peoples. The practices termed "white magic" were intended to combat the influences of black magic, achieving good instead of evil. A primitive people would use black magic against the elements, against their enemies. The same people would use white magic to prevent illness, thunderstorms, droughts, and other evils.

Out of these early forms of magic grew many curious customs. In time of illness the medicine man applied his lips to the part that pained and "sucked out the evil." It is still a natural instinct to suck a bruised finger—still a nursery remedy to "kiss it and make it well" (see p. 23). The rain-maker also made his appearance; charm words and spells were invented; talismans, amulets, and good-luck charms appeared in great profusion. Man entered upon an era of superstitious bondage from which he has never wholly escaped.

The Spread of Superstition.—Untold are the crimes that have been committed in the name of superstition! Untold are the victims who have died upon the sacrificial altar—human sacrifices to man-made gods and man-made superstitions! A trail of blood and blackness stretches out across the ages to show the path that superstition has taken.

Nor did Christianity dispel the ignorance and superstitious fears which held man in bondage. We find the fear of the "evil eye" still persisting. We find definite charms, and spells, and incantations for the purpose of warding off evil influences. Religion took one path; superstition another. Sometimes a curious superstitious notion found its way into the religious practices, was accepted, became a religious rite—*and has survived.*

(Courtesy of Metropolitan Museum of Art)

"The Sun Vow."
MacNeil, American, 19th Century.

(Courtesy of Metropolitan Museum of Art)

"Cherub."
French, 18th Century.

The narrow-minded ignorance of the Middle Ages gave rise to many atrocities—blots upon the pages of history, but blots carefully erased from the pages of schoolbooks. Thousands of men and women were killed for no other reason than that they were supposed to be exerting an "evil influence." Infants born with too-bright eyes or with little faces that seemed "wise and canny" to the superstitious were sacrificed for fear that they might be evil spirits born into the world through some unsuspecting woman. An old woman mumbling to herself in the street would cause a panic which invariably ended in some horrible massacre of elderly people.

> The mediæval community cooped up between the narrow walls of dark little cities and villages, at the mercy of a thousand unknown forces of nature, was always in a state of panic. Disease, a solar eclipse, a stroke of lightning, a flood, all these were not the result of impersonal natural laws, but the direct manifestation of an evil will. The community at large (with that strange sense of justice which is an integral part of all slightly civilized groups of human beings) was for ever looking for someone whose personal wickedness had caused the disaster.

One of the most familiar forms of superstitious massacres is that of the burning of women and girls as witches. Writing in the June, 1923, number of *Mentor,* Hendrik van Loon says:

> The witch game was played with human lives, and the odds were a hundred to one against the victim.

It would be difficult to estimate the vast numbers of men and women who met death as wizards and witches. There is very little doubt, however, that the great majority of the victims were women. In 1515, during a witchcraft craze in Europe, thousands of women were burned—very few men. Van Loon says:

> During the first half of the 17th century, one energetic witch-hunter (by the name of Carpzou) alone passed the sentence of death on more than fifteen thousand witches. At this rate, the number of victims must have run into several million—which seems incredi-

ble. More conservative historians place it at two or three hundred thousand—which is quite enough.

The two groups of women who appear to have suffered most were the young women who refused to marry and preferred to live alone, and the elderly women who mumbled to themselves or otherwise acted "witchly." Only occasionally was a young married woman burned as a witch, unless, as was sometimes the case, the husband tired of her and for purposes of his own directed suspicion upon her.

One of the most familiar characters born of superstition is the witch who rides upon broom sticks. There are still many people who believe that witches prowl about on Hallowe'en.

In the 17th century the spark of superstition found its way across the Atlantic, was fanned into flame in Salem with the result that innocent persons were sacrificed to ease the superstitious hysteria of the masses. The Salem witchcraft delusion is much exaggerated, however. It lasted less than a year and comparatively few people were murdered; but it seems more appalling to us than most witchcraft crazes because it is closer, both in time and in place.

A curious thing about the Salem "witches" is that

several of them actually confessed. Of course, in mediæval Europe many of the men and women accused of being wizards or witches confessed under torture, but in Salem women confessed of their own accord. It would appear that the superstitious notions of the people, being contagious, so affected these poor souls accused of witchcraft that they actually believed themselves to be "possessed" and could not deny the accusation when arrested. Ignorant fear and superstition would have persuaded these women that they actually were witches, just as superstition caused Ferdinand IV to die of fright.

The story is that in 1312 Peter and John de Carvajal were condemned to death for murder on circumstantial evidence. They were sentenced to be thrown from the summit to jagged depths below. Ferdinand IV, then King of Spain, resisted obstinately every attempt to induce him to grant a pardon.

Standing upon the spot from which they were to be thrown, the two men called upon God to witness their innocence, appealing to His high tribunal to prove it. They summoned the King to appear before this tribunal in thirty days. His Majesty laughed at the summons and gave the sign to proceed with the execution.

In a few days the King fell ill. He retired to his country residence, ostensibly to rest but really to shake off remembrance of the summons which somehow persisted. He could not be diverted. He became more and more ill, and on the thirtieth day he was found dead in bed—a victim to the superstitious dread which had gripped his heart from the moment the summons had been uttered.

The witchcraft crazes represent only one, though an appalling and conspicuous, phase of superstition. Following in their wake were many practices intended to ward off evil influences, many absurd and curious customs, many superstitious notions concerning things lucky and things unlucky.

Even in this age of science we are not entirely free from

superstition. We have our lucky coins, our unlucky Fridays and our wishbones. We have our palm-readers and our crystal-gazers, our birth omens and wedding omens. We still cast a bit of salt over the shoulder, still pick up a fallen horseshoe, still have our delusions concerning broken mirrors, black cats, and unlucky thirteens.

> Ever since the beginning of time [says Van Loon], man has run to crystal-gazers, and fortune-tellers and soothsayers and necromancers to get secret information about the events of the immediate future . He is doing it to day. Look at the advertising pages of any of the great English dailies and you will see what we mean. Spook doctors offer their services to bereaved parents and to ruined business men. Yogis, with and without turbans, are ready to tell the smitten girl just what sort of husband the handsome young man will make.

Some of the world's greatest thinkers have been slaves to superstition. Sir Walter Scott, for instance, would not visit Melrose Abbey at night because of the superstitious dread of bogies and ghosts. Napoleon had a horror of black cats. Peter the Great would not cross bridges because of a superstitious fear. Cotton Mather, American clergyman and author, took an active part in the witchcraft persecutions at Salem. The great Blackstone, on whose teachings England's law and our own are based, openly declared that witches existed and that he believed they caused evil—a belief voiced also, at his inspiration, by many prominent lawyers and ministers of his day.

Witchcraft delusions belong to the dark ages of the past. Magical rites and practices for the purpose of warding off evil are confined solely to savages. Nevertheless, there are few persons to-day who do not have their pet superstitions—harmless superstitions, the most of which, however, have their origins buried in paganism, in savagery. We find these superstitions prevalent even among the most highly educated people. In a recent experiment it was found that only thirty-two students out of two thousand were unable to quote a superstition in which they truthfully believed.

As one authority says:

> Few persons, no matter how rational, are not given to superstition. . . . One reason why superstition has not yet died out among lettered and intelligent people is because it is contagious. In Colonial days in Salem even the learned professors and lawyers believed in witchcraft. It was "in the air." Children brought up in atmosphere of credulity rarely rise above it.

We find superstitious notions in famous literature. In "Evangeline," Longefellow says: "Happy art thou, as if every day thou hadst picked up a horseshoe," Goldsmith tells us in "The Vicar of Wakefield" that the "girls had their omens" and that "true love knots lurked at the bottom of every tea-cup." Herrick writes:

> My ear tingles, some there be,
> That are snarling now at me.

The "Arabian Nights" abounds with magical tales, and in our fairy tales we read of mice that turn to horses, pumpkins that become fairy chariots, boys that climb beanstalks to kill evil giants, pussies that wear seven-league boots.

Just as these tales are relics of old fears and superstitions, many of our modern customs and beliefs are relics, remnants, of the superstitions that characterized early life. Why is thirteen regarded as an unlucky number? What makes Friday different from any other day? What is the significance of the horseshoe? Why do we say "God bless you!" to a person who has sneezed?

Harmless superstitions—a sort of luxury to the modern mind. Where did they come from? How did they originate? What do they mean? In this chapter we will concern ourselves with the superstitions that are still prevalent and popular, superstitions that many people still observe.

GOOD-LUCK OMENS

In savage life the general use of talismans and amulets is to guard against the "evil eye." We find this fear, in one form or another, prevalent in almost all parts of the world, not only among savages but among civilized peoples. The Dutch, the Irish, the Italians, the Egyptians, the Chinese—all fear the evil eye and have charms for the purpose of warding off its evil influence. The Dutch place broad strips of black paint upon their farmhouses; the Irish have special "charm phrases"; the Chinese expectorate over the shoulder to frighten away the Evil One. We find similar customs almost universally prevalent.

The amulet, intended for protection against the evil eye, is usually just a bit of stone, a shell, or image of carved wood. But in modern life these amulets have taken the form of good-luck charms and are offered in such guise as miniature wishbones or horseshoes, little china pigs or elephants. Men wear them on their watch chains; women wear them on ribbons around their necks.

In savage life the amulet or talisman is a charm intended to exert a magical influence upon evil spirits and frighten them away. In modern life the good luck charm is intended to attract good rather than to repel evil. The transition has given rise to the custom of accepting certain objects and certain happenings as good luck omens. The most familiar of these omens will presently be discussed.

The word "luck" itself appears to have been derived from an old Anglo-Saxon verb meaning "to catch." It is analogous to the German word *Glück,* indicating "a good catch."

The Lucky Horseshoe.—One of the most familiar good-luck omens, and one widely prevalent, is that concerning the finding of a horseshoe. There are many fascinating legends connected with this omen, some of which reach back into antiquity.

The horseshoe closely resembles the conventional figure for the *yoni* (phallic symbol) in modern Hindu temples.

Phallic ornaments, since the early days of sex-worship, have been used to avert evil influences. In North Africa, for instance, we find phallic charms above the entrances of houses and over tent doors. The natives inform us that these charms, very similar in shape to the horseshoe, drive away the evil eye. It is probable that the good luck attributed to the horseshoe is in some way connected with the good luck of the phallic charms.

Some authorities are of the opinion that the horseshoe is regarded as a good luck omen because it resembles the crescent moon. There have been many peoples who considered the crescent moon extremely lucky, and it is barely possible that the horseshoe, because it looks like the crescent moon, is considered lucky by these people too. The belief would have spread quickly elsewhere, been carried to other peoples, and become a popular notion.

One writer says that the horseshoe, "wherever used as an amulet or charm, is the handy conventional representative of the crescent, and that the Buddist crescent emblem is a horseshoe with the curve pointed like a Gothic arch."

The exact origin of the iron horseshoe is not known. Prof. N. S. Shaler believes that it was invented in the 4th century A.D. and that it originated in Greece. However, some very ancient iron horseshoes have been found in the south of Scotland. Appian makes mention of iron shoes for horses; and in a mosaic portraying the Battle of Issus (unearthed at Pompeii in 1831) is the figure of a horse which appeared to be shod with iron shoes similar to those in modern use. There seems to be abundant evidence that the ancients protected the feet of their beasts of burden.

When the horseshoe began to be used as a good luck charm is not known. Possibly no definite date could be set, as the belief appears to be a slow development. It may have grown out of the phallic ornaments and belief in their power to charm. It may have grown out of the crescent moon, long regarded as a good luck omen. The Irish say that the horse was in the stable where Christ was born, and that the horseshoe was therefore given magical power. Almost every country has a different legend or tradition concerning this omen.

> The Romans had the custom of driving nails into cottage walls as an antidote against the plague [says one writer]. Both this practice and the later one of nailing up horseshoes, have been thought by some to have originated from the rite of Passover. Blood sprinkled upon doorposts and lintel at the time of the great Jewish feast formed the chief points of an arch and it may be that with this in mind the people adopted the horseshoe as an arch-shaped talisman, and it thus became generally emblematic of good luck.

It is interesting to note, in this connection, that the peasants of the west of Scotland have for centuries had the custom of training the boughs of certain trees to form an arch over the farmyard gate to protect the cattle from evil.

Iron has always been regarded as a protective agent and a good-luck charm. In Scandinavia, iron is the historic charm against the wiles of sorcerers. Among many ancient peoples iron was regarded as a protection against evil spirits; many regarded it as a protection against the plague. Pliny says that iron coffin nails, affixed to the lintel of the door, protect the people within from spirits that may be prowling in the neighbourhood. Pliny also remarks that there is no more excellent protection against illness than the cast-off horseshoe found in the road, and he advises it not only as a protective charm but as a healing agent.

The Chinese have for ages had the superstitious notion that to hang crooked horseshoe nails on a string around a child's neck is to ward off illness and evil influences. The Scotch fisherman, highly superstitious, carries with him always a bit of iron—"for luck"—or tacks it above the door at home to insure his safe return.

The horseshoe superstition captivated the public fancy, and the finding of a horseshoe became a general omen of good luck. The one outstanding exception to this widely prevalent superstition is the Bohemian belief that to pick up a horseshoe is to pick up bad luck; but even among the Bohemians it is believed that a nailed-up horseshoe will cure lunacy and help to prevent others from losing their minds.

There is an ancient Saxon superstition that witches cannot practise their wiles upon persons in the open air, and to cause harm or injury to a person they must enter the home of that person. It would appear that horseshoes were placed at the outer entrance to homes, rather than inside, because of this superstitious notion. It is still customary to tack up a horseshoe on the outside of a door.

The horseshoe superstition is still widely prevalent. There are many people even to-day who believe that the finding of a cast-off horseshoe is an omen of good luck. Miniature horseshoes, in the form of charms, are worn on ribbons and on watch fobs. Nor is the superstition in any sense limited; we find it among the educated as among the uneducated. Indeed, this horseshoe superstition appears to have been a favourite during the last five centuries among writers, teachers, physicians, and intellectuals generally.

In the 18th century, for instance, Dr. Robert James, an English physician, discovered a fever powder for which he became famous and through which he attained great success. Having once found a horseshoe at Westminster Bridge, Doctor James ascribed his success to that omen, and consequently he adopted the horseshoe as a family crest.

Before leaving the subject of the horseshoe, it is interesting to note that in some countries the blacksmith was credited with supernatural powers. Some writers, in fact, advance the theory that the horseshoe is regarded as a good-luck omen because the blacksmith, in the rôle of wizard or witchdoctor, used it as a charm in performing his "white magic." In Russia blacksmiths at one time enjoyed a reputation as magicians, and oaths were taken upon the anvil instead of the Bible.

The Four-Leafed Clover.—A superstition as widely prevalent as that of the good-luck horseshoe is the belief that a four-leafed clover portends fortune and happiness. This is a very old superstition, and its origin is lost in antiquity.

The old legend is that Eve, upon being ejected from Paradise, took a four-leafed clover with her. Because the clover was a bit of green from the garden of paradise, its presence in one's own garden came to be looked upon as an omen of good luck.

Herrick, in his "Hesperides" (1648) mentions the four-leafed clover and indicates the custom of strewing these good-luck omens before the bride to insure her happiness. We quote:

> The showers of roses, lucky foure-leav'd grasse
> The while the cloud of younglings sing,
> And drown ye with a flowrie spring.

A Curious Luck Custom.—Among the ancients, spittle was esteemed a charm against all evil. Pliny tells us that spitting was superstitiously observed by people to avert the influences of witchcraft. Theocritus says, "Thrice on my breast I spit to guard me safe from fascinating charms." The Boxers always spit into their hands to insure success in all their undertakings.

The custom of spitting on money for luck is a relic of the time when bodies and property were "anointed with the grease of animals as a sign of ownership and affluence." Spitting, in other words, was a mode of consecrating or anointing. It became accepted generally as a method of insuring good luck or success in an undertaking, and also of insuring one's property against theft from others. Some early peoples spit upon property to prevent witches or other evil influences from luring it away.

To spit on a coin "for luck" is still a custom among people of a highly superstitious sort.

The Magic of the Tides.—Primitive peoples marvelled at the changing of the tides, even as we do to-day. Why were the tides sometimes low, sometimes high? Why did the rollings and the rockings never cease? Where did the waves come from and where did they go? What was the great secret of the sea?

It was in an effort to solve this secret that early man evolved the superstitious notion that that the incoming tide brought luck, prosperity, happiness, and that the outgoing tide portended evil to some person or persons living along the coast. An ancient belief, usually accredited to Aristotle, is that no one can die until ebb tide. However, the superstition goes back very much farther and can be traced to a period several generations before the appearance of Aristotle. Primitive men, at a very early period, regarded the flowing tide as a symbol of life and death, and as the tide ebbed slowly outward they believed that life ebbed slowly with it. If one of their number died, they attributed it to the outgoing tide. If a child were born as the tide came in, the superstition was strengthened.

Dickens was evidently acquainted with this superstition, popular among coast peoples, for he has Mr. Peggotty say (in "David Copperfield"): "People can't die along the coast, except when the tide's pretty nigh out. They can't be born unless it's pretty nigh in—not properly born till flood."

Shakespeare must have been familiar with this superstition too, for he has his Falstaff die "even just between twelve and one, even at the turning o' the tide." (Henry V, Act II, Scene III.)

Casting the Tooth over the Shoulder.—A custom widely prevalent among children, and practised also by superstitious grown-ups, is to cast a tooth backward over the left shoulder and make a wish, firmly believing that the wish will come true.

Among certain Australian and African tribes, one or more of a boy's front teeth are knocked out at the ceremonies of initiation to which he must submit before he is able to enjoy the rights and privileges of a full-grown man.

These teeth are buried under a tree, near the roots, the whereabouts of which the boy never knows. While the teeth are being buried the boy's father usually chants a song of hope that the boy may become as strong and stalwart as the tree beside which the teeth will lie for ever.

It is customary, in many parts of the world, to throw the tooth in some corner where a mouse or rat will find it, "in the hope that the remaining teeth with acquire the whiteness and firmness of the teeth of the rodents." In Germany, to give one example, it is practically a universal custom to go behind the stove and throw the tooth backward over the head, saying, "Mouse give me your iron tooth; I will give you my bone tooth."

The modern custom is to cast the tooth over the left shoulder and make a wish, not necessarily for a son as strong and stalwart as a tree, or teeth as white and firm as a rodent's, but for anything one would like to have. If the tooth cannot be found after it has been cast over the shoulder, one may interpret it as a good-luck omen. The wish will surely come true!

BAD LUCK OMENS

Fear of the unknown and dread of the evil eye led early man to avoid whatever seemed, to his superstitious mind, an omen of bad luck. He saw signs of warning in the simplest happenings. Whatever he feared or could not understand he accepted as an agent of evii and hence something to be shunned.

Some of the early superstitions, originally concerned with the evil eye and with customs for banishing or destroying its influence, have survived and are still observed. The survivals have taken the form of bad luck omens such as the black cat, the spilling of salt, the number thirteen, etc. And, of course, there are methods for overcoming the bad luck promised by these omens, as casting a pinch of the salt over the shoulder, or whispering a benediction after the sneeze.

The Unlucky Number Thirteen.—

> And Neolithic man was counting, and falling under the spell of numbers [says Wells]. He was beginning to use tallies, and wondering at the triangularity of three and the squareness of four, and why some quantities like twelve were easy to divide in all sorts of ways, and others, like thirteen, impossible. Twelve became a noble, generous and familiar number to him, and thirteen rather an outcast and disreputable one.

Outcast it has remained ever since! One of the most widespread of superstitious notions is that thirteen is unlucky, and so general is this notion that many hotels do not have a room number thirteen.

Precisely how the superstition originated no one knows. In Scandinavian mythology there are twelve Aesir or Demigods, and the old legend is that Loki came among them, making the thirteenth. This Loki was cruel and evil, according to the story, and among the Demigods he became "the chief author of human misfortunes." Because he was evil, and because he was the thirteenth, the number thirteen came to be looked upon as an omen of ill luck.

Another explanation as to the origin of this superstition is that the Valkyrs, or Virgins, who waited upon the heroes in Valhalla were thirteen in number. Many writers believe that from this source sprang the common superstition concerning the bad luck of the number thirteen, especially in connection with guests at a table.

The most popular explanation, however, is that there were thirteen persons at the Last Supper, Judas being frequently represented as the thirteenth guest. Not a few authorities offer this as the true origin of the superstition, although this writer is inclined to believe that the notion goes back much farther.

The superstition regarding the number thirteen is universal. We find it in France, England, throughout practically the whole of Europe, and in America. It has long been a matter of etiquette in France to avoid having exactly thirteen guests at a dinner or party, and the *pique-*

assiette (corresponding to the English "trencher friend" or "sponger" and to the American "stop-gap") is known also as the *quatorzième*, as he usually is invited to fill the fourteenth seat at the table.

The number seven appears also to have been regarded with superstitious awe by early peoples, although it was considered lucky by as many as considered it unlucky. One writer says:

> It is hard to escape the conclusion that magic had something to do with the constant recurrence of the number seven in antiquity. We have the seven caves of the Aztecs, the seven ecstasies of Zoroast, the seventh-day Sabbath, the seven days of the week, the seven golden candlesticks of Solomon's temple.

Another writer says:

> Seven was a sacred number among the Acadians, Assyrians, and Babylonians. The "unlucky days" of the "Farmers' Almanac" are based upon this ancient cult.

Among various early peoples, the seventh son of a seventh son was believed gifted with supernatural powers. When such an infant was born, the nurse placed a worm in each of its hands, enclosed in a bit of muslin. The hands were tied up until the worms died, and then the tiny fists were allowed to open. The dead worms were thrown away, but it was believed that locked up in the child's hands were miraculous powers of healing and protecting. When the boy grew to manhood he was regarded as a wizard.

There are still many people who believe that the number seven portends good luck, just as the number thirteen portends ill luck.

The Black Cat.—The black cat is the traditional companion of witches. Because of this old tradition, the black cat has become an omen of misfortune and ill luck, and a popular notion is that unhappiness will follow quickly in the wake of the black cat that crosses one's path.

There is an ancient superstition that spirits are able to assume the forms of black animals, particularly black cats.

An old black-letter book called "Beware the Cat!" (1584) gives warning that black cats are witches in disguise, and that killing the cats does not necessarily mean killing the witches, for a witch can take on the body of a cat nine times.

This old notion concerning the nine lives of a cat goes back to ancient Egypt. The cat-headed goddess, Pasht, was said to have nine lives. It is amazing how a thought will persist through many ages and come at last to be accepted as truth. Even to-day there are many who believe the cat has nine lives, though few realize that this superstitious belief is based upon Pasht, mother cat of the witches, believed by the Egyptians to have nine lives.

The black cat is the traditional companion of witches—because of an old superstitious notion that witches are given the power to assume the form of a black cat nine times.

The Egyptians did not fear the black cat, but rather reverenced it. A cemetery sheltering the mummies of thousands of black cats has been unearthed, and not very long ago a cargo of these mummified black cats were sent to England.

But because of the general notion that witches and evil spirits assumed the form of the black cat, this animal came gradually to be looked upon as a bad omen, and the superstition that the black cat was unlucky became widespread. Women who believed themselves witches became fond of the cats and used them in their divinations. In the Middle Ages the brain of a black cat was considered as essential ingredient in all recipes of the witches and witch doctors.

To-day the black cat is not feared as it was in earlier times, but there are many superstitious people who still regard it as an unlucky omen, and who believe that not only the black cat, but all cats, have nine lives.

Unlucky Days and Seasons.—The belief in lucky and unlucky days is very ancient. This belief appears to have been taught first by the magicians of ancient Chaldea, and history tells us that similar beliefs affected almost every detail of primitive life in Babylonia. The natives of Madagascar have since the earliest times believed in lucky and unlucky days of birth, and if a child is born on what they consider the unlucky day, it is killed.

The poet Hesiod who, it is believed, lived about 1000 B.C., distinguished lucky days from others in his poem called "Works and Days." He declared that the thirteenth day was unlucky for sowing, but favourable for planting.

Among many early peoples we find the superstitious belief that it is best to sow one's seed at the full of the moon. Among others we find the belief that it is best to gather in the harvest when the moon is full and mellow. Still others regard the crescent moon as a fortunate omen. In South Africa it is to this day considered unlucky to begin a journey or undertake a work of importance during the last quarter of the moon.

The Romans marked their lucky days with a piece of chalk, their unlucky days with charcoal. From this custom of marking unlucky days with charcoal arose the phrase "black-letter day." We still refer to "black-letter days," but with us, instead of portending evil, the "black-letter day" is a day remembered with regret because of some unfortunate occurrence connected with it.

"Blue Monday" is a very old phrase still in general usage. In early days those whose affairs of business occupied them on Sunday were considered entitled to a holiday on Monday. On Monday, therefore, while others were busy at their tasks, these people who worked on Sunday had a day of rest, during which they usually lazed rather than indulged in any pleasures. Because the churches throughout Europe were decorated with blue on the first Monday before Lent—which was a holiday or "lazy day"

(Courtesy of Metropolitan Museum of Art)

French school, early 14th Century. Virgin and child.

(*Courtesy of Metropolitan Museum of Art*)

"The Bouquet."
A water colour by E. A. Duez. (*19th Century.*)

for everyone—this day of rest for the Sunday workers came to be known as "Blue Monday."

We still use the phrase, but its meaning has become somewhat modified. We now speak of a "Blue Monday" when we wish to convey the thought that we are lazy, tired, melancholy—in *need* of, rather than enjoying, a holiday.

The fear of Friday is quite as old as the fear of the number thirteen. An ancient proverb says:

> Friday's moon,
> Come when it will, it comes too soon.

The origin of the superstition concerning Friday is traced by most authorities to the crucifixion of Chirst on that day. But there are some writers who advance the theory that Friday is regarded as an unlucky day because it was on Friday that Adam and Eve partook of the forbidden fruit. It is quite probable that this popular old legend gave rise to the superstitious notions concerning Friday.

In his "Sex and Sex Worship" Wall says:

> Among some nations in Asia the first day of the week was named in honour of the god Saturn, which would make the last day of the week Friday; at that time, however, this last day was sacred to the goddess Mylitta, the Assyrian form of the goddess Venus; this day was consecrated to marriages, and to festivals during which practices were indulged in that are now considered indecent when done in public, but which at that time were done publicly in honour of Venus (Mylitta) in her temples.
>
> This day therefore became accursed to the early Christians, because the church considered the sexual rites in honour of the goddess Venus as a gross affront to their own Virgin.

This explanation of Friday's disrepute explains also the inevitable fish on Friday. As a symbol of the *yoni*, the fish was consecrated to the goddess Mylitta. But the early Christians, despising the pagan goddess and the sexual rites, ate the fish at their feast on Virgin's Day (Freya Day, or Friday). "The fish is still eaten, but as a fast, on the Virgin's Day by an overwhelming majority of Christians."

Although we are still accustomed to refer to Friday as an unlucky day, it would seem that we in the United States should regard it as a particularly lucky day. It was on a Friday, August 3, 1492, that Columbus set sail from the Port of Palos, Spain, on his great voyage of discovery. It was on a Friday, October 12th, that land was sighted. On Friday, November 10, 1620, the *Mayflower* reached the harbour of Provincetown, and on Friday, December 22, 1620, the Plymouth fathers landed upon the famous Plymouth Rock. A century later, on a Friday, February 22, 1732, George Washington was born. It would seem that all good things happened to young America on the traditional bad-luck day!

The Broken Mirror.—One of the most common of modern superstitions is that to break a mirror invites death, or seven years of bad luck.

Since very early times the mirror has been used in divination, in attempts to read the future or the past. In ancient Greece divination performed by means of water and a mirror was so popular and so widely practised that it was given a definite name—"catoptomancy." There are still seers and fortune tellers who "see" the past and the future in crystals and mirrors.

An early belief was that one saw the will of the gods in the mirror. To break a mirror accidentally, therefore, was interpreted as an effort on the part of the gods to prevent the person from seeing into the future. This was construed as a warning that the future held unpleasant things. Among highly superstitious people the breaking of the mirror came to be looked upon as a death omen. Somehow this superstitious belief has prevailed and still exists even among educated people.

It is related of Napoleon that on one occasion when he was campaigning in Italy he broke accidentally a mirror which hung over Josephine's portrait. Instantly he conceived the superstitious notion that she had died, and he couldn't rest until he returned home and saw for himself that she was well and alive. Superstition sometimes clouds even a brilliant mind.

The curious notion that to break a mirror brings seven years of bad luck originated with the Romans about the first century of the Christian Era. They believed that the health of a person changed every seven years, and as the mirror reflected the health, or appearance, of the person, to break it meant to break the health for a period of seven years. Hence the belief in seven years of bad luck.

There are many people who believe a falling window blind a bad omen—usually a forewarning of death in the house. We can readily understand how a window blind, falling suddenly and for apparently no reason, would strike terror into the hearts of superstitious people. Early man, keen as an animal trained to the jungle, could sense the slightest rustle near his cave, the faintest approach of beast or man. Fear of enemies made man sensitive to every sound, alert, fearful. As he slowly developed man lost much of his keenness, but he has never lost entirely his fear of unexplained sounds, of rustlings and noises that seem to come from nowhere. A blind falling suddenly and noisily in an empty room makes the bravest person tense and alert for a moment. We can understand how superstitious people would have accepted this falling blind as an omen of ill luck—of death. The superstition, like many others, has survived and is a part of modern life.

Dread of a Drowning Person.—One of the most inhuman of all superstitions is that which forbids the rescue of a person who is drowning because it invites misfortune to the rescuer.

The general notion among superstitious peoples everywhere is that if a man is drowning, it is the intention of the gods that he do so. To rescue the man is to defeat the purpose of the gods—cheat them—and hence win their enmity.

Tylor tells of an occasion in 1864 when fishermen in Bohemia actually refused to snatch a drowning man from the water as they believed they would endanger their own lives by doing so. The same superstition exists among the boatmen of the Danube, among the French and English sailors.

Another explanation of this curious superstition is that "the water spirit requires tribute" and that to deny the spirit this tribute is to invite misfortune and disaster. This, according to some authorities, accounts for the reluctance among primitive seaside peoples to rescue a drowning person from the water. A familiar old rhyme is:

> Save a stranger from the sea
> And he'll turn your enemy!

Some Death Omens.—An ancient belief is that the howling of dogs portends death and calamities. This appears to be a relic of the time when men made deities of animals. As a deity, the dog was supposed to be able to foresee death and give warning of it by howling or barking. In the Odyssey the dogs of Eumæus are described as terrified at the sight of Minerva, although at the time she was invisible to Telemachus.

Among sailors we find the belief that sharks following a ship also portend death. There is scarcely a sailor who does not believe that if a shark follows a ship someone aboard is going to die. The truth is that sharks follow a ship for the refuse that is thrown overboard.

Man has always feared death and he has imagined omens, or warnings, in the simplest things. Ringing in the ears, for instance, has been regarded as a sign of impending death for many generations. To place three chairs in a row accidentally means a death in the family. If a sick person is changed from one room to another it is a sure sign that he will die. He who counts the carriages at a passing funeral will die within the year. An open umbrella, held over the head indoors, indicates approaching death. Scores of superstitions like these exist among peoples everywhere.

In Europe, the country people always turn the mirror to the wall when someone lies dead in the house. They believe that whoever looks into a mirror when there is death in the house will die also. This custom of turning the mirrors to the wall, evidently to avoid seeing the evil spirits which cause death, originated among the early Irish, but quickly spread among superstitious peoples everywhere. The custom is practised even in the United States among various peoples, and frequently all pictures hanging on the walls, as well as all mirrors, are turned around.

There are several superstitious reasons for planting yew trees in churchyards. One reason is that the yew is symbolic, typifying the doctrine of resurrection by its unchanging verdure. Another reason is that some species of yew trees are gloomy and poisonous, and hence just right for the churchyard.

The ringing of bells or death knells for the deceased is very ancient. Bells themselves are very old, dating back many centuries before Christ—indeed, going back even farther than the biblical record. In ancient times bells were rung only when important people died, but with the coming of Christianity it was the custom to ring death bells "for all good Christians."

Some authorities believe that the ringing of bells at times of death originated in the desire to frighten away the evil spirits that lurk about a dead body, the fearsome, invisible ghosts that wait to pounce upon the soul.

To Change One's Luck in Cards.—A current superstition is that to change one's seat during a card game is to change one's luck. An unlucky player will often ask permission to change seats with a lucky player. "Maybe my luck will change!" he laughs—little realizing that he is expressing an old primitive thought.

To the primitive mind, any sort of change or substitution represents escape from danger or from ill luck. Thus among many savages an ill man will change his name in an effort to frighten away the evil spirits that are causing him his pain. Among the Dyaks a man changes his name after recovering from an illness in the hope of thus "getting rid of his former personality and its liability to disease."

In Amboina, if a couple have lost several children the father gives the next child to another woman, firmly believing that the change will enable the child to live. In Ceramlaut a barren woman changes her name believing that the change also affects her personality and her bodily functions. Among many savages the boy is given another name at puberty, to symbolize the change in status from boy to man.

To-day, based upon the same primitive notion, seats are changed by players to change their luck.

A superstition at Monte Carlo is that immediately after a suicide, everyone who plays against the bank will win. So thoroughly do the gamblers believe in this superstition that as soon as news of a suicide is heard there is a great rush for tables. One can easily understand how a superstition of this nature would have originated. The news of a suicide would depress the gamblers and cause them to leave the tables. To counteract this affect, wily persons evidently caused the superstition to be circulated that to play against the bank after a suicide is to win.

Among the more popular card superstitions we find that to drop a card while playing is a bad omen. There are some superstitious players who actually refuse to continue after a card has been dropped in the game. Another popular superstition is that one who plays with a cross-eyed partner cannot possibly win. The notion among players is that cross-eyes frighten away luck.

Salt Superstitions.—No one knows the exact origin of salt, or how its use first became known to man. In Finnish mythology we read that the mighty god of the sky, Ukko, struck fire in the heavens. A spark from this celestial fire fell into the ocean and turned to salt. Another old legend is that the oceans are made up of the tears of all those who have suffered since the world began; and as tears are salt, the oceans' waters are salt.

We know that salt was used long before the Christian Era, and that it was highly valued by those who included it in their dietary. Wells indicates that salt was probably being traded even in Neolithic times, pointing out that "on a meat dietary men can live without salt, but grain-consuming people need it just as herbivorous animals need it."

Among the Israelites salt was valued as an item of diet. They believed that no meal was complete without a bit of salt to help digest it, although *how* it helped they never attempted to explain. Homer called salt divine, and Plato described it as a substance valued by the gods.

At one time salt was regarded as being almost as valuable as gold, and soldiers, officials, and working people in Greece and Rome received all or part of their pay in salt. Money paid for labour or service was termed *salarium*, from whence comes our word *salary*, meaning money paid for services rendered. From this custom of paying with salt comes also the popular phrase "to earn one's salt."

It was a custom in early times to place salt before strangers as a token or pledge of friendship. To eat a person's salt, therefore, came to be used as the popular expression for accepting a person's hospitality. "Take a pinch of salt with me" was the popular method of inviting a friend or acquaintance to one's home to partake of one's hospitality.

In Oriental lands salt was offered to guests as a token of hospitality, and if any particles fell to the ground while being presented it was accounted an omen of ill luck. The belief was that a quarrel or a dispute would follow.

One authority says:

> The widespread notion that the spilling of salt produces evil consequences is supposed to have originated in the tradition that Judas overturned a salt-cellar at the Paschal Supper as portrayed in Leonardo da Vinci's painting. But it appears more probable that the belief is due to the sacred character of salt in early times. Any one having the misfortune to spill salt was formerly supposed to

incur the anger of all good spirits and to be rendered susceptible to the malevolent influences of demons.

Among the Germans we find the old saying "Whoever spills salt arouses enmity." Among the Romans we find the belief that to spill salt is to cause quarrels or disputes, and it was the custom to exclaim, when salt was spilled, "May the gods avert the omen!" An old tradition says that if salt is thrown over the left shoulder it will appease the devil, who will otherwise make enemies of friends whenever salt is spilled.

These old salt superstitions are found in many widely separated countries. Long ago they captured the public fancy, and they have survived. We still find many people who believe that to spill salt is an omen of a quarrel or of lost friendship, and that to cast a bit of the salt over the left shoulder is to "avert the omen."

"God Bless You!"—The ancients gave much thought and contemplation to the sneeze. Where did it come from? What did it portend? Was it a lucky or an unlucky omen?

Among those early peoples who believed the soul dwelt inside the head, any function of the head was respected. The sneeze was regarded by many as a sign from the soul—an omen—a warning. Some regarded it as a lucky omen, others as an unlucky omen. The Greeks, Romans, and Egyptians considered the sneeze a kind of divinity or oracle which warned them in times of danger, which foretold future good or evil. Sneezing to the right was considered lucky, to the left, unlucky.

In early life there were so many omens and superstitions concerning the sneeze that it would be impossible to consider them all here. St. Augustine tells us that in his time there were so many sneeze omens, and they were regarded with such utter faith, that a man would return to bed instantly if he happened to sneeze while putting on his shoes, or upon any other occasion that, according to the omen, was supposed to forewarn of ill luck.

An old Flemish belief was that a sneeze during conversation proved the truth of a remark. This is one of the oldest superstitions in connection with the sneeze, and it was prevalent among the Greeks, the Romans, and the Egyptians. In the Odyssey we read that the Princess Penelope, unhappy because of the importunities of her suitors, prayed that her husband Ulysses be returned to her. As she ended the prayer her son Telemachus sneezed, whereupon Penelope felt vastly relieved, accepting it as an omen that her prayer would be answered.

Just before the battle of Salamis (480 B.C.), the Athenian commander Themistocles stood upon the deck of his gallery offering a sacrifice to the gods. A sneeze was heard which was hailed by Euphrantides, the soothsayer, as an omen from the gods that the battle would end in victory for them. Themistocles was greatly heartened by this "lucky" omen.

The custom of uttering a benediction after the sneeze is universal. Its origin is obscure, and each country seems to have its own particular legend concering it. Among the Romans, for instance, we find the belief that the sneeze expelled evil spirits. To sneeze, therefore, was regarded somewhat in the light of a lucky effort on the part of the person to rid his system of evil spirits, and those present at the time would say, "Good luck to you." Many references to this salutation after sneezing are found in the writings of ancient Roman authors.

There is an old legend that before the time of Jacob men sneezed only once, and expired. But the patriarch interceded in the behalf of man and obtained a relaxation of this law on condition that a prayer or benediction follow every sneeze. Some writers offer this old legend as an explanation of the modern sneeze benedition, "God bless you!"

We quote, for instance, from a recent writer on this subject who says:

> After the creation, God decreed that every living person should sneeze but once—and that at the instant of the sneeze his soul

should depart from his body. Jacob it seems was a strenuous objector to being so unceremoniously eliminated from this earth's joys and he earnestly entreated the Lord to grant him and his children the favour of being excepted from the rule. This favour was granted and in return Jacob praised God each time his children sneezed. The Princes of the Earth, hearing of the decree, implored favour likewise—therefore the danger of the sneeze was averted to all if a blessing was asked each time. Hence, to this day, "God bless you" has a meaning with all nations of the earth.

There can be no doubt that the phrase "God bless you!" is very ancient and traces its way into remote antiquity. There was a common notion among many primitive peoples that the sneeze was a sign of impending death, and therefore when anyone sneezed the customary phrase was "God help you!" or its equivalent.

In Iceland, tradition tells us, there was once a dreadful scourge known as the Black Pest. The mortality was great and one after another the people succumbed. In a certain household it was observed by a brother and sister that everyone around them who succumbed to the scourge was first attacked by sneezing. Therefore when they themselves sneezed they cried, "God help me!" Because of this prayer they were allowed to live, and the story is that of all the inhabitants of the district, this brother and sister were the only ones who survived. Through all succeeding generations the Icelanders have continued the custom of saying, "God help me!" when they themselves sneeze—"God help you!" when others sneeze.

Carlo Signonio, the Italian historian,

voices the belief that the practice [of saying "God bless you!" after sneezing] began in the sixth century during the pontificate of Gregory the Great. At this period a virulent pestilence raged in Italy which proved fatal to those who sneezed. The Pope, therefore, ordered prayers to be said against it, accompanied by signs of the cross.

It was during this era that the custom of crying "God bless you!" to persons who sneezed became definitely established.

The phrase, or benediction, is still in general use.

GEM SUPERSTITION

The popular superstitions concerning gems are really survivals of the primitive superstitions concerning amulets worn for protective purposes. The amulet (from the Arab word *hamala,* meaning "to carry") is anything hung around the neck, wrists, ankles, or in any way attached to the person for the purpose of warding off evil or protecting against illness. The gem amulets of modern life carry the same significance.

Amber is one of the oldest of all gem amulets. As a charm it has stories and traditions without end. It is said to change colour with the state of one's health, and is therefore an excellent indicator of one's condition. There is also a superstition that amber will prevent illness, and that it will prove a special protection against throat diseases if worn on a ribbon around the neck.

Coral also changes colour according to the state of health. As an amulet coral is declared lucky, and we are told that "to hang coral about an infant's neck will save it from falls and sickness." During the Middle Ages coral was worn as a protection from witches and witchcraft.

For a long time opals were regarded as lucky gems and were supposed to possess supernatural powers. They were worn as charms by many people until Sir Walter Scott, in his "Anne of Geierstein" introduced them as unlucky amulets, inviting misfortune and unhappiness to the wearer. This bit of fictional belief that the opal is unlucky became superstitious fact to the mass mind, and "unlucky" the opal has remained ever since.

The sapphire has always been a symbol of good luck. The ancients believed that to wear the sapphire was to invite the favour of the gods. The diamond was also considered lucky, particularly among the Italians. In Oriental countries the favourite good-luck amulet is the turquoise, which is usually carved with the name of Allah or a verse from the Koran for additional enchantment.

It is a general belief that pearls bring bad luck. However, history tells us that Venus favoured pearls more than any other gems, and that the Romans and Greeks wore pearls to win the favour of the goddess. The Orientals believe that pearls have medicinal properties, and that to wear them greatly improves the clearness and beauty of the skin.

The custom of wearing one's birthstone as a lucky gem amulet still prevails. Following are the birthstones that are supposed to bring good luck to the wearers:

January	Garnet	July	Ruby
February	Amethyst	August	Sardonyx
March	Bloodstone	September	Sapphire
April	Diamond	October	Opal
May	Emerald	November	Topaz
June	Agate	December	Turquoise

FLOWER SUPERSTITIONS

From the very first, nature's gift of flowers captured the heart of man. He watched the tiny buds open their velvet petals to the sun. He saw the slender life stems sway gently in the breeze, and drank of the perfume that flooded his senses. Red, green, and yellow things growing in wild profusion. Pretty, harmless things that tasted good when one nibbled them.

Man soon came to know and love the flowers that made their appearance at different seasons of the year. There were times when the world was ugly and barren; times when the world was brightly carpeted with flowers and creeping vines. Man learned to recognize the flowers that portended mild, pleasant weather. He watched when the flowers withered and knew that the cold spell was not far off.

And sometimes man wandered long on barren lands, across cold and cheerless stretches. Where were the gay growing things that meant warmth and sunshine, the laughing bits of colour that filled the world with perfume? He followed the path that led southward and came at last to the cheerful spot where flowers grew. And here he made his home.

At an early period flowers found their way into various religious ceremonies, into courtship customs, into harvest and season festivals. The beauty and fragrance of the blossoms won for them an enduring place in the heart and in the sentiments of mankind.

We are all familiar with the conspicuous part flowers have played in love and courtship. In Egypt, Rome, Greece, among the South Sea Islanders, even among savages that roam jungle wastes—wherever we tread our way through the mazes of man's history—we find the flower silently symbolizing the blossoming of love. Wall says:

> The Hawaiian women decorate themselves with wreaths and garlands of odorous flowers; Cleopatra is identified by both ancient and modern writers with the utmost luxury in the use of perfumery and flowers, and our modern women delight in receiving gifts of flowers and rare perfumes.

In Rome and in Greece flowers spoke not only in the language of love, but in eloquent tones of beauty and decoration. Crowning with flowers was accounted a high honour, and wreaths of myrtle and ivy were awarded victors in games. Among the Athenians the violet was the favourite flower, and the hyacinth and laurel were early favourites.

Egypt loved its roses. In a gold box, beautifully jewelled, in Tutankhamen's tomb was found a mass of roses, still exuding a faint perfume after thousands of years of preservation. Egypt plucked its roses from the banks of the Nile where they grew in great profusion at the time of Tutankhamen. Rome also loved its roses, and we are told that Roman youths sent baskets of roses tied with ribbons to the maidens they admired—much in the modern manner!

In Egypt it was customary to present each dinner guest

with a small garland of flowers. This custom is traced also among the Greeks and Romans. Thus has the flower expressed not only love, beauty, tenderness, but hospitality.

Through the ages, each flower has taken a single significance; and to-day flowers are symbols that speak a language as eloquent as any invented by man. There is a flower that expresses tenderness, another that carries the message of love. There is a flower that breathes of kind remembrance and a flower that tells of hope. From several

sources we have accumulated this list of popular flowers and their hidden meanings:

Acacia	Friendship
Acacia, yellow	Awakening love
Almond Blossoms	Indiscretion
Anemone	Forsaken
Apple Blossoms	Hope, awakening
Aster, China	Variety
Auricula, Scarlet	Luxury, extravagance
Bachelor's-button	Celibacy
Balm	Sympathy
Balsamine	Impatience
Bramble	Envy
Buttercup	Ingratitude
Carnation	Love, promise, beauty
Catchfly	Artifice
Cedar	Thoughtfulness

Chrysanthemum	Wealth, abundance
Clover	Hope
Columbine	Constancy
Cowslip	Divinity
Crocus	Cheerfulness
Cypress	Mourning
Daffodil	Self-love
Dahlia	Elegance, dignity
Daisy	Innocence
Dandelion	Coquetry
Flax	Kindness
Flowering Reed	Confidence
Forget-me-not	Remembrance, true love
Fuchsia	Humble love
Geranium	Faith, friendship (also ingenuity)
Grape Blossoms	Mirth, jollity
Harebell	Grief
Hawthorne	Hope, love
Hazel	Peace, reconciliation
Heath	Solitude
Heliotrope	Undying devotion
Holly	Friendship, happiness
Hollyhock	Ambition
Honeysuckle	Generosity
Hyacinth	Play, joyousness
Iris	A message
Ivy	Friendship
Jasmine	Amiability
Jonquil	Desire
Larkspur	Fickleness
Laurel	Glory
Lavender	Acknowledgment
Lilac	Youth, tenderness
Lily	Purity, majesty
Lily-of-the-valley	Return to happiness, humility (as marringe flower, symbolizes happiness)
Locust	Eternal love
Lotus	Eloquence
Lupine	Sorrow
Marguerite	Innocence
Marigold	Jealousy
Mignonette	High character
Mimosa	Sensitiveness
Mistletoe	Perseverance

Moss	Maternal love
Myrtle	Love, triumph
Narcissus	Self-love, egotism
Oleander	Warning
Orange Blossoms	Chastity, purity (also signifies fruitfulness)
Orchid	A belle
Pansy	Tenderness, thoughtfulness
Passion Flower	Religious fervour
Pea, Sweet	Departure
Peony	Bashfulness
Periwinkle	Remembrance
Phlox	Souls united
Poppy, Red	Consolation
Poppy, White	Oblivion
Primrose	Childhood, youth (also indicates inconstancy)
Rose	Love, grace, beauty
Rose, Bridal	Happiness
Rose, China	Grace
Rose, Moss	Superiority
Rose, White	Sadness, misfortune, purity
Rose, Yellow	Infidelity
Rosemary	Remembrance
Sage	Domestic virtues
Snowdrop	Consolation
Sunflower	False riches
Sunflower, Dwarf	Devotion
Sweetbrier	Poetry, beauty
Sycamore	Curiosity
Tulip	Love
Tulip, Red	Passion
Violet	Modesty
Wallflower	Fidelity, sincerity
Water Lily	Eloquence
Weeping Willow	Forsaken
Wormwood	Absence, bitterness
Yew	Sorrow, penitence

Bachelor's-buttons.—There are some interesting traditions concerning the origins of flowers. Of the bachelor's-button, for instance, it is related among the peasants of Europe that at one time this little flower exerted a magical influence over lovers. It was the custom for young men to carry a bachelor's-button or two in their pockets, to insure their safety and happiness in love.

According to the old tradition, the blossom was to be picked early in the morning with the dew still upon it. It was placed in the pocket where it was permitted to remain for twenty-four hours. Upon being taken from the pocket, if it were still bright and fresh—still "true blue"—the wearer would be happy in marriage with the girl he loved. If the flower faded and died in his pocket the marriage would bring misery and unhappiness. Because the flower so frequently faded and superstitious men remained bachelors rather than marry and court unhappiness, the blossom came to be known as the "bachelor's-button." The familiar expression "true blue" originated with this superstition.

Carnation.—The carnation is an old and popular flower, having been cultivated for more than two thousand years. It is a hardy flower, and thrives even in wind and cold.

There are many meanings hidden in the petals of carnations. When worn for decoration they express a love of beauty. They are worn also to express love—the white carnation being the love symbol of Mothers' Day. When carnations are sent to a young woman by her sweetheart they carry the message of promised happiness, devotion, constancy.

Chrysanthemum.—This is a brightly coloured, late-season flower which blossoms almost until the first of the year. Most chrysanthemums are yellow in colour, some yellow tinged with red. But new chrysanthemums have recently been produced, some as small as buttons, some as large as footballs, in a variety of colourful types.

The original home of the chrysanthemum is China. About two thousand years ago the flower was introduced from China to Japan, where it quickly became a favourite. To-day the chrysanthemum is as popular with the Japanese as the traditional cherry blossom.

The chrysanthemum is a favourite in the United States, though it is used more for interior decoration than for personal adornment. Because it is a late flower which blooms at about the time the national football games are being played, it is usually worn by the young women who attend. One of the reasons for its choice, undoubtedly, is that it is one of the hardiest flowers known and will not wilt in the sun as quickly as violets or roses.

Dahlia.—This flower derives its name from the Swedish botanist, Dahl. It was originally grown in Mexico, but is now grown in the United States. It is not a particularly popular flower, but because it expresses dignity and elegance it is used frequently for decorative purposes.

Various schools use the dahlia as an emblem.

Forget-me-not.—We are all familiar with the pretty blue flowers known as forget-me-nots. There is a delightful old legend concerning the origin and naming of these flowers.

It is preserved in German tradition that a knight and his lady love walked on the banks of the Danube the evening before their wedding day. The young lady saw a spray of beautiful blue flowers which the water apparently had dislodged, and which in a moment would be swept by the current down the stream. The flowers were so pretty that she could not see them wasted so, and she begged her lover to save them for her. He plunged into the water and grasped the flowers, but the water, as though defeated of its purpose, swirled angrily around him and suddenly swept him away with the current. As he struggled vainly to reach the shore, the knight cried to the weeping lady, "*Vergissmeinnicht!*" (Forget-me-not!) And so was the pretty blue flower given its name.

Another old tradition, now forgotten, is that a farewell gift of forget-me-nots presented on February 29th to one who departs upon a trip, brings happiness and contentment to the donor. And furthermore it insures the safety of the traveller. For a long time it was customary for friends to exchange forget-me-nots on February 29th, whether they went on trips or not; but the custom has fallen into desuetude.

Hyacinth.—"If I had but two loaves of bread I would sell one of them and buy white hyacinths to feed my soul." So did the great Elbert Hubbard express himself—he who saw beauty everywhere around him, he who had the great good fortune to know and understand the gifts of nature.

The hyacinth was once an insignificant and commonplace wild flower, with no particular beauty. It was found originally in Greece and Asia Minor, and was not brought into western Europe until the beginning of the 16th century. Dutch horticulturists experimented with the clustered flower and cultivated this simple member of the lily family until it developed into a flower of rare beauty. To-day hyacinths are grown in pink, rose, yellow, scarlet, and pure white, exquisite and highly cultivated blossoms. The finest bulbs are still grown in Holland where, as you know, gardening is a national industry.

Ancient Greece has bequeathed us this tale concerning the fragrant hyacinth. The god Apollo was on one occasion playing a game of quoits with a young mortal called Hyacinthus. Apollo dearly loved this young mortal and his happiest hours were passed in his company. While they played thus in joyous companionship, the west wind came trembling by, and Zephyrus, god of the wind, looked on in jealous anger. He hated Apollo, and in a fit of rage he caused the quoits to be blown aside. One of the quoits flew with great force against the head of Hyacinthus and inflicted a mortal wound.

In a few moments Hyacinthus died in Apollo's arms, while Zephyrus disappeared. The god grieved at the death of his friend and he decided to cause some earthly thing to grow in his memory. And so he caused beautiful clustered blossoms to spring from the drops of blood that had fallen from his friend's head, calling them hyacinths in memory of Hyacinthus.

Lily.—From the earliest times the lily has been associated with purity, truth, honour. No other flower has ever had so great a religious significance. For centuries, artists have pictured the angel Gabriel coming to the Virgin Mary with a spray of lilies in his hand, to announce that she is to be the mother of the Christ-child. Italian artists particularly have made use of the lily as a symbol of truth, purity, and innocence.

Christianity adopted the lily as the symbol of the Resurrection, and as such it is the traditional Easter flower. The exquisite lily with its tall, slender green stalk, its crowning blossoms of pure white, its delicate fragrance, is a fitting symbol of the Easter spirit. It carries a message of purity, of majesty, of solemn joy.

Churches are decorated with white lilies at Easter time. These lilies originated in Japan and for a long time their beauty was known only to the Japanese. But about 300 years ago a flower-loving sea captain carried some of the rare white flowers to the Bermudas, from whence they gradually travelled to all parts of the world. But it is still in Bermuda that the lily is cultivated, grown in great shining white fields and shipped to the United States in time to fill the Easter demand.

The lily-of-the-valley is a beautiful flower composed of tiny white bells that nestle comfortably on broad leaves. It has a rare, delicate perfume. Though the lily-of-the-valley blossoms naturally in Europe, Asia, and America in the spring, the demand for the dainty flower for bridal bouquets, decorations, etc., is so great that hothouse cultivation is necessary. The hothouse variety is quite as dainty and lovely as that which blossoms naturally in the spring.

Laurel.—Poets have long sung to us of the flowering laurel—favourite of the ancient Greeks and Romans. In Greece twigs of the laurel tree were entwined to form a crown with which victors in the Pythian games were rewarded. And a high honour it was, indeed, so to receive the laurel crown of victory!

Borrowing from this ancient custom, the people of the Middle Ages crowned their poets with laurel wreaths.

(Courtesy of Metropolitan Museum of Art)

"The Competitor."
By McKenzie, American, 19th Century.

(Courtesy of Metropolitan Museum of Art)

Egyptian balls of wood, 20th Dynasty. Found at Lisht, North Pyramid.

Laurel came to be associated with all that means glory, honour, triumph, success. It was used also for decorative purposes, particularly at the time of the harvest festival, symbolizing gratitude for, and happiness in, the bounties of the land.

The story of the laurel's origin is interesting. Greek traditions tell us that the nymph Daphne was pursued by Apollo. The nymph prayed that he turn into a tree—which, promptly he did. Tradition says that it was a laurel tree into which Apollo was transformed, and so the laurel tree has been sacred to the god ever since.

Marigold.—In the Middle Ages pretty golden-yellow blossoms made their appearance in great profusion in certain parts of southern Europe. Delighted with the lovely golden flowers, the people decided to call them "Mary's gold," in honour of the Virgin Mary. From the phrase "Mary's gold" the blossoms came to be known as marigolds. They bloom late and are hardy. They are used generally for indoor decorative purposes.

Mignonette.—There was a pretty and fragrant flower in ancient Egypt which was known as *reseda,* which means "to assuage." For centuries this flower was known to no country but Egypt, and for an incredibly long time it grew in wildness, uncultivated and unnoticed.

It was not until the 18th century that the flower was introduced into France from Egypt, where it immediately became popular under the name of mignonette. During the same century it became popular also in England. The mignonette is not particularly popular in this country, although the perfume is an old favourite.

Orange Blossoms.—"Significantly from one of the most prolific of all fruit-bearing trees, orange blossoms are plainly a symbol meant to bring fruitfulness to the union," says one authority, discussing the custom of wearing orange blossoms at weddings.

This custom appears to have been introduced into Europe at the time of the Crusades. Even at that early date, sprigs of the blossoms were worn as a crown on the bridal veil, a practice which is said to be Saracenic in origin.

The orange tree bears fruit and flowers at the same time, therefore its blossoms make an excellent symbol of fruitfulness, productiveness. The language of the orange blossoms is purity, chastity, which makes them ideal as bridal blossoms.

Rose.—There is probably no flower as popular and as beloved as the rose. As one writer expresses it: "From the time of Midas, the King of Phrygia, whose rose gardens were the wonder of the ancient world, until to-day, the rose has reigned queen of flowers."

An old tradition tells us that Venus, hurrying to Adonis with nectar, stepped upon a thorn while alighting from her chariot. Blood rushed from the wound and stained the bush, and a little nectar was spilled over it also. Where both blood and nectar mingled on the bush a beautiful red rose made its appearance.

Because of this tradition the rose has been dedicated to Venus, and is a symbol of joy, love, beauty. Still another old tradition tells us that Cupid gave a rose to Hippocrates, the god of silence, "to bribe him not to reveal the indiscretions of Venus."

It is said that the Sybarites used to sleep on mattresses stuffed with rose petals. From this long-forgotten custom came the phrase, now familiar everywhere, to sleep on a "bed of roses." In its modern significance the phrase means to have an easy life, to be comfortable, wealthy, satisfied.

SOME MISCELLANEOUS SUPERSTITIONS AND ORIGINS

There are many little things we do and say today simply because others do and say those things, but how many of us actually know what they mean, how they originated?

The phrase "Adam's apple," for instance, is used constantly by people who haven't the slightest notion as to how the phrase originated. The story is that a piece of the forbidden apple lodged in Adam's throat, and that all men have this lump in the throat as a reminder of Adam's sin. The origin of the name is, of course, obvious.

The custom of "knocking on wood" appears to have originated in the custom of touching wood upon every occasion of happiness or good fortune in gratitude to Christ who died upon a wooden cross. Through some perverted notion of the mass mind, the custom of touching or "knocking" on wood came to be looked upon as a means of warding off ill luck. The superstition has remained and the custom is still observed. A similar type of superstition is found in Sweden where fishermen do not dare to mention to anyone during the course of the day how many fish they have caught, for they believe that if they do so they will catch no more fish that day.

We have a rather peculiar superstition, or rather tradition, that "to eat garlic gives strength." This can be traced back to ancient times in Egypt, when the pyramids were being built. The workmen were given great quantities of onions and garlic to eat, because of the belief that this food would make them stronger. Herodotus in an account of the building of the pyramids says that the workmen ate "*raphanus,* onions and garlic."

It is curious to see how logical and customary things gradually become elaborated into superstitions that are accepted, believed. For example, it is customary for children, if not carefully watched, to fall out of bed. What could be simpler to understand? The child is left alone, it rolls over and over until it finally rolls off the bed altogether. But there has existed for many centuries the superstition that a child falls out of bed at the will of the spirits that hover about it. If a baby does not fall out of bed before it is eleven months old, it will be a fool. Another curious superstition is that if a baby should happen to look into a glass before its first birthday, it will die. There are, indeed, many superstitious notions concerning infants, a few of which we list here:

If a baby smiles in its sleep, it is talking with angels.

If a child cries at birth and lifts one hand, it is born to command.

If a child's nails are cut with scissors before it is a year old, it will grow up to be a thief.

If a child cries on its first birthday, it will be unhappy throughout life.

If a child cries during baptism do not be alarmed. It is simply the devil going out of it.

If you want your child to rise in the world, carry it upstairs the day it is born.

This familiar old rhyme preserves the old superstitions concerning the personalities of various children on various birthdays:

> Monday's child is fair of face,
> Tuesday's child is full of grace,
> Wednesday's child is sour and sad,
> Thursday's child is merry and glad,
> Friday's child is loving and giving,
> Saturday's child must work for a living,
> But the child that is born on the Sabbath day
> Is blithe and bonny, good and gay.

Superstitious people believe in omens concerning the weather and the seasons. Some of the more familiar omens are:

If March comes in like a lamb it goes out like a lion.

If it rains on Easter, it will rain seven Sundays thereafter.

If it storms on Friday, it will storm again before Monday.

If the sun rises red, there will be a hot day on the morrow.

If one sees a rainbow, it is a sign of showers.

Heavy snowstorms indicate an excellent spring crop.

Large, bright stars in the winter promise a frost for the following day.

A disk or ring around the moon indicates rain or snow.

There are, of course, many bridal and wedding superstitions, some of which have already been discussed in the chapter devoted to weddings. Here are a few of the more popular superstitions, still current:

If you marry on Wednesday you will be happy; if you marry on Friday or Saturday you will be unhappy.

A double wedding means unhappiness to one of the couples.

It is bad luck to try on a wedding gown before the ceremony.

To lose the wedding ring is an omen of unhappiness.

A bride, to be happy, should step over the church sill with her right foot.

An amusing combination of warning and superstition: If you are cross when you are young, you will be an old maid!

Dreams have always interested man, and it is not surprising that through the centuries many superstitions should have been evolved concerning the things that man sees in his dreams. According to the popular notion, dreams go by contraries. For instance, to dream that someone hates you is supposed to indicate that you have gained a new friend. Here are some of the familiar dream superstitions:

Dream of death and you will hear from the living.

Dream of eggs and you will quarrel with a friend.

Dream of a nest and you will receive a gift.

Dream of a fire and you will have ill luck.

Dream of a great blaze in your home, and you will receive money.

Dream of men and you will be lucky; of women, and you will be unlucky.

Dream of marriage and you will attend a funeral.

Dream of a funeral and you will attend a marriage.

Dream of gold and you will see prosperity.

Dream of flowers and you will be ill.

Dream of a ship or an anchor and you will have good luck.

Dream of bread and you will have happiness.

Dream of a snowstorm and you will hear of the death of a relative.

Dream of an heir and you will have a misfortune.

Dream of babies and you will be unlucky.

Dream of rain and good luck is in store for you.

Dream of teeth and there will be sickness in your family.

Dream of having a tooth drawn and you will lose a friend.

Dream of catching fish and you will be very lucky.

Dream of pigs and you will have lifelong happiness.

Dream of a white horse and bad luck is on the way.

Dream of a black horse and there will soon be either a funeral or a wedding.

Dream of cutting hay and you are going to be successful in society.

Dream of a hat and you will win in whatever you undertake.

Dream of dogs and horses and you will have good luck.

Dream of a dead mother and you will have sorrow.

Dream the same thing three times in succession and it will positively come true.

It would fill a volume to quote here all the dream superstitions of the various countries. Practically all superstitious people believe in dreams, and there are many who are not superstitious otherwise but believe that dreams have "meanings." There are several so-called Dream Books which pretend to explain authoritatively the meanings of dreams.

There is a proverbial saying that when a person's ears burn someone is talking about him. One writer on superstitions says, "If your right ear burns, someone is talking well of you. If your left ear burns, he is talking ill."

This superstition is of great antiquity and is mentioned by Pliny. He says, "If our ears do glow and tingle some there be that in our absence doe talk of us."

Frequently we hear the expression "to roast" a person.

A scolding is spoken of as a "roasting." This is a relic of cannibalism when human beings actually were roasted for food. Thus among the Samoans, who at one time practiced cannibalism, to speak of "roasting" a person is the very worst language that can be used. It carries with it a grim significance. We have borrowed the phrase, have given it a place in our vocabulary of slang, and use it to indicate a scolding.

Some Food Origins.—It is said that coffee was discovered by the Sheik Omar, though whether the tale is authentic or not is still in doubt. The story is that the Sheik, starving in the desert, found some bitter berries growing on a shrub. He tried to improve their taste by roasting them, but he found to his surprise that they became very hard. To soften them he dropped them into boiling water, but they would not become soft again. The liquid, he noticed, became dark in colour. Finally, in desperation, the Sheik drank the liquid, and so discovered coffee.

According to Lamb ("A Dissertation on Roast Pig") the custom of roasting food to improve its flavour originated by accident. Bo-bo, a Chinese boy, burned down his father's hut. As he was digging among the embers, his fingers came in contact with a pig which had been roasted in the conflagration. He put his burned fingers in his mouth to cool them and tasted—for the first time—crackling.

Of course, this is just a myth made popular by Lamb. The true story of the origin of roasting or cooking food goes back very much farther. It is very possible that man discovered the value of "putting food through fire" when he began to make animal sacrifices to the deities. We can imagine a tribe of primitive men frightened by a great storm, or a drought, or some other calamity. Believing that in some way they have angered the deities of their tribe, they decide to soothe their ruffled feelings by making gift offerings in the form of food.

To leave the food on a scaffold or on the ground would be unsafe. The prowling animals would get it before the gods. Therefore they conceived the idea of burning the food so that its fragrant smoke would rise up to the sky and delight the nostrils of the deities.

But the burning food delighted the nostrils of mere mortals, too! And so we find man cooking his own food, roasting in fire the meats he had formerly eaten raw (See chap. XIII).

Someday someone may write a book on the meanings and origins of our words for various foods—bread, coffee, cake, potatoes, meat, carrots, onions. Behind each name there is a long history and an interesting origin. To give but one example, let us choose the word "halibut." In the old Saxon days a fish was called a "but." Taken into the German language, the word came to be "Butte." In England, at a later date, the word "halibut" was originated, meaning "holy fish," *i.e.*, fish that is eaten as a holiday dish on feast days. The halibut is still a special holiday fish in England.

Heaven and Hell.—We have already discussed at length the notions concerning a heaven and a hell. Now let us see how the words themselves originated, what they mean.

Ralph Waldo Trine tells us that the word heaven means *harmony*. The word *hell* originally meant to build a wall around, to separate. Thus to be *helled* off meant to be shut off.

Public Libraries.—The public library does not belong to modernism as many of us are inclined to think. Recent excavations at Nippur in Babylon have laid bare a library dating from about 3000 B. C.—meaning that this library is about 5000 years old! The "books" are clay tablets upon which are inscribed important information which the scribes of the day wished to preserve.

The greatest library of antiquity was that of Alexandria. The "books" were in the form of great parchment rolls, indexed and placed on shelves for all the world like a modern library. Vast quantities of these parchment rolls were housed at the Alexandrian library where students, teachers, and everyone who could read came for "research."

The library was founded by the Ptolemies and was destroyed in the early centuries of the Christian Era. Its loss is a great misfortune, for the parchment rolls and their information would have been of inestimable value to the modern student of ancient times.

Bookkeeping is very ancient. But the earliest bookkeeping was simply entry of items on a clay tablet or a parchment roll. It was not until 1495 that Luca di Borgo, in Venice, wrote in detail of double-entry bookkeeping and its advantages. An English book on the subject, the first of its kind to appear, was published in London in the year 1543 and was written by a bookkeeper known as John Gowgne.

Pin Money.—For a long time after the invention of pins, in the early 14th century, makers were allowed to sell them only on the 1st and 2d of January. The reason for this regulation was that women, delighted with the novelty and the usefulness of the pins, spent money intended for household purposes to secure them. They were extremely expensive, and only the wealthy could really afford them, but everyone bought. Therefore the regulation became necessary, and the custom originated of placing aside a bit of money every now and then so that one would have sufficient to buy pins on January 1st and 2d. This money came to be known as "pin money."

The phrase has remained, and even we frequently refer to small amounts of money, intended for trifles, as "pin money."

The Barber's Pole; Tipping.—Why do barbers use red-and-white poles as a sign of their profession? Have you ever wondered? Have you ever guessed?

It was at one time customary for barbers to perform minor operations in surgery. During the era when bleeding was regarded as a cure for most ills, it was to the barber that people applied to be bled. It was necessary, in this operation, for the patient to grasp a staff or pole, and such a pole, with bandaging to tie the patient's arm, was always kept in readiness.

When the pole was not in use the bandaging or tape was fastened to it and both were placed at the door as a sign, or symbol, that the barber was proficient in bleeding. As a later development it became customary to use a pole painted with stripes around it, instead of the identical pole used in the operations. Red stripes were used to indicate blood-soaked bandages.

Thus the red-and-white barber poles are relics of the crude staffs and bandages used by barbers in ancient times during bleeding operations.

Tipping appears to have originated with barbers, for we are told that they received no definite payment for the bleeding operation. The patient tipped the barber whatever he was able to afford, or whatever he felt the operation was worth. England took up the custom of tipping, or feeing, finding it an excellent means of securing quick and efficient service. There appeared presently small boxes hung conspicuously in inns and road houses, above which appeared signs bearing the slogan "*T*o *I*nsure *P*romptness." From the initial letters of these three words is derived our word "tip." The box "To Insure Promptness" has disappeared, but the tip has remained, developed, and become a universal custom.

How Ireland Got Its Name.—There is an old Celtic legend which tells us how the name of Ireland originated.

According to this old legend, the famous Emerald Isle was originally altogether submerged, except during brief periods every seventh year. During the time the island appeared above the surface of the water it looked so green and beautiful and tempting that many bold people attempted to build homes and remain upon it. But always, after the brief period, the lovely green island was swallowed up by the sea again and disappeared for another seven years.

Then, on one great occasion, there appeared a heavenly apparition, and it was declared to all that the island could be rescued from the sea only by planting a shaft of iron in its heart the next time it appeared above the water. Iron was believed at that time a sacred and luck-bringing metal.

When the island appeared above the water the next time, a bold and daring adventurer proceeded upon it and buried his sword in its heart. The spell was dissolved. The island was not swallowed up by the waves again, as it had been so many times before, but settled itself comfortably upon the surface of the sea—and there it has remained ever since.

Because of this myth the island came to be known as Iron-land, or Ireland. One writer says it is because of this tradition that "iron is always accounted lucky by the Irish, and when a bit of iron is found in the form of a horseshoe it is nailed for luck above the house door."

Man's Lighting Devices.—Man has always feared the dark, for it was in the dark of night, way back in primitive times, that fearsome animals stole upon the tribe and carried off one or two struggling humans. It was, indeed, in the dark of night that most of the terrible things of primitive life happened to man. And so, man has always attempted to pierce this darkness, to dispel it with light of his own making.

The first lighting apparatus was simply a burning brand snatched from the campfire. The earliest lamp was a hollowed stone, shell, or skull filled with animal fat or fish oil as fuel, and reeds, rushes, or a twist of vegetable fibre as the wick. Lamps such as these are used by the Eskimo even to-day.

In Greece and Rome the dim, smoky lamp made its appearance at a fairly early date. It was a shallow dish, round or oval in shape, with a handle at one end and a spout for the wick at the other. It was made of baked earth or metal, and the wick was made of tow or cloth. These lamps, used chiefly by students and teachers, are the traditional "lamps of learning" to which reference is frequently made.

Candles are of great antiquity. They were at first simply crude cylinders of wax or solid fatty matter rolled around a vegetable fibre or bit of twisted cloth for a wick.

It was not until 1783 that the flat lamp wick was introduced by M. Legers of Paris. It made possible for the first time a smokeless lamp, and it had a spur wheel for regulating the flame and adjusting the wick. In 1784 a Swedish chemist improved this invention, and soon afterward the use of the glass chimney was discovered.

The early New England colonists used a flat, iron, pear-shaped lamp known as the "Betty Lamp." But Benjamin Franklin contrived a very much superior lamp of two round wick tubes, suggesting wicks of braided cotton. About 1865 the double burner was introduced and became extremely popular.

The next step in the development of illumination came in 1817 when gas light began to be used in the United States for the first time. This proved to be the best light thus far invented, and its use quickly spread. The electric light replaced gas light, and is superior to any other kind of illumination. It is safe, bright, attractive, and less expensive than even candlelight.

The Story of Coinage.—One of the most deeply rooted customs of civilized man is the use of coins, and government notes representing coin, in the business of buying and selling. From Robert Mushet's "History of Coinage" we quote the following:

> Money is a measure of value and medium of exchange; coinage is the art of fabricating money.
>
> As soon as nations emerge from a state of barbarism, when simple barter no longer suffices to meet their wants, they will invent some common or conventional measure of value by which to exchange their products and carry on their commerce. In the rude ages of society, cattle are said to have been the common medium of commerce; and

among the patriarchs of old they were the measure of man's wealth and greatness. The armour of Diomede, says Homer, cost only nine oxen; but that of Glaucus cost a hundred oxen. In some countries, in former times, salt was the measure of value and instrument of exchange; and in others shells formed the circulating medium. But as the necessities of nations multiply, and their commercial transactions extend, they soon discover the inadequacy of these means, and will search for something of a more steady and durable character, which shall serve both as a circulating medium, as well as a medium of exchange with other countries trading with them.

From a very early period metals, as possessing that character in a high degree, were chosen to perform these important functions. They are not only less perishable than other articles, but they can, without loss, be divided into any number of parts, and be united again by fusion; they can be hammered or rolled into plates, and moulded into any shape; and occupying less bulk than other articles, they are easily transported from place to place.

Thus briefly and completely does Mr. Mushet, an authority, give the reasons for the use of gold and silver as coinage for a means of exchange and for use in commercial transactions. Copper and iron as well as gold and silver were used by ancient peoples, but gradually the two latter metals alone remained and took the form of coins.

The bills with which we are familiar are simply promissory notes given by the government and entitling the bearer to gold or silver on demand. The gold and silver, which would be cumbersome and inconvenient to carry around in bulk, are kept in the treasury and the light bills carried in their place. Of course, the bills are accepted as "legal tender" by everyone because the government promises to pay gold or silver to the holder on demand.

The history of money and of coinage is fascinating, and we have barely touched upon it here. There are many interesting books on the subject, however, and most of them are available at the public libraries.

Wall Paper.—Few of us realize how wall paper came into being. The story is an interesting one.

For a long time the walls in homes were covered with rich tapestries to hide the bareness. These tapestries were made by hand and were, of course, extremely valuable. Therefore only the wealthy could afford them.

In feudal times the walls in the castles and in the homes of the mighty were covered with rare and costly tapestries, while the walls of those whose homes were humble had to remain bare and ugly. This condition remained for many centuries, until finally some clever persons conceived the notion of imitating tapestries in heavy paper and covering bare walls in this manner. In 1790 John B. Howell established the first wall-paper factory in the United States. These paper imitations of tapestries were at first quite expensive, though very much less expensive, of course, than actual tapestries. After much experimenting a cheap type of wall paper was perfected, and by the beginning of the 19th century pretty and colourful papers for the walls came into general use.

To-day wall papers are made, not only in imitation of rare old tapestries, but in floral and conventional designs. Some papers are even of pure white, or cream, or solid tones of blue, yellow, pink, etc. The art of creating wall papers has reached a high degree of perfection, and now even people in the most humble circumstances can afford to have the walls of their homes neatly, if not extravagantly, covered.

Days of the Week.—How did the days come to get their names? What does Friday mean, Tuesday, Sunday?

The names of the days of the week are Anglo-Saxon in origin and have the following meanings:

Sunday: The Sun's day, in honour of the sun.

Monday: The Moon's day, in honour of the moon.

Tuesday: Tiw's day, in honour of Tiw, an old Teutonic deity.

Wednesday: Wodan's day, in honour of Wodan, the old Teuton and Norse god. (Some believe it means Venus' day, in honour of Venus.)

Thursday: Thor's day, in honour of Thor, the Norse god of thunder.

Friday: Freya's day, in honour of the German virgin goddess.

Saturday: Saturn's day, in honour of the god Saturn.

Tuesday was once known as Marsday, for the Teuton god of war (Tiw) was considered identical with the Roman god of war, Mars.

THE NAMING OF THE STATES

It is interesting to trace the origins of the name that our states bear. The following table gives the names of the states in alphabetical order, with the origin and meaning of the names beside them. We are indebted to Compton's "Pictured Encyclopedia" for most of this information:

Alabama: From an old Creek Indian word meaning "place of rest."

Arizona: From an Indian word meaning "place of small springs."

Arkansas: From the name of an old Indian tribe; no particular meaning that is known.

California: From *caliento forno* (hot furnace) originally applied to Lower California. Probably also from the name of a fabled island in Spanish romance.

Colorado: From a Spanish word meaning "reddish colour"; first applied to the Colorado river and later to the entire state.

Connecticut: From the name "Quonoktacut" given to the river by the Indians.

Delaware: From Lord de la Warr, first governor of Virginia.

Florida: From *Pascua florida* (flowery feast) Spanish for "Easter Sunday."

Georgia: In honour of King George II of England.

Idaho: From an old Indian word, meaning "gem of the hills."

Illinois: From French interpretation of the Indian word "Illini," meaning *men.*

Indiana: From the word "Indian." The meaning of the name is probably "land of the Indians."

Iowa: From an Indian name meaning "sleepy waters"—a name given by the Indians first to the river, and later applied to the state.

Kansas: From an Indian tribe called "Kanzas." The meaning of the word is "wind people."

Kentucky: From an Indian name "Kentake" meaning "prairie" (uncertain).

Louisiana: In honour of King Louis XIV of France.

Maine: From charter of 1622 where land is called "Province of Maine," probably from name of Province in France.

Maryland: In honour of Queen Maria of England.

Massachusetts: From Indian name meaning "great hills."

Michigan: From Indian name meaning "great water."

Minnesota: From Indian name meaning "clouded water."

Mississippi: From Indian name meaning "gathering waters."

Missouri: From Indian name meaning "muddy stream."

Montana: From Spanish word meaning "mountain."

Nebraska: From a Sioux Indian name meaning "shallow water."

Nevada: From a Spanish word meaning "snowy."

New Hampshire: Named for the county of Hampshire in England.

New Jersey: Named for the island of Jersey in the English channel.

New Mexico: From the Indian name "Mexitl," an old Aztec divinity.

New York: In honour of the Duke of York (later James II of England).

North Carolina: In honour of Charles II of England.

North Dakota: From Indian name meaning "allies."

Ohio: From Indian name meaning "beautiful river."

Oklahoma: From Choctaw Indian name meaning "red people."

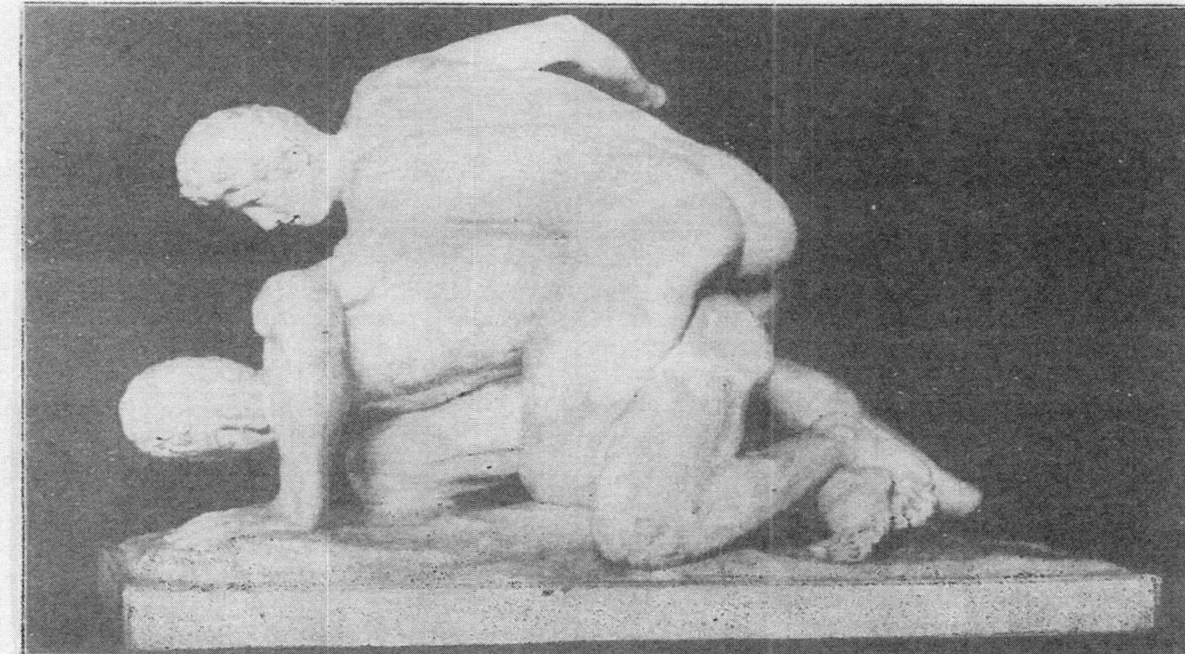

(Courtesy of Metropolitan Museum of Art)

The two wrestlers, Roman.

(Courtesy of Metropolitan Museum of Art)

Old Athenian box of the school of the "Meidias Painter." Exterior shows girl athlete balancing a stick.

Oregon: From name given to Columbia River, popularized in "Thanatopsis" (Bryant).

Pennsylvania: In honour of the founder, William Penn. The name is the Latin form for "Penn's woods."

Rhode Island: From the Dutch "Roode Eylandt," meaning "red island."

South Carolina: In honour of Charles II of England.

South Dakota: From Indian name meaning "allies."

Tennessee: From Indian name given to the river, meaning unknown.

Texas: Named for the Texas tribe of Indians.

Utah: Named for the tribe of Ute Indians.

Vermont: From a French word meaning "green mountains."

Virginia: In honour of Elizabeth, virgin queen of England.

Washington: In honour of George Washington.

Wisconsin: From Indian name meaning "meeting of the rivers."

Wyoming: Named for the Wyoming valley in Pennsylvania (scene of the Indian massacre of 1778).

POPULAR PHRASES

There are many phrases which we use constantly in our conversation without knowing what they mean or how they originated. Some of these phrases have become "slang," although at one time they carried an important and dignified meaning. There are old and interesting traditions behind most of these popular phrases.

The phrase "blue blood," for instance, can be traced back to the time of the Moorish conquest. There are old families of Spain that trace their pedigrees even beyond the time of the conquest, claiming that at that time the blood of the common people was of a muddy hue, while those who belonged to the pedigreed families had blood of pure blue. Now it is customary to refer to people with notable pedigrees as "blue-blooded."

We speak of "lynching" people, but how many people know how the word originated? During the Revolutionary War an American planter by the name of Charles Lynch illegally put to death some Tories. Thereafter, whenever any one was hanged or otherwise put to death without the sanction of the law, the event was referred to as a "lynching." Through constant usage the word has become familiarized and is now a part of the language.

The phrase "bury the hatchet" obviously derives from the actual ceremony of burying the hatchet, practised symbolically by the Indians to indicate their willingness to be friendly. One writer says:

Tickling the soles of a prisoner—a form of torture practised by the early Chinese. From this custom has come our popular expression "tickled to death."

> The Great Spirit commanded the North American Indians when they smoked the calumet, or peace-pipe, to bury their hatchets, scalping knives and war-clubs in the ground that all thought of hostility might be buried out of sight.

We still use the phrase "bury the hatchet" when we wish to indicate peacefulness, friendly relations, usually after a quarrel.

You Are a Brick.—In his "Life of Agesilaus" (King of Sparta) Plutarch tells this story, which indicates the origin of the phrase "a perfect brick" or "you are a brick" as used in modern slang:

On a certain occasion an ambassador from Esperus, on a diplomatic mission, was shown by the king over his capital. The ambassador knew of the monarch's fame, knew that though only nominally king of Sparta, he was ruler of Greece, and he had looked to see massive walls rearing aloft their embattled towers for the defense of the town, but he found nothing of the kind. He marvelled much at this, and spoke of it to the king. The following conversation took place:

"Sire," he said, "I have visited most of the principal towns and I find no walls reared for defense. Why is this?"

"Indeed, Sir Ambassador," replied Agesilaus, "thou canst not have looked carefully. Come with me tomorrow morning and I will show you the walls of Sparta."

Accordingly on the following morning the King led his guest out upon the plain, where the army was drawn up in full array, and pointing proudly to the serried hosts, he said:

"There thou beholdest the walls of Sparta—ten thousand men, and every man a brick!"

A Feather in One's Cap.—Among the Sioux Indians of North America it was the ambition of every young brave to earn the "feather"—the greatest honour possible. The "feather" was awarded for distinction, for bravery in war, etc., and it was highly coveted. When won, it was worn on the head, and each new feather was added to it. Thus the value of an Indian brave was estimated by the number of feathers in his "cap."

We find this same custom among the Hungarians. In the Lansdowne manuscript in the British Museum we find a description of Hungary in 1599 in which the writer says:

> It hath been an ancient custom among them that none should wear a fether but he who had killed a Turk, to whom onlie it was lawful to shew the number of his slain enemys by the number of fethers in his cappe.

From customs such as these has originated the now familiar phrase "to wear a feather in one's hat."

When in Rome, Do as the Romans Do.—This old phrase is used constantly in modern life to indicate adapting oneself to one's environment. It has an ancient origin that can be traced in Church history to the time of St. Austin.

The story is that Milan and Rome differed in the matter of keeping the Sabbath. At Milan the old custom prevailed of making of Saturday a festival. In Rome the Sabbath was kept as a fast day. St. Austin, who had occasion to visit both Rome and Milan did not bother much about the matter, but it perplexed and annoyed his mother, Monica. Therefore he agreed to go to St. Ambrose for advice, and the legend is that St. Ambrose said to him: "When I am at Rome I fast as the Romans do; when I am at Milan I do not fast. So likewise you, whatever church you come to, observe the custom of the place if you would neither give offence to others nor take offence from them."

A Thorn in My Side.—Among savage peoples it is customary to use a curious expression of some sort in reference to one's wife, for to use her right name would bring misfortune and unhappiness to the household. Thus, among the Tuyangs a man never uttered his wife's name but referred to her by a special word which, when translated, means "my dull thorn" or "the thorn in my ribs."

It would appear that our phrase "a thorn in my side" originated with this old Tuyang custom.

Kick the Bucket.—The phrase "to kick the bucket" is slang for death, but it has a perfectly legitimate origin.

The Egyptian word for kick is *Khekh*, meaning to recoil, to return, to send back. Therefore to *Khekh* the bucket in the Egyptian hieroglyphics indicates or symbolizes the return of an empty bucket—*i.e.*, a body without life. The Egyptians used the bucket constantly in their hieroglyphics as a symbol of death.

This is but one instance of slang interpretation of the symbol language. A lifetime might well be spent in gathering the lore and the tales of various countries and interpreting them in relation to modern usage.

The Greenhorn.—This familiar slang phrase had its origin during the reign of Louis XIV of France. A law was passed compelling all bankrupt Hebrews to wear small pointed caps or hats made of green cloth. This green cap was the badge of bankruptcy, and its purpose was to warn people from doing business with the wearer.

For a period of about twenty years these green hats were worn, and if an insolvent Jew appeared in the streets without one, he was liable to be seized by his creditors and thrust into a dungeon.

Progress and tolerance have robbed the expression of its original meaning, but the phrase "greenhorn" has remained and is used now to denote a person "bankrupt" in brains rather than in business.

Baker's Dozen.—This phrase carries us back to the time when there was much difficulty concerning "short weight" in bread. The City of London made special provision that an extra piece of bread be given after weight, so that there would be no difficulty.

Consequently twelve pieces of bread, with one extra piece to prevent insufficient weight, came to be known familiarly as the "baker's dozen." The phrase is still in use, but is more familiar in England than it is in the United States.

Nothing New under the Sun.—Here is a popular phrase which traces its origin back to the sacred narrative. In Ecclesiastes (I, 9) we read:

> That which hath been is the same which will be; and that which hath been done is the same which will be done; and there is nothing new under the sun.

In the Book of Job we find another familiar phrase—"Skin of your teeth." Both these phrases are in constant use to-day.

The phrase "catch our hare before we cook him" is an old English proverb made popular by Hannah Glasse. Hannah was a cook of no little reputation, and in 1747 she published a cookery book filled with rare and interesting old recipes. In one recipe, of which the hare is the principal ingredient, she says, "And we must catch our hare before we cook him."

Adding Insult to Injury.—Many of us use this phrase, but few know how it originated. There is little doubt that the now popular expression originated in this bit of philosophic humour by Phaedrus, known as "The Bald Man and the Fly":

> A fly bit the bare pate of a bald man who, endeavoring to crush it, gave himself a heavy blow. Then said the fly, jeeringly: "You wanted to revenge the sting of a tiny insect with death; what will you do to yourself, who have added insult to injury?"

Blarney.—The famous Blarney Stone is a relic of an ancient castle of Blarney in Ireland.

> It is a triangular stone suspended from the north angle of the castle, about twenty feet from the top. According to a tradition of the country, the castle was besieged by the English under Carew, Earl of Totness, who, having concluded an armistice with the commander of the castle on condition of its surrender, waited for the fulfilment of the terms, but was put off from day to day with soft speeches instead, until he became the jest of Elizabeth's ministers and the dupe of the Lord of Blarney.

From this story comes our slang term "blarney" referring to jesting or to untruths. And "kissing the Blarney Stone" has become a popular synonym for flattery and for smooth, deceitful words.

Pouring Oil on Troubled Waters.—In his "Natural History" Pliny (1st century of Christian Era) speaks of the excellent results to be secured through pouring oil on troubled waters, indicating that as oil will smooth a stormy sea so will soft words smooth a ruffled, angry personality. Another interesting account of the so-called "phenomenon" is noted in Bede's "Ecclesiastical History" (book 3, chapter 15) written in Latin more than eleven centuries ago.

The familiar phrase "No royal road to learning" is accredited to Euclid, father of mathematics, who was born at Alexandria about 300 B.C. On one occasion the famous mathematician was asked, by Ptolemy Soter, who was then his student and later became the King of Egypt, if geometry could not be made easier. Euclid without a moment's hesitation replied, "There is no royal road to learning!"

There's Many a Slip.—A tradition tells us that Ancæus, King of the Leleges in Samos (an island in the Grecian Archipelago) planted a vineyard. Because he oppressed and ill-treated his slaves; one of them prophesied to him that he would never live to taste the wine.

When the wine was made the King sent for the slave who had made this prophecy and said, "What do you think of your prophecy now?" The slave looked at him intently for a moment, and said, "There's many a slip 'twixt the cup and the lip." At this moment a man rushed in to inform Ancæus that a wild boar had broken into his favourite vineyard and was laying it waste. The King placed his cup aside, untasted, and hurried out to attack the boar and drive it from his vineyard. In the encounter he was killed, and the slave's prophecy was fulfilled.

Robbing Peter to Pay Paul.—This phrase had its origin in the rivalry which existed between St. Peter's Cathedral (now Westminster Abbey) and St. Paul's Cathedral in London.

The story is that in 1550 an appropriation was made from St. Peter's to make up a deficiency found in the accounts of St. Paul's. This action instantly met with opposition, and the people demanded, "Why rob St. Peter to pay St. Paul?"

For a while the phrase was forgotten, lost, but it was revived in the 18th century upon the death of William Pitt (Earl Chatham). Both the cemetery of St. Paul's and the cemetery of St. Peter's (Westminster Abbey) claimed the honour of his burial. The City of London argued that so great a statesman should be buried in the sacred earth of St. Paul's, but Parliament declared that if he were not buried in Westminster Abbey they would again be "robbing St. Peter to pay St. Paul." Finally the dispute was settled in favour of Westminster Abbey, and since then the phrase "robbing Peter to pay Paul" has been in popular use.

Blackball.—The blackball is a vote by ballot against the election of a candidate for membership in a club or other association. The origin is interesting.

In ancient times, small black and white balls were used to represent votes against and for a candidate. This method of using balls is now obsolete, but the word "blackball" remains and is used in the manner indicated.

The origin of the word "windfall" in the sense of "good luck" dates back to the time of William the Conqueror. It was at that time a criminal offence to cut timber in the forests, and only such timber could be gathered as the wind had blown down. A great windstorm was hailed by the peasants as a piece of great good fortune, for there would be much timber to gather after the storm. This good fortune was referred to as a "windfall," and the word has been preserved with its original meaning to this very day, although the modern application refers to luck in general, rather than to luck in gathering timber.

Man in the Moon.—Harold Bayley in his "Lost Language of Symbolism" advances a theory for the origin of the myth of a man in the moon. He tells us that the Egyptians personified the moon as masculine, and identified it with Troth, the pathfinder and awakener of sleeping minds. Presumably it is the face of Troth—the man in the moon—that we see!

Plutarch wrote a treatise on the "Face in the Moon" in which he relates an interesting fable. The good, he says, go to the moon and enjoy perfect tranquillity. But "should anyone whose purification was incomplete attempt to force his way thither, he was frightened away by the apparition of a terrifying and appalling face." Mr. Bayley suggests that this myth was probably originated to deter premature entrance into the next world "by the unlawful method of suicide."

Science tells us that the Man in the Moon is really nothing more nor less than great mountains which can be seen distinctly through powerful magnifying glasses

Crocodile's Tears.—There is an old tradition that crocodiles moan and sigh like a person in distress when they wish to lure travellers to the spot. It is said that they even shed tears while in the very act of devouring the prey.

Because of this tale, which has never definitely been proved true, hypocritical tears are called "crocodile's tears." The phrase is frequently used in modern life.

The odd simile "dead as a doornail" is explained by one authority in this manner:

> Doors of the 16th and 17th centuries were furnished with nails upon which the knockers fell; hence the phrase is used to denote one irrecoverably dead—death as reiterated strokes on the head would produce.

Shakespeare uses the phrase. He has Pistol remark to Falstaff that the King is as dead as "the nail in the door."

From Æsop's Fables.—Æsop, from whom we quote probably more than from any other writer, is supposed to have lived from about 620 to 560 B.C. He was a slave, said to have belonged to Iadmon of Samons. Despite the hardships of his life he was able to write of the things he saw and heard about him, and he has bequeathed us a rare legacy of simple, wholesome philosophy. Many of the proverbs, familiar phrases, and even some of the slang we use to-day originated with the slave Æsop who lived thousands of years ago.

Here, for instance, is a typical Æsop fable called "The Fox and the Lion":

> A fox who had never seen a lion, when by chance he met him for the first time, was so terrified that he almost died of fright. When he met him the second time, he was still afraid, but managed to disguise his fear. When he saw him the third time, he was so much emboldened that he went up to him and asked him how he did. Familiarity breeds contempt.

That last sentence, "Familiarity breeds contempt," is quoted frequently to-day. It is but one of the keen, sugar-coated bits of wisdom that is part of our inheritance from

Æsop. Some of the other phrases which he originated, and which we quote to-day, are:

Look before you leap.
Figures are not always facts.
Winter finds out what Summer lays by.
There is no arguing a coward into courage.
Men are blind to their own faults.
Give me less of your currying and more of your corn.
Grasp at the shadow and lose the substance.
Those who cry loudest are not always the most hurt.
A tyrant never wants a plea.
Better save a man from dying than salve him when dead.
They who lay traps for others are often caught by their own bait.
It serves you right (an idiomatic phrase originated by Æsop).
For me a dry crust with liberty against a king's luxury with a chain.
Pride shall have a fall.
Slow and steady wins the race.
One man's meat is another man's poison.
Necessity is the mother of Invention.
Keep to your place and your place will keep you.
Example is better than precept.
There can be little liking where there is no likeness.
Better be wise by the misfortunes of others than by your own.
What are blessings in freedom are curses in slavery.
Quality comes before quantity.
The lights of heaven are never blown out.
A bird in the hand is worth two in the bush.
He who plays a trick must be prepared to take a joke.
Union is strength.
Revenge is too dearly purchased at the price of liberty.
Honesty is the best policy.
Nip evil in the bud. Spare the rod and spoil the child.
The smaller the mind the greater the conceit.
It is one thing to propose, another to execute.
One good turn deserves another.
Facts speak plainer than words.
Wise men say nothing in dangerous times.

These are just a handful of the more familiar of Æsop's sayings. What a wealth of wisdom to crowd into one short lifetime! And behind each of these sayings is a delightful fable, a myth, a story if you will—the sugar coating that makes his wisdom easy to take, pleasant to swallow. He writes of bears, of lions, of dogs, of mice, of mountains, but mirrored in his tales are the doings and sayings of human beings. And we cannot fail to see that the doings and sayings of the human beings of his day are not so far removed from the doings and sayings of to-day.

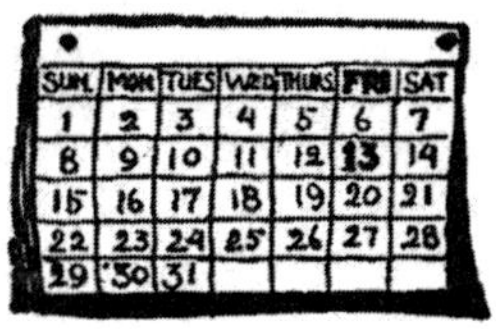

CHAPTER XX

SURVIVALS IN GAMES

If the earth were struck by one of Mr. Wells's comets, and if, in consequence, every human being now alive were to lose all the knowledge and habits which he had acquired from preceding generations (though retaining unchanged all his own powers of invention and memory and habituation) nine-tenths of the inhabitants of London and New York would be dead in a month, and 99 per cent of the remaining tenth would be dead in six months. They would have no language to express their thoughts, and no thoughts but vague reveries. They could not read notices, or drive motors or horses. They would wander about, led by the inarticulate cries of a few naturally dominant individuals, drowning themselves, as thirst came on, in hundreds at the riverside landing places, looting those shops where the smell of decaying food attracted them, and perhaps at the end stumbling upon the expedient of cannibalism. Even in the country districts men could not invent, in time to preserve their lives, methods of growing food, or taming animals, or making fire, or so clothing themselves as to endure a northern winter.

—GRAHAM WALLAS.

PLAYING WITH LIFE

MAN woke to life in a strange world. He saw animals of many species, and creatures of his own kind. But for one long age he lived a life within himself, finding food when he was hungry, searching shelter when storms rocked the earth, climbing to a safe sleeping-place when the sun dropped behind the mountains. He shunned the animals that prowled everywhere about him; and shunned with even greater fear the creatures like himself.

But gradually man became accustomed to the world in which he found himself. He paused for a moment to watch a lion mother play with her cubs. He looked into the sky and saw birds riding on the wind. He passed through a jungle and heard monkeys jabbering in the treetops, mimicking one another, swinging from slender branches high above the ground. He studied the ants that hurried in battalions across a square inch of earth; peered into a hollow tree which swarmed with insect life; watched a pair of brown bears roll together gleefully on a slope.

And man moved closer to his own kind. Nature taught him companionship.

In companionship play was inevitable. All creatures of the earth play when they are together. At first it was with curious bits of shell that man amused himself, colourful bits of mystery swept up by the sea; and with sticks that crossed through some curious freak of nature; with stones that were marked in unusual ways; with nuts that fell from the treetops—with the many wonderful things of nature.

And while man played so in primitive times he learned about the world in which he lived. He played with life. He had the whole world for his playground, and all the glorious gifts of nature for his playthings. Unlike the cubs that rolled on the ground, the monkeys that jabbered in the treetops, he learned while he played. Reason entered play as it entered every other development of human life.

There came a time when man tired of the knucklebones, the dice, the skulls with which he played. He began to play with his own gifts—running races with feet as fleet as any animal's, wrestling, matching his skill and strength against the skill and strength of others. He discovered his voice and matched it with the voice of the birds, the animals. Here was a new kind of play. And here again man reasoned while he played, learned, developed.

Then came playthings of man's own invention—balls to throw and catch, clubs to serve more peaceful purposes than warring, draughts, kites, dolls, clever playthings that no lion mother ever invented for her cubs, that no monkeys ever enjoyed in their treetops. These playthings of man's creation came to be used in games reasoned out by the mind of man—ball, draughts, chess—games in which skill and reason are necessary. Through these games man developed. While lions still romped and monkeys still jabbered, man reasoned out ever more skillful games to play, ever more difficult games to tax his powers of reasoning. And as a tool is sharpened by constant use, so were man's reasoning powers sharpened through use in his games of skill.

Throughout the long ages man has played with life and with the things of life. There was a time when he played with forked branches cut from the tree, and from this play there developed the use of the fork, the important discovery of the plough. There was a time when man played with shells over which he drew vegetable fibres, bits of twisted moss—and from this play evolved the harp, the lyre, and other musical instruments. Man played with kites, and the sailboat resulted. Man played with the lightning, and electricity was harnessed. Man played with the air waves, and the radio made its bow.

And so through long ages of development man has played, and learned, and made the world more interesting. We have to-day mechanical toys that are marvels of science and invention; racing cars that put to shame the chariots of another age; dolls that walk, and talk, and sleep. But they are playthings—just as the little wooden doll fondled by an Egyptian baby of long ago, or a string of shells dangled by some primitive infant, were playthings. The difference is in man and his development rather than in the playthings themselves.

After all, we are but children playing at being grown up. The many popular games we play to-day are but elaborate survivals of the early playdays of humanity.

THE GAMES OF GREECE AND ROME

It is to Greece that we must look for the greatest development of the ancient games.

The earliest games of which we have any record are those at the funeral of Patroclus, which form the subject of the 23rd Iliad.

They are noteworthy as showing that Greek games were in their origin clearly connected with religion; either, as here, a part of the funeral rites, or else instituted in honor of a god, or as a thank-offering for a victory gained or a calamity averted, or in expiation

The high bicycle which was popular about 1880

of some crime. Each of the great contests was held near some shrine or sacred place and is associated with some deity or mythical hero. . . . The games of the Iliad and those of the Odyssey at the court of Alcinous are also of interest as showing at what an early date the distinctive forms of Greek athletics—boxing, wrestling, putting the weight, the foot and the chariot race—were determined. ("Encyclopædia Britannica.")

The Olympian games of Greece are more familiar to us than any other game of antiquity. Olympia was a spot in the rich plain of Eli, naturally enclosed, where the games took place and where statues of the victorious athletes were erected. Games were held every four years at Olympia, the chief sports being foot races, boxing, wrestling, javelin throwing, quoit throwing, jumping, chariot and horse racing. Every recurring fourth year was known as the "Olympiad" meaning the year in which the Olympian games took place, and starting from the year 776 B. C., when the Eleians engraved the name of Coroebus as the victor in the foot race, we have an unbroken record of games held regularly for over a thousand years.

The Greeks had also the Pythian games (from Pytho, the original name for Delphi) which were limited to musical competitions. The prize was a chaplet of laurel. In the Nemean games a wreath of wild celery was the coveted prize. The Isthmian games, held on the Isthmus of Corinth, included gymnastic, equestrian and musical contests, and the prize was a crown of pine. Our authority says of these games that

> Their early importance is attested by the law of Solon which bestowed a reward of 100 drachmae on every Athenian who gained a victory.

The Romans were as fond of games and sports as were the Greeks, but their spectacles and exhibitions were really shadows of the Olympia and the Pythia. As in everything else, the Romans patterned themselves after their Greek neighbours.

Concerning the *Ludi Publici* of the Romans, the Encyclopædia Britannica says:

As in Greece they were intimately connected with religion. At the beginning of each civil year it was the duty of the consuls to vow to the gods games for the safety of the commonwealth, and the expenses were defrayed by the treasury. Thus, at no cost to themselves, the Romans were enabled to indulge at the same time their religious feelings and their love of amusement.

Their taste for games naturally grew till it became a passion, and under the Empire games were looked upon by the mob as one of the two necessities of life. . . . But though public games played as important a part in Roman as in Greek history and must be studied by the Roman historian as an integral factor in social and political life, yet, regarded solely as exhibitions, they are comparatively devoid of interest, and we sympathize with Pliny who asks his friend how any man of sense can go day after day to view the same dreary round of fights and races.

As early as the 6th century B. C. there were "reformers" who objected to the games which were so extravagant in display and which were regarded as a necessity by the masses. Xenophanes complains that "the wrestler's strength is preferred to the wisdom of the philosopher." And as everyone knows Euripides "holds up to scorn the brawny, swaggering athlete."

The cup and ball, a great favourite in the time of Henry III, of France.

GAMES WITH BALLS

The ball is one of the oldest playthings of man. The ancient Egyptians made balls of leather or skin, sewed with string crosswise and stuffed with bran or with husks of corn. These balls were very similar to the modern baseballs, lacking only the cork centre. Some of the ancient balls found at Thebes are about three inches in diameter. Others are very much larger and are made of string or of the stalks of rushes, plaited together to form a circular mass and covered with leather.

The Egyptians played handball—throwing and catching it as children play to-day. This game of handball is probably the oldest ball game known, but the ball itself gave origin to many popular pastimes.

Most authorities accredit the discovery of the ball to Greece, although it is now definitely known that the Egyptians had and used balls at a very much earlier period. Herodotus attributes the invention to the Lydians. Many writers are of the opinion that a woman name Anagalla, a native of Corcyra, was the first to make a ball for the purpose of pastime.

An old tradition is that Anagalla presented the ball she created to Nausicaä, the daughter of Alcinous, King of Phæacia. In Homer we read that Nausicaä was playing at ball with her maidens when Odysseus first saw her in the land of the Phæacians:

> O'er the green mead the sporting virgins play,
> Their shining veils unbound, along the skies,
> Tost and retost, the ball incessant flies.

Baseball.—Of all the games played with balls, there is probably none as popular and as great a favourite as baseball. It is the national game of the United States. It is popular also throughout Canada and Japan.

The origin of the game is somewhat obscure, although authorities are strongly of the opinion that it is a development of the old English game of rounders. The name, of course, is derived from the bases which play an important part in the game, and the ball that is used.

The first appearance of any game similar to baseball in this country was in the early 19th century. A game known as "One old Cat" was popular with schoolboys in the North Atlantic states. It was played by three boys, each fielding and batting in turn, runs being scored by the batsman running to a single base and back again without being cried "out." There were also modifications of this game with four, six, and eight players.

As the game developed it came to be known as town-ball, and in 1833 the Olympic Town-Ball Club was organized in Philadelphia. The first actual matches between organized baseball clubs took place about 1840 and in the neighbourhood of New York. It was in 1843 that the Washington Baseball Club was founded, but not until two years later were the first regular rules drawn up by the Knicker Baseball Club. The first National Association was organized in 1858, and the first entirely professional baseball club, the Cincinnati Red Stockings, was organized ten years later.

For the game of baseball a smooth, level field about 150 yards long and 100 yards broad is required. Upon this field a square, familiarly known as the "diamond," is marked with white chalk. The sides of this square measure 30 yards each, and the nearest corner is distant about 30 yards from the limit of the field. This corner is marked with a plate called the home base. At the other three corners are white canvas bags, about 15 inches square, filled with some soft material, and attached to the ground with pegs. These are known as the first base, second base, and third base, beginning at the right as one looks toward the field.

The game of baseball is played by two sides of nine men each. Each side has nine turns at bat, or innings, unless the leading side at bat does not need the last half of the ninth inning to win the game. A tie at the end of the ninth inning makes additional innings necessary.

Three batsmen are put out in each inning, and the side scoring the greatest number of runs—complete encircling of the bases without being put out—wins. The runner who is not put out but fails to reach the home base is "left on base" but does not score a run. The game generally takes about two hours.

The players consist of the pitcher and catcher on the fielding side; the first baseman, second baseman, third baseman, and shortstop (infielders); and the left fielder, centre fielder and right fielder (outfielders). The players usually wear shoes with three-cornered spikes.

The umpire has absolute jurisdiction over all points of the game. There is usually one umpire who officiates at the game of baseball, but in all important games there are two. One stands behind the catcher to call the good and bad balls pitched; the other is posted in the infield to give decisions on the plays at the bases.

The implements of the game are balls made of yarn wound upon a small core of vulcanized rubber and covered with white leather. The bat is made of ash or some other hard wood.

Basketball.—A game with balls particularly adapted to the outdoors is basketball; but it is most frequently played in the winter in an indoor gymnasium.

This game was invented in 1891 by James Naismith, an instructor in the gymnasium of the Young Men's Christian Association training school at Springfield, Mass. At first it was not popular, but suddenly it attracted the public fancy and became a favourite gymnasium game both here and in England. It is played with equal enthusiasm by men and women.

The game of basketball is played on a marked-off space about 60 feet by 40 feet. Dimensions are sometimes larger when the game is played in the open air. Directly in the middle of each short side, and 10 feet above the ground, is placed a metal ring 16 by 18 inches in diameter, from which is suspended a net. Behind this "basket," at a distance of about 6 inches, is a backboard.

An inflated, leather-covered ball is used. The purpose of the game is to propel this ball into the opponents' basket by striking it with the open hands. The opponents' basket is the goal, and the side wins that scores the most goals during two periods of play divided by a short interval of rest.

In indoor matches there are generally teams of five, in positions opposing one another. A referee has supervision

(Courtesy of Metropolitan Museum of Art)

An Egyptian game board with drawer for draughts.

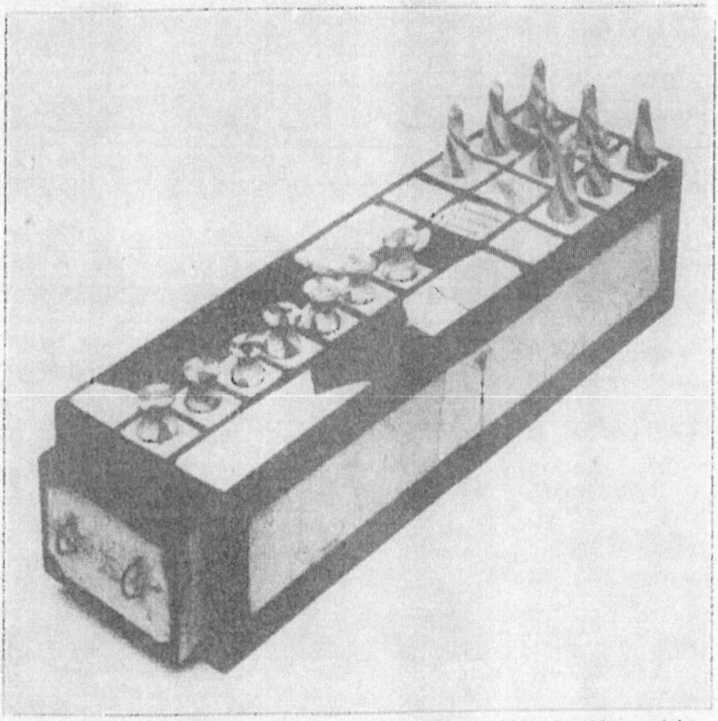

(Courtesy of Metropolitan Museum of Art)

Egyptian game board, with men in position.

(Courtesy of Metropolitan Museum of Art)

Egyptian dice, 18th–20th Dynasty.

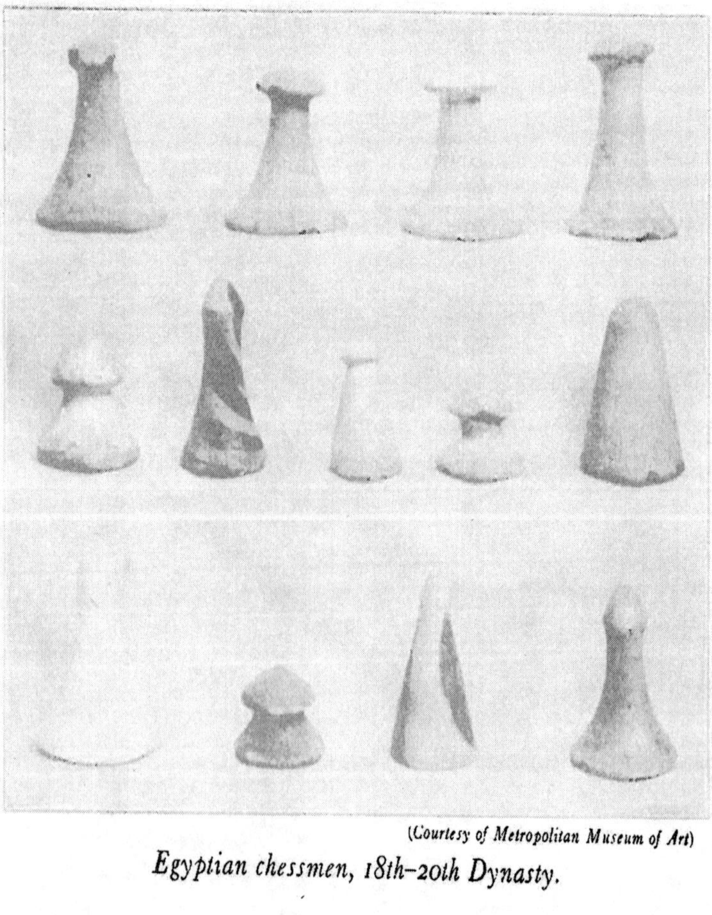

(Courtesy of Metropolitan Museum of Art)

Egyptian chessmen, 18th–20th Dynasty.

of the game and decides when goals have properly been scored, and an umpire watches for fouls. There are also the scorer and the timekeeper.

To start the game, the referee tosses the ball into the air above the heads of the players, who stand within a four foot ring in the centre of the floor. The players jump into the air for possession of the ball and attempt to bat it towards the opposing goal. The ball continues in play until a foul is made, or until it falls into one of the baskets. After a goal has been scored the referee once again puts the ball into play by tossing it over the players' heads.

A foul is an infringement of a rule of the game. When a foul has been made, a player of the opposing side is allowed what is known as a "free throw." This means that he is permitted to make a throw for his opponents' basket from a point of fifteen feet distant from it, and without interference from the other players. If the goal is scored from this "free throw" it counts one point. A goal scored while the ball is in play counts two points.

In basketball the principal qualifications are accuracy, quickness of movement and judgment. Excellent team work is necessary for full enjoyment of the game.

Billiards.—An indoor game of skill, played with balls, is called billiards. The name is said to have originated in the French *bille* (related to the English *billet*) meaning "a stick." The game is played on a rectangular table with small balls and a stick known as the cue.

In "Modern Billiards" it is said that Catkire More, King of Ireland in the 2d century, left "fifty-five billiard balls of brass, with the pools and cues of the same materials" when he died. In the same book we read of the travels of Anacharsis through Greece, about 400 B.C., during which he saw players amusing themselves at a game very similar to the modern game of billiards.

The origin of the game is not definitely known. In Cotton's "Compleat Gamester," an interesting old work published in 1674, we read that "this most gentile, cleanly and ingenious game" was first played in Italy. But as we read further in the same book we discover that he mentions Spain also as its birthplace!

The English knew the game of billiards at a very early date. Shakespeare has Cleopatra say, in the absence of Antony:

> Let us to billiards;
> Come, Charmian.
> ("Antony and Cleopatra," act II, scene 5.)

There seems to be an intimate connection between the lawn game of croquet and billiards. Indeed, some authorities insist that billiards itself was at one time played upon the lawn, and they insist that in this form it was introduced into Europe from the Orient by the Crusaders. Hidden in the forgotten origin of billiards, perhaps there is a connection between the green lawn of croquet and the green baize cloth of the billiard table.

Cotton seems to indicate the connection between croquet and billiards, between the green lawn and the green table, in this bit of verse quoted from his book:

> Billiards from Spain at first derived its name,
> Both an ingenious and a cleanly game.
> One gamester leads (the table green as grass)
> And each like warriors, strive to gain the Pass.

Billiards in the United States is played on a pocketless table, though the English type of table with six pockets is occasionally used here. The "three-ball carom game" is the recognized form of American billiards. The table is marked with a centre spot, a red spot and a white spot. The centre spot is on the centre of an imaginary line dividing the table longitudinally into halves. The spot for the red ball and the spot for the white ball are marked on the same line, halfway between the centre spot and the end cushions.

The right to play first is decided by "stringing." The opponent's white ball and the red ball, being spotted, the player plays from within the imaginary line. Each carom counts one point; a miss counts one to the opponent. A ball is re-spotted on its proper spot if it has been forced off the table. Should red be forced off the table and the red spot be occupied, it is placed on the white spot. The centre spot is used when both spots are occupied and a ball has been forced off the table.

If a carom be made, and the ball afterwards jumps off the table, it is spotted and the count allowed. If the striker moves a ball not his own before he strikes, he cannot count but may play for safety. If he does so after making a carom, the carom does not count, he forfeits one, and his break is ended. If he touches his own ball before he plays he forfeits a point, and cannot play the stroke. Should he, however, touch his ball a second time, the opponent has the option of having the balls replaced as exactly as possible, or of playing on them as they are left. It is a foul stroke to play with the wrong ball, but if the offence is not detected before a second stroke has been made, the player may continue. (Condensed quotation from the "Encyclopædia Britannica.")

Bowling.—The pastime of bowling appears to be an invention of the Middle Ages. At first it was an outdoor game, played upon the green, but later it became an indoor game played upon an alley with wooden balls and nine or ten wooden pins.

Bowling greens are said to have originated in England, though some authorities claim that they first made their appearance in Germany. The inconvenience and awkwardness of playing on the green led to the creation of alleys. Nevertheless, the game was played on the green until the year 1840, the Dutch inhabitants of New Amsterdam being great enthusiasts. Their favourite bowling place was the square just north of the Battery in New York, still known as Bowling Green.

The bowling alley is built up of alternate strips of pine and maple wood, and is about 60 feet in length. On each side of the alley is a 9-inch gutter to catch the balls that are bowled wide.

Originally 9 pins set up in diamond form were used in the game, but during the early part of the 19th century excessive betting became so troublesome to the authorities that the game of "nine-pins" as it was called was prohibited by law. This prohibition made the game more popular than ever, and in an effort to evade the law the game of "ten-pins" was invented. The game is precisely the same, except that 10 pins are used instead of 9.

To play the game, the 10 pins are set up in the form of a right-angled triangle in four rows. Four pins are at the back, three in front of this row, then two and one as a head pin. As many may play on a side as is desired, five being the customary number for championship teams.

The balls are provided with holes for the thumb and the middle finger. Each player rolls three balls, called a *frame,* and ten frames usually constitute a game. Scoring is estimated in the following manner:

If all ten pins are knocked down by the first ball the player makes what is known as a *strike.* This scores him 10 plus whatever he may make with the first two balls of his next frame.

If he should then make another strike, 10 more are added to his score, making 20, to which are added the pins he may knock down with the first ball of the third frame.

If he should make still another strike, on his third frame, he scores 30 as the first frame.

If this high average is kept up the player scores the maximum, 300 in the 10 frames.

But if all three balls are used and no strike or spare is scored, the player records only the number of pins overturned. The spare is scored when the player knocks down all pins with two balls, and he may then add the pins made by the first ball to those of his second frame.

In bowling, scores are kept on properly lined score boards and entries are made after every play. Of course, the person showing the largest score at the close of the game is the winner.

Football.—

There is not much doubt that the word football comes down to us, through Teutonic channels, from a series of words, each meaning a foot [says Monckton], but it is a grievous mistake to suppose that the word meant, originally, a ball that was kicked with the feet, although this is the meaning universally assigned to it. The word meant a ball-game which was played by individuals on foot as opposed to those on horseback. Possibly the fact that the ball gradually came to be of such size and nature as to be capable of being kicked with the foot, may have had something to do with the final nomenclature.

The game of football is very old, and is a particular favourite in England. In the United States it ranks second only to the baseball game in popularity. The origin of the game is disputed.

There are several writers who assert that the game of football was introduced into England by the Romans, but there does not seem to be any definite proof to substantiate this belief. The Romans, it is true, borrowed their games to a great extent from the Greeks, and Pollux does mention a Greek game of ball which has often been looked upon as the origin of football. But no definite facts have been, or can be, traced.

Fitzstephen is the first English writer to mention a game similar to football. In his famous "Survey of London," an 11th century manuscript, he mentions two games, either one of which may be accepted as a prototype of football. He says among other things that the London schoolboys "played at the celebrated game of ball."

The next mention of the game is in the time of Edward II. Owing to great disturbances created in the streets of London by mobs who collected to play or to watch the game, an edict was passed in the early 14th century which prohibited football altogether. But authorities tried in vain to put a stop to the popular game, and despite all efforts it persisted.

A game called Calcio, very similar to football, was played in Florence in the 15th century, and became very popular there. In France, too, the game of football soon made its appearance, but it was in England that the game had its greatest development.

It was not, however, until about 1850 that clubs began

to be formed for purposes of arranging football matches. Cambridge was one of the first clubs formed, with Sheffield and Hallam in close succession. The famous Blackheath and Richmond Clubs were not long in following.

As for the game of football itself, it would be ridiculous even to attempt to describe the game here. To those who do not understand it, football seems as though it were played practically with no science and with but few rules. As a matter of fact it is to-day one of the most scientific of all ball games, and requires great skill and perseverance in coaching. A college team will practise carefully sixty or seventy separate plays before it feels ready to meet an opposing team.

The main requisites for a football player are speed, dexterity, skill in dodging, running, good judgment, perseverance. There is no question that it is a difficult game, and more dangerous than most games played with balls; but a knowledge of the rules of the game, skill developed through practice, and a fair amount of strength generally make a good player. During a recent Army-Navy game the players were so well matched that the game was a tie from beginning to end, and rather monotonous to the spectators because there was not a player conspicuously superior to the others.

Golf.—"The origin of golf seems wrapped in mystery, the honour apparently lying between Scotland and the Netherlands," says Charles Evans. The game is very ancient, and has one of the most interesting histories of any ball game.

The name itself has a variety of spellings. It has been known variously as Goff and Goffe, as Gauf and Goufe, as Gaoff and Gaulf, as Gowff and Gowlf. The last is probably the genuine old pronunciation which gives us our modern name. It possibly derives from the Dutch *kolf,* meaning a club.

The origin of golf is buried in antiquity, but we can be reasonably certain that the Dutch were among the first to play the game to any extent. It is possibly a derivative from one of the ancient ball games of Greece, although we cannot be definite. The first actual appearance of the game appears to be in Holland, and there are many old Dutch pictures which show the game of golf being played.

By 1457 the game had become very popular in Scotland. Mention of the game is made in an Act of the Scotch Parliament in 1457, indicating that the popularity of the game was threatening to interfere with the important pursuit of archery. The game of "Goff" is referred to as an "unprofitabill sport," but it is amusing to note that King James IV, responsible for the Act prohibiting golf, set his people a bad example by indulging in the sport himself!

A game called *choule* was played in Belgium as early as 1353. Balls and iron clubs were used, and the game consisted essentially in hitting the balls with the clubs toward a fixed mark. But though this game was played with club and ball, authorities have proved conclusively that it had no connection with the game of golf which was developing elsewhere.

We trace the greatest development of golf in Scotland. James V was very partial to the "Ancient and Royal Game of Goff," and his daughter, Mary Stuart, was an ardent golfer. Tradition tells us that a few days after the death of her husband she "was seen playing golf and paille-maille in the fields outside Seton," which, her enemies declared, was proof of her indifference.

Charles I was devoted to gaming of all kinds, but particularly to golf. It was while he was on the links at Leith, in 1642, that he received news of the Irish rebellion. Later as a prisoner at Newcastle, he found diversion in playing "the royal game." We are told that

> The King was nowhere treated with more honour than at Newcastle, as he himself confessed, both he and his train having liberty to go abroad and play at goff in the Shield Field, without the walls.

During the 17th and 18th centuries the development of golf was marked. By the beginning of the 19th century it was a game of universal popularity. In 1834 William IV became the patron of St. Andrew's Golf Club, St. Andrew's being at that time, as it is even now, the most famous seat of the game. In 1863 the Prince of Wales (Edward VII) requested that he be elected captain of the club.

Monckton says:

> The great delight of this ancient game of "gowff" is that it was, and always will be, a game in which old and young can join on equal footing. Unlike such strenuous pastimes as football or hockey, a good wind and some training are not essentials to the enjoyment of a game, although doubtless such attributes do add to the potential skill of any possible club wielder. This is the reason why golf has endured, and will endure, throughout the ages.

Briefly, the game of golf may be defined as consisting in hitting the ball over a great extent of country, "preferably of that sand-hill nature which is found at the sea-side." The ball is finally hit or "put" into a little hole cut in the turf. The place of the hole in the turf is marked with a flag.

On a full course the recognized number of holes is 18. They are at varying distances apart, from 100 yards to a distance as great as a half-mile. A number of different "clubs," cleverly devised to suit the different positions in which the ball may be found, are used for the various strokes. Thus there is one "club" for driving the ball, another for propelling it from a bad spot in the "rough."

Every player, in golf, plays with his own ball and with no interference from his opponent. The object of each is to hit the ball from the starting point into each successive hole with the fewest strokes. At the end of the course of 18 holes the player who has won the majority of holes is the winner.

TERMS USED IN THE GAME OF GOLF

Baff: To strike the ground with the club when playing, and so loft the ball unduly.

Baffy: A short wooden club, with laid-back face, for lofting shots.

Golf became very popular in the 16th Century, when it was played with great enthusiasm by the courtiers of England and France.

Bogey: The number of strokes which a good average player should take to each hole.
Brassy: A wooden club with a brass sole.
Bulger: A driver in which the face bulges into a convex shape.
Bunker: A sand pit.
Caddie: The person who carries the clubs and watches the ball.
Cleek: Iron-headed club, almost straight-faced, capable of the longest shot of any of the clubs with iron heads.
Dead: Ball is "dead" when so near the hole that the putting it in the next stroke is a "dead" certainty.
Divot: Piece of turf cut out in the act of hitting the ball.
Dormy: A side is said to be "dormy" when it has the same number of holes to the good as remain to be played, so that it cannot be beaten.
Driver: A straight-faced wooden club used for longest shots, generally used only at the tee.
Fozzle: A badly missed or bungled stroke.
Fore: A cry of warning to people in front.
Foursome: A match in which four persons engage, two on each side.
Green: The smoothly rolled, closely cut area which terminates the hole.
Grip: The part of club shaft which is held in the hands while playing.
Half shot: A shot played with something less than a full swing.
Handicap: The strokes which a player receives either in match play or competition.
Hanging: Said of a ball that lies on a slope inclining downward in regard to the direction in which it is wished to drive.
Hazard: A general term for bunker, whin, long grass, roads, water, and all kinds of bad ground.
Heel: To hit the ball with the "heel" of the club, *i.e.,* the part of the face nearest the shaft.
Honour: Privilege of striking off first from the tee.
Iron: Any iron-headed club.
Lie: Angle of the club-head with the shaft.
Like: The stroke which makes the player's score equal to his opponent's in the course of playing a hole.
Line: Direction in which the hole toward which the player is progressing lies with reference to present position of his ball.
Mashie: Iron club with short head.
Match play: Play in which score is reckoned by holes won and lost.
Medal play: Play in which score is reckoned by the total of strokes taken on the round.
Niblick: Short, stiff club with a laid-back iron head, used for

getting the ball out of a bad lie (*lie* means position of ball or ground, as well as angle of club-head).

Odd: A stroke more than opponent has played.

Press: To strive to hit harder than you can hit with accuracy.

Pull (or hook): To hit the ball with a cut across it, so that it flies curving to the left.

Putt: To play the strokes on the green.

Putter: A straight-faced club used for putting, usually with iron head.

Rub-of-the-green: A chance deflection of the ball.

Run up: To send the ball low and close to the ground. Opposite of lofting.

Slice: To hit a ball with a cut across it, so that it flies to the right

Stance: Position of the player when addressing the ball. Reference made to "a good stance," a "bad stance." Also means position relative to each other of the player's feet.

Tee: Little mound of sand on which ball is placed for the first shot to each hole.

Teeing ground: The place marked as the limit, outside of which it is not permitted to drive the ball off.

Up: A player is said to be "one up," "two up," etc., when he is so many holes to the good of his opponent.

Wrist shot: A shot less in length than a half-shot but longer than a putt, made almost entirely with the wrists.

Hockey.—Hockey is a popular outdoor game, played by women as well as men. As played to-day, field hockey is a development of a game known in the British Isles for centuries under the names "hurley," "shinty," and "bandy."

A cricket ball, painted white, is used. The sticks are hooked clubs not more than two inches wide. These clubs have a flat face along the crook. The hockey team usually consists of 11 players—5 forwards, 3 halfbacks, 2 backs and a goal keeper. The game is divided into two intervals of about 30 minutes each, and the teams change sides at the end of each interval.

The well-equipped hockey player wears strips of felt to protect his knees and shins. This is particularly essential in ice hockey—a newer development of the game. The same rules apply to ice hockey as to field hockey, but there are seven players to a side instead of eleven.

Ice hockey calls for great skill in the art of skating, an

also for very close team work. It is rather a dangerous game and no one should attempt it who is not entirely "at home" on the ice.

Both *hockey* and *croquet* appear to be derived from an old French word *hocquet* meaning a "crooked stick." The game itself is similar in its rudiments to some of the ball games already discussed, and with a knowledge of the science of the game, and a natural skill and dexterity, the game can easily be mastered. Space does not permit of a complete discussion of the game here.

Polo.—A Persian writer of the 11th century refers to this ancient game as the "Game of the Kings." It was, indeed, played by kings and queens and emperors with great enthusiasm. We are told that Shirin, the beautiful wife of Khosura Parviz (last great king of the Sassanian dynasty, who reigned about 600 A.D.) "joined the ladies of her court in matching her skill with the ball and stick against the Shah."

It was about 600 A.D. that polo became popular with the Chinese. In these days of the Tang Dynasty it was played with a light wooden ball. We are told that everyone of importance played polo, and that at night the grounds were lighted with candles for the "fans." From one account we quote:

> A Prince of the Tang dynasty taught his ladies to play polo on donkeys with rich saddles and bridles incrusted with jewels. . . . Emperors received the heroes of the polo teams in audience; and one royal lover of the game requested four candidates for official positions to play a tournament, and then he awarded the post to the winner,

It was among the Chinese that the game had its greatest development. An Emperor who reigned about 1160 insisted that the game be played regularly. When it rained he had the ground covered with oiled cloth and sprinkled with sand. He played polo constantly, never tiring of the game.

Polo is not as popular with us as are most of the other ball games. It is like hockey, but played on horseback.

The game requires great skill, a knowledge of horses, quickness, excellent judgment.

Tennis.—Monckton gives an excellent history of the game of tennis in his book, "Pastimes in Times Past." The following is a condensed quotation from his writings:

> The origin of the word "tennis" is doubtful. The game was imported into England from France in very early times, though the exact date is not known nor, probably, ever will be. But whether the French nation invented the game, or whether, as some have supposed, it is an adaptation of a ball game introduced from the East after the Crusades, perhaps from the Byzantines, is a matter for surmise.
>
> Given a ball and two opposing sides of players, it does not need much originality in order to devise a game in which a net, or its early mud-wall equivalent, would form a feature, while boundaries would follow of swift necessity.
>
> Tennis was well known in Chaucer's time. . . . It was only the upper classes who could afford to play the game at all, since both racquets and balls were dear; not to mention any question of the scarcity of tennis courts.
>
> But as the years rolled by, courts became much more common; though the various hazards, such as the grille, tambour, and chases did not exert their sway over the game all at once. . . . Not long afterwards, however, the game began to fall into disrepute, mainly on account of the large amount of betting and cheating which used to take place in these public courts; to such an extent, indeed, that the name *"Nacquet"*—the French word for a marker—became synonymous with the word "cheat." It was the old, old story of the evils of betting and gambling—the same evils which, at the commencement of the 18th century led to the suppression of the good old English game of bowls.
>
> But markers, or professional players, were not always of the male sex. One lady has been termed the Joan of Arc of tennis, because of her skill and because she was a contemporary of the Maid of Orleans. This Jean Margot, who flourished about 1427, came to Paris from the Province of Hainault. "She was twenty-eight to thirty years of age, and played better at hand ball than any man had seen; and with that, she played both forehanded and backhanded very powerfully, very cleverly, and very cunningly, as any man could, and there were few men she could not beat except the very best players. . . .
>
> We are not told what became of this mediæval amazon of the tennis court; but as she is described as being both young and pretty,

and with no recorded political views, no doubt she came to an end more fortunate than the stake of her namesake.

The exact period at which the game of Lawn Tennis was first "invented" is again a matter of uncertainty. A passage in the sporting magazine of 1793 reads as follows: "Field Tennis threatens ere long to bowl out cricket. The former game is now patronised by Sir Peter Burrel." It was therefore no new invention, but a mere revival, which about the year 1874 came into existence in England. . . . Since 1875 lawn tennis has steadily looked upwards.

From other sources we learn that in early mediæval times the game of tennis was known as Pame, or Paume. The word is from the Latin *palma* which signifies "palm of the hand." Thus in England the game, which was played with the bare palm, came to be known as palm play. This game of palm play was particularly popular in France among the fashionable men and women.

One authority says:

During the reign of Charles V, palm play, which may properly enough be denominated hand-tennis, was exceedingly fashionable in France, being played by nobility for large sums of money.

During the 16th century tennis courts became common in England. Maître Perlin, a distinguished French ecclesiastic, in his "Description of England and Scotland," written in 1558, says:

Whilst I remained in England, there were many garrisons all over the country; the people make good cheer and dearly love junketing; and you will see many rich taverns . . . for here you may commonly see artisans such as hatters and joiners, playing tennis for a crown, which is not often seen elsewhere, particularly on a working day.

Henry VII of England was fond of tennis and an enthusiastic player. James I commended tennis as a "game befitting a prince" and highly recommended it to his son. Charles II and Henry VIII frequently played the game, and their wardrobes are said to have contained special kinds of dresses for tennis-playing.

It is undoubtedly to Major Wingfield, who reintroduced

tennis in England in 1874, that we owe gratitude for the greatest development of this favourite game. In the following year the first code of rules for playing lawn tennis were drawn up, and under the supervision of Major Wingfield tennis clubs were founded. Monckton says:

> Let us express our thanks to Major Wingfield for having evolved, from the history of the past, a game which the present generation unites in saying is the king of games, and was, and is, the game of kings.

Originally the game of tennis was played with the open palm—hence the name palm play. But it became the custom later to wear gloves so that the ball would rebound more forcibly. Even the gloves did not satisfy the players, and soon it became customary to bind cords and tendons around the hands. From these cords and tendons it was just a step to the racket.

Most authorities accredit the discovery or invention of rackets to the Italians. The word "racket" itself is derived either from the Latin *retis,* meaning a net, or from the Low German *racken,* meaning to stretch. Evidently rackets were in use as early as Chaucer's time, for we find this sentence in a work written about 1380:

> But canstrow playen racket to and fro?

It would appear that hair was used to stuff tennis balls in the 15th and 16th centuries. In "Much Ado About Nothing" we discover the following conversation.

> *Don Pedro:* Hath any man seen him at the Barber's?
> *Claudio:* No; but the Barber's man hath been seen with him, and the old ornament of his cheek hath already stuffed tennis balls.

And in an old play called "Merry Tricks," dated 1611, we find this mention of tennis balls:

> Thy beard shall serve to stuff those tennis balls by which I get me heat at tennis.

Many tennis players must have wondered what the word "love" means in the scoring of tennis points. It is used in the sense of "nothing." Singer, in a note to his rare old work on "Playing Cards" tells us that there is an old Scotch word "luff" which means "nothing." In discussing this matter Monckton says:

> Out in the East, a similar word bearing the same sense has been in constant use for ages; and as tennis may have come from the East, this origin is as likely as any other.

The word "volley" is from the French *à la volée,* meaning "on the fly." The word "sette" (now "set") originally meant a collection or number of persons or things, and we can see how the word would have been applied to a collection of games, like a "sette of tennis." As for the word "court," it is a survival of the time when tennis was the game of nobility and was actually played on the courts that surrounded castles.

PLAYING THE GAME OF TENNIS

(Condensed from Compton's Pictured Encyclopedia)

The object of the game is for the player on one side of the net to send the ball into his opponent's court in such a manner that it cannot be returned. . . . At the start of a match of singles—as the game is called when two persons play—one player "serves" while the other "receives." The server stands with both feet behind the base line, tosses the ball into the air, and by striking it with the racket sends it over the net into his opponent's service court diagonally opposite. If the first ball is a "fault" he tries with a second ball. The receiver must hit the ball on the first bound, attempting to drive it back over the net so that it will fall within the court. If he fails to return it over the net or sends it outside the court, he loses the point. . . . The ball often passes back and forth across the net several times before one of the players fails to return it. The service alternates, first from the right then from the left court, and a player continues to serve until he wins or loses a game.

The first point won makes the score 15, the second point 30, the third 40 and the fourth wins the game, unless each player has scored 40. In that case the score is "deuce" and in order to win the game thereafter one player or the other must take two points in succession. The scores "15 to 0" and "30 to 0" are called as "15 love," "30 love," etc., the opposite are "love 15," etc. The first of the two points after "deuce" is called "advantage in" if won by the server, and "advantage out" if won by the striker-out.

The principal strokes that a player uses in returning the ball are the "forehand drive," the "backhand," the "volley," the "lob," and the "overhead smash." . . . Service gives opportunity for many skilful strokes. . . . There are many "fine points" in lawn tennis and much opportunity for the study of technique. Quickness of mind, eye, and limb are essential—and endurance, too, for a fast match between skilful opponents calls for the strenuous exercise of virtually every muscle in the body.

The game of "doubles" is very similar to "singles" except that there are four players instead of two.

Chess.—Chess is one of the oldest and most interesting of indoor games. It is warfare in miniature, a game of skill pure and simple, and undoubtedly more ancient than any game of which we have record.

The origin of chess, like the origins of most games, is lost in countless legends of the past. Practically every country in the world, savage and civilized, has some game which can be closely identified with our game of chess, and all of these games trace their way into remote antiquity.

Very possibly the game of chess developed from primitive games played with dice. The die is one of the oldest playthings of man, evolved from the knucklebones with which man amused himself in the very dawn of life. The antiquary Thomas Hyde records, in his "Syntagma," the opinion that the game of "odd and even" played with pebbles in primitive times, is nearly coeval with the creation of man.

The pebbles of early man were soon marked to identify those that meant good fortune, those that meant ill fortune. In Africa the savages have for centuries used pebbles marked like dice to discover before a war or battle whether they will be successful or not. These marked pebbles were the first dice.

In Egypt the ancients amused themselves with dice of bone or ivory, marked with small circles to represent units. Such dice have been discovered at Thebes. It may have been out of the games played with these dice that the early

(Courtesy of Metropolitan Museum of Art)

Playing card of the 15th Century, German. Wild woman and unicorn

Egyptians conceived the idea of playing with "men" in miniature warfare, establishing the first crude game of chess. King Rameses is portrayed on the walls of his palace at Thebes engaged with the ladies of his household in a game which closely resembles chess. The pieces or the "men" used in the game stand about 1½ inches high and each stands upon a circular base.

But we cannot be certain that the game of chess originated with the Egyptians. Authorities attribute it variously to the Greeks, the Romans, the Babylonians, the Jews, the Persians, the Hindus, the Irish, the Welsh, even the Chinese and the Arabians. There are some who declare King Solomon invented the game; others who insist that the philosopher Xerxes gave it to the world; still others, that the Mandarin Hansing was the originator. Even Aristotle has been called the "father of chess"!

In his interesting "Museum of Antiquity," L. W. Yaggy says of ancient Greece:

> The so-called "game of cities" seems to have resembled our chess or draughts. The board was divided into five parts. Each player tried to checkmate the other by the skilful use of his men.

Of all the explanations offered, the one that seems most credible is that the game originated among the Hindus. The authorities who are best qualified to judge are of the opinion that Hindustan was the cradle of chess, the game having been known there from time immemorial by the name of *chaturanga*. This old name means the four *angas*, or members, of an army.

Chaturanga is a Sanskrit word which was gradually corrupted to *shatrang*. This later word is really Persian in origin and is now in colloquial use throughout India. The word "chess" is evidently derived from it.

There are many chess legends from the 1st to the 10th centuries during the Christian Era, but as they are not authoritative historically and are based upon no authentic facts, we need not dwell upon them here. It was apparently not until about the 12th century that the game became popular in Europe. The Spaniards probably learned the game from their Moslem conquerors, and the Italians from the Byzantines, but for a long time the game was played only by a few because of its intricacies and because of the skill necessitated. Gradually, however, knowledge of the game spread, more and more people became skilled in it, and finally, toward the close of the 12th century, it became a popular and favourite indoor game.

Chessboards were originally uncoloured. About the beginning of the 13th century the first checkered chess-boards made their appearance. The words "check" and "mate" used in chess are simply phonetic equivalents for the Persian words *Shah* (a king) and *mat* (he is dead)—the phrase *shah mat* meaning "The King is dead." From this we derive such words as checkerboard, checkmate, and as Skeat points out in "Curious Survivals," even our word "check" meaning a slip of paper which checks a certain amount of money expended against our account at the bank.

William the Conqueror, Henry I, John, and Edward I were chess players. Napoleon is said to have been fond of the game. Among the most famous chess players of more recent times are:

Philidor, who played blindfolded in London, and whose book "*Analyse des échecs*" (1749) was long regarded an authority.

Count van Nyevelt, who played about 1880.

J. Allgaier, the German player who flourished from 1763 to 1823.

Deschapelles, who was also a brilliant whist player and who was famous during the first half of the 19th century.

Mahé de Bourdonnais, pupil of Deschapelles and greatest player of France in the 19th century.

Macdonnell, who was the greatest English champion.

Sarratt, also a great English champion, replaced by Lewis, his student.

Stauton, who won many times in famous matches with French champions during the 19th century.

Morsphy, famous American player of 19th century, seldom surpassed by players of any nationality.

Pillsbury, leading American master after Morsphy. Died in 1906.

Chess is a game of skill, and it entails subtle variations which cannot possibly be discussed in a brief outline of games such as is given here. As a pastime the game of chess is easily learned, but great practice is required before any amount of skill or mastery is acquired.

The board is divided into 64 checkered squares. The pieces consist of King, Queen, two Rooks (or Castles), two Knights, and two Bishops. The eight men in front are called the Pawns. There is one black side, one white side. At the beginning of the game the Queen stands on a square of her own colour.

The King may move in any direction, only one square at a time, except in castling. Two Kings can never be on adjacent squares. The Queen moves in any direction whether square or diagonal, backward or forward. There is no limit to her range over vacant squares. She takes opponents, but a piece of her own color stops her.

The Rooks may not move diagonally but only in straight lines, forward or backward. Their range, like the Queen's, is unlimited with the same exceptions. The Bishops move diagonally, in any direction, forward or backward.

The Knights move differently. They move from one corner of any rectangle of three squares by two to the opposite corner. A move may be in any direction, and no obstacle is recognized if the squares between happen to be occupied. The Knight always moves to a square of a different color.

The Pawn for the first move may advance either one or two squares straight forward, but afterwards only one square. The Pawn can never move backwards, but can capture only diagonally. A Pawn moves like a Rook, captures like a Bishop, but only one square at a time. (Condensed from the "Encyclopædia Britannica.")

Dominoes.—Most authorities are of the opinion that the familiar game of dominoes originated in Italy. It was unknown until the 18th century. The name is said to be derived from the ebony backing, resembling the black cloak called *domino.*

The game is played with 28 oblong pieces, the faces of which are of ivory divided into two squares and marked in each half with the value—*i.e.,* each half is marked with one or more black pips, usually up to six. The most popular form of the domino game is called the Draw game. Here are detailed directions for playing the game, quoted in condensed form from our authorities:

> Shuffle the dominoes face downward. The lead is usually decided by drawing for the highest domino, but sometimes it is held that any doublet takes precedence. The dominoes are reshuffled, and each player draws at random the number of dominoes required for the particular form of the game, usually seven. The dominoes left behind are called the "stock."
>
> To play a domino is called a "pose." The leader poses first, generally playing his highest domino. At the end of the game the player wins or loses according to the number of pips in the dominoes he has remaining. By some rules the player after playing a double may play another domino that matches—*i.e.,* if he plays a double six, he may play another domino with six at one end. The second player must match the leader's pose by putting one of his dominoes in juxtaposition at one end. In other words, if the leader plays four-five, the second player must play a domino which contains either a four or a five in one of its halves. The four is applied to the four, the five to the five.
>
> Doubles are played crosswise. A double, of course, is a domino in which both halves are alike. If the player cannot match he says "go" and his opponent plays. But in the usual Draw game the player who cannot match draws from the stock until he takes a domino with which he can play.
>
> The player who succeeds in posing all his dominoes calls "Domino," and wins the game. He scores as many points as there are pips on his opponent's remaining dominoes. A game is usually 100 points.

Mah-Jong.—A Chinese game which is enjoying a tremendous vogue at the present time is called Mah-Jong, meaning "Sparrow." It is probably the oldest game existing in China to-day. It is older even than "Choke-choo-hong-ki," the chess game invented, it is said, by the mandarin Hansing to amuse his soldiers. This was in

174 B.C. The game of Mah-Jong, which is known by a variety of names, was invented by a Chinese who lived about the time of Confucius—550 B.C.

The game was first played in Ninpgo, although there are some writers who claim Canton for its birthplace. The name of the inventor is not definitely known, and probably never will be. Through the long ages the game has slumbered in China, suddenly to be revived, carried across the ocean, and made the fad of fashionable America.

A set of Mah-Jong consists of 144 tiles which resemble dominoes. Each tile is composed of two layers, the top one of bamboo, the bottom of ivory or bone. It is said that the original set was made of bamboo and deer horn, the former signifying good health and the latter high official position. But because of the poor wearing quality of deer horn, ivory or bone has been used as a substitute

The game of Mah-Jong is played by four persons, each for himself. There is no partnership as there is in card games. The game is very fascinating, requires a keenness and quickness of mind, and it helps develop a retentive memory. Because of its great educational value in these respects it is being encouraged in this country and is already one of the most popular pastimes.

Mah-Jong is an elaborate and complicated game and could not be mastered by such brief directions as we could give here. Anyone desirous of learning the game should procure an authoritative volume on this one subject alone. The instructions are lengthy; there are many penalties, rules, regulations, etc.

A variation of Mah-Jong is Pung-Chow. Both games are apparently of the same origin and are played with the same kind of dominoes in practically the same way—but somehow they have been given different names.

GAMES WITH CARDS

Playing cards are of obscure origin, and there are many nations that are credited with being their birthplace. However, the view generally accepted is that playing cards came to us from Asia.

Some authorities tell us that cards were used in Hindustan in ancient times, although no definite facts seem to be available. The tradition is that both Hindus and Moslems used round playing cards for their amusement, marked with "curious and fantastic inscriptions."

Monckton says that practically nothing is known of the history of cards before the 14th century. However, we learn from other authorities that the Chinese played cards as early as 1120. (M. Abel Remusat.) In the Chinese dictionary, *"Ching-tsze-tung,"* it is recorded that cards were invented in the reign of Seun-ho (1120) for the amusement of his concubines.

We know, also, that cards were popular in France toward the close of the 14th century. In an edict of the Provost of Paris, 1397, the working people are forbidden "to play at tennis, bowls, dice, cards or nine-pins on working days." A pack of cards is mentioned by the name they still retain in France—*Jeux de cartes*—by Charles Poupart, treasurer of the household to Charles VI of France (1393).

The first cards were generally rectangular or square in shape, though sometimes they were circular. During the 14th century the game of cards became for the first time popular, and various card games made their appearance in different parts of Europe. Towards the beginning of the 15th century there was a passion for gaming and gambling in France.

"The first mention of cards in the New World is found in the letters of Herrara, a companion of Cortes, who describes the interest manifested by the Aztecs in the card games of the Spanish soldiers." ("Encyclopædia Britannica.") It was not until the 18th century, however, that card games were played to any great extent on this continent.

The early packs consisted usually of eighty-six cards,

among which was an unnumbered card called the "Fou"—*i.e.*, the Fool, now known as the Joker. The sun, moon, justice, charity, and countless other emblems or symbols were used to embellish the cards, and the court cards of King, Queen, Knight, and Knave were almost always used. Most authorities are agreed that the origin and use of emblematic cards are in some distant way connected with chess and chessmen.

The earliest cards were executed by hand, like those designed for Charles VI. Monckton says:

> The earliest packs were painted on thin vellum, a substance which the destructive hand of time, not to mention hard usage, would quickly ruin. . . . It was not until three or four thicknesses of card were put together, that the name of the game was changed from *Pagina* to *Carta*, a Latin word from which the English "card" is derived.

In the 15th century wood engraving was introduced in Europe and the manufacture of cards began. This enabled the poorer classes to indulge in the card games for the first time. Prior to the introduction of cheap engraved cards only those who were wealthy enough to afford packs of cards were able to play. For a long time cards were on boards like chess pieces.

The marks on the suits of the earliest German cards are hearts, bells, leaves, and acorns. The next suits in the historical story of cards are marked with swords, batons, cups, and money. These suits are common on the Italian cards of the 15th century. In the next century the French cards bore these four suits, which are still in use to-day: hearts, clubs, spades, and diamonds. The symbol language of cards seems to suggest a military origin.

There are so many card games that it would be impossible to consider them all here. There are, for instance, poker, euchre, whist, pinochle, bridge. And there are usually several variations of each game. The most popular card game at the present time appears to be bridge, and it is with a discussion of bridge that we will close our story of games.

Bridge.—The game of bridge is supposed to have developed from the game known as whist. The country of its origin is unknown. According to a popular notion, bridge originated in Russia and the very name is derived from the word *Biritch* meaning Russian Whist. There are no facts to substantiate this theory, however, and we cannot accept it as authentic.

Some connect the game with a pastime called *Khedive* enjoyed in Turkey and Egypt. Others insist that the name is derived from the Tartar word *birintch* which means "the town crier." Many claim Denmark as the birthplace of the game.

It was in Turkey, however, that the game of Bridge first attracted public favour and became a popular amusement. One writer suggests that the name may be a corruption of the Turkish *Bir-uch* meaning "one-three." This seems to be the most plausible origin of the name.

According to M. Jean Boussac, Bridge was introduced to England about 1893, after having been played by the Turks, the Russians, the French. He quotes *Le Figaro*, November 26, 1893, to prove his statement. The following year Bridge was already a popular and favourite game in England, and from that period until the present day its development has been rapid. The rules of the game were definitely compiled by a joint committee of the Portland and Turf Clubs in 1895.

Ordinary bridge is played with four players. In each hand the partner of the dealer takes no part in the play. After the first lead his cards are placed on the table, exposed, and played by the dealer as in the game called Dummy Whist. The trump suit is selected by the dealer or his partner without consultation, the former having the first option.

In Bridge the value of tricks and honours varies with each suit declared as trumps. The honours are reckoned on a scale which is somewhat involved, and which must be learned through actual practice in the game. The score for honours does not count toward winning or losing the rubber, but it is added afterward to the trick score in order to determine the value of the rubber. There are also scores for holding no trumps (chicane) and for winning all the tricks except one (slam).

At the opening of the play partners are arranged, cards shuffled and dealt. The last card is not turned but is placed face downward on the table. The dealer cannot lose the deal through a misdeal. After the cards are dealt, the dealer makes the trump or no-trump declaration, or passes the choice to his partner. After the declaration either adversary may double, the leader having first option. The effect of doubling is that each trick is worth twice as many points as before. But the scores for honours, chicanes, and slams are unaltered.

If the declaration is doubled, the dealer and his partner may redouble, thus making each trick worth four times as much as at first. The declarer always has first option. The value of a trick is limited to 100 points.

There are many rules, regulations and penalties in the game of bridge and there are variations of the game, such as Auction Bridge, Dummy Bridge, Draw Bridge, etc. It is a game that abounds with countless little subtleties that can be acquired only through practice. It is impossible to give full directions for playing the game here, and we have barely touched upon the fundamentals.

AUTHORITIES CONSULTED

ARMYTAGE, FENELLA F. — *Old Court Customs*

AVEBURY, JOHN LUBBOCK — *Marriage, Totemism and Religion*

AVEBURY, JOHN LUBBOCK — *The Origin of Civilization*

BAYLEY, HAROLD — *The Lost Language of Symbolism*

BEARNE, CATHERINE — *Pictures of the Old French Court*

BERGEN, FANNY D. — *Current Superstitions*

BERRY, EDWARD W. — *Environment of the Ape Man*

BLANCHARD, MME. — *Speech*

BOAS, FRANZ — *Development of Folk-tales and Myths*

BOAS, FRANZ — *The Mind of Primitive Man*

BOHN, HENRY G. — *The Handbook of Games*

BOSE, P. N. — *Epochs of Civilization*

BOURKE, JOHN G. — *Vesper Hours of the Stone Age*

BOUTET DE MONVEL, ROGER — *Beau Brummell and His Times*

BRAND, JOHN — *Popular Antiquities*

BREASTED, JAMES HENRY — *The Origins of Civilization*

BRIFFAULT, ROBERT — *The Making of Humanity*

BURGE, LORENZO — *Pre-Glacial Man and the Aryan Race*

BURNE, CHARLOTTE S. — *Origins of Popular Superstitions and Customs*

CAMDEN, WILLIAM — *Ancient and Modern Manners of the Irish*

CARUS, PAUL — *Animal Symbolism*

CARUS, PAUL — *Chinese Life and Customs*

CHAMBERS, ROBERT — *The Book of Days*

CHATTO, WILLIAM ANDREW — *Facts on the Origin and History of Playing Cards*

CHESTERFIELD, PHILIP DORMER STANHOPE, 4TH EARL OF — *Letters to His Son*

CHURCHWARD, ALBERT — *Origin and Evolution of Primitive Man*

CHURCHWARD, ALBERT — *Signs and Symbols of Primordial Man*

CLODD, EDWARD — *The Childhood of Religions*

Clodd, Edward . . . *Magic in Names and Other Things*
Colbert, E. . . . . . *Humanity in Its Origin and Early Growth*
Compton's Pictured Encyclopædia
Crawley, Ernest . . . *The Mystic Rose; a Study of Primitive Marriage*
Customs of the World (Edited by W. Hutchinson)
Cutler, Harry G. . . *Panorama of Nations*
Dadachanzi, R. K. . . *Origin of Phallism*
Darwin, Charles . . . *Descent of Man*
Darwin, Charles . . . *Origin of Species*
Dawson, John W. . . *Fossil Men and Their Modern Representatives*
Dean, Amos . . . . . *History of Civilization*
Denison, Thomas Stewart *The Primitive Aryans of America*
Denton, Clara J. . . *Holiday Facts and Fancies*
Dobbins, Frank S. . . *Story of the World's Worship*
Doran, John . . . . . *Habits and Men*
Dore, Henry . . . . . *Researches into Chinese Superstition*
Earle, Alice Morse . . *Customs and Fashions in Old New England*
Earlf, Alice Morse . . *Two Centuries of Costume in America*
Eichler, Lillian . . . *The Book of Etiquette*
Elliot, Frances . . . *Old Court Life in France*
Ellis, Havelock . . . *Studies in the Psychology of Sex*
Farrar, James A. . . . *Primitive Manners and Customs*
Fielding, William John *The Caveman Within Us*
Franklin, Ruth Barker . *Significant Aspects of Ancient and Mediæval Civilization*
Frazer, Sir James George *The Golden Bough*
Frazer, Sir James George *Popular Superstitions of the Ancients*
Freeman, Frederick . . *Civilization and Barbarism*
Frere, Thomas . . . *Hoyle's Games*
Goldenweiser, A. A. . . *Origin of Totemism*
Goldsmith, Milton . . *Signs, Omens and Superstitions*
Gomme, G. Laurence . . *Heredity and Tradition*
Goodrich, Samuel G. . . *Manners, Customs and Antiquities of the Indians of North and South America*
Gorham, Charles T. *Christianity and Civilization*

GRANT, JAMES . . . . *Mysteries of All Nations; Rise and Progress of Superstition*
GUNNING, WILLIAM D. . *Life-History of our Planet*
HAMILTON, AUGUSTA (LADY) *Marriage Rites and Customs of All Nations*
HODGIN, CHARLES E. . . *A Study of Spoken Language*
HODGKIN, JOHN ELLIOT . *Monograms, Ancient and Modern*
HONE, WILLIAM . . . *The Every-day Book*
HONE, WILLIAM . . . *The Table Book*
HONE, WILLIAM . . . *The Year Book*
HOPE, THOMAS . . . *Costume of the Ancients*
HOYLE, EDMUND . . . *Rules for Playing Fashionable Games*
HUGON, CECILE . . . *Social France in the XVIII Century*
HULL, ERNEST R. . . . *Civilization and Culture*
HUNT, ROBERT . . . *Popular Romances of the West of England*
JACKSON, A. V. WILLIAMS . *Philology*
JAMES, EDWIN OLIVER . . *An Introduction to Anthropology*
JEWISH ENCYCLOPÆDIA
KNOWLSON, T. SHARPER . *Origins of Popular Superstitions and Customs*
LANG, ANDREW . . . *Custom and Myth*
LANG, ANDREW . . . *Social Origins*
LAWRENCE, ROBERT M. . *Magic of the Horse-Shoe; Other Folk-Lore Notes*
LEFEVRE, DE MORSAN . . *Manners and Customs of the Romans*
LETOURNEAU, CH. . . . *Evolution of Marriage and of the Family*
LOCKWOOD, INGERSOLL . . *Superstition*
LOWIE, ROBERT H. . . . *A New Conception of Totemism (In American Anthropologist, vol. 13, p. 189)*
LYELL, CHARLES . . . *Geological Evidences of the Antiquity of Man*
MCCABE, JOSEPH . . . *Evolution of Civilization*
MCLENNAN, JOHN FERGUSON *Studies in Ancient History*
MALLERY, GARRICK . . *Customs of Courtesy*
MARSHALL, FREDERIC . . *International Vanities*
MASSEY, GERALD . . . *A Book of the Beginnings*
MIGEOD, FREDERICK WM. H. *Earliest Man*
MILLER, CLAUDE . . . *Outdoor Sports and Games*

MITCHELL, ARTHUR . . *The Past in the Present*
MONBODDO, LORD . . . *Origin and Progress of Language*
MONCKTON, O. PAUL . . *Pastimes in Times Past*
NADAILLAC, JEAN F. ALBERT DE P. (MARQUIS DE NADAILLAC) . . . . . *Manners and Monuments of Prehistoric Peoples*
OSBORN, HENRY FAIRFIELD . *Origin and Evolution of Life*
PARDOE, MISS . . . . *Louis the Fourteenth*
PARSONS, ELSIE CLEWS . . *Fear and Conventionality*
PARSONS, FRANK ALVAH . *Psychology of Dress*
PATTEN, HELEN PHILBROOK *The Year's Festivals*
PAYNE, GEORGE HENRY . *The Child in Human Progress*
PECK, CHARLES HARVEY . *Our World*
PLINY, THE ELDER . . *Natural History*
POST, EMILY . . . . *Etiquette*
RAWLINSON, GEORGE . . *Origin of Nations*
REDDALL, HENRY FREDERIC . *Fact, Fancy and Fable*
RIPLEY, WILLIAM Z. . . *Races of Europe*
ROBINSON, JAMES HARVEY . *The Mind in the Making*
ROBINSON, JOHN . . . *The Savage*
RODD, JAMES RENNELL . . *Customs and Lore of Modern Greece*
ST. DENIS, LOUIS ETIENNE . *Napoleon from the Tuileries to St. Helena*
SCHIEFFELIN, SAMUEL B. . *The Foundations of History*
SMITH, HORATIO . . . *Festivals, Games and Amusements; Ancient and Modern*
SPENCER, HERBERT . . . *Principles of Sociology*
STRUTT, JOSEPH . . . *Sports and Pastimes of People of England*
SWINTON, WILLIAM . . *Outlines of the World's History*
TARDE, GABRIEL . . . *The Laws of Imitation*
THOMAS, WM. I. . . . *Source Book for Social Origins*
TITTLE, WALTER . . . *Colonial Holidays*
TYLOR, EDWARD B. . . *Primitive Culture*
VUILLIER, GASTON . . . *History of Dancing*
WAKEFIELD, PRISCILLA . . *Sketches of Human Manners*
WALLAS, GRAHAM . . . *Our Social Heritage*
WALLS, O. A. . . . . *Sex and Sex Worship*
WELLS, H. G. . . . . *Outline of History*
WESTERMARCK, EDWARD . *History of Human Marriage*
WIDNEY, J. P. . . . . *Race Life of the Aryan People*
WILLIAMSON, GEORGE CHARLES *Curious Survivals*
WILSON, DANIEL . . . *Prehistoric Man*

WOOD, JOHN GEORGE . . *Uncivilized Races of Men*

Ceremonies and Religious Customs of the World
Customs of the World (edited by W. Hutchinson)
Compton's Pictured Encyclopædia
Encyclopædia Britannica
Jewish Encyclopædia

Reference has also been made to hundreds of authoritative magazine articles, too numerous to be mentioned here.

INDEX